'This compelling book shows definitively how an ancient, abiding and often murderous hatred, antisemitism, has found, in recent decades, a new and politically-acceptable, even fashionable, way to attack Jews – antizionism.'

Walter Reich, *Yitzhak Rabin Memorial Professor of International Affairs, Ethics and Human Behavior, The George Washington University, USA*

'David Hirsh, a leading sociologist of contemporary antisemitism, and eleven other authors at the forefront of the struggle against it show how Jews pay the price for redemption when Israel becomes the symbol of ultimate evil. Their book is indispensable for understanding the startling revival of antisemitism in our time.'

Chad Alan Goldberg, *Martindale-Bascom Professor of Sociology, University of Wisconsin–Madison, USA; award-winning author of* Citizens and Paupers: Relief, Rights, Race, from the Freedmen's Bureau to Workfare *(2008) and* Modernity and the Jews in Western Social Thought *(2017)*

THE REBIRTH OF ANTISEMITISM IN THE 21ST CENTURY

The Rebirth of Antisemitism in the 21st Century is about the rise of antizionism and antisemitism in the first two decades of the 21st century, with a focus on the UK.

It is written by the activist-intellectuals, both Jewish and not, who led the opposition to the campaign for an academic boycott of Israel. Their experiences convinced them that the boycott movement, and the antizionism upon which it was based, was fuelled by, and in turn fuelled, antisemitism. The book shows how the level of hostility towards Israel exceeded the hostility which is levelled against other states. And it shows how the quality of that hostility tended to resonate with antisemitic tropes, images and emotions. Antizionism positioned Israel as symbolic of everything that good people oppose, it made Palestinians into an abstract symbol of the oppressed and it positioned most Jews as saboteurs of social 'progress'. The book shows how antisemitism broke into mainstream politics and how it contaminated the Labour Party as it made a bid for Downing Street.

This book will be of interest to scholars and students researching antizionism, antisemitism and the Labour Party in the UK.

David Hirsh is Senior Lecturer in Sociology at Goldsmiths, University of London, and Academic Director of the London Centre for the Study of Contemporary Antisemitism. His previous books include *Contemporary Left Antisemitism* (Routledge, 2017) and *Law against Genocide: Cosmopolitan Trials* (2003).

Studies in Contemporary Antisemitism
Series editors

David Hirsh, *Senior Lecturer in Sociology, Goldsmiths, University of London and Academic Director of the London Centre for the Study of Contemporary Antisemitism* and Rosa Freedman, *Professor in the School of Law, University of Reading and Research Fellow at the London Centre for the Study of Contemporary Antisemitism*

Published in conjunction with the London Centre for the Study of Contemporary Antisemitism, *Studies in Contemporary Antisemitism* is a timely, multidisciplinary book series, drawing primarily, but not exclusively, on the social sciences and the humanities. The series encourages academically rigorous and critical publications across several disciplines and that are explicit in understanding and opposing the presence and ascendancy of contemporary antisemitism in both its theoretical and empirical manifestations. The series provides a unique opportunity to offer an intellectual home for a diversity of works that, taken together, crystallize around the study of contemporary antisemitism. The series consists of research monographs, edited collections and short form titles.

Nazis, Islamic Antisemitism, and the Middle East
The 1948 Arab war against Israel and the aftershocks of WW II
Matthias Küntzel

Mapping the New Left Antisemitism
The Fathom Essays
Edited by Alan Johnson

The Rebirth of Antisemitism in the 21st Century
From the Academic Boycott Campaign into the Mainstream
Edited by David Hirsh

For more information about this series, please visit: www.routledge.com/studies-in-contemporary-antisemitism/ book-series/SICA

THE REBIRTH OF ANTISEMITISM IN THE 21ST CENTURY

From the Academic Boycott Campaign into the Mainstream

Edited by David Hirsh

Routledge
Taylor & Francis Group

LONDON AND NEW YORK

Designed cover image: © Mina Kupfermann

First published 2024
by Routledge
4 Park Square, Milton Park, Abingdon, Oxon OX14 4RN

and by Routledge
605 Third Avenue, New York, NY 10158

Routledge is an imprint of the Taylor & Francis Group, an informa business

British Library Cataloguing-in-Publication Data
A catalogue record for this book is available from the British Library

Library of Congress Cataloging-in-Publication Data
Names: Hirsh, David, editor.
Title: The rebirth of Antisemitism in the 21st century : from the academic boycott campaign into the mainstream / edited by David Hirsh.
Description: First. | New York, NY : Routledge, 2024. | Series: Studies in contemporary antisemitism | Includes bibliographical references and index.
Identifiers: LCCN 2023026079 (print) | LCCN 2023026080 (ebook) | ISBN 9781032119793 (hardback) | ISBN 9781032116624 (paperback) | ISBN 9781003222477 (ebook)
Subjects: LCSH: Antisemitism--History--21st century. | Antisemitism--Great Britain--History--21st century. | Labour Party (Great Britain)--History--21st century. | Zionism--History--21st century. | Zionism--Great Britain--History--21st century.
Classification: LCC DS145 .R43 2024 (print) | LCC DS145 (ebook) | DDC 305.892/40410905--dc23/eng/20230729
LC record available at https://lccn.loc.gov/2023026079
LC ebook record available at https://lccn.loc.gov/2023026080

ISBN: 978-1-032-11979-3 (hbk)
ISBN: 978-1-032-11662-4 (pbk)
ISBN: 978-1-003-22247-7 (ebk)

DOI: 10.4324/9781003222477

Typeset in Sabon
by Deanta Global Publishing Services, Chennai, India

CONTENTS

LIST OF CONTRIBUTORS

Matthew Bolton is working on the 'Decoding Antisemitism' project in Berlin. He has a PhD in Philosophy from Roehampton. He, along with Frederick Harry Pitts, is the co-author of *Corbynism, a Critical Approach*. His articles have been published in *Philosophy & Social Criticism*, *Journal of Contemporary Antisemitism*, *British Politics* and *Political Quarterly*.

Sarah Annes Brown is Professor of English Literature at Anglia Ruskin. She has published on the reception of Ovid, adaptations and sources of Shakespeare, and science fiction and fantasy. Her recent book is *Shakespeare and Science Fiction*. She has published several short articles and book reviews relating to antisemitism on *Fathom* and *Engage* websites.

David Hirsh is Senior Lecturer in Sociology at Goldsmiths, University of London, and Academic Director of the London Centre for the Study of Contemporary Antisemitism. His first monograph developed a sociological account of crimes against humanity and cosmopolitan law and his second did similar work on contemporary left antisemitism.

Anthony Julius is Deputy Chairman of Mishcon de Reya and has a Chair of Law and the Arts at UCL. He represented Deborah Lipstadt against David Irving and Ronnie Fraser against UCU. He wrote *Trials of the Diaspora* and his biography of the patriarch Abraham will be published in 2024.

Lesley Klaff is Senior Lecturer in Law at Sheffield Hallam University and is the editor in chief of the *Journal of Contemporary Antisemitism*. She writes on contemporary and campus antisemitism and she has done ground-breaking work on Holocaust distortion and inversion, and on the legal construction of Jewish identity and antisemitism.

Hilary Miller has an MA in Human Rights Studies from Columbia and a degree in Political Science from the University of Wisconsin–Madison. She was a researcher on the Freedom of Religion or Belief Project at City University, New York, and has worked with NGOs on the Human Rights Council in Geneva.

David Seymour is Senior Lecturer in Law at City Law School, University of London. His work focuses on critical theory and Holocaust memory. He has also written on Law and the Arts, Brexit and the recent COVID pandemic.

Philip Spencer is Emeritus Professor in Holocaust and Genocide Studies at Kingston University and Visiting Professor in Politics at Birkbeck, University of London. He wrote *Genocide since 1945*, and with Robert Fine, *Antisemitism and the Left: On the Return of the Jewish Question* and with Howard Wollman, *Nationalism: A Critical Introduction*.

Karin Stögner is Professor of Sociology at the University of Passau, Germany, and works on questions of the intersectionality of ideologies, especially antisemitism, sexism, racism and nationalism. She is the author of *Antisemitismus und Sexismus. Historisch-gesellschaftliche Konstellationen* (2014) and co-editor of *Kritische Theorie und Feminismus* (2022).

John Strawson is Professor of Law at the University of East London. He writes on international law and Middle East Studies, with a focus on postcolonialism, Islam, and Palestine and Israel. He has taught at Birzeit University (Palestine) and the Institute of Social Studies (The Hague Netherlands).

Izabella Tabarovsky is Senior Advisor with the Kennan Institute (Wilson Center) and Fellow with the London Centre for the Study of Contemporary Antisemitism. She is a contributing writer at Tablet Magazine and writes on Soviet antizionism, antisemitism, Soviet Jewry, Holocaust in the USSR, Stalin and politics of historical memory.

Mira Vogel is Senior Lecturer in Education at King's College London. When colleagues across academic fields need to develop themselves in the areas of curriculum design, teaching strategies, assessment approaches, inclusive educational practice or education for sustainability, they may encounter Mira.

FIRST PREFACE

Esprit d'escalier: reminiscences of a silent observer of the UCU conference[1]

Robert Fine

Engage, 30 May 2009

> 'The tones are mellow but they give me a shiver and make me feel my Jewishness in a new way.'

The opening refrain of the proposers of the 'this is not a boycott' motion was: 'We shall not be intimidated'. There was little chance of that. Opponents of the motion barely got a word in. Between demagoguery and good will there wasn't a lot of room for argument.

Demagoguery was represented by three professional Israel-haters. One I remember from the 1980s calling for the 'no platforming' of Zionist organisations on campus, including Jewish societies active in the Anti-Nazi League. They have been hawking their wares for many years. The Palestinians are suffering, so let's boycott Israeli academics. Mmm? It follows like breakfast follows day. But it did give us the opportunity to study the punitive mind at work. It knows only one register – guilt, and only one response – punishment. All other modalities and distinctions are lost.

The language of guilt, as Roland Barthes observed, allows those who declare it to describe and condemn at one stroke. It knows only how to endow its victims with epithets. It is ignorant of everything about their actions save the guilty category into which they are forced to fit. All else must be excluded. Especially compassion. Nothing is allowed into this Manichean world other than the criminal guilt of Israel and the appropriateness of Israel as a target for basic punitive instincts.

Good will was represented by the executive of the union. The President reported she was shocked by her visit to Gaza. I have no doubt I would have been too. Shocked at finding the lives of ordinary men and women made intensely difficult by the cruelties of war, sanctions and security.

Shocked at the problems students faced in graduating, shocked they had to keep their mobile phones on so that they could be alerted to troubles outside the classroom. Good will declared that something must be done and that a boycott of Israeli academics is what is to be done. Not so for other international motions. They were different. There was no call to boycott Sudanese academics for their complicity in the genocide in Darfur, or Ethiopian academics for complicity in the blood bath in Somalia, or Chinese academics for complicity in the extinction of Tibetan culture. Everywhere else well established norms of trade union solidarity applied, as they used in the 1980s when most unions here supported direct links with (not a boycott of) the fledgling independent unions in South Africa. But in Israel we were asked to consider cutting links with our fellow academics and trade unionists. And the majority of the union exec supported it out of good will and philanthropy and with the skill of moving onto next business.

Demagoguery and good will are a potent couple. One offspring was simplicity. Villain nations and victim nations; those we embrace and those we learn to hate; those whose voices we want to hear and those whose voices we wish to exclude lest they disturb the world we have constructed.

The other offspring was duplicity. Weasel words such as 'criticism of Israel is not as such antisemitic'. Of course, criticism of Israel is not as such antisemitic. But some criticism of Israel is antisemitic. It was in the Doctors Trials in Russia in 1953. It was in the expulsion of Zionists from Poland in 1968. It is in the daubing of synagogue walls in East London with antizionist graffiti in 2008. It is in the inclusion of the Protocols of the Elders of Zion and the use of black-shirted straight arm salutes among armed groups dedicated to fighting 'Zionism'. Weasel words noted 'the apparent complicity of most of the Israeli academy'. They did not inform us what our Israeli colleagues are meant to be complicit with. But the good news is that any sense of our own complicity – e.g. for working for a state that is now fighting a war in Iraq of which many of us strongly disapprove – is projected onto the Israeli other. We punish, therefore we are absolved. Self-righteousness is so much easier than self-criticism.

I found myself imagining there were a campaign to boycott British academic institutions to punish us for our complicity in the Iraq war. How would the union respond to holding British academic institutions and the corporate academic body responsible for what our government has done, or to targeting those individual academics in the UK who supported the war or did not oppose it? If not us, why them?

This brought me back to those words: 'we shall not be intimidated'. They seemed to resonate with history. Intimidated by whom? The UCU annual conference is a bastion of support for equalities, academic freedom and anti-discrimination. Both in word and deed. If there is one thing we all deplore it is racism. Could it be, however, that the forbidden word, the word whose utterance is identical to intimidation, is antisemitism? One speaker who used it was, albeit mildly, jeered. The jeer had its own voice. It is no longer antisemitism that is a problem, it is talk of antisemitism. Talk of antisemitism serves only to silence rightful criticism. Antisemitism was real in the past; today it is just a ruse. It is not part of our battle against racism, it is a diversion from it. This way of thinking has crept into both academic literature and our academic union.

The proposal our union overwhelmingly voted for noted 'legal attempts to prevent UCU debating boycott of Israeli academic institutions'. Doubtless, this was a crucial exemplar of intimidation. It failed to note that legal opinions have warned the union that it would be going down a discriminatory road if it endorsed a boycott of academics based merely on their national membership. It failed to note that these legal opinions have appealed not to anti-trade union laws but to anti-discrimination laws – our laws, the laws the union uses in its daily activities. They have appealed to the Race Relations Act, not to the ghosts of Thatcher. Instead of being worried about discriminating against Israeli academics and determining not to do so in the future, instead of listening to the warning, the union has been encouraged to discredit those who raise the issue.

No alternatives were placed on the agenda. We could create links with independent trade unionists, both Palestinian and Israeli. We could support trade unionists on both sides even in the face of obstruction or repression from their own respective governments and political leaders. We could embrace an anti-racism in which what matters is not whether someone is a Palestinian trade unionist or an Israeli trade unionist but a fellow trade unionist in need of solidarity. We could stand against the irresponsibility of those whose charge of complicity is merely verbal here but may have lethal consequences in the Middle East. We could have an international strategy based not on the instant self-certainty of those who know from afar which nation is guilty and which nation is innocent but on supporting anti-racism and trade union democracy wherever they make their stand. We could imagine a way forward that does something positive for peace and make us proud of our union. Instead we had a boycott motion, pretending not to be a boycott motion. Its potential to cause damage to our union and to the values of academic freedom, trade union solidarity and anti-racism most members of our union share, is the shame of it.

The Middle East has more than its fair share of violence and fundamentalist thinking. It is quite possible that the struggles for power now going on will get worse. Few of us are experts enough to know. However, to hold Israel uniquely culpable or uniquely responsible for the suffering of Palestinians, and then to make no distinction between the Israeli state and civil society, and then to focus punitive action against what is arguably the most progressive sector of Israeli society, and finally to justify this selective treatment on the grounds that Israel is a democracy – this is to swallow whole the politics and prejudices of some of the most nationalistic forces in the area.

I was born and brought up as an English Jew. The younger son of first and second generation immigrants. In my youth I thought of myself as Jewish rather than English and this self-consciousness has never gone away. For many years I have been involved in socialist organisations, academic research and teaching, and a personal life in which Jewishness has only played a bit part. I used to visit Israel, where I have relatives and friends, but I haven't been back for some years now – in part because I disapprove of the occupation and the militarism that has accompanied it. I think it has damaged Israeli society from within as well as adding to the suffering many Palestinian men and women have had to endure throughout the Middle East. Over the last few years, however, we have had to listen to the grotesque vilification of Israel and exaggeration of its crimes. We have had to resist relentless calls to exclude Israeli academics from our campuses, editorial boards and research networks. With an increasing sense of adversity we have honed our arguments. Now for the third time our own union has chosen to go down the road of considering 'the appropriateness of continued educational links with Israeli academic institutions'. The tones are mellow but they give me a shiver and make me feel my Jewishness in a new way.

Let's only hope that in our own union good will gets wise and demagoguery gets shafted. I also hope that next time I won't be the silent observer indulging in this esprit d'escalier.

Robert Fine
Warwick University's delegate to UCU Congress
30 May 2008

Note

1 Robert Fine. Esprit D''escalier: Reminiscences of a Silent Observer of the UCU Conference, (Engage, 30 May 2008) https://engageonline.wordpress.com/2008/05/30/esprit-descalier-reminiscences-of-a-silent-observer-of-the-ucu-conference-robert-fine-30-may-2008/ [accessed 16 February 2023].

SECOND PREFACE

I guess it doesn't matter any more[1]

Norman Geras

normblog, 30 April 2009

Things can take a surprising turn. 'Not all criticism of Israel is anti-Semitic' is a truth that has been often stated. To which it has just as often been pointed out in reply that this truth doesn't license the inference that all criticism of Israel is *not* anti-Semitic; for it yields only the proposition that *some* criticism of Israel is not anti-Semitic, and this is compatible with some other criticism of Israel being indeed anti-Semitic. In fact, there is such other, anti-Semitic, criticism of Israel, and not merely criticism but also downright hostility and hatred. None of that should by now surprise anyone, I know. The logical relationships are pretty straightforward and the relevant facts of the matter are all easy to come by.

What is surprising is something else. Those of us who have been pointing out the logical compatibility between 'Not all criticism of Israel is anti-Semitic' and 'Some critical attitudes towards Israel nonetheless are anti-Semitic' have perhaps rather too much taken it for granted that emphasis on this latter thought might put anti-racist liberals and leftists on their guard - on their guard against countenancing, associating themselves with, giving a free pass to, attitudes towards Israel of an anti-Semitic kind. It would seem to be an important concern for anti-racist liberals and other people of progressive outlook to have, for reasons of a quite general kind which I hope I don't need to explain. Yet this may have been a naïve and too sanguine expectation on our part.

For there is a third proposition that increasingly captures, I will not say the spirit of the times, but the spirit of a significant sector of contemporary opinion. This third proposition may be formulated as follows:

It doesn't matter if criticism of and attitudes to Israel are anti-Semitic, so long as they are *also* anti-Zionist.

In other words, racist animus against Israel is getting an easy ride from more and more commentators just on condition that it chimes in with the narrative of Israel as a usurper-colonialist and racist state. It's as if the taint of anti-Semitic racism isn't strong enough to worry the easy-riders (much less to put a question in their minds about anti-Zionism itself); instead the 'truths' of anti-Zionism are taken as, so to say, cleansing in their effects, so that Jew-hatred is not allowed to deflect anyone from the proper business of denouncing Israel.

This thought was prompted, following Mahmoud Ahmadinejad's recent speech at the Geneva conference (which I have characterized <u>here</u>[2]), by a letter to the Guardian from Ghada Karmi, in which (scroll down) she says:

> Mahmoud Ahmadinejad's UN speech on 21 April struck many as obnoxious, but in terms of understanding the 1948 roots of the Middle East conflict he was spot on. Vilifying him may feel good, but it is a diversion [from] the real issue.

Got that? 'Vilifying' him. And not the real issue. You couldn't ask for anything clearer. The guy can deny the Holocaust and look forward to wiping Israel from the page of history, he can give out Jews-controlling-the-world talk, but to react against this is vilification and a diversion from the real issue. Karmi is perhaps unfamiliar with the circumstance of there being more than one real issue.

Take a look next at <u>Martin Jacques in the New Statesman.</u>[3] After warming up with the irony of 'a people who suffered from racism on such an enormous scale... themselves display[ing] *the same kind of attitude* towards the Palestinians' (my italics) - Jacques expresses himself nonplussed by, he can't think of a good reason for, the boycott of and the walkout at the Geneva conference. Just think about that walkout: it's not enough for Jacques that a guy with Ahmadinejad's Holocaust-denying record is a keynote speaker at this conference and that his speech, as both prepared and delivered, contains clear anti-Semitic tropes. If it can be fitted into an anti-Zionist narrative, this doesn't matter.

The same 'balance' of considerations is to be found in the column by Seumas Milne and the Guardian leader to which I drew attention[4] last week: Ahmadinejad's speech may have been repugnant and <u>inflammatory</u>[5]; but justifying a walkout when the speech is contextualized by reference to the colonialist-settler story that is Israel? It would seem not. Declining to sit and listen to a Holocaust-denier is in those circumstances, for Milne, itself the symptom of racism. Meanwhile, the newspaper for which he writes is careful to observe that the speech of Ahmadinejad, displaying 'the views of a crude anti-semite', might <u>colour</u>[6] how his remarks on the establishment of Israel are taken. Never lose sight of the main thing, hey? Israel, not anti-Semitism - even if and when there is anti-Semitism. As the man <u>said</u>[7], I guess it doesn't matter any more.

The Guardian, let it be remembered, now opens its <u>opinion pages</u>[8] and its <u>opinion website</u>[9] to the spokesmen of Hamas, an organization that propagates hatred of Jews and endorses the poisonous myths of 'The Protocols of the Elders of Zion' <u>in its charter</u>[10]. It might be said in the paper's defence that Hamas is the political representative of a section of the Palestinian people and the Guardian is simply fulfilling its journalistic duty in reporting the views of leading members of that organization. But this is not *reporting*; it is providing a platform - for the views of an organization with 'crude Jew-hatred in its founding documents - and that is something different.

On Saturday, to bring the story up to date, <u>Mark Brown let it be known</u>[11] that the Guardian was making available a reading of Caryl Churchill's *Seven Jewish Children*. He noted that the play has been controversial and that part of the controversy centres on whether it is anti-Semitic. Readers will now be able to 'make their own judgment'. One wonders whether the decision to make the play available in this form reflects a judgement by the paper itself that *Seven Jewish Children* is *not* anti-Semitic. I mean, if it either is or even just might be anti-Semitic (I've put forward <u>seven reasons here</u>[12] for thinking that it is), you'd hope the Guardian would have some qualms about helping to put it about. Things are now such, however, that it's impossible to form a view about whether Churchill's play has been judged by those concerned not to be anti-Semitic, or whether the possibility of its being so is thought not to matter because... so long as it's anti-Zionist, who cares whether it's anti-Semitic? Given the emerging track record at the Guardian, how could one tell?

Notes

1 Norman Geras. I Guess It Doesn"t Matter Any More (*Normblog*, 30 April 2009). https://normblog.typepad.com/normblog/2009/04/i-guess-it-doesnt-matter-any-more.html [accessed 16 February 2023].

2 *These were all links to websites in the original blog. Replaced here by references*. Norman Geras. Ag Pleez Ahmadinejad (*normblog*, 23 April 2009). https://normblog.typepad.com/normblog/2009/04/ag-pleez-ahmadinejad.html [accessed 16 February 2023].

3 Martin Jaques. Face to Face with History (New Statesman 23 April 2009). http://www.newstatesman.com/international-politics/2009/04/racism-israel-conference-face, now accessible via https://web.archive.org/web/20210222195359/http://www.newstatesman.com:80/international-politics/2009/04/racism-israel-conference-face [accessed 16 February 2023].

4 Ag Pleez Ahmadinejad *ibid*.

5 Seumas Milne. What Credibility Is There in Geneva"s All-White Boycott? (The Guardian 23 April 2009). https://www.theguardian.com/commentisfree/2009/apr/23/un-race-conference-walkout-ahmadinejad [accessed 16 February 2023].

6 Editorial. How Ahmadinejad''s Latest Speech Got Lost in Translation (The Guardian 22 April 2009). https://www.theguardian.com/commentisfree/2009/apr/22/mahmoud-ahmadinejad-iran-farsi-speech [accessed 16 February 2023].

7 The link here is to a YouTube video, long gone. We are assuming it linked to the song, written by Paul Anka and recorded by Buddy Holly on 21 October 1958, "I guess it doesn't matter anymore"; but perhaps it linked to a cover version.

8 Mousa Abu Marzook. A Decisive Loss for Israel (The Guardian 22 January 2009). https://www.theguardian.com/commentisfree/2009/jan/22/gaza-israel -palestine-hamas-obama [accessed 16 February 2023].

9 Bassem Naeem. Hamas Condemns the Holocaust. (The Guardian 12 May 2008). https://www.theguardian.com/commentisfree/2008/may/12/hamascondemnsth eholocaust> [accessed 16 February 2023].

10 Norman Geras. The protocols of Comment is Free (normblog 13 May 2008). https://normblog.typepad.com/normblog/2008/05/the-protocols-o.html [accessed 16 February 2023].

11 Mark Brown. Churchill''s Children: Guardian reading for Caryl Churchill''s Gaza play (The Guardian 25 April 2009). https://www.theguardian.com/stage /2009/apr/25/israel-gaza-play-caryl-churchill-website [accessed 16 February 2023].

12 Norman Geras. Seven Themes for Caryl Churchill (normblog 23 March 2009). https://normblog.typepad.com/normblog/2009/03/seven-themes-for-caryl -churchill.html [accessed 16 February 2023).

INTRODUCTION

David Hirsh

In this introduction, I will begin with some discussion of the two prefaces, by Robert Fine and Norman Geras. They were friends and mentors to many of us, and are sadly no longer alive. They are both widely and deeply missed, and when people who knew them gather today, there is often speculation about the extent to which they might be surprised, or not, to see how the phenomena they were worried about in public life have developed. They are missed as friends, but also as intellectual leaders and teachers. This volume begins with short extracts of their writing. What they say with precision and eloquence introduces what this book is about with great, expressive accuracy.

In this introduction, I go on to discuss something about the concept of this multi-authored book. It looks back at what was in a sense a rather small and local struggle, over a proposal that people in universities in Britain should boycott their colleagues in Israeli universities. We are taking the time to reflect because this struggle, the antisemitism that fuelled it, what it told us about our politics and our intellectual frameworks and the ways in which it changed the people who participated in it, turned out neither to be so small nor so local as it had at first appeared.

I go on to introduce the chapters that follow and the people who wrote them. They are diverse in their disciplines, in their understandings and in their political and scholarly traditions. But in their courage, their clarity, their knowledge, their thoughtfulness and their solidarity, they are all similarly magnificent.

DOI: 10.4324/9781003222477-1

FIGURE 0.1 Witness.

Note: The cover image is detail from this work, by Mina Kupfermann, called 'Witness'. Standing at nearly 3 metres tall, from a distance it depicts a catastrophic event; a single eruption of antisemitism through time. Upon closer inspection, hidden in the artwork are hundreds of pieces of antisemitic social media material from many different sources.

Source: Kupfermann M (2019) Witness. Digital image © Mina Kupfermann.

Robert Fine and Norman Geras

The *First Preface* of this book was a report of the University and College Union (UCU) Congress 2008. It was written by Robert Fine, who had been a delegate from Warwick University UCU that year, and it was published on the *Engage* website on 30 May. It is clear from the writing that his memory of the experience was fresh, as was his anger.

Robert Fine was a widely respected and senior sociologist. His book on Marx's understanding of democracy and law is still used to teach students; his work on the struggle against apartheid in South Africa was both groundbreaking and prescient; he had edited a book about the policing of the 1984–1985 miners' strike; his cosmopolitan social theory, drawing on Hegel, Marx and Arendt, was original and influential. He considered himself to be a Marxist, and he never stopped paying his monthly dues to the Trotskyist group *Workers' Liberty*.

The experience of being a delegate at this conference made him feel alien within a place where he thought, without question, that he belonged: his union. For a whole career, he had attended union meetings, he had discussed strategy, he had been part of organising strikes and he would never have dreamed of crossing a picket line. It was deep within his identity that he was part of the union.

He knew before he went to this conference that he would be on the losing side in votes on motions for a boycott of Israel, and he had a sophisticated understanding of how left antisemitism was encroaching into the union. It was not that, which got under his skin, that year in Manchester. Throughout his political life on the left, and as a Marxist, he was well used to finding himself in small and marginalised minorities. His clarity on issues relating to democracy in particular, and the threat of totalitarian thinking within the left – his anti-Stalinism – made him no stranger either to losing votes or to being denounced. He was well aware of the undemocratic, and the anti-democratic, culture with which democratic politics co-exists, and struggles, inside the left.

But there was something happening at this congress that made him feel that he was being constructed as an enemy of the union, and as an enemy of the left, and that this hostile construction of him was being accepted within the mainstream as a kind of common sense: by too many of his fellow trade unionists, his fellow academics, his fellow sociologists; and by too many of his old comrades and friends.

It seems to be a common experience of antisemitism that Jews who felt they were at home in a social space are suddenly and surprisingly confronted by an expanding culture that treats them as not being at home. Well, many racialised people were never allowed to feel themselves to be at home at all, so perhaps the shock of alienation at a specific moment is, in a horrible sense, indicative of relative privilege. Nevertheless, this is a specific phenomenon. Dreyfus thought he was accepted as an army officer. German Jews felt themselves to be at home, until they did not. Jewish Communists felt themselves to be at home in Prague until Slansky and 11 of his Jewish comrades were charged with the crimes of bourgeois Jewish nationalism and Zionism, and hanged. Jewish feminists felt themselves to be at home in the Spare Rib collective, until, following the 1982 Israeli invasion of Lebanon, they were given antizionist loyalty tests.

Robert Fine never gave up resisting the alienation that he experienced in UCU and he never accepted being pushed out of the left. He remained confident in his reading of Marx, as an unambiguous supporter of the project to complete the Enlightenment and to make its values real and concrete for humanity as a whole, never to overthrow the Enlightenment or to traduce it as 'bourgeois' and so obsolete. In 2008, he had already made the following points about connections between Marx's critique of left antisemitism and our own predicament on today's left:

First, modern, political anti-Semitism is a creature of the left as well as the right. We should abandon any fond hope that the universalism of the left inures it to anti-Semitic temptations. Second, there is a strong tradition of anti-Semitism on the Left. Indeed, the most intelligent and radical currents of the left (including Marx) have placed the battle against anti-Semitism at the centre of their political thinking. Third, the significance of anti-Semitism on the Left lies not only in what was known as the Jewish question as such, but in helping to sow the seeds of totalitarian thinking and practice in anti-capitalist and anti-imperialist circles. And finally, there is a deep and enduring connection between the reconstruction of socialism as an enlightened, cosmopolitan radicalism and the overcoming of anti-Semitism in all its shapes and forms.[1]

Robert Fine's writings on antisemitism culminated in his 2017 book, with Philip Spencer, *Antisemitism and the Left: On the Return of the Jewish Question*. His thinking was always situated in his membership of the left and it always spoke to, rather than about, the left. He did not often articulate his anger or his humiliation with such visceral clarity as in this piece of writing. Afterwards, he returned to his more familiar, patient, academic style, although his writing was always clear and was always written to be read, to impact how people were thinking. This piece of writing is especially important for its rare, naked, *emotional* clarity.

Robert died, before his time, in 2018. I am so pleased to be able to include him, and his voice, in this book.

The *Second Preface* was written by Norman Geras, 11 months later. Norm's piece is as expressively furious as Robert's and yet his is as characteristically Geras as the other was characteristically Fine. The two Marxist profs had been born within two years of each other, towards the end of the Second World War, Geras was in Rhodesia, later liberated as Zimbabwe, and Fine in London. They were both veterans of the 1968 left, the movement against the Vietnam War, the anti-apartheid struggle and the Trotskyist left. Geras was also drawn towards the study of antisemitism towards the end of his academic career, publishing *The Contract of Mutual Indifference* at the very close of the 20th century. It focused, as did Fine's work, on trying to understand the totalitarianism that had so marked that century. It was a moral and political philosophy of the Holocaust. It re-worked the *social contract*, a concept with which philosophers had theorised the foundations of modern human community, into a concept of profound social negligence, which he thought was the pre-requisite for the dissolution of human community that made the Holocaust possible.

In the ways Fine and Geras treated totalitarianism as profound, and not as a contingent or random detour from the alleged progress of human history, they echoed Gillian Rose too. She was taken by the idea of the two cities that had been held to represent the two key aspects of human community, Athens, representing reason, and Jerusalem, representing love. Rose proposed that there should now be a third city to represent a third aspect of human community: Auschwitz, representing terror.[2]

The *Second Preface* by Geras is sharp, accurate and clear, written in the style of English analytic philosophy, and it feels so watertight that nobody could argue with it. But it is also edged with a dry, almost unarticulated English outrage; he cannot believe that the things he describes are really happening, and yet he writes about them in a way that makes the weary familiarity and the relentless, stupid repetitiveness of this antisemitism quite clear.

In his retirement, Norm was a pioneer of the new, groundbreaking, but by now already obsolete, practice of blogging. He wrote in normblog (normblog .typepad.com) pretty well every day, sometimes about the Australian cricket team that he loved, or his Manchester United where he had a season ticket, but more often about other issues of the day that appeared to him to be important. One of the foundations of the medium of blogging, as can be seen in this piece, was the *hyperlink*, by which one could not only reference other sources, but also allowed the reader to get straight to them via a click of the mouse. This facilitated community, since blogs related to other blogs and people with similar interests found each other. Reading this piece now is evocative of the style of the medium and also of the moment. We could see what was happening, it was obvious, but there was also a feeling that most people could not see it at all. Normblog was one of the central pillars of a much larger, organic, loosely constituted community of anti-totalitarian, social democratic blogs and websites, and the activists behind them. *Engage*, the website that we founded to organise opposition to the Israel boycott campaign, was another. Norman Geras was the main author of the *Euston Manifesto*,[3] an initiative to organise and define that community.

Paragraph 7 of the *Euston Manifesto*:

For a two-state solution: We recognize the right of both the Israeli and the Palestinian peoples to self-determination within the framework of a two-state solution. There can be no reasonable resolution of the Israeli-Palestinian conflict that subordinates or eliminates the legitimate rights and interests of one of the sides to the dispute.

Paragraph 8 articulated opposition to racism, but adds:

The recent resurgence of another, very old form of racism, anti-Semitism, is not yet properly acknowledged in left and liberal circles. Some exploit the legitimate grievances of the Palestinian people under occupation by Israel, and conceal prejudice against the Jewish people behind the formula of "anti-Zionism". We oppose this type of racism too, as should go without saying.

The first passage positions the manifesto with respect to the Israeli and Jewish right, with its aspiration to consolidate some or all of the West Bank as Israeli territory, and the antizionist left, which dreams that Israel should be dismantled altogether. The second passage positions the manifesto as acknowledging and opposing a resurgence of antisemitism, and specifically that which appears in the form of antizionism.

One might argue that the ways in which these boundaries were articulated look today a little threadbare. Does the 'two state solution' have a reality beyond its symbolic one, as a method of articulating a democratic and liberal politics with respect to Israel and the Palestinians? If it has become utopian, in the sense of being impossible, then it does not articulate much of a politics; perhaps more an abstract ethics. But on the other hand, it is much less utopian than the 'democratic secular state' which is the best that antizionism promises. If a democratic secular state could come about by agreement between Palestinians and Israelis, then who would argue? But Israel does not agree, and for good reasons. So in the *realpolitik* of the ostensibly pro-Palestine movement, the 'democratic secular state' formula becomes a polite way of advocating the dismantling of Israel without the agreement of Israelis, which means conquest. Whatever might result from such a fantasised military defeat of Israel, it would not, in reality, be either a democratic or a secular state.

The phrasing of Paragraph 7 is also interesting with hindsight. First, arguments rage about the relationship between antisemitism and racism. Some say that Jews are white and so antisemitism is not even a racism; others say that antisemitism is no ordinary racism because it has inherent genocidal potential. Some say we should emphasise the similarities between antisemitism and racism so that anti-racists take it seriously; but sometimes the emphasis on antisemitism's similarity with racism becomes a way of putting Jews in their place and reining them in from always claiming a special and superior oppression.

And then Paragraph 8 of the *Euston Manifesto* characterises antizionist antisemitism as a deliberate exploitation of Palestinian grievance to 'conceal' antisemitism inside a more palatable form, 'criticism of Israel'. But it seems clear that people like Jeremy Corbyn, for example, genuinely think of themselves as the very best opponents of antisemitism, and their outrage at being called antisemitic is genuine. They do not believe that they are exploiting antizionism or concealing antisemitism, they just do not see the relationship. On the other hand, the clarity and the intensity of the antisemitism that sections of the ostensibly anti-racist left are now willing to defend makes this assumption of good faith feel implausible.

The Norman Geras piece that we chose to include as the *Second Preface* of this book focuses on the straightforward little slippages of logic by which antizionism claims to oppose antisemitism. Norm had already written, in the run up to the 2008 UCU Congress that Fine had attended, a piece on the *Engage* website that chased the different formulations around their circles, the 2008 version of which was:

'Criticism of Israel or Israeli policy are [sic] not, as such, anti-semitic'.

Geras writes:

This may be seen as successor to the claim embodied in an earlier motion: namely, that 'criticism of Israel cannot be construed as anti-semitic'.

...in saying this they blithely pass over and indeed seek to obscure:

(a) that those of us opposing the boycott have never claimed that criticism of Israel is necessarily anti-Semitic;

(b) that, even if it isn't necessarily so, there is, these days, some anti-Semitic criticism of Israel about, which, as avowed anti-racists, the boycotters of UCU should feel an obligation to counteract rather than just behaving as if it had no relevance to the campaign they are relentlessly pursuing;

(c) that what they are themselves proposing – a boycott directed at the academics of one country and one country only – is aimed at academics who are mostly Jewish, and that they have never been able to come up with a satisfactory account of why the academics of countries other than Israel which have appalling human rights records should not be the subject of their boycotting efforts;

(d) that a boycott which punishes Israeli academics goes beyond 'criticism'.[4]

This book turns to consider seriously the question of 'criticism of Israel' in the final chapter, by Anthony Julius. He focuses on what has happened to liberal Zionism and he offers some personal 'criticism of Israel'. I turn at the end of this introduction to contextualise some of the difficulties of thinking about Zionism in a serious way, while also being immersed in a humiliating and relentless struggle against an antisemitism that characterises our Zionism, without our consent and without our input, as racism: as the worst thing on earth.

The *Second Preface* generalises Norm's outrage at the acceptance of antisemitic discourse within mainstream left and liberal circles, as exemplified by what was considered appropriate in the *Guardian* newspaper. His example of the piece by Seumas Milne, who was later to become Jeremy Corbyn's Chief of Communications, was especially redolent of another significant turn that was happening at that time, the construction of Jews as white. A predictable outcome of that is the construction of concern about antisemitism as a white concern, and hence, potentially, as a racist concern.

President Mahmoud Ahmadinejad of Iran was well known for his Holocaust denial, his antisemitic conspiracy fantasies and his threats against Israel; he was the president of a regime for which antisemitism was an important organising principle and which financed and armed antisemitic movements like Hamas and Hezbollah.

The 2001 *Durban World Conference against Racism* had been infamous for its acceptance of antisemitism as delegates worked to define Zionism as the global target for all antiracist activism, following the fall of apartheid. Chapter 3 of this book, by David Hirsh and Hilary Miller, looks at the significance of that event in re-consolidating and re-legitimising antizionism, after a lull during the peace process.

When Ahmadinejad addressed the *Durban Review Conference* in Geneva 2009, a number of ambassadors from democratic states walked out. Seaumas Milne wrote this up under the headline: 'What credibility is there in Geneva's all-white boycott?'[5]

To call outrage about the antisemitism of those who rule Iran 'white' was to trivialise it. It set opposing antisemitism in opposition to opposing racism and it portrayed opposition to antisemitism as a bad faith, cynical manoeuvre, aimed at weakening the conference against racism.

Milne could not even contemplate the more straightforward possible explanation: that states protested the antisemitic president not because they were 'white', or because they were 'imperialist', or because they were cynical, or because they were racist, but because they were democratic; and the concomitant would have been that the states that refused to protest Ahmadienjad's antisemitism simply did not find it to be significantly objectionable.

Norman Geras could see all this clearly, he could articulate it brilliantly in just a few lines and, which was new at the time, he could publish it within an hour or two of thinking through a specific point, connection or argument.

This book

This book is published 23 years after what many have remembered as the final collapse of the peace process between Israel and the Palestinians at the Taba Summit in January 2001. The *Durban* conference took place at the beginning of September that year. *Al Qaeda* attacked the *World Trade Centre* in New York, and the *Pentagon* and the *White House* in Washington, DC, the following week, on 11 September.

The campaign to exclude our Israeli academic colleagues from our universities, journals and conferences around the world was made public the following spring. A letter was published in the *Guardian* newspaper on 6 April, signed by 123 academics, which called for a 'moratorium' on European funding for Israeli universities:

> Despite widespread international condemnation for its policy of violent repression against the Palestinian people in the occupied territories, the Israeli government appears impervious to moral appeals … . Would it not therefore be timely if at both national and European level a moratorium was called upon any further … support unless and until Israel abides by UN resolutions and opens serious peace negotiations with the Palestinians.[6]

An opinion piece by Hilary and Steven Rose was published in the same paper in July 2002, calling for a boycott of Israeli academic institutions.[7] It appeared under the headline 'the choice is to do nothing or try to bring about change', offering a false dichotomy that is so characteristic of this politics. There were always a huge number of things, other than boycotting Israel, that might be done to help bring about peace between Israel and the Palestinians.

Genuine solidarity is about finding what 'we', who are perhaps comfortable, can do to help 'them', who are suffering. Solidarity begins 'there', not 'here', and it relates primarily to the needs of others; it is about material help rather than using people far away to perform our own identities. In 2014, a student president in Ohio made a video of herself pouring a bucket of blood over her own head in order, she said, to 'send a message of student concern about the genocide in Gaza'.[8]

When we make solidarity, we should listen carefully and respectfully, but there is always a diversity of voices and positions to listen to; solidarity must always also be a responsibility to engage, and to think for ourselves. Solidarity changes 'us' as it changes 'them', it is never genuinely a passive or a one-way responsibility to 'answer a call' or to obey those who say they speak in the name of the oppressed. Solidarity must be a relationship with people with whom we identify, who are closer to the violence and the oppression than we are. It should be about fostering links, communication, confidence and critical engagement between us and them but also between them and them. Solidarity can also be simple and practical: sending books, teaching and speaking in Palestine and in Israel, working with Israelis and with Palestinians; forging links between trade unions, academic bodies, universities, schools and civil society.

Engagement between Israeli and Palestinian academics prepared the way for the *The Oslo Process*, which was also facilitated partly by academics from third countries. Genuine solidarity is about campaigning against violence and oppression, including racism and antisemitism. Solidarity with Israelis and Palestinians is about relating to the reality of diversity within

Israel and Palestine, not treating each nation as a single monolith wrapped in a national flag.

We, who are far away from the violence, we who are professionally involved in the work of thinking things through coherently and in context, have a special responsibility to get things right, to think about the consequences of our actions, to be a force for good and for peace.

If you were brought up in a refugee camp under the occupation of a Jewish army, it might be understandable, though by no means inevitable, if you find your way towards antisemitic thinking. If you were brought up under the threat of suicide bombs, and missiles, and with hostile Arab neighbours, it might be understandable, though by no means inevitable, if you were to internalise a hostility to Arabs. But we, in our comfortable academic lives, do not have such reasons or excuses to vicariously embrace a politics of violence and exclusion or antisemitism and racism. In fact, many Palestinians and Israelis find their way to more enlightened worldviews than those of boycott or racism and antisemitism or violence, or uncritical patriotism.

But the politics of boycott is to a large extent a 'not in my name' politics far away from the conflict and it addresses the needs of the boycotters more than those of people closer to danger. In much of the left, the politics of socialism, a positive constructive project, has been replaced by the politics of resistance and of critique, a negative symbolic enterprise concerned primarily with asserting innocence. It is also infantilising insofar as it contents itself with opposition, often moralistic, often ineffectual. In their *Guardian* op-ed, Rose and Rose talk about boycotts as a method of expressing 'moral outrage', as a way of 'shaming', and as 'ethical refusal'.

The effect of the false dichotomies – moral or not moral, ethical or shamed, do nothing or support the boycott, support the boycott or support Israel – is to divide the world into those who are with us and those who are against us, those who are inside the community of the good and those who put themselves outside of it by their immorality. 'Every rational person knows...', they tell us; and 'what is self-evident is...' and we tense, knowing we are somehow going to be constructed outside of the community of the rational.

They know, already, the key arguments against their boycott, and they work in advance to make them appear insignificant. The suggestion that their boycott of Israeli universities is comparable to the Nazi boycott of Jewish shops, they say, is grotesque. They do not quite say why. But they say it with confidence. They say such suggestions 'match hate emails' accusing them of antisemitism, as though that was a reason. And they say:

> If the supporters of the Israeli government cannot distinguish between being opposed to Israeli state policy and being anti-semitic, it is scarcely surprising that real anti-semites conflate the two.

Notice how the Roses transfer the agency of what they call 'real' antisemites and they deftly transfer all responsibility for antisemitism onto Jews whose bad behaviour, they think, is the root cause of it.

But they are also setting into stone the axiom that people who worry about antisemitism are supporters of the Israeli government. If you worry about antisemitism, say the antizionists, then you must support the government, and if you support the government, then that is why you say you are worried about antisemitism. Good people, it follows, do neither, because worrying about antisemitism has been constructed as a lie, told by people who support the Israeli government, to de-legitimise criticism of it. Later, I was to call this standard response to an allegation of antisemitism, the *Livingstone Formulation*.[9] From the beginning of the boycott campaign, the *Livingstone Formulation* is packaged in with the case for the exclusion of Israelis from our campuses. Anyone who does not support the exclusion is, from here onwards, to be recognised as a supporter of the Israeli government, and as an apologist for its racist, apartheid, colonialist, Nazi, evil.

It was not until 18 long years later that the Equalities and Human Rights Commission (EHRC) reported on antisemitism in the Corbyn-led Labour Party, making it clear that amongst the things that constituted 'types of antisemitic conduct that amounted to unlawful harassment' was:

> Suggesting that complaints of antisemitism are fake or smears. Labour Party agents denied antisemitism in the Party and made comments dismissing complaints as 'smears' and 'fake'. This conduct may target Jewish members as deliberately making up antisemitism complaints to undermine the Labour Party, and ignores legitimate and genuine complaints of antisemitism in the Party.[10]

It is the relentless allegation of bad faith that makes Jews who speak up about antisemitism on the left into pariahs, people who are recognised as inauthentic on the left, because their real allegiance is to the Israeli government, whoever that may be at any particular moment.

And naturally, in response to its findings, the EHRC itself was denounced as a secret supporter of the Israeli government. The hashtag '#ItWasAScam' still circulates on social media, referring to the suggestion that there was no issue of antisemitism in Corbyn's Labour Party, and explaining the complaints about antisemitism as a conspiracy hatched by supporters of the Israeli government. Jeremy Corbyn himself lost the Labour whip since he responded, on the very day of the publication of the EHRC report, with rhetoric that could be interpreted as being structurally identical to that which the report had explicitly defined as amounting to 'unlawful harassment of Jews'. Corbyn said:

the scale of the problem was... dramatically overstated for political reasons by our opponents inside and outside the party, as well as by much of the media.[11]

Antisemitism is not rational and it is never true. It follows, then, that antisemitism can only be defended in ways that are extraneous to the claims it makes and to the forms it takes. Corbyn cannot defend his record, either, by reference to what actually happened in the party under his leadership, because what actually happened is clear, and it does not vindicate him. He cannot respond to what was actually said about him, about his supporters, and about their politics, because what was said was true. In the end, all he can do is defend antisemitism by antisemitic means: that is, by reference to an unseen enemy that was so powerful that it succeeded in 'dramatically overstating' allegations that were not true, and in persuading the EHRC, the Jewish Community, and enough of the electorate to believe these 'dramatic overstatements'; and crucially, because there were enough Jews inside the Labour Party who were lying about their experience of antisemitism in order to harm Corbyn politically. Because it is conspiracy fantasy, it is unfalsifiable, and cannot be dented at all by any amount of evidence or argument.

The *leitmotif* of the *Livingstone Formulation*, embedded inside the rhetoric of the boycott, and of antizionism itself, sits ready to de-legitimise in advance any talk about antisemitism.

Following the *Guardian* letter and the Roses' op-ed, there were boycott motions at both of the academic trade union conferences in the Spring of 2003, the Association of University Teachers (AUT) and the National Association of Teachers in Further and Higher Education (NATFHE).

Later, the boycotters were rather candid about what they thought were the reasons for the defeat of their motions at AUT Council in 2003. Sue Blackwell said to the press:

> One of the reasons we didn't win ... was that there was no clear public call from Palestinians for the boycott. Now we have that, in writing.[12]

In 2016, Ilan Pappé, on a public platform, responded to a claim from Ruba Salih that the boycott had been launched 'by the Palestinians in 2005'. The following exchange can be seen on YouTube.[13]

'Yes, yes,' Pappé replies, making a face to show that he knows it is not true, 'not really, but yes, OK, for historical records, yes'. Ruba Salih smiles at him and reiterates, 'That's important'. Pappé replies to her, nodding and smiling, quietly, embarrassed, patronisingly, knowingly: 'It's not true but it's important'.[14]

Boycott Divestment and Sanctions (BDS) does not come from Palestine in the way that it is often presented, as a kind of authentic 'call from the oppressed'. It was actually first pushed in London, by academic antizionists, and it was exported to Palestinian 'civil society organisations', from where it was re-imported. The call had to come from 'civil society', because neither the Palestinian Authority nor Hamas wanted to issue it. As we will see in Chapter 4, the Durban conference of 2001 was also a key source of the boycott 'call'.

The boycott motions were brought back to the academic unions in 2005, and were passed. The decision made by AUT Council in 2005 to embrace the boycott galvanised significant opposition. We set up *Engage* to organise that opposition. The *Engage* website, edited by me, created a space where information and ideas could be marshalled to help people formulate their arguments against the boycott; and the fightback within the structures of the union was organised by Jon Pike, a senior lecturer at the Open University. Both of us have continued to work as academics but neither of us have progressed beyond 'Senior Lecturer' in the 19 years since.

This book consists of essays that have been written two decades later, mainly by people who participated in that defence against the boycott campaign. The book is partly about their experiences. It is informed by their experiences and the ways that those experiences changed them. But it is also a collection of writing that is crafted inside the diverse academic disciplines within which those people work. If this book manages to interweave academic analysis with personal memoir and reflection, then it will have achieved what the editor had in mind when he conceived it.

This book documents and theorises the relationship between this boycott movement and the antisemitism from which it found itself quite unable to disassociate. The book engages more broadly with the emergence of antisemitism into the British mainstream in the first two decades of the 21st century. This antisemitism begins as a political phenomenon and it leads with rhetoric that takes the form of hostility to Israel. The book addresses the central issue of how a movement that thought of itself as anti-racist became a significant vehicle for a renewal of antisemitism, which then flowed more widely into respectable society.

Antizionism and this kind of antisemitism are also global phenomena but the influence of their British heritage is significant. The *Camp David Peace Summit* had collapsed in July 2000, the *Second Intifada* had erupted in September and the Taba Summit had collapsed in January 2001. The Durban *World Conference against Racism*, where there was a formidable campaign to designate Zionism as the key racism on the planet, took place in the first week of September 2001 and the 9/11 attacks happened the following week.

The book looks back from a time in which the boycott campaign has succeeded in gaining a foothold in the academic trade unions in Britain and in which a safe space for antisemitism has been staked out and defended by a core of union activists and officials; and in which the wider union member-ship, and liberal and left opinion more generally, had allowed that to happen.

The book is the product of 20 years of practical engagement, through which provisional understandings were proposed, tested by events and dis-cussion, refined and developed. These chapters are distilled from two dec-ades of thinking and of struggle. They are written by people, both Jewish and not Jewish, whose understandings of antisemitism were sharpened by their experiences of being targeted by it.

The writers of this book are academics, lawyers and activists who had, to one extent or another, hitherto felt comfortable and at home in their fields. The experiences of being transformed, without their consent, into 'Zionist scholars', 'Zionist lawyers' and 'Zionist activists', were unexpected, trans-formative and traumatic. The word 'Zionist', when applied by antizionism in this way, means 'dishonest' and 'racist'. An assumption is set up that this designation as 'Zionist' applies to those Jews, and other opponents of the boycott and its antisemitism, who do not disavow the campaign or the state of Israel.

Because we, not least the authors of this book, failed to stop the rise of this antisemitism in the academic unions, it spread, as we had feared it would, to the wider labour movement and into the Labour Party. The same antizionist antisemitism which had been licensed by the boycott campaign was normalised at the centre of British public life when Jeremy Corbyn, himself a lifelong adherent to this politics, and a supporter of BDS, became *Leader of Her Majesty's Opposition*.

Populist politics was on the rise into the 2010s, notably in Italy, France, Austria, Hungary, Poland, USA, Brazil, Turkey and Russia. This was the global context in which the Corbyn and Brexit movements emerged in Britain, the former taking control of the Labour Party and the latter, the Conservative Party. They presented as each other's bitterest enemies, but they were in some ways similar. Each sought to focus popular anger against a liberal, metropolitan, establishment, which was accused of being con-nected more intimately to a global system of elites than to 'their own people'.

Both left and right populism fuelled cynicism towards democratic insti-tutions, cultures and principles and they offered charismatic leaders, onto whom supporters could project their own diverse fantasies. Hostility to Zionism was as emblematic for Corbyn as hostility to unlimited migration and to European institutions were for Johnson. The symbolic corrupting power of Zionism, and of Europe respectively, over British life functioned as a way of imagining and feeling the disloyalty of Britain's own elites, to the authentic interests of 'the people'.

The Corbyn movement was defeated, narrowly in June 2017 and deci-sively two and a half years later, after years of Parliamentary Brexit stale-mate. Johnson won the election by attracting the votes of those who were repelled by Corbyn and voters who, either with enthusiasm or bored fatalism, agreed to 'Get Brexit Done'.

Largely discredited and on the retreat from the Labour Party, the antisemitic component of the Corbyn movement has been re-grouping and consolidating back on campus and on the fringes of the left, where it came from. It is possible that the apparent ebb of populism globally, and in Britain, might turn out to be temporary. There are significant numbers of activists and intellectuals in Britain who have 'learnt' that between 'us' and 'progress' sits 'Zionism', and the institutions of the Jewish community, and 'Zionist' activists. There may also emerge openings on the right for antisemitism amongst people who have 'learnt' that a cosmopolitan, educated, metropolitan, liberal, elite stands between them and their own utopian and nostalgic vision of a Great again Britain.

This book, rooted in the case study of a specific set of events, develops diverse conceptual tools and frameworks to explain a number of aspects of how widespread concern for the rights of Palestinians coalesced, at least for some, into an antisemitic ideology. The aim of this book is to help the reader to understand how antisemitism re-ignited in the 21st century, after it had apparently been doused by the shame that Europeans felt after the Holocaust. If this is a lull in populism rather than a decline, the antisemitism that is the focus of this book might turn out to have been more significant than we currently hope.

The chapters

The first two chapters of this book focus on some of the pre-history of the 21st century antizionism that underpinned the boycott movement. Izabella Tabarovsky was not with us in Britain at the time of the rise of the boycott movement, but she was shaped, in significant part, by her personal and intellectual engagement with antizionism. She was born in the Soviet Union in 1970, in Novosibirsk, where her father worked at the Siberian branch of the Academy of Sciences. In 1987, she went to study in Moscow and in 1989, with her family, she emigrated to the United States. She wrote in 2019:

> The Soviet anti-Zionist campaign I personally experienced began in 1967 and lasted essentially through the end of the empire. In that time, hundreds of books and thousands of articles were published painting Zionism as a racist ideology. Anti-Zionist caricatures using classic anti-Semitic imagery peppered the pages of Soviet newspapers. They equated Zionism with Nazism, fascism, American imperialism, German militarism, and apartheid. They compared Zionism to the Ku Klux Klan. The "Zionist" of those cartoons was easily recognizable as a stereotypical Jew of the Nazi propaganda.

...

We, the Jews who lived with all of it ... were targets of anti-Semitic insults in the streets. Our educational and professional opportunities were diminished. When I was deciding what college I wanted to apply to to study foreign languages, I learned that my top two schools were off limits to me: They prepared students for careers in foreign service, and these were closed to the untrustworthy Jews. The third school, a teachers' college, was a possibility but it, too, initially rejected me, even though I had scored in the top five at my entrance exams.[15]

There was very little understanding of Soviet antizionism by those who supported the boycott campaign in the academic unions. In particular, there was no awareness that the key elements of the post-2003 boycott discourse were prefigured in rhetoric developed in Moscow in the 1960s and 1970s: the claims that Israel was key to the system of global imperialism or that it was an apartheid state, or that it was colonialist, or that the Zionists were the new Nazis. The ease with which antizionism mirrored the tropes and emotions of antisemitism, not least its conspiracy fantasy and its blood libels, was prefigured in the Soviet ideology; the ways in which opposition to Zionism slipped into a symbolic discourse of opposition to oppression in general, and the ways in which antizionism's Zionism was analogous to 'the Jews' of earlier anti-Jewish ideologies. Izabella Tabarovsky traces, describes and evidences some of these similarities between the 20th century Soviet totalitarianism and 21st century antizionism.

Contemporary antizionism is quite unaware of its own many faceted relationship to antisemitism: its similarities of form, with its blood libels and child-killing accusations, its conspiracy fantasy and accusations of globally powerful pro-Israel lobbies; its common heritage; because the unique intensity of anger with Israel, and its symbolic focus, can only be explained by reference to already existing antisemitism; and even if antizionism was not caused by antisemitism, it will certainly nurture it for the future. The plausibility of antizionism's denials is increased by its genuine innocence, in the sense of the absence of self-awareness. The Soviet heritage becomes more significant, then, because it demonstrates that today's innocent, anti-racist antizionism is descended from an explicitly antisemitic political culture. The boycott ideology in 21st century Britain has many points of similarity to the antizionism that was pieced together by an explicitly antisemitic totalitarian movement. This is a fact that the boycotters do not want to know and it begs questions that they do not want to answer.

There is an important further similarity between contemporary antizionism and its Stalinist ancestor: antisemitic Soviet antizionism mobilised the same absolute denials and counter-accusations of Jewish bad faith when it was accused of antisemitism as its ostensibly anti-racist academic descendants fancy themselves to have thought of decades later. In 1952, Rudolph Slansky, who had himself been the General Secretary of the Communist Party of Czechoslovakia, was faced with an antisemitic purge by his 'comrades'. Slansky was removed from power, and the following 'confession' was extracted under torture:

> I deliberately shielded Zionism by publicly speaking out against the people who pointed to the hostile activities of Zionists and by describing these people as anti-Semites so that these people were in the end prosecuted and persecuted. I thus created an atmosphere in which people were afraid to oppose Zionism.[16]

Slansky and the Jewish Communists close to him were hanged.

As David Seymour points out, new anti-Jewish movements typically begin by denouncing the older ones that came before them as being based on mere prejudice, but this does not prevent them from *reconstructing* the emotionally virulent cores of those discredited hatreds. If today's antizionists knew their own history, they would know that they are not the first people to pick up and use elements of antisemitic rhetoric, while denying that they are doing so.[17]

Philip Spencer's chapter is a look at how the left in Britain in 2003 on campus found itself in a position in which it was ready to embrace antisemitic politics and to scorn those who raised the alarm, accusing them of betraying the underpinning principle of trade unionism, solidarity. Spencer's chapter is also, to an extent, a political accounting of his own political tradition. His positive memories of the *Anti-Nazi League* (ANL) in the late 1970s are first hand: he was there, and he was a member of the *Socialist Workers Party* (SWP) that was its prime mover and organiser. The ANL was a 'Popular Front', a big broad campaign, attracting support in the fight against the fascistic far right from everyone who would join. There was a lot of cool music and culture, there were bishops of the Church of England, there were community and youth groups and there were the self-defence organisations of people targeted by fascistic politics, and they came together under the ANL's banner. That included Jews. The name of the organisation welcomed them in. The *Union of Jewish Students* (UJS) and other Jewish groups, and many individuals, participated. They fought 'Nazis' out of self-defence, but also out of solidarity with others targeted.

The *New Left* of the 1960s was an amorphous and diverse movement that was united by their dissatisfaction with official Communism. Philip Spencer asks in his chapter how it was that the anti-Stalinist *New Left* of the 1960s, and the big popular movement against Nazism of the 1970s and 1980s, was ready by the 21st century to abandon any kind of serious understanding of antisemitism in the face of the temptations of a new anti-imperialism. The problem was that the Iranian revolution and the Arab Nationalist and Jihadi Islamist movements, which were fighting hard against the 'imperialist' USA and its allies, and were challenging their 'bourgeois' values too, were also antisemitic. If the radical left of the 1990s had recognised antisemitism as a red line that unambiguously divided democratic from undemocratic politics, they would have closed themselves off from the militancy and the energy, the layers of young people and the armed states and movements that they were drawn to and tempted by.

Spencer asks how the radical left could navigate a world in which anti-imperialism had been split away from anti-fascism and anti-antisemitism. But perhaps more unsettling still, Spencer also shows that the radical left's opposition to antisemitism, its support for Jews, even against Nazism itself, was never as reliable or clear as the left likes to remember. Izabella Tabarovsky and Philip Spencer, in their different ways, both excavate the antisemitic heritage of the left that was so open to embracing antizionism in 2003, and so closed to hearing concerns about the antisemitism with which it was associated.

Chapter 4 is by David Hirsh and Hilary Miller. Hilary Miller was in the generation that went to university in Donald Trump's America. That generation saw the 'Unite the Right' rally in Charlottesville in August 2017, where the 'alt-right' chanted 'The Jews will not replace us' and the president declared that there were 'very fine people on both sides' of the protests; it saw the murderous attack on the *Tree of Life* Synagogue in Pittsburgh in October 2018, and it was confronted by the fact that the specifically anti-semitic aspect of these events was of little interest to the people they looked to, on the left, for solidarity. In a polarised America, a cohort of Jewish students was conscious of being caught between the populist right and the populist left.

Chapter 4 focuses on the huge UN, NGO and youth '*World Conference against Racism*' in 2001. It took place in Durban, in a South Africa glowing and energised from its recent liberation from apartheid rule. At Durban, a formidable campaign to construct Zionism as the key symbolic form of racism in the world came to a focus. Antizionism, went the plan, would take the place in the global anti-racist movement that had been occupied by the anti-apartheid movement. One outcome of the pushing of the apartheid analogy for Israel was that if it was accepted, then a Boycott, Divestment and Sanctions (BDS) campaign against Israel would seem like an obvious strategy.

The Durban conference came a few months after the collapse of the peace process between the Israelis and the Palestinians. This collapse was presented by the radicals as inevitable, due to the essential dishonesty of the ostensibly rational and liberal politics upon which it was based. The radials portrayed 'bourgeois' democracy as a facade, whose function is to hide the real nature of the huge, global system of exploitation, which they called by various names, such as 'capitalism', 'modernity' and 'imperialism'. To the extent that everything in the world became explicable by reference to this single, global, structure of oppressive power, and to the extent that meta-explanation functioned more and more as conspiracy fantasy, it is no surprise that 'Zionism' came to appear as a plausible key to the whole model.

Durban was followed, a week later, by the 9/11 attacks on the USA. Al Qaeda targeted the World Trade Centre, at the symbolic heart of capitalism, the Pentagon, the symbolic heart of military imperialism, and the White House, which symbolised democratic political power. If Durban heralded a reconstituted political antizionism for a new century, with heritage from the Russian 20th century totalitarian movement, then 9/11 announced the emergence of a new Jihadi Islamist antisemitism, with heritage also from the German 20th century totalitarian movement.[18]

At Durban, the hard antizionism of the UN *Zionism=Racism* era, which had been kept marginal in democratic spaces, elbowed its way back into the mainstream of democratic thinking. From Durban, it was taken back to every country, and in particular by young people, who would fight hard to normalise the new variant of antizionism as they rose up their respective career ladders in politics, academia, human rights law, diplomacy, the women's movement and the NGOs.

Hirsh and Miller look at the anatomy of 'Durban antizionism' and they focus on a question that is picked up right across this collection, not least by David Seymour in Chapter 4, on the relationship between antizionism and antisemitism. We are used to thinking about antisemitism in an intuitively naive way as a hatred of Jews that motivates a movement to discriminate against them or to eradicate them. If antizionism is an anti-Jewish ideology, it seems to be an unusual one in that it does not recognise itself as such. Antizionists appear to be completely comfortable in their own view of themselves, as consistent opponents of antisemitism. It might simply not be as unusual as it seems in this respect. We have become more and more used to thinking of racism, for example, or sexism, being caused by social structures whose existence most social actors would categorically deny. We are used to the concepts of institutional and cultural racism, which are not caused by individual hatreds. Ironically, the people who are most likely to hold these sophisticated understandings of racism and sexism may be the least likely to understand themselves in these ways when they consider antisemitism.

Hirsh and Miller revisit the debate between those who think of antisemitism as fundamentally one single 'longest hatred', and those who insist that each antisemitic episode, in different times and different places, should be understood as distinct. For them, this debate sheds some light on the question of agency. If antisemitism is really an ahistorial fact about human history, then does not antisemitism become rather mystical? But if there are specific and discreet antisemitic movements, even if they draw upon older ones, then those movements are built by human beings; and antisemitism is mobilised by them for some reason that they perceive. This model might help with the perplexing question of who is responsible for an antisemitism that is carried by people who are unaware of doing so.

Hirsh and Miller's chapter builds a bridge from the two backstory chapters towards two more conceptual chapters, by David Seymour and by Karin Stögner.

David Seymour, an academic lawyer, had been a witness at the Ronnie Fraser trial against UCU. The key part of his evidence was about the antisemitic discourse that circulated daily around the union-hosted and moderated email list. His evidence was clear and compelling, and it included some detail about the serious effect that antisemitism in the union had on his own well-being and health. In its judgment, the tribunal said that as a witness, he was impressive, careful, thoughtful and courteous, unlike some of the rest of us, who

> appeared to misunderstand the nature of the proceedings and seemed more disposed to score points or play to the gallery rather than providing straightforward answers to the clear questions put to them.[19]

It made little difference, the tribunal listened as little to him as it did to Ronnie's other witnesses. It did not refer to the content of David's evidence, only to its form. The experience of antisemitism in UCU was not entirely new for him. He had been through something similar at South Bank Poly in 1986, as a student, in a struggle over the antisemitic *Nation of Islam* leader Louis Farrakhan. There already, he had found that the assumption that left-wing antiracists would rally round when Jews were drawing attention to antisemitism was unfounded.

Seymour identifies within contemporary *Critical Theory*, a turn away from understanding antisemitism as a social phenomenon, which mirrors the essentialism and the mystical thinking that is inherent in antisemitism itself. The social nature of antisemitism is of crucial importance, he argues, because it situates a particular episode or form of antisemitism squarely in the social situation of which it is a part. The ahistorical understanding of antisemitism as 'the longest hatred' tends to miss the particularities of this or that specific antisemitism, and so it cannot but *mystify* it. Seymour makes the case for re-concretising, for focusing in on the context of an antisemitic movement, on aspects that are material and far from mystical: Who is constructing and embracing it, for what purpose, and how they are doing it?

He makes the case for returning in the direction of classic *Critical Theory* understandings of antisemitism as being symptomatic of contradictions that are inherent within the workings of capitalism itself. He quotes Adorno:

'even a lie tells a truth about society'. Antisemitism mystifies capitalism, but it is an expression of something real, even if it is not a true or a just expression of it. In our time, there is a real conflict between Israelis and Palestinians, but antizionism is a way of making sense of that real conflict by using the mystifying language and demonic shapes of antisemitism. It is the antisemite who sees the world through that mystifying lens, they are not passive in that. It is not the bad behaviour of Israel that makes people describe reality in the language of antisemitism, nor does antisemitism just spill over us, mystically, from the universe. Antizionism is not just a quantitative exaggeration, it is not just too much criticism; it is a qualitative departure from reality, it is a different thing altogether from criticism.

Seymour focuses on Ben Gidley, David Feldman and Brendan McGeever's 2020 effort to describe and understand the antisemitism that had mushroomed inside Corbyn's Labour Party. Seymour argues that they do not dig deeply enough to find the social processes that conditioned this antisemitism, and so they satisfy themselves with a rather abstract analogy. They say that antisemitism is like a reservoir, which endures from one time to another, and appears in one context and another, and sometimes it spills its hateful tropes, images and ideas into one of those new contexts.

Seymour wants to anchor the analysis of this social phenomenon back to the social anatomy of the context, of the time in which it occurred, back to the social relations and to the human agency that made the specific events and ways of thinking significant. He wants to focus on the specific context of the 2015 Labour Party and the wider society with which it connected. How did the social relations of that moment tempt people to pick up obsolete and neutralised fragments of antisemitic material and use them to construct something new? How did the historical fragments become virulent again? What need was this new antizionism addressing for the social agents who were constructing it and who were setting it to work? Yes, artefacts of antisemitism do get preserved in the reservoirs of culture, both conscious and unconscious, and yes, they preserve with them some emotionally virulent potential. But the reservoirs are not the antisemitism. The antisemitism is the act of re-creating mystificatory anti-Jewish ideologies, and putting them to work.

Karin Stögner was not with us in Britain during the boycott campaign, but was doing her PhD in Germany, engaging with some of the key intellectual underpinnings of antizionism. Her work is at the forefront of the scholarly defence of the concept of 'intersectionality', both against those who argue that it is antisemitic in its essence, and also against those who mobilise the concept in a way that excludes antisemitism as a relevant structure of power.

In simple terms, social theory groups together people who have similar relations of power and subordination to each other. For example, people who have similar economic power may be thought of as making up classes. The concept of 'class' is more than just an arbitrary grouping together of people in an income distribution, it also implies a community of common experience and sometimes also of collective agency. Other groups of people may be subordinated by a common process, for example of gendering or of racialisation, and they may feel they have experiences in common, and they may act collectively. The strength of these kinds of big, broad categorisations is that they delineate social structures, which are held to explain social phenomena, and they may be key to addressing shared injustices.

People may occupy unique positions, or they are grouped into quanta, on a quantitative scale of class, gendered or racialised power. But qualitatively, every person is unique. That uniqueness is enhanced by the ways in which common structures intersect with others to produce new situations, and those new situations intersect with each other.

To understand somebody's experience completely, and their position in the world, you have to study them as unique individuals. But the danger then is that you would lose the analytic power of the big, broad-brush structures of power, and the huge communities of solidarity that they, at least sometimes, produce. You could sketch the unique lives of every individual, but you would lose the analytic power to say anything about structure; or you could group individuals together as being subject to huge structures, and then you would lose their uniqueness.

The concept of intersectionality worked to sharpen the structural explanatory potential of structures of power, by creating a more granular understanding of reality. Black women, in general, experienced the world differently to white women but also differently to black men. The subordination that they were subject to at the intersection of racism and gender created something qualitatively different, which could not be predicted *a priori* from knowledge of the two intersecting structures. Racism added to gender was not a simple quantitative calculation, it created a new, specific, qualitative community of experience amongst black women.

But in Chapter 5, Karin Stögner shows that later sometimes the term 'intersectionality' came to be used to describe an opposite way of thinking. More and more structures of 'oppression' were taken into account. How could one do justice to the unique experience of black, working class, lesbian and disabled women? There emerged so many new, unique, qualitative communities of experience, and of resistance, that the explanatory powers of class, racism and gender were in danger of being diminished. The answer that some embraced was to go back to treating 'oppression' as being quantitative rather than qualitative. This aimed to trade granular, qualitative observation for structural clarity. But this framework requires judgments as to what counts as oppression, and how much; and what does not count as oppression. Those who decided that Jews were white, and were also likely to be colonialist oppressors of Palestinians, if they did not explicitly disavow Zionism, were sometimes excluded from the community of the oppressed altogether.

Karin Stögner shows how this shift from thinking about structures of domination to thinking about membership of marginalised groups also made it more difficult to see power structures *within* marginal groups clearly, which, she says, eventually leads to a form of 'anti-intersectionality'. Stögner returns, at the end of her chapter, to her defence of (Crenshaw's) intersectionality, arguing that one should not write off a concept when it is applied contrary to the meaning that originally gave it such value. Understanding antisemitism, she argues, is greatly aided by the concept of intersectionality because antisemitism is itself a 'thoroughly intersectional ideology', which excludes Jews from all of the key categories of social life, nation, class, gender and race.

John Strawson was one of the most serious pro-Palestine activists in academia in the 1990s, and therefore it follows that he was one of the first people who was boycotted as a result of the campaign to boycott Israeli universities – because he also had links with like-minded colleagues in Israel. A legal scholar at the University of East London, Strawson nurtured and participated in postgraduate law teaching at Beirzeit University in Ramallah, partly in the hope of educating a cadre of Palestinian lawyers who would be well placed to contribute to writing a constitution of the new state. It turned out that John's proud and courageous record of working in solidarity with Palestinian freedom did not help him to gain a hearing for what he had to say about the counter-productivity of the boycott; rather, his position against the boycott undermined his legitimacy, in the eyes of many, as a supporter of Palestinian rights. This is because the boycott was not about Palestine but about Israel; and it was not even about Israel as it exists in all its complexity but about a fantasy, in Britain and elsewhere, of Israel.

In Chapter 6, John Strawson argues that there was a concomitant phenomenon to the breaking free of 'criticism of Israel' and floating off into the realms of antizionism and antisemitism; it was that Palestine Solidarity also broke free from a concern with Palestine as it exists, materially in the world. Insofar as Israel became the ideal-type oppressor, Palestine assumed, in the Western, and the Middle Eastern, imagination, mythic status as the ideal-type oppressed. Far away from the refugee camps, in which generations of Palestinians were confined by ostensibly friendly state regimes, the Keffiyeh was worn and the Palestinian flag was waved, but not so much in solidarity with the country as in symbolic defiance of Israel; defiance not so much against the concrete and contradictory reality of Israel but against Israel as a symbol of evil. This was the era of the politics of resistance and of 'not in my name', an era in which confidence in its ability to make the world better was drained from radical movements. Palestine was hollowed out, in the imagination of those who performed their rage against Israel and it was employed as a floating signifier. Spraying 'Free Palestine' on Jewish sites became an iconic statement. The idea and symbols of Palestine were, to borrow a term which was often used against opponents of antisemitism, 'weaponized'.

John Strawson says that for those of them who knew Palestine and were fiercely committed to ending the occupation and creating a Palestinian state, it became evident that actual solidarity was not on the agenda. This chapter examines how the narratives of the academic boycott of Israel were to displace Palestine and undermine solidarity with it. It shows how the boycott campaign, which was ostensibly mounted for the benefit of Palestine, actually undermined support for Palestine and has contributed to the increasing isolation and marginalisation of Palestinians today.

Lesley Klaff is a legal scholar, the editor of the *Journal of Contemporary Antisemitism* and was a witness in the Fraser case. She has recently been denounced as an asset of Israel and as a Zionist witch hunter for standing up against antisemitic rhetoric in her university. She continues, with great tenacity and courage, to oppose antisemitic motions in her UCU branch. Her Chapter 7 is a legal treatment of the ways in which recent adjudications have constructed Jewish identity as a protected characteristic. She analyses the implications of the Fraser Tribunal Judgment, as well as an adjudication of the *Office of the Independent Adjudicator for Higher Education*, on institutional antisemitism at Sheffield Hallam University, and the groundbreaking *Equality and Human Rights Commission (EHRC)* report on Labour antisemitism in the Corbyn period.

Jewishness is recognised in English law, unusually, as a protected characteristic in two aspects. Jews are protected as members of both a religion and also a 'racial group'. But when Jews have been targeted by an assumption that they are Zionist, meaning dishonest, and supporters of apartheid and colonialism, the courts have found it difficult to fit this into either of the above protections. In 2006, the High Court accepted Ken Livingstone's argument that hostility to Israel is wholly distinct from antisemitism when it overturned a lower judgment against him. Lesley Klaff explores what progress was made from this simplistic position in the three cases she examines.

Sarah Annes-Brown, a scholar of English literature, was with us in the campaign against the boycott of Israeli universities from the beginning up until the Fraser trial, and beyond. She is not Jewish, but she saw what was going on with a clear, analytical eye and she dug her heels in and she fought for what she believed in; not only against antisemitism, but also for a rational politics and a trade unionism of solidarity and of collective interest. She followed the logic of taking responsibility all the way to an elected position on the UCU National Executive Committee.

Her Chapter 8 explores the difference between teaching and activism; it looks at teaching in a world of antisemitism and antisemitism activism, and at activism in the context of teaching. As an academic, one's research and one's writing appear in a context of all of these. Interestingly, our opponents in the boycott campaign find themselves in similar positions, although they seem to approach the dilemmas with more confidence. They proudly declare that there is no such thing as neutrality, and they will teach and write with explicit political commitment, which is better than the only other option, they declare, which is to do so with implicit, hidden values.

Sarah Annes-Brown's central case study is the 10-minute play by Caryl Churchill, published and performed in February following the conflict between Israel and Hamas in Gaza over New Year, 2008–2009: 'Seven Jewish Children: a Play for Gaza'. The chapter begins with a discussion of literary criticism and teaching literary criticism. It focuses on letting the text speak in its ambiguity, and letting the students make their judgements in open and respectful discussion. She asks whether this openness can survive the discussion of something both as important and as contested as contemporary antisemitism. One's instincts as a participant in charged debates are different from good practice as a more detached English literature academic.

She shows how the discussion hots up when matters of interpretation become matters of recognising, or not recognising antisemitism. She shows how as the stakes feel higher, and the evidence mounts up, the happy disinterest of the academic gives way to a sharper dilemma. 'I was aware', she writes, 'of a tension between my own understanding of the antisemitic menace of the play and a more professional appreciation of its literary quality, nuance and ambiguity'.

In Chapter 9, Mira Vogel also draws on teaching experience, and learning and teaching theory, to think about how one might hope to get a better hearing for knowledge about antisemitism from people who at first do not see it, and from people who feel anger and betrayal just at hearing a discussion of it. Mira Vogel was a learning and teaching technologist, developer and theorist at Goldsmiths, University of London, at the time of the big debates in UCU, the same campus where I was teaching. She was a hugely strong ally and friend. I felt brave and confident walking onto campuses around the world and talking about these issues, but the hardest place to do it is on one's own campus, where one's own colleagues embrace antisemitic rhetoric and thinking. I was happy to have Mira around. She was a Green Party member, and she set up a sister website to *Engage*, *Greens Engage*, to fight antisemitism there. For doing that, she was subjected to a long, but ultimately unsuccessful, disciplinary process against her; she fought off baseless accusations of dishonesty and racism which flowed from her sharp and reasoned opposition to antisemitism. She later went to UCL and then to King's and was a witness at the Fraser trial.

Vogel explores an idea that has been identified in teaching theory as a 'threshold concept'. This is the one concept that, when grasped successfully, alters one's perspective and brings together different ideas which previously seemed unrelated and incoherent. Once this step forward is taken, it cannot be lost. Antisemitism on campus is not indicated by an attainment gap, like racism frequently is, it manifests itself in other forms of exclusion and humiliation. Her chapter works through the thought experiment of treating the problem of persuading people about important concepts during debates about boycotts and antisemitism in a union in a similar way to which one would think about helping students to grasp a threshold concept in the classroom or lecture theatre.

Matthew Bolton is one of the most talented early career social theorists I know. He wrote, with Frederick Harry Pitts, *Corbynism: A Critical Approach*, which was a critique of the Corbyn leadership from the point of view of Marxist Critical Theory. It was a left, materialist critique of what they characterised as a moralist worldview and politics built around a romanticisation of the figure of Corbyn himself. Politically and personally, both authors paid a heavy price of contempt and ostracism from many of the people around them.

Boltons's Chapter 10 explores the academic variant of contemporary antisemitism through a case study of a particular debate between Andreas Malm and Anslem Jappe. I cannot improve upon his own introduction, as follows:

> The panel opened with Toscano's presentation, before Malm was invited to make his contribution. Flexing a sculpted bicep behind his head, seemingly clad in a Taqqiyah prayer cap, Malm immediately announced that he had just unwillingly 'extricated' himself from a Palestine solidarity demonstration in Malmö in order to join the discussion, and 'confessed' that he was too choked with 'emotion,' too 'seething' and 'boiling,' to focus on the topic at hand. The only thing Malm wanted to discuss, he said, the thing he could 'not stop himself' from saying, was
>
>> "How do we assess the current conjuncture in the Palestinian struggle for liberation? How do we express our admiration for the heroes of the resistance in Gaza, headed by Mohammed Deif? How do we understand the drift of the Zionist entity ever further into the extreme proto-genocidal right? And how does this relate to general trends of fascist-isation in the global north?... How do we learn the lessons from the Palestinian resistance and apply it as a model on other fronts [particularly the ecological crisis]?"
>
> At this point Anselm Jappe intervened, declaring that he 'was not here to hear hate speeches against the Jewish state,' and that if the discussion did not return to the proposed topic – namely Covid, climate and the state – he and his co-authors would leave the Zoom panel. Malm responded with a withering 'oh yeah, you're German, right?'

This passage offers an introduction to a whole number of issues that Bolton addresses: the symbolic centrality of Israel and Palestine to every other issue relating to oppression; how elite academics in social theory can profess uncritical admiration for an antisemitic movement; the meaning of the accusation that Israel is genocidal and fascist; Palestinian resistance as an ideal type of all resistance; how anybody who questions such claims is swiped aside with *ad hominem* attacks; and how Holocaust memory fits in to this discourse.

***

The reader might expect the last chapter to be, in a sense, a comfortable chapter, bringing together the themes of the book, underlining some key conclusions, reassuring readers that they have understood what they need to understand, demonstrating that the different chapters are in fact coherent with each other on the important points. This concluding chapter is not that. It is, in a sense, a rather challenging and unsettling chapter. It reopens a difficult issue that the whole of this book has gone to some lengths to close, and it leaves it open.

In 2017, I was giving expert witness testimony in South Africa, in a case that concerned a radio broadcast that featured examples of every antisemitic trope that I knew of. My job was to explain how the programme was antisemitic. I said that its notion of 'Zionism', as a movement that exploited black diamond and gold miners in South Africa so that it could pay for the colonisation of Palestine, was fictional. Just as 'race' is not found objectively in the world prior to the racist discourse that constructs it, so antizionism invents the 'Zionism' in opposition to which it creates its own antisemitic worldview. The Zionism of antizionism only touches tangentially the actual, contradictory and diverse relationships that diaspora Jews have with Israel. During the Fraser trial, Anthony Julius characterised these relationships as constituting a 'non-contingent and rationally intelligible' aspect of most Jewish identities.

'Yes', asked one of the tribunal members, impatiently, but 'What is Zionism, *really*?'

It is a question that brings out the stubbornness in me. I could have explained that different Jews have different notions of what Zionism *really* is; and antisemites have their particular notions too. Some Jews understand Zionism in religious terms, as a return to the places where the Torah stories, which they re-read every week in synagogue, played out; a return that followed a driving out and a long exile. Others understand it as a response to European, Russian and Middle Eastern antisemitism. It may also be understood as the key story of the survival and re-birth of a people existentially threatened and significantly depleted, and as a home for those whose feelings of being at home elsewhere had been devastatingly dismantled. And many people's 'Zionism' contains elements of all of these, and more. I probably did, a bit grudgingly, give an answer like that.

But my first answer was that, in the context of a discussion about antisemitism, it does not matter what Zionism, a relationship between Jews and Israel as an idea, as a movement, as a Yishuv (a state in embryo) and as a state, *really* is. In the context of antisemitism all that matters is the antizionist caricature of Zionism that is thrust upon Jews without their collaboration or consent.

This answer does not preclude the possibility that some Jews may collaborate with or even pioneer the imposition of such an antizionist Zionism onto their fellow Jews. Antizionism sets up its assumption that Jews are Zionists, even while it offers a humiliating exceptional path that allows them to disavow Israel, to bear witness against their fellow Jews, and to content themselves with a prefabricated antizionist identity that promises to allow them to remain within the community of the good.

When antizionism speaks of Zionists, the meaning of the word is clear: racists and supporters of apartheid and imperialism; inauthentic individuals; people who separate themselves off from humanity, 'chosen people' in the antisemitic tradition of the phrase, who think they are better than everybody else. Antizionism's Zionism takes everything stupid, vulgar and evil and thrusts it into the hearts of mainstream Jewry.

Zionists are caricatured in similar terms to the other nation that is defined as inauthentic and vulgar, that is the USA. In our time, we may add Ukraine, to the short list of nations characterised as imposter, essentially imperialist, pseudo-nations; and it is not accidental that the Jewish President, in some tellings of the story, is made 'racially' identical to the 'white' 'European' Zionists of Israel: they are all said to be 'Khazars'. These anti-nations are said to be the ones that failed to learn the lessons of Auschwitz or of colonialism, and who cling on to the worst of ethnic nationalism, while the rest of the world has moved on. Zionism is made symbolic of all that civilised and progressive people disavow.

This is the context in which we have refused to answer for what Zionism *really* is. Antizionism fights hard to construct itself as nothing but a legitimate engagement with the Israel–Palestine conflict. It angrily rejects consideration of its own relationship with older anti-Jewish ideologies, insisting that such consideration is itself nothing but a disguised engagement with the Israel–Palestine conflict. Our Zionism is our business, it is not up for debate with antisemites.

We do not treat antisemitic railing against Jewish financiers as an opportunity to debate the rights and wrongs of finance capital; we do not explain the benefits of socialism to somebody who hates Jewish Communists. If somebody says Jews are ugly, we do not reach for pictures of Paul Newman and Gal Gadot. If somebody cannot see anything good in Israel, we do not make them read Amos Oz, or take them to Tel Aviv Pride or show them that their phone has Israeli-designed software. Jews do not have to be good for antisemitism to be bad. Jews are diverse, and some of them *are* bad, an observation that is already a critique of antisemitism.

Antizionism refuses to consider any discussion about antisemitism by framing everything as a question about Israel and Palestine. There is very little discussion about Israel and Palestine in this book, but there is a lot of discussion about how Israel and Palestine are thought about and talked about in places far away from the conflict.

In this chapter, Anthony Julius, who identifies as English, Jewish, liberal and Zionist, considers the state, and the concept, of liberal Zionism.

He writes in the context outlined in this book, of the 21st century consolidation of antizionism, an intellectual framework that is, to one extent or another, widely accepted as legitimate in left and liberal circles. This is an antizionism that is distinct from a critical engagement with Israel, and which amounts to an anti-Jewish worldview or ideology. Julius is a leader of the intellectual and material opposition to antizionism; following on from his previous landmark contribution to the critique of literary antisemitism and his part in buttressing democratic guarantees against explicit Holocaust Denial.

The context of this chapter is also a catastrophic decline in hope, both in Israel and outside it, that a 'two state solution' will address the root causes of the conflict between Israel and its neighbours, and will remove some of the specific complexities of liberal Zionism. This is related to the sustained strengthening of populist and anti-liberal parties in the Knesset and in government in Israel, and to a decline of the Israeli left.

The days when Benjamin Netanyahu seemed to be a uniquely illiberal figure in democratic politics are long gone. We have seen populism gush into mainstream political cultures in many democracies, and semi-democracies. 'Bibi' has been outshone, not least by the 45th president of the USA, in his vulgarity, his dishonesty and in his occupation of political ground that had previously, and to a liberal way of thinking rightly, appeared to lie beyond the boundaries of legitimate discourse. The context of re-founding liberal Zionism is the need to re-address liberalism in general.

Julius introduces his chapter:

> The imperative to resist the academic boycott was so strong, and the justifications of an anti-academic boycott stance so plain, the prompt to self-interrogation was just not felt.

The defence against antizionism, and against the recognisable antisemitic effects that inevitably seep from it, plays out rhetorically as a struggle of framing. Antizionism positions itself as a movement that sides with the Palestinians against their oppressors, and it works hard to construct the raising of the issue of antisemitism, in the words of the Fraser judgment, as 'an impermissible attempt to achieve a political end'. Insofar as antizionists succeed in this project, opponents of antisemitism feel pressured to demonstrate good faith because for them good faith is not assumed. One must pay for entry to the 'community of the good' by professing acceptable positions on Israel, but even then, no criticism of Israel is ever strong enough. Like Winston in room 101, the 'Zionist' finally realises that only a complete disavowal will do. Antizionism requires that we accept its framing that this is a debate between supporters of Israel and supporters of Palestine; in that context, discussion about antisemitism is made into an illegitimate ad hominem attack, and if it appears, it is interpreted as a bad faith move. The Israel versus Palestine binary also de-legitimises any kind of cosmopolitan framework, which recognises political diversity within the opposing nations, and there are forces that deserve solidarity within both of them. Antizionism is a nationalist framework that insists one must pick a flag.

Anthony Julius and Deborah Lipstadt famously ran their defence against David Irving's libel suit by refusing to allow him to make the trial into a debate about whether the Holocaust happened. Instead of addressing the antisemite's 'Jewish Question', they addressed the antisemitism question. The defence focused on Irving's writing, demonstrating that it was based on tampered evidence and twisted narrative.

We have always related to antizionism's antisemitism in an analogous way. We never sought to respond to antizionism's portrayal of Israel as uniquely evil by showing that Israel is good. Just as we did not object to real scholarship on the Holocaust, we never objected to discussion about Israel and Palestine. But we refused to respond to antisemitism by understanding it as existing on a single continuum with 'criticism of Israel'.

We addressed antizionism as a phenomenon that was mobilised, in the first place, in the diaspora, and which threatened the social spaces where it was tolerated by normalising a culture that was hostile to Jews and by degrading the democratic norms of those spaces. In the context of the antisemitic assault on the right of Jews to participate as equal citizens, for example in UCU, or in Corbyn's Labour Party, we felt antizionism as an attack on us, not only as an attack on Israel. Ours was a movement of self-defence, not an Israel solidarity movement. The struggle against Nazi antisemitism was not a defence of banking, Bolshevism, homosexuality or Jazz, it was a defence of Jews and it was a defence of a democratic and pluralist Germany.

It is as a free person that Anthony Julius, in this chapter, self-interrogates; he does not do so under antisemitic coercion. He asserts his rational autonomous subjectivity, in the face of those who denounce this Enlightenment aspiration itself as the root of all oppression. How could a Zionism elucidated under such circumstances be anything but liberal? And how could the assertion of rational autonomous subjectivity be anything but provisional, partial, a self-conscious reach towards a future where there may be fewer barriers to it?

But perhaps Zionism is a thing of the past? Our great grandparents were Zionists when they aspired to build a state of which they could be full citizens. Herzl thought that this would liberate us from the trauma-induced neurosis that he thought antisemitism nurtured within us.

Yet anti-Jewish ideology has not gone away. Zionists, those Jews who refuse to disavow Israel, are now made symbolic of all that corrupts the world; Israel becomes the key to history; Zionism is said to be the block in the road between 'the people' and utopia. Those who dream at their Pesach seder of 'Next Year in Jerusalem' are outnumbered a hundred times by those who yearn for the destruction of Israel and for the 'liberation' of Jerusalem.

What, then, is the meaning of the self-interrogation of we proud Englishmen about Zionism, we, who have a right to asylum in Israel should we ever need it, or even if we do not? When English Jews became Zionist, they did not emigrate; embracing Zionism was arguably key to making them feel able to stay. Then perhaps it is antizionism, not Zionism, that threatens to force us to choose between our Britishness and our Zionism.

Israel has not become an ordinary nation state with ordinary liberal norms, as was envisaged by Herzl. Antizionism is not only the ideology by which hostility to Israel 'spills over' into the diaspora, it is also a cause, as well as an effect, of hostility to Israel and of Israel's inability to normalise. And neither has the provisional consolidation of Israel put an end to antisemitism.

Antizionism talks about Zionism or 'the Zionist entity' out of a refusal to recognise Israel as permanent. An ideology can be wrong and it can be defeated but a nation state just exists, and then the aspiration to dismantle it becomes genocidal. So long as antizionism prevents Israel from existing, Jews are forced to think about Zionism. Ironically, since the protocols were published as a response to the Basel Zionist congresses, to this day, Zionism is a response to antizionism, not the other way round.

Is that why we feel the need to elucidate our vision of Zionism? And is that why diaspora Jews feel the need to insist on their rights to do so, to be legitimately concerned with what Israel is, what it is becoming, what it could become, what it must not become and what it could never, surely (are we sure?), become?

Israel as an end of prophecy? A homeland where Jews can stop wandering and become ordinary? Or is it supposed to make us extraordinary? The life raft state that is never itself rescued, full of refugees who will never be taken home, because it was demonstrated to them that the places they felt at home were no such thing? And how indignant does the other, more essentialist nationalist soul of Zionism fume at the suggestion that Jews might have wanted to go home to Iraq, or Petersburg, or Breslau, and that their real home is anything but the Israel that finds its legitimacy purely in its ancient, mystical and indigenous authenticity?

It is within the complexity of these intersecting contexts, and in the shadow of uncertainty about the future, that you are offered the last chapter to read, not to consolidate the views that have been presented in this book, but to unsettle them a little.

David Hirsh
February 2023

Warm thanks to Andrew Apostolou, Eve Garrard, Greg Schwarz and Jo De Guia for their help in reading and preparing this manuscript.

Notes

1 Robert Fine, Karl Marx and the Radical Critique of Anti-Semitism. *Engage Journal* 2, 2006. https://engageonline.wordpress.com/2015/11/04/karl-marx-and-the-radical-critique-of-anti-semitism-robert-fine-engage-journal-issue-2-may-2006/ (accessed 14 February 2023).
2 Gillian Rose, Athens and Jerusalem: A Tale of Three Cities. *Social & Legal Studies*, 3(3), 333–348, 1994. https://doi.org/10.1177/096466399400300302 (accessed 17 February 2023).
3 Norman Geras, *The Euston Manifesto.* EustonManifesto.org, 25 may 2006. https://eustonmanifesto.org/the-euston-manifesto/ (accessed 17 February 2023).
4 Noman Geras, Criticism of Israel or Israeli Policy Are Not, As Such, Anti-semitic: A Commentary by Norman Geras. *Engage*, 20 April 2008. https://engageonline.wordpress.com/2008/04/20/criticism-of-israel-or-israeli-policy-are-not-as-such-anti-semitic-a-commentary-by-norman-geras/ (accessed 17 February 2023).
5 Seumas Milne, What Credibility Is There in Geneva's All-White Boycott? *The Guardian*, 23 April 2009. https://www.theguardian.com/commentisfree/2009/apr/23/un-race-conference-walkout-ahmadinejad (accessed 16 February 2023).
6 Hilary Rose and Steven Rose, More Pressure for Mid-East Peace. *The Guardian*, 2002. https://www.theguardian.com/world/2002/apr/06/israel.guardianletters (accessed 24 March 2021).
7 Hilary Rose and Steven Rose, Why We Launched the Boycott of Israeli Institutions. *The Guardian*, 2002. https://www.theguardian.com/world/2002/jul/15/comment.stevenrose (accessed 14 February 2023).
8 Daniel Mael, Student Body Prez Dumps Bucket of Blood on Herself to Target Israel in 'Ice Bucket Challenge'. *Truth Revolt*, 2014. https://web.archive.org/web/20140916071321/http://www.truthrevolt.org/news/ohio-univ-student-body-prez-dumps-bucket-blood-herself-target-israel-ice-bucket-challenge (accessed 14 February 2023).
9 David Hirsh, How Raising the Issue of Antisemitism Puts You Outside the Community of the Progressive: The Livingstone Formulation. In: Eunice G. Pollack, ed., *Anti-Zionism and Antisemitism: Past & Present*, Boston: Academic Studies Press, 2016. https://engageonline.wordpress.com/2016/04/29/the-livingstone-formulation-david-hirsh-2/ (accessed 26 February 2023).
10 EHRC, Investigation into Antisemitism in the Labour Party, Equality and Human Rights Commission 2020. https://www.equalityhumanrights.com/en/publication-download/investigation-antisemitism-labour-party (accessed 14 February 2023).

11 Peter Walker and Jessica Elgot, Jeremy Corbyn Rejects Overall Findings of EHRC Report on Antisemitism in Labour. *The Guardian*, 2020. https://www.theguardian.com/politics/2020/oct/29/jeremy-corbyn-rejects-findings-of-report-on-antisemitism-in-labour (accessed 14 February 2023).

12 Polly Curtis, Boycott Call Resurfaces. *The Guardian*, 2005. https://www.theguardian.com/education/2005/apr/05/internationaleducationnews.highereducation (accessed 14 February 2023).

13 David Collier, Ilan Pappe Destroys BDS, Claims Its Central Pillar Is Not True. *YouTube*, 28 August 2016. https://www.youtube.com/watch?v=IjPJSvTezSo (accessed 19 February 2023).

14 David Collier, *It's Not True But It's Important*. David-collier.com 2016. http://david-collier.com/?p=2229 (accessed 17 October 2016).

15 Izabella Tabarovsky, We Soviet Jews Lived through State-sponsored Anti-Zionism. We Know How It Is Weaponized. *Forward*, 7 March 2019. https://forward.com/opinion/420508/the-ussr-was-famous-for-state-sponsored-anti-zionism-is-america-heading-in/?amp=1 (accessed 21 February 2023).

16 Colin Shindler, Israel and the European Left: Between Solidarity and Delegitimization. *Continuum*, 2011, pp 145146.

17 David Seymour, Disavowal. Distinction and Repetition: Alain Badiou and the Radical Tradition of Antisemitism. In: J. G. Campbell and L. D. Klaff, eds. *Unity and Diversity in Contemporary Antisemitism: The Bristol-Sheffield Colloquium on Contemporary Antisemitism*, Boston: Academic Studies Press, 2019, pp. 203218.

18 Matthias Küntzel, *Nazis, Islamic Antisemitism, and the Middle East: The 1948 Arab War against Israel and the Aftershocks of WWII*, Routledge, 2023.

19 Judgment of the Employment Tribunal Between: *Mr R Fraser v. University and College Union*, Case Numbers 2203390/2011 (25 March 2013). www.judiciary.gov.uk/judgments/fraser-uni-college-union/ (accessed 23 February 2023).

1

DEMONISATION BLUEPRINTS

Soviet conspiracist antizionism in contemporary left-wing discourse[1]

Izabella Tabarovsky

The 2001 UN Conference against Racism at Durban offers a stark illustration of the ease with which progressive antizionism devolves into dehumanisation of the Jews. In Durban, self-described anti-racists – including international NGOs Human Rights Watch and Amnesty International – stood by as Jewish participants were harassed and prevented from speaking. Booths displayed posters picturing Jews with hooked noses and bloodied hands, and ones equating Zionism with Nazism.[2] *Protocols of the Elders of Zion* were distributed, along with flyers bearing Hitler's photo, captioned 'What if I had won?'[3] The security situation deteriorated, threatening Jewish attendees' physical safety. What began with a demonisation of Israel quickly turned into a demonisation of 'Jews of the entire world', who were portrayed as 'accomplices of this evil regime'. By the end of the conference, demonisation became personal, as human rights activists 'could no longer show their Jewish colleagues respect': their very Jewishness 'shamed the anti-racist cause'.[4]

Durban may have been an extreme example of Jews being subjected to antisemitic demonisation in an ostensibly left-wing space, but it wasn't an exception. Progressives cross the supposedly clear line they claim separates antizionism from antisemitism with distressing regularity. From the antisemitic scandal that destroyed the Women's March national organisation[5] to Jeremy Corbyn's Labour Party, which UK's Equality and Human Rights Commission found guilty of antisemitism and 'political interference in antisemitism complaints'[6] to Congresswoman Ilhan Omar suggesting that American Jews had dual loyalties[7] and bought political influence,[8] and that Israel 'hypnotised' the world against seeing its 'evil'[9] to a climate change group demanding that organisers of a Washington, DC, voting rally remove

DOI: 10.4324/9781003222477-2

Jewish groups from it because they were 'Zionists'[10] to prominent Muslim American leader Zahra Biloo pronouncing the entirety of American Jewry – from the Anti-Defamation League to Hillel to 'Zionist synagogues' – enemies of American Muslims,[11] instances of progressive antisemitism have become the mainstay of Jewish experience in the United States, Britain and elsewhere in the West.

If the line separating antizionism and antisemitism is as clear as the left insists, why do some of its most prominent activists, politicians and intellectuals cross it so frequently?

In this chapter, I argue that they do so because the form of antizionism they choose to engage in is, in fact, grounded in antisemitic conspiracy theory. Despite the fact that non-antisemitic criticism of Israel and Zionism is possible, and countless people, including Israelis and the Jewish diaspora, engage in it daily, parts of the left which are becoming increasingly influential have opted for a worldview, explanatory logic and rhetorical devices that are not just similar to but rooted in the deadly tropes of the antisemitic theories of the *Protocols of the Elders of Zion* and Nazi theory. It is a style of antizionism that was formulated and infused into the global hard-left discourse by the USSR through a massive international propaganda campaign, which it ran between 1967 and approximately 1988.[12]

That campaign presented Zionism in demonising, conspiracist terms and associated Israel with all of humanity's greatest evils such as racism, settler colonialism, imperialism, fascism, Nazism and apartheid. It asserted that Zionists controlled the world's finances, politics and media. It routinely invented blood libel-like stories about Israelis. It claimed that Zionists collaborated with the Nazis and were complicit in the Holocaust; that they incited antisemitism and were themselves antisemitic; and that they complained about antisemitism in order to smear the left. It inverted the Holocaust, presenting Israelis as the Nazis. In reinventing these age-old deadly fantasies for the global left, it drew on far-right conspiracy theories, including those disseminated by the Nazis in the Arab states. As we will see in this chapter, the most important ideologues of this campaign personally held antisemitic views.

The adoption of these tropes by the left began in the 1970s. Michael Billig, a scholar of conspiracy theory, observed that in the late 1970s and early 1980s, the British antizionist hard-left deployed openly antisemitic tropes and noted that one in particular, which equated Zionism with Nazism, had Soviet origins. In fact, every antizionist trope that he quotes from the British left-wing reproduced portions of Soviet conspiratorial antizionist discourse.[13] Another scholar of conspiracy theory, Jovan Byford, notes that in the 1970s and the 1980s, 'the far-left in Britain and on the continent viewed Middle Eastern politics almost exclusively through the prism of Soviet antizionism'. He classifies this as conspiracy theory, noting that Soviet antizionism motifs persist today both 'in the anti-Israel propaganda in the Middle East' and, somewhat sanitised, 'in the discourse of a segment of the contemporary liberal and leftist intelligentsia'.[14]

Perhaps the most trenchant critique of left-wing antisemitism at the time came from a committed British socialist, Steve Cohen. Cohen was no Zionist. When Israel invaded Lebanon in 1982, he said he sat down to write a condemnation, went 'to the left press as source material – and became horrified by what I was reading'.[15] In 1984, he published his influential book *That's Funny, You Don't Look Antisemitic*, dissecting his left-wing comrades' conspiratorial antisemitic discourse posing as criticism of Israel. Among other things, he referred to a similarity between the British left's antizionist rhetoric and that propagated by the USSR at the time.[16] More recently, Daniel Randall, also a British socialist, has offered a detailed analysis tracing contemporary far-left antisemitic antizionism back to the Soviet antizionist campaigns and has issued an urgent appeal to abandon this legacy.[17]

What is different today compared to the 1970s and the 1980s is that Soviet-style conspiracist antizionism is no longer a fringe, hard-left phenomenon. It is increasingly moving into the mainstream. As the history I discuss below demonstrates, the danger of this development cannot be overestimated. It contains seeds of anti-Jewish discrimination and violence, and they are bearing fruit. During the May 2021 confrontation between Israel and Hamas, Jews were beaten in the streets of American and European cities to the cheers and encouragement from celebrities whose social media following exceeded the total number of Jews on the planet, while Alexandria Ocasio-Cortez, Rashida Tlaib and other stars of progressive politics advanced conspiracy tropes and deadly fantasies on the floor of the US Congress.[18]

In this chapter, I explore the ideological roots of Soviet-style conspiracist antizionist rhetoric that is taking over the American liberal mainstream. I will look at the background of the people who produced it and the ideology that guided them. I will also look at the mechanisms that the USSR used to transmit its conspiracist antizionism to the global left. Finally, I will examine how that ideology nourished the post-Soviet generation of Russian neo-Nazis, who have grown to be a crucial part of the transnational extremist movement. I will conclude by considering the implications that the contemporary left faces in making itself an heir and standard bearer of this tradition.

The Paris trial

On 24 April 1973, a Paris court indicted 43-year-old Robert Legagneux, a senior functionary in the French Communist Party and the Soviet embassy employee in charge of its French-language weekly publication *U.R.S.S.*, 'for inciting racial hatred and violence'.[19] The problem arose with the publication of an article titled 'The School of Obscurantism', originally carried by the Soviet news agency Novosti, in *U.R.S.S.* in September of 1972. Testifying in court, Jacob Kaplan, the Grand Rabbi of France who survived the Nazi occupation and stood against Vichy government's treatment of Jews,[20] stated that the article was 'the most violently antisemitic statement published in France since the end of Nazism'.

In its content and rhetorical approach, the article was a typical representative of the antizionist smear genre that had blossomed in the USSR in the wake of the Six Day War. It opened by drawing a parallel between the 1948 massacre at Deir Yassin by the paramilitary troops of Etzel and Lehi and the 1968 Song Mi massacre of Vietnamese civilians by the American military – a misleading analogy that did little to explicate and much to anger.[21] It then equated Israel with Nazi Germany by accusing it of treating the Muslim citizens in the 'occupied Arab lands of the Lebanon, Syria and Jordan' the same way that Nazi Germany had treated Jews – another spurious equation, which is today known as Holocaust inversion. Today, wrote M. Zandenberg, the author of the piece, it was the Jews who were throwing Arabs 'into ghettos, behind the barbed wire of concentration camps'.

How did 'the Zionist state' produce such cold-blooded 'mercenaries', Zandenberg asked. He answered: Israeli children are taught from elementary school to say that the only way to treat an Arab is to kill him – an idea that they learn from Jewish holy books. To 'prove' his point, he offered a collection of quotes from the books of Jewish legal code – *Shulchan Aruch*, *Orach Chayim* and *Yoreh De'ah* – which, he said, served as 'manuals' for Israeli military's action. These quotes, he claimed, demonstrated that Judaism preached racial superiority of the 'God-chosen people' over others and instilled in Jews hate for non-Jews. Israeli soldiers who failed to obey these laws, he claimed, were severely punished.[22]

The article was an obvious case of lies and defamation, and the French International League against Racism and Anti-Semitism (LICRA), the interfaith organisation Rencontres entre Chrétiens et Juifs, and the Israeli embassy in Paris protested. In response, the Soviets doubled down. In a piece titled 'What Are Zionists Not Satisfied About?', which Novosti circulated internationally in French, English and Italian, writer Nikolai Rebrov went straight for the conspiracies. 'Israeli hierarchies', he wrote, had always tried to conceal the contents of their most important religious books from the rest of the world. (Only a Soviet writer living in a country where Jewish religious texts were censored – or one who was ignorant about the subject – could hope to convince his readers that a well-known text such as the *Shulchan Aruch* was secret.) The 'worshippers of Yahweh' (a mocking Soviet reference to Israelis and religious Jews) deceived the public about their 'religious ideology', 'hypnotising' it with propaganda as they tried to humanise Zionism.

To prove that the 'racist' religious Jewish concept of 'chosenness' and the supposed resulting desire for world hegemony were what inspired the imaginary Zionist 'genocide' against the Arab people, Rebrov added a few 'religious' quotes of his own that were similar in spirit to ones in Zandenberg's article. He concluded by saying that Zionists cry about antisemitism and racism, but 'they are the ones who put the Arabs in concentration camps, reservations and ghettos to protect "the purity of the Jewish race"'. [23]

There is no room in this chapter to analyse the tropes used in the two pieces in their entirety. Many – from the false, misleading and demonising analogies to the easily-identifiable elements of classic antisemitic conspiracy theory – are a staple of contemporary left-wing discourse. They have been debunked by others in our own time. The point is that the articles provided enough material for LICRA and Rencontres to sue for racial defamation and incitement to discrimination, hatred or racial violence. Since the Soviet embassy enjoyed diplomatic immunity, the plaintiffs sued Legagneux, who oversaw the publication of the *U.R.S.S.* Only the first article, which was published by a French-language magazine domiciled in France, figured in the proceedings.

The trial attracted considerable media attention. The plaintiffs drew on an illustrious group of witnesses, including the aforementioned Grand Rabbi of France and René Cassin, a Nobel Peace Prize-winning French jurist who had been a driving force behind the Universal Declaration of Human Rights. [24]

But the high point of the trial came when Grigory Svirsky, a Soviet writer living in Israel, testified about the source of Zandenberg's article. It turned out that Zandenberg borrowed entire passages – typos included – from a 1906 pamphlet called *The Jewish Question … or the Impossibility of Granting Full Rights to Jews*, authored by S. Rossov, a member of the ultra-nationalist, antisemitic Black Hundreds movement which incited pogroms in pre-revolutionary Russia. [25] The only difference between 'The School of Obscurantism' and the 1906 pamphlet was that whenever the former used the word 'Jew', the latter used the word 'Zionist'. [26]

Rossov's source of supposed religious quotes in his pamphlet is important. He had lifted them from translations by Alexei Shmakov – one of the most prominent Russian Black Hundredists who dedicated his life to unmasking the Jewish conspiracy that he believed was strangling Russia. A lawyer by training, Shmakov defended pogromists in court and appeared as a private prosecutor in the notorious 1913 Mendel Beilis blood libel trial. (When Beilis was acquitted, Shmakov reportedly exclaimed: 'All is lost; a terrible blow for Russia'. [27]) Shmakov believed that the source of Jewish iniquity lay in 'secret' Jewish texts and took the trouble of 'translating' them himself, not only twisting the original Hebrew but also adding entire paragraphs of his own in the process. [28]

Nothing could be more embarrassing for the Soviet Union, which positioned itself as the vanguard of the global struggle against racism, than to be caught spreading right-wing, racist, antisemitic propaganda in Europe. Evidently, recognising that it had no case and wishing for it all to go away, the defence called no witnesses. Legagneux's attempt to argue that the article constituted a criticism of Israel did not impress the court.[29] However, his testimony helped lift the curtain over the process that Moscow used to deliver its anti-Israel rants to Europe. Legagneux testified that, although he was in charge of the bulletin, he had no say over its contents; Moscow sent the articles to him in French for automatic inclusion. The bulletin was sent to other embassies, and news organisations had explicit permission to reprint its contents.

Recognising that Legagneux was but a cog in the Soviet propaganda machine, the court ordered him to pay a symbolic sum and to publicise the verdict in the next issue of *U.R.S.S.* ('in the same place and in the same type as the incriminating article') and in six French newspapers selected by the plaintiff.[30]

The people behind the propaganda

The presence of the reactionary Black Hundreds propaganda in the article that triggered the Paris trial and in the one that sought to defend it was hardly an exception. In the early 1980s, Ruth Okuneva, the Soviet historian and educator, sent a letter to Leonid Brezhnev, the general secretary of the Communist Party, expressing concern with the proliferation of antisemitic tropes in Soviet publications. She supplemented her letter with several pages of what she called 'strange analogies'. Placed next to some 200 quotes from Soviet antizionist bestsellers in these pages were incredibly similar-sounding quotes from Hitler, Himmler, Goebbels and prominent Black Hundredists.[31]

The similarity was shocking and, as Okuneva pointed out, entirely out of line with the Leninist legacy that the Soviet Union overtly claimed. Lenin had condemned the racist antisemitism of the Black Hundreds, viewing it as a tool of class oppression. In his view, there was no room for such rhetoric in the socialist state. How did such antisemitic language find its way into mainstream Soviet publications 65 years after the revolution? The General Secretary didn't respond to Okuneva's letter. But we can venture an answer today. In order to do that, we need to look at some of the individuals who were part of the group that produced this kind of literature – the Zionologists.

The Zionologists

The men and women who produced most of Soviet antizionist propaganda were part of a loose Great Russian nationalist movement, which arose in the late 1950s and gained strength in the 1960s. It was called the Russian Party, even though it never became an actual political party. In a sense, the movement arose out of the same brooding atmosphere which gave birth to the liberal dissident movement. But instead of looking to Western liberal democracy for answers, members of the Russian Party looked to the extreme right and Russia's pre-revolutionary past. There they found a rich inventory of antisemitic screeds that matched their own hard-core antisemitism.

Some members of the movement could not conceal their hatred for the Soviet regime and ended up in the same labour camps as their liberal coun terparts. But many learned to marry their ultra-nationalist, antisemitic and xenophobic views to the system's Marxist-Leninist language, gaining considerable influence among Soviet communist elites, the security appara- tus and sections of the media and publishing industry.[32] In the 1960s, the officially banned *Protocols of the Elders of Zion* circulated freely among the Komsomol elites (the powerful youth division of the Soviet Communist apparatus) where several prominent Zionologists took their start. Members of the Russian Party read White Guard émigrés who popularised the Judeo- Bolshevism myth – the antisemitic fabrication claiming that Jews instigated the 1917 revolution and subjugated Russia, which became central to Nazi propaganda. Some read *Mein Kampf.*

Their 'knowledge' about the Jews became highly sought after in the wake of the Six Day War. The defeat of the Soviet Arab allies at the hands of Israel, which gave Soviet leadership a sense that it was losing ground in the critically important Middle East arena, threw the socialist bloc into a crisis. Israel's victory also gave a powerful boost to the Jewish national movement at home, which, in turn, stimulated the influential Soviet Jewry movement abroad, thrusting the plight of Soviet Jews into the heart of Cold War politics. The one common denominator in all of these events was Jews. Conditioned by decades of a political culture where conspiracism – including of the antise- mitic kind – and paranoia ran wild, the Soviet security and party apparatus were ripe for embracing a notion that a massive Jewish/Zionist international conspiracy was operating against them at home and abroad. It was against this background that the group known as 'Zionologists' gained prominence.

The man behind the Paris trial article

One of the most prominent Soviet Zionologists was Yevgeny Yevseyev. It was only decades after the Paris trial concluded that the Russian historian Gennady Kostyrchenko discovered that he, and not a 'M. Zandenberg', was the real author of the incriminating article that sparked it.[33] By the time U.R.S.S. included his pseudonymous piece in its bulletin in September of 1972, he had already made a name for himself as an author of *Fascism under the Blue Star,*[34] whose obviously antisemitic tropes – including the equation of Zionism with fascism, which in 1971 still shocked the Western public – attracted opprobrium in the West.

Yevseyev's background is typical of several prominent Zionologists. He had been trained as an 'Arabist' – a Middle East specialist with knowledge of Arabic – at prestigious Moscow institutions that groomed a trustworthy cadre for the Soviet foreign policy establishment. Graduating in 1958, he received a plum appointment in the Middle East section of the Ministry of Foreign Affairs (MFA), and the same year joined the Soviet embassy in Cairo, where he rose from Arabic interpreter to third secretary. Returning to Moscow in 1963, he defended his doctoral dissertation, 'Arab Nationalism and Arab Socialism in United Arab Republic's Political Practice'. He then left the diplomatic service (some claim that he was dismissed) and joined the Soviet Academy of Sciences – specifically, the Institute of Philosophy, where he reported to Yelena Modrzhinskaya, who headed the department of Scientific Criticism of Anticommunism and was herself an important figure in Soviet Zionology. (Modrzhinskaya's biography included serving as an NKVD intelligence officer under Stalin henchman Lavrenty Beria, being stationed in Soviet intelligence residency in London, and being privy to the intelligence received from the Cambridge Five spy ring.[35] One of her contributions to the late-Soviet antizionist campaign was *The Poison of Zionism*, a slim volume illustrated with *Der Stürmer*-like cartoons.[36])

Despite switching to the Academy of Sciences, Yevseyev retained high-level connections at the KGB, the Central Committee and the MFA, as well as important membership in the Soviet-Palestinian Society. Being a nephew of Boris Ponomarev, a powerful chief of the International Department of the CPSU Central Committee, who played a central role in formulating Soviet foreign policy (including Soviet relations with foreign left-wing parties), probably helped him to stay relevant.[37] It is likely because of Yevseyev's high-level connections and notoriety that the KGB classified his name during the Paris trial.[38]

The Institute of Philosophy conferred academic credentials and gave scholarly cover for Yevseyev's antizionist 'critique'. From this perch, he authored numerous articles demonising Zionism and promulgating the use of the now-familiar tropes equating Zionism with Nazism, fascism and racism. He lectured widely to Soviet audiences.[39] In 1973, he delivered a lecture in Arabic titled 'Middle East in Zionist and Imperialist Plans' at a Soviet-sponsored conference in Cairo.[40] In 1978, he defended his next-level dissertation 'Zionism in the System of Anticommunism'. The dissertation became a sensation among Russian nationalists but caused protests on the part of true scholars.[41] Because of the controversy, the dissertation was published in a very small print run of 500 copies. (Brezhnev's son-in-law, Deputy Minister of Internal Affairs, arranged for the use of the Ministry's print shop for these purposes.) Some of the copies were sent via the MFA to Soviet embassies.[42]

In 1981, his *Fascism under the Blue Star* was republished, with some additions, as *Racism under the Blue Star.*

As the Paris trial incident demonstrates, Yevseyev used Russian pre-revolutionary pogromist literature as a source of information on Jews and Zionists. His background as a Middle East specialist helps explain an additional case of antisemitic plagiarism identified by the writer Emanuel Litvinoff. In 1969, he was found to have borrowed fake statistics about American Jews from a 1957 pamphlet called *America – A Zionist Colony*, which was published in Cairo. According to Litvinoff, in 1957, Egypt's anti-Jewish propaganda was overseen by Johannes van Leers, a Nazi fugitive, who served under Hitler, published for Goebbels and later converted to Islam. Appointed by Egypt's president Gamal Abdel Nasser to head the Institute for the Study of Zionism in Cairo, he oversaw the publication of hundreds of antisemitic publications.[43]

Yevseyev's unpublished personal notes confirmed that his 'scholarly' antizionism matched his personal antisemitism. In the notes he complained about what he viewed as a Jewish stranglehold on Soviet state structures, the press, literature, art, medicine and the legal profession. He was insulted by what he viewed as the 'ridiculing' of the Russian people by Soviet Jewish stand-up comics. He suggested that the Soviet 'Jewish question' be solved through the following process: introducing discriminatory measures against Jews; letting those Jews who oppose them emigrate; closing emigration completely after two years; and forbidding Jews who chose to stay from communicating with Jews abroad ever again. Those who broke the communication taboo were to be 'severely punished'.[44]

Milovanov's club

Yevseyev's background highlights an important link that existed between Soviet Zionologists and the Soviet Middle East foreign policy establishment. As a group, Zionologists coalesced around senior functionary Ivan Milovanov, who was in charge of the Middle East section at the CPSU Central Committee's International Department (which was headed by the aforementioned Ponomarev, Yevseyev's uncle). Milovanov personally signed off on all publications related to 'international Zionism'.[45]

Working directly under Milovanov was Yuri Ivanov, the founding father of Soviet Zionology who oversaw the Central Committee's relationship with Israeli communists. He had an excellent knowledge of English and travelled in the Middle East, including Israel. It was on Milovanov's urging that he wrote, in 1969, *Beware: Zionism!* – the foundational text of Soviet antizionism, which sold some 800,000 copies in the USSR and was translated into at least 16 languages.[46] (I have personally seen copies of the book in Russian, English, Arabic, French, Ukrainian, Estonian, Slovak and Polish.)

The book's singular achievement was to fit classic antisemitic conspiracy theory into the only philosophical framework permitted in the USSR – the Marxist-Leninist one – and rewrite it as antizionist critique. 'Ivanov managed to supply a strong theoretical foundation for openly criticising Zionism with the help of Marx's and Lenin's works, which no one could argue against', Vladimir Bolshakov, another prominent Zionologist, recalled in his memoirs. The Marxist-Leninist framework, to be sure, was limiting, but even 'the little' that Ivanov did manage to say within it was received as a 'true sensation', Bolshakov wrote, likely hinting at the response among his fellow antisemitic Russian nationalists.[47] Ivanov's obsessive focus on Zionists earned him a moniker among his Central Committee's colleagues – 'the Soviet Union's main kikologist'. The moniker showed that for Soviet apparatchiks, there was no substantive difference between 'kikes' and Zionists.[48]

Another prominent Soviet Zionologist, Valery Yemelyanov, was also part of the Soviet foreign policy establishment, having served as Khrushchev's advisor on the Middle East. This background, combined with his excellent knowledge of Arabic, helped him acquire high-level contacts in the Arab world, which is where he picked up his 'knowledge' about Zionism.[49] As a popular speaker on the Moscow Communist Party lecture circuit in the early 1970s, he gave talks in the style of *Protocols of the Elders of Zion*, unmasking the 'Judeo-Masonic plot' to take over the world. Yemelyanov's book *De-Zionization*, which reproduced the *Protocols* and included his vision for establishing a Worldwide Antizionist-Antimasonic Front, an organisation with observer status at the UN, was serialised in Arabic in the Syrian newspaper *Al-Baath* in 1978–1979.[50] The text found its way to Syria, thanks to PLO representatives.[51] Apparently, the book was too overtly antisemitic even for Soviet censors. The Russian version of the book was printed with the help of PLO's Paris-based Free Palestine Press.[52]

In assessing the Zionologists' work, Russian scholar Nikolai Mitrokhin notes that part of their objective was to 'justify Soviet pro-Arab and anti-Israel policy' to the Soviet public.[53] Their connections in the Arab world and knowledge of Arabic gave them access to Nazi-influenced Arab antisemitic propaganda, which only confirmed their pre-existing antisemitic beliefs. Kostyrchenko believes that in lobbying the Kremlin to harden its antizionist stance, which they regularly did, they were motivated by the interests of their Arab contacts, going so far as to call them Arab states' 'agents of influence'.[54]

Whatever domestic and foreign policy dynamics that motivated the massive Soviet anti-Israel propaganda campaign, Zionologists' most important and long-lasting contribution to global anti-Jewish discourse was to make antisemitic conspiracy theory, typically associated with the far-right, not only palatable to the Western hard-left but also politically useful to it. In the next section, I will discuss some of the ways in which this propaganda reached its global audiences.

Reaching global audiences

The role of Novosti

The Paris trial illustrated two ways in which Soviet propaganda reached the West: Soviet embassy publications and the powerful international network of the Novosti press agency, also known as the APN.

Novosti was a crucial player in the Soviet foreign propaganda machine. Established with the KGB's help, intelligence officers comprised of a significant portion of its editorial staff. It was active in 110 countries and maintained connections with 140 major international and national agencies.[55] Testifying to the significance of the agency, the Novosti chair was a ministerial-level position.

Novosti played a central role in helping strategise and execute the global Soviet antizionist campaign. One of the tools at its disposal was the printing and distribution of pocket-size pamphlets in foreign languages, which delivered Soviet view of Jews and Zionism to foreign audiences. In my personal collection, I have the following English-language Novosti pamphlets, each of which was likely published in numerous other languages as well:

1. *Zionism: An Instrument of Imperialist Reaction. Soviet Opinion on Events in the Middle East and Adventures of International Zionism* (1970)
2. *Anti-Sovietism – Profession of Zionists*, by Vladimir Bolshakov (1971)
3. *Soviet Jews Reject Zionist Protection: Novosti Press Agency Roundtable, Discussion February 5, 1971* (1971)
4. *Deceived by Zionism* (1971)[56]
5. *The Deceived Testify Concerning the Plight of Immigrants in Israel* (1971)
6. *Letters from Europe, January-March 1971*, by Aron Vergelis (1971)
7. *Soviet Jews: Fact and Fiction* (year unknown)
8. *Tel Aviv Fails in Africa* (1975)
9. *Israel: The Reality behind the Myth* (1980)
10. *Zionism Counts on Terror*, by Sergey Sedov (1984)
11. *Enemy of Peace and Progress: On the Criminal Policy of Israel's Zionist Regime* (1984)
12. *Washington and Tel Aviv against the Arabs* (1984)
13. *Criminal Alliance of Zionism and Nazism* (1985)
14. *Zionism: Words and Deeds*, by the Antizionist Committee of the Soviet Public Opinion (1987)

A 27 January 1971 memorandum from Novosti chairman Ivan Udaltsov to the CPSU Central Committee offers a peek into Novosti's 'continuous efforts' to 'counter Zionist propaganda' abroad. Udaltsov reported on Novosti commentators' appearances on foreign TV stations, including in the UK, where they argued that Soviet Jews enjoyed equal status. In his words, these appearances were covered by international press, including UPI, the *Guardian* and American Jewish publications.

Udaltsov's explanation of how Novosti worked to 'expose the truth' about Zionism is filled with characteristic conspiracist tropes. For example, he reported on the placement in the *New York Times* of an article titled 'The Fuehrers and Storm Troopers of Neo-racism', which explored 'the spiritual kinship of Zionism and fascism'. (More on this below.) Novosti also distributed to foreign audiences materials on 'how Zionists, by provoking antisemitism, recruit volunteers for the Israeli army'; on top-level American political circles supposedly providing cover to the Jewish Defense League (JDL), a Meir Kahane-led far-right fringe Jewish group that terrorised Soviet offices and representatives in its campaign for Soviet Jewry; and on Zionists' supposed 'subversive activities' during the 1968 Prague Spring, a reform attempt by Czech communists, which Moscow crushed.

Udaltsov's memo also offered a peek into how the Soviets compelled their Jewish citizens to participate in their antizionist campaign. Udaltsov was writing at a critical time, immediately after the trial in Leningrad of a group of young Jewish activists who, frustrated with their inability to receive permission to emigrate, had attempted to hijack an empty airplane to fly abroad.[57] The trial, which resulted in two death sentences, provoked massive protests abroad, forcing authorities to commute the death sentences to 15 years in prison camps. But the damage had been done, and an international conference on Soviet Jewry was to open in Brussels shortly after, promising more negative press.

To neutralise negative coverage, Novosti planned to send Aron Vergelis, editor-in-chief of the official Soviet Yiddish-language journal *Sovetish heymland* ('Soviet motherland'), on a European tour and he was expected to give press conferences at Novosti's Swiss and Belgian bureaus. In parallel, Novosti planned to organise protests against the Brussels conference by Soviet Jews at home, including having them sign a letter of protest to be delivered to European editors; and planned to hold a press roundtable at *Sovetish heymland* on Soviet Jews' equal status. Novosti also planned to deliver propaganda materials to Soviet embassies and Novosti bureaus, including a special film it produced about the status of Soviet Jewry and a series of presentations on the difficult life of 'toiling Jews' in the West and 'on the failures of Zionist propaganda, which is aimed at inciting antisemitism'.

Some of the specific deliverables that Udaltsov reported are easily traceable. Vergelis did appear at a Novosti press conference in Geneva on 7 January 1971[58] – an event that the World Jewish Congress condemned as a staged performance by 'a few tame, paid, intimidated and frightened [Soviet] Jews' with the purpose of 'cover[ing] up the actions taken by the Soviet authorities against the Jewish population of some 3 million'.[59] The press roundtable at *Sovetish heymland*'s Moscow offices also took place, with Vergelis and other usual go-to Jews condemning Zionism and praising the Soviet Jewish policy. (These events provided source material for the Novosti pamphlet *Soviet Jews Reject Zionist Protection*.)[60]

The placing of a *New York Times* piece on 23 January 1971, was, undoubtedly, the single most important achievement for Udaltsov's reporting period. To the credit of the paper's editors, they changed the bombastic title of the piece to the more anodyne 'A Soviet View on Jews', and surrounded it, above and below, with columns by two prominent leaders of the Soviet Jewry movement, William Korey and Morris Abram. The author of the Novosti piece, Spartak Beglov, built the article around the condemnation of Kahane and the JDL. It was a perspective that would have earned him easy agreement from most American Jews – a fact that Soviet propagandists understood well. But the real point of the article was to introduce Soviet 'Zionism is Nazism' smears to the *Times'* massive audiences. While ostensibly focused on Kahane, Beglov tagged every American Jew identifying with Israel as a 'Zionist fanatic' and member of a fifth column standing in the way of peace between the United States and the USSR.[61]

Soviet embassies abroad

Some insights into the role of Soviet embassies in propagating antizionist demonisation can be gleaned from correspondence between the long-serving Soviet ambassador to the United States, Anatoly Dobrynin, and his superiors in Moscow.

In a 7 July 1970 memo titled 'Some thoughts on fighting hostile, anti-Soviet and anti-socialist-bloc activities by American Zionist and pro-Zionist circles', Dobrynin provided Moscow with an analysis of Zionists' success at penetrating the American establishment. He attributed the success to several factors: the all-powerful Israel lobby; the 'excessive public activity' of more than 300 Jewish organisations; the presence of a large number of Jews in influential positions in American media, business and AFL-CIO leadership; and support from the Pentagon. Having tapped into several antisemitic tropes at once and confirmed Moscow's belief that a powerful Zionist conspiracy operated against it in Washington, Dobrynin noted that the Zionist element 'had struck deep roots in the American soil' and that fighting it successfully required 'a unified and carefully coordinated plan'.

In February of 1971, Moscow directed Dobrynin to study closely the American Jewish community and American Zionist organisations, paying particular attention to the ways Zionists 'manipulated American public opinion' in general and members of Congress in particular. The embassy was to work to undermine Zionist influence among Republicans and Democrats; investigate Zionist connections with the 'American monopolistic capital'; and to study financial and industrial enterprises controlled by 'Jewish capital'. It was the embassy's task to take note of any contradictions among American Jews with regards to the Soviet Union, Israel and the Nixon administration, and to propose ideas for using these 'to discredit and weaken the unity of anti-Soviet Zionist forces'.

The embassy was further tasked with demonstrating to the American public that Zionists were hostile to American national interests and undermined the all-important relationship between the two superpowers (a talking point which also appeared in Beglov's *New York Times* article). Dobrynin was to report on any instances of antisemitism in the United States, particularly among the political elites, propose ways to use these in Soviet antizionist propaganda and work with progressive American Jewish and mainstream press to expose hostile Zionist actions.

Dobrynin responded soon after by reporting on the establishment of a special propaganda council at the embassy tasked with aggravating divisions along the Zionist/Israel line among American Jewry, as well as between Zionists and the non-Jewish population of the US and other Western countries; raising questions about Zionists' loyalty to Israel; helping deepen disagreements between American and Israeli governments; and exposing to ordinary Americans 'the brazen face of the leaders of the newly-minted Zionist "higher race" from Tel Aviv'.[62]

Dobrynin's correspondence illustrates the degree to which Soviet antizionist ideology had imbibed classic antisemitic conspiracism. Tropes about Jewish disloyalty are here as well, presenting Jews as foreign elements in America who stood in the way of peace. The conspiracy fantasy of an all-powerful Israel lobby is a direct reflection of the *Protocols of the Elders of Zion*, a book that fed Soviet Zionologists' conspiracy theories. Some of the proposed actions, such as sowing discord among American Jews and driving a wedge between Jews and non-Jews in America, sound outright malicious. (Israeli investigative journalist Ronen Bergman reported on a KGB operation attempting to drive a wedge between American Jews and Blacks, as well as a series of other 'active measures' seeking to undermine Jewish communities worldwide.[63])

This exchange also illustrates the fact that although Soviet officials seemed to understand that the American Jewish opinion on Israel and Zionism was hardly united (hence Moscow was directing Dobrynin to work with progressive Jews and to deepen divisions within the Jewish community), they nevertheless posited the presence of an 'excessive' number of Jews in influential positions' as an explanation for America's 'pro-Zionist' policy, as though every American Jew was a channel of Zionist influence. Soviet antizionist ideology held that mainstream American Jewish organisations were cogs in the streamlined and unified international Zionist machine, unquestioningly obeying the World Zionist Organization and the Jewish Agency. It is a notion that is both absurd to anyone who understands the diversity and independence of American Jewish organisations and indicative of the damaging conspiracism that infected Soviet thinking and that Soviet propaganda was selling worldwide, including to the Western left.

Building an echo-chamber with the Western left

Another important channel for delivering the Soviet conspiracist perspective on Zionism to Western audiences was direct engagement with the Western left, often conducted via a special department within CPSU's Central Committee which handled relations with foreign Communist parties. Moscow first learned that foreign Communists were sensitive to the 'Jewish question' after an outcry that followed the revelations of Stalin's secret murder in 1952 of prominent Soviet Jewish cultural figures. Another vociferous protest by foreign comrades came in 1963, when the Ukrainian branch of the Soviet Academy of Sciences published an openly antisemitic book *Judaism without Embellishment*.[64] These events embarrassed Khrushchev and taught him, and other Soviet leaders, that they had to carefully manage Jewish-related issues.

Thus, the Central Committee was alerted in the spring of 1966 that leaders of the Communist Party of Great Britain (CPGB) approached the Soviet Embassy in London, requesting help in preparing a statement 'on the status of the Jewish population in the USSR'. Their appeal was a result of questions raised by Jewish Communists in the wake of a new spate of reports of anti-Jewish discrimination in the USSR. In response, the Soviet ambassador in the UK was to impart the 'correct' perspective on Soviet Jewry to British comrades, and Novosti was to send relevant 'informational materials and articles' to be passed on to the CPGB leadership.[65]

The same year, the Central Committee learned that a volume was published in Italy criticising the Soviet Jewish policy. Aggravating the situation in Moscow's eyes was that a senior Jewish-Italian Communist, Umberto Terracini, had contributed to it. The Politburo of the Italian Communist Party (ICP) met with Soviet embassy representatives to express regret over the incident, while Moscow instructed Novosti to supply the ICP with propaganda materials on Soviet Jews and a subscription to the *Sovetish Heymland*. (One wonders what the Jewish-Italian comrades thought of Moscow gifting them a Yiddish-language journal.) Moscow also proposed sending a member of the journal's editorial board 'to appear before a large audience' in Italy.[66]

Moscow also built a strong relationship with the American Communist Party (CPUSA). One example of the two parties' cooperation in the sphere of the Jewish question and antizionist propaganda appears in a 19 November 1971 memorandum, which informed the Central Committee that Hyman Lumer, a member of the political committee of CPUSA's National Committee and editor-in-chief of CPUSA's *Political Affairs* theoretical journal, was coming to Moscow to attend a conference on Trotskyism and requested help in preparing 'materials for unmasking the Zionist anti-Soviet campaign'. Lumer planned to incorporate these materials in a series of articles and a pamphlet intended 'for wide distribution within the US'. The Central Committee memo proposed that Lumer meet with the usual go-to Soviet Jews who knew how to communicate the Soviet party line to foreigners (the group included the ubiquitous Vergelis of the *Sovetish Heymland*). The material Lumer collected during this trip appeared in his 1973 book *Zionism: Its Role in World Politics*.[67]

Lumer was generally a prolific writer holding a clear Moscow line on Jews and Zionism, while avoiding the themes that were immediately identifiable in the West as antisemitic, such as demonising Jewish religious literature. Examples of his writings can be found in the pamphlet *'Soviet Antisemitism': A Cold War Myth*[68] and *Zionism: Is It Racist?*[69] Moscow, in turn, republished Lumer's output in at least two Russian-language collected volumes on Zionism, which included contributions by other foreign leftists.[70] These two volumes illustrate the mechanism through which Moscow's ideologues created a global antizionist echo-chamber: Lumer and other foreign leftists learned the 'correct' position on Zionism, Israel and Jews from their Soviet handlers and conveyed this position to their own constituencies via home publications. The latter, in turn, were republished in the USSR, where Soviet domestic propaganda could claim that the world's 'progressive forces' saw eye to eye with Moscow on Israel and Zionism.

Facilitating the workings of the antizionist echo-chamber, undoubtedly, was Moscow's generous financing, whose purpose was to ensure outward unity on all key political questions. For example, between 1958 and 1980, CPUSA received $28 million in subsidies from Moscow. Annual subsidies grew each year after that, to reach $3 million in 1988. (The money was used, among other things, to publish CPUSA's *People's Daily World*).[71]

Between 1950 and 1990, Moscow provided PCF, the French communist party, with $50 million in direct subsidies. In 1987 and 1988, it also supplied PCF with free newsprint to publish its organ *L'Humanité* and paid the salary and expenses of *L'Humanité*'s Moscow correspondent.[72] It also financed the publication of CPGB's organ the *Morning Star* – until 1974, with direct cash infusions, and after that with daily 'bulk orders of copies' from Moscow'.[73] The latter was a typical way in which Moscow propped up friendly Western hard-left publications. And since these were the only foreign newspapers and journals accessible to the Soviet reader, the approach helped to build the eco-chamber effect on critical issues.[74] The arrangement was crucial for Western leftist publications: when Moscow abruptly terminated its purchases of the *Morning Star* in 1989 (at the time it was buying 6,000 copies per day), with only a weeks' notice, it caused 'huge financial disruption'.[75]

That the parties had to toe Moscow's line as a condition of the subsidies is clear from the experience of CPUSA's long-serving General Secretary Gus Hall, whose criticism of Gorbachev's reform led Moscow to drop its financ-ing from $3 million in 1988 to zero in 1989. (In 1989, Moscow still allo-cated a total of $22 million to 73 foreign communist parties, workers parties and revolutionary groups.[76]) It helps explain why Italian comrades were so apologetic about the 1966 book on Soviet Jewish policy: with Moscow hav-ing allocated $5.7 million to the PCI that year, it was important to assuage the sponsor's concern with a senior Italian communist's contribution to an 'anti-Soviet' volume.[77]

Two high-profile alumni of that Soviet-devised and Soviet-financed prop-aganda system continue to influence contemporary left-wing politics, includ-ing in the sphere of Zionism and Israel. One is Angela Davis, a member of the CPUSA from 1969 to 1991, who became a star not in small part, thanks to Soviet efforts. (According to CIA estimates, in 1971 Moscow devoted some 5% of their propaganda efforts to her.[78]) Davis famously refused to speak for jailed Soviet Jewish activists because they were 'Zionist fascists[79]'. As the author Scott A. Shay observes, Davis continues to advocate conspira-cist antizionist views, which hold Zionism as a universal evil responsible as much for the problems in Gaza as for the problems of policing in Ferguson and Baltimore.[80]

The second figure is Andrew Murray, who served as a Special Political Advisor to Jeremy Corbyn during the years when Corbyn's Labour Party was plagued by a horrific antisemitism scandal in which antisemitism often posed as antizionism. (This scandal eventually brought Corbyn down.) Murray spent 35 years in the CPGB starting in 1976, and held an unwa-vering pro-Soviet position. During those years, he not only wrote for the Soviet-financed *Morning Star*, but in 1986 and 1987 he also worked directly for Novosti.[81] His Soviet-style, conspiracist antizionist views are well-documented.[82]

Both Moscow and the Western parties it financed denied the existence of the financial support. Had it become broadly known, it would have under-mined the appearance of solidarity. It might also have caused not a little bit of indignation among increasingly restless Soviet citizens, who would have had difficulty understanding why Moscow spent hundreds of millions of dollars to support the revolutionary fantasies of the Western left while they, who already knew what happens after the revolution, lived in humiliating poverty and unfreedom.

Redefining Zionism

One of the lasting contributions of Soviet antizionist propaganda to the Western left's anti-Israel discourse was to decouple Zionism from its original meaning. It was Soviet propaganda that developed what Steve Cohen, the British socialist and author, called 'transcendental' antizionism – an antizionism that 'transcends anything done by the Israeli state', which continues to dominate the worldview of parts of contemporary left. This form of antizionism, Cohen argued, could

> easily exist without Israel, without Zion and even without Zionism. [...] Anti-Zionism without Zion has the same transcendental qualities as anti-Semitism without Jews; it has no necessary relationship to anything a real Zionist, or real Jew is doing. It exists in the air quite apart from material reality – except for the reality it creates for itself.[83]

While Soviet officials always claimed that their antizionist position was consistent with that of Lenin, in fact, by the 1960s, they had radically redefined the meaning of Zionism. Scholar Lukasz Hirszowicz demonstrated this by examining the evolution of the definitions of *Zionism* in Soviet encyclopedias and encyclopedic dictionaries between the 1920s to the 1970s.

Hirszowicz observed that early Soviet definitions, while 'tendentious and imperfect', could still help the reader grasp the actual meaning of Zionism. The definitions noted that Zionism arose in response to antisemitism and that it held a view (erroneous and harmful, from the Marxist-Leninist perspective) that Jews were a nation. The definitions were 'not particularly virulent', nor did they contain references to Zionism as 'racist or fascist'. Importantly, wrote Hirszowicz, no one reading the early definitions would have viewed Zionism as 'a force of universal significance': the reader would have recognised that it was limited in its relevance to Jews, Palestine and the Middle East.

By the mid-1960s, this began to change. References to Zionism as a response to antisemitism disappeared, as did the Zionist view of Jews as a nation. Soviet dictionaries now associated Zionism exclusively with the Jewish bourgeoisie, presenting it as inimical to the interests of the working class. Importantly, Zionism acquired a clear international and conspiracist dimension. It was described as a 'far-flung system of organisations' connected to 'imperialist states' and 'monopolistic circles'. Zionism's 'specific objectives and activities' became 'global and regional, precisely in that order', wrote Hirszowicz. The idea of 'international Zionism' as a nefarious global network that is hostile to the Soviet Union appeared at this time.

These later entries also began to incorporate demonising language, describing 'international Zionism' as a 'shock detachment of imperialism, colonialism and neo-colonialism'; 'an essential ally of imperialism in its global struggle against the world liberation movement'; and 'the gendarme of imperialism' in the Middle East. In American–Soviet relations, Zionism was said to conduct 'subversive activities against the détente' – in other words, being an enemy of peace. Zionism was 'extremist in its nationalism, chauvinistic and racist', allying itself with 'a whole assortment of reactionary forces, including Nazi Germany and Italy'. Zionists were said to employ 'terrorist methods and resort to criminal means of gathering funds'. It was an ideology that 'progressive Jews' regarded as a 'variety of fascism'.[84]

This change is hardly surprising: some of the entries were written by the Zionologists who formulated this exact theory of international Zionist conspiracy. The inclusion of these terms in official reference books, however, is significant. Not because they set the trends in public discourse: they didn't. In setting trends, the press was ahead of them by years. But, as Hirszowicz noted, Soviet reference books were massive undertakings organised from the top. They required approval of countless government-appointed scholars, functionaries and censors. Inclusion of conspiracist and abusive antizionist language in these volumes indicated official approval. So while those wishing to believe that there was no antisemitism in the USSR might claim, for example, that the antisemitic piece that sparked the Paris trial was a result of individual editorial oversight, they could not make the same claim about an entry in the Big Soviet Encyclopedia.

Antizionism as a political tool

The conspiracist, 'transcendental' Soviet antizionism was born in response to specific challenges Soviet leadership faced at home and abroad. The Cold War, the intensifying competition in the Middle East, the war for allegiances in the developing world, the growing Jewish national movement at home and the Soviet Jewry movement abroad, all these challenges arose nearly simultaneously, demanding urgent solutions and proactive propaganda support.

Conspiracist antizionism proved to be a multipurpose propaganda device capable of addressing all these problems at once. Cleverly constructed, it provided authorities with an opening to deny that it was antisemitic. After all, if one analysed Soviet propaganda carefully, the only Jews and Jewish institutions it demonised were those that could be classified as hostile to the socialist vision: religious, capitalist and nationalist. Demonisation of political enemies was an integral part of Soviet political culture. If capitalism, nationalism and religion as whole were fair game, why couldn't one attack their specific Jewish variants?

The answer, of course, is that demonisation of the Jews has such a long history that demonisation of *some* Jews immediately thrusts the door wide open to demonising the people as a whole. Moreover, it serves as a dog whistle for antisemites. It is hardly an accident that it was members of the antisemitic right-wing Russian nationalist movement that responded with such zeal to the authorities' need to develop a propagandistic weapon against Zionists and Israel.

Although the Soviets always denied that their propaganda was antisemitic, internally there was an awareness that the problem existed. Within the Academy of Sciences, moderate critics of Zionism protested the Zionologists' output, which they viewed as a profanation of scholarship. In 1976, the Institute of Oriental Studies, a central player in the development and legitimisation of Soviet antizionist propaganda, organised an internal conference to tease out the thorny issue of antizionism versus antisemitism. At the conference, the moderate antizionists attacked the extremists. (When one of the radicals stood up to defend her Zionologist colleague by referencing his father's heroic death in World War II, someone in the audience quipped: 'Was it the Zionists who killed him?')[85]

Among Soviet leadership, too, there were those who understood that the campaign went against the original internationalist principles articulated by Lenin. A behind-the-scenes tug-of-war developed between conservative supporters of Zionologists in the party and the security services apparatus and their opponents. With time, some of the Zionologists found themselves losing positions and even had trouble publishing some of their most extreme work. The Central Committee resisted Zionologists' ongoing urging to harden its antizionist propaganda even further, recognising and fearing that it might lead to pogroms.[86] (Zionologists, in turn, explained the hesitation by blaming the actually and allegedly Jewish wives of several top Kremlin officials who – naturally! – acted as a channel of Zionist influence on their husbands.)

And yet, the Soviet antizionist campaign continued unabated. The reasons for continuing with it would have been complex, but one of them, undoubtedly, was the fact that conspiracist antizionism had simply proven too useful a tool to give up. Antizionism helped Moscow bond both with its Arab allies and the Western hard-left of all shades. Having appointed Zionism as a scapegoat for humanity's greatest evils, Soviet propaganda could score points by equating it with racism in African radio broadcasts and with Ukrainian nationalism on Kyiv TV. Mutual satisfaction and goodwill were guaranteed when Soviet leaders signed joint communiqués with visiting Third World leaders that concluded with the boilerplate condemnations of 'imperialism, Zionism, and world reaction'.

Conspiratorial antizionism that the left inherited from Soviet propaganda continues to be a highly effective political tool. In her analysis of the conference in Durban, Anne Bayefsky noted the political dimension of antisemitism that was present at the event:

> One and the same states sought to minimize or exclude references to the Holocaust and redefine or ignore antisemitism, as sought to isolate

the state of Israel from the global community as a racist practitioner of apartheid and crimes against humanity [...] Success on the political battlefield was to be accomplished by using the language of human rights to demonize and then dismember the opponent.[87]

Conspiracist antizionist rhetoric helps today's progressives make important political alliances and fundraise. It helps create an illusion of a just cause and generate votes. 'Conspiracy theorists are above all propagandists', noted Quassim Cassam, a scholar of conspiracy theory, observing that their theories 'tend to be politics-based rather than evidence-based'.[88] Like classic antisemitic conspiracy theory, the antizionist conspiracy theory offers simplistic and seductive explanations of world events, offering an illusion of easy clarity where, in fact, none is to be found.

The far-left meets the far-right

The propagandistic, conspiratorial antizionism that is gaining influence among the mainstream left poses real dangers. In his *Confronting Antisemitism on the Left*, Randall, the socialist activist, warns that 'the current carriers' of these ideas 'entrench conspiracy-theorist modes of thought that will render the left ideologically hindered and ineffectual, including when it comes to fighting rising antisemitism from the far-right'.[89]

It is an astute observation. But I believe that the situation is even more dire than that. By aligning itself under the banners of conspiracist antizionism, the left is, in fact, legitimising and empowering the extremist far-right. The genealogy of conspiracist antizionism, which goes back to 20th century antisemitic conspiracy theory, means that it contains the same seeds of anti-Jewish violence that produced pogroms, which drove four million Jews out of the Russian empire, and the Nazi genocide. From Durban to the anti-Jewish attacks of May 2021 in American and European cities, the relationship between conspiracist demonology of Zionism and the physical danger for Jews is obvious.

Ominously, conspiracist antizionism that the Soviets pushed to the global left also has a record of radicalising its consumers towards right-wing extremism. Political scientist Andreas Umland tells a disturbing story about a well-known Russian neo-Nazi and admirer of Hitler, Alexander Barkashov. During his 1972–1974 army service, Barkashov became radicalised after undergoing 'a specially designed brainwashing procedure', in which Soviet antizionist literature 'played a prominent role'. The procedure was applied in the expectation that he would be deployed to the Middle East to support Egypt in its war against Israel, which did not happen. After the army, Barkashov founded a karate club which became the nucleus of his future Russian neo-Nazi party. To help educate the members, he provided them with Soviet antizionist publications.[90]

Today, books by Soviet Zionologists are being republished by right-wing Russian presses that also peddle antisemitic classics. After the USSR fell apart, some Soviet authors no longer felt the need to conceal their antisemitic views. Others, on the contrary, added an 'antizionist' gloss to their books and supplied them with introductions denying that they were antisemitic.[91] The same Soviet antizionist literature whose ideas continue to infect left-wing discourse is being used to educate a new generation of the Russian neo-Nazis. The latter, in turn, are influencing the deadly transnational white nationalist movement. When David Duke, one of the most influential voices in that movement, visited Russia in 2001, he expressed a view that Russia could help solve the 'crisis faced by the White World' – among other things, because 'Russians have a greater knowledge than Westerners of the power of International Zionism'.[92]

It is a fair assumption that Soviet antizionist materials are now circulating among the Western neo-Nazis. For example, I have seen a Soviet film, which the KGB commissioned in 1973 as part of its antizionist campaign and ultimately prohibited because of its obvious antisemitic content, surface on the internet complete with English subtitles and an English-language introduction expressing regret that Soviet authorities hadn't had enough courage to stamp out the evil of the Jewish/Zionist conspiracy that the film depicted. I have also seen Ivanov's *Beware: Zionism!*, obviously retyped from the original English translation and made available in a PDF file on a suspicious-looking, anonymous site.[93] With the increasingly important role that the Russian far-right plays in transnational extremism, it is highly likely that the knowledge it picked up from Soviet antizionists has been conveyed to others.[94] It helps explain the warm embrace that the neo-Nazi far-right has extended to the conspiracist antizionist far-left. For example, Duke has praised both Ilhan Omar and Jeremy Corbyn for their anti-Israel stance.[95] Steven Cohen described an embarrassing, and telling, 1980 episode, in which the *Socialist Worker*, the organ of the British far-left Socialist Workers Party, published a letter from an organiser for the fascist National Front, because they were incapable of distinguishing his antizionist rant from those of their left-wing comrades.[96]

This history makes clear that those on the far-left who embrace and propagate conspiracist antizionism face a massive moral problem. Influential players among it have staked their political future, funding and social capital on ideas that trace their ideological roots to late-Soviet KGB, Stalin, Hitler and the Russian pogromists. It incorporates the same conspiracist worldview, explanatory logic and antisemitic motifs that characterise the *Protocols of the Elders of Zion* and *Mein Kampf.* These tropes do not lose their antisemitic charge because those espousing them claim that they are not antisemitic, only antizionist.

Like their Soviet predecessors, the most radical portions of the left may be unwilling to give up the immediate, and illusory, political benefits of this deadly philosophy. But the rest of the left doesn't have to follow this fringe.

It can disavow this murderous legacy. Political victories won with the help of antisemitism are morally corrupt and not ones that are worth winning. Importantly, abandoning conspiracist antizionism doesn't mean stopping opposition to Israel and Zionism. But it does mean committing to the concept of criticism as opposed to demonisation. It means learning about the complex reality on the ground in Israel rather than embracing an easy conspiracist explanation. It means learning to use reality-based arguments rather than those rooted in a conspiracy theory. There isn't a shortage of material that shows the way to do it. All that's required is courage and political will.

Notes

1 A version of this chapter was first published as follows: Izabella Tabarovsky,Demonization Blueprints: Soviet Conspiracist Antizionism in Contemporary Left-Wing Discourse. *Journal of Contemporary Antisemitism*, 5(1), 1–20, 2022. https://doi.org/10.26613/jca/5.1.97 (accessed 2 May 2023). It is reproduced here with the permission of the journal.

2 Anne Bayefsky, The UN World Conference against Racism: A Racist Antiracism Conference: Proceedings of the Annual Meeting. *American Society of International Law*, 96, 67, 2002.

3 Alan Rosenbaum, Learning Lessons from the Antisemitic Durban Conference. *The Jerusalem Post*, 1 July 2021. https://www.jpost.com/diaspora/antisemitism/learning-lessons-from-the-antisemitic-durban-conference-672583 (accessed 6 February 2022).

4 Joëlle Fiss, *The Durban Diaries: What Really Happened at the UN Conference against Racism* American Jewish Committee, 2008, p. 3. On cancellation of the Holocaust revision session, see p. 23 and on bodyguards, p. 29.

5 Farah Stockman, Women's March Roiled by Accusations of Antisemitism. *New York Times*, 23 December 2018. https://www.nytimes.com/2018/12/23/us/womens-march-anti-semitism.html (accessed 6 February 2022).

6 Labour Suspends Jeremy Corbyn over Reaction of Antisemitism Report. *BBC*, 29 October 2020, https://www.bbc.com/news/uk-politics-54730425 (accessed 6 February 2022).

7 Karen Zraick, 'Ilhan Omar's Latest Remarks on Israel Draw Criticism. *New York Times*, 1 March 2019. https://www.nytimes.com/2019/03/01/us/politics/ilhan-omar-israel.html (accessed 6 February 2022).

8 Ron Kampeas, Freshman Rep Ilhan Omar Says AIPAC Pays Politicians to Be Pro-Israel. *Jewish Telegraphic Agency*, 10 February 2019. https://www.jta.org/quick-reads/ilhan-omar-says-aipac-pays-politicians-to-be-pro-israel (accessed 6 February 2022).

9 Ilhan Omar Defends 2012 Tweet Accusing Israel of "Hypnotizing the World. *The Times of Israel*, 17 January 2019. https://www.timesofisrael.com/rep-ilhan-omar-defends-2012-tweet-accusing-israel-of-hypnotizing-the-world/ (accessed 6 February 2022).

10 Ron Kampeas. Environmental Group Quits Democracy Rally Because 'Zionist' Groups Are Present. *Jewish Telegraphic Agency*, 20 October 2021. https://www.jta.org/2021/10/20/politics/environmental-group-quits-democracy-rally-because-zionist-groups-are-present (accessed 6 February 2022).

11 Aaron Bandler. CAIR SF Head Says 'Zionist Organizations' Are the Enemy, Warns of 'Zionist Synagogues'. *The Jewish Journal*, 8 December 2021.

https://jewishjournal.com/news/343182/cair-sf-head-says-zionist-organizations-are-the-enemy-warns-of-zionist-synagogues/ (accessed 6 February 2022).

12 For an overview of Soviet antizionist campaigns of 1967–1988, see Izabella Tabarovsky, Soviet Antizionism and Contemporary Left Antisemitism. *Fathom*, May 2019. https://fathomjournal.org/soviet-anti-zionism-and-contemporary-left-antisemitism/ (accessed 6 February 2002) and Izabella Tabarovsky. Understanding the Real Origin of that *New York Times* Cartoon. *Tablet*, 6 June 2019. https://www.tabletmag.com/sections/arts-letters/articles/soviet-anti-semitic-cartoons (accessed February 6, 2002).

13 Michael Billig, Anti-Semitic Themes and the British Far Left: Some Social-Psychological Observations on Indirect Aspects of the Conspiracy Tradition. In: C. F. Graumann and S. Moscovici, eds., *Changing Conceptions of Conspiracy*, New York: Springer-Verlag, 1987, pp. 115–136.

14 Jovan Byford, *Conspiracy Theories: A Critical Introduction*, Palgrave Macmillan, 2011, pp. 62–65.

15 Steve Cohen, That's Funny, You Don't Look Antisemitic: An Anti-racist Analysis of Left Antisemitism. *Engage*, 2005, p. ix.

16 Cohen, p. 32, 38–39.

17 Daniel Randall, *Confronting Antisemitism on the Left: Arguments for Socialists*, No Pasaran Media, 2021, pp. 76–116.

18 Seth Mandel, The Jews Who Are Complicit in Jew Hatred. *Commentary*, July/August 2021. https://www.commentary.org/articles/seth-mandel/jews-complicit-in-jew-hatred/ (accessed 10 February 2022).

19 Nan Robertson, Paris Court Rules Reds Defamed Jews. *New York Times*, April 25, 1973, https://www.nytimes.com/1973/04/25/archives/paris-court-rules-reds-defamed-jews-defense-plea-rejected.html (accessed 17 February 2022).

20 The Associated Press, Jacob Kaplan; A French Grand Rabbi, 99. *New York Times*, 8 December 1994. https://www.nytimes.com/1994/12/08/obituaries/jacob-kaplan-a-french-grand-rabbi-99.html (accessed 7 February 2022).

21 A recent book contests that the 1948 events at Deir Yassin qualify as a civilian massacre. Eliezer Tauber, *A Massacre That Never Was*, The Toby Press, 2021.

22 Emanuel Litvinoff, *Soviet Antisemitism: The Paris Trial*, London: Wildwood House, 1974, pp. 16–18.

23 Litvinoff, pp. 18–21.

24 Nobel Prize, *René Cassin: Facts*. https://www.nobelprize.org/prizes/peace/1968/cassin/facts/ (accessed 7 February 2022).

25 Litvinoff, pp. 67–71. Gennady Kostyrchenko. *Tainaya politika: ot Brezhneva do Gorbacheva. Chast I: Vlast – Yevreiski vopros, intelligentsiya*, Moskva: Mezhdunarodniye otnosheniya, 2019, p. 500.

26 Litvinoff, pp. 22, 70.

27 Mendel Beilis, *Blood Libel: The Life and Memory of Mendel Beilis*, Chicago: Beilis Publishing, 2011.

28 Kostyrchenko, pp. 500–501; Grigory Svirsky, *Khozhdeniye v shtrafniki*: Parizhskii tribunal. O moikh dushevnykh druzyakh – yedinomyslakh. In: *Shtrafniki*. http://shtrafniki.narod.ru/svirski-frames.files/tribunal.html (accessed 7 February 2022).

29 Litvinoff, pp. 100–102, 116.

30 Litvinoff, p. 115.

31 Ruth Okuneva, Antisemitic Notions: Strange Analogies. In: Theodore Freedman, ed., *Anti-Semitism in the Soviet Union: Its Roots and Consequences*, New York: Freedom Library Press of the Anti-defamation League of B'nai B'rith, New York, 1984, pp. 266–381.

32 Nikolai Mitrokhin, *Russkaya partiya: dvizheniye russkikh natsionalistov v SSSR, 1953–1985 gody*, M: Novoye literaturnoye obozreniye, 2003.
33 Kostyrchenko, p. 501.
34 Yevgeny Yevseyev, *Fashizm pod goluboi zvezdoi*, Moskva: Molodaya gvardiya, 1971.
35 Kostyrchenko, p. 537; Nikolai Dolgopolov. Razvedchitsa Yelena Modrzhinskaya znala: nemtsy napadut 22 iyuya. *Vechernyaya Moskva*, 21 June 2014. https:// vm.ru/society/193689-razvedchica-elena-modrzhinskaya-znala-nemcy-napadut -22-iyunya, (accessed 8 February 2022). On Modrzhinskaya's involvement in the Cambridge Five affair, see Nigel West and Oleg Tsarev, eds. 39.Elena Mdrzhinskaya's Report, April 1943 in 'Part IV: NKVD Reports'. In: *Triplex: More Secrets from the Cambridge Spies*, New Haven: Yale University Press, 2009, Kindle edition.
36 Yelena Modrzhinskaya and Vladimir Lapsky. *Yad sionizma*, M. Pedagogika, 1983.
37 Yevseyev's bio: Kostyrchenko, pp. 527–538. On Yevseyev's membership in the Soviet–Palestinian society, see p. 537.
38 Kostyrchenko, p. 501.
39 Mitrokhin, p. 404.
40 Kostyrchenko, pp. 527–538.
41 Mitrokhin, p. 406.
42 Kostyrchenko, p. 537.
43 Emanuel Litvinoff, Soviet Antizionism or Antisemitism? *Soviet Jewish Affairs*, 3(4), 12, 1968. On van Leers heading Nasser's Institute for the Study of Zionism, see Kevin Coogan, audio interview with Dave Emory, *For the Record*, 5 August 2002. https://spitfirelist.com/for-the-record/ftr-371-interview-with-kevin-coo-gan/ (accessed 21 February 2022).
44 Kostyrchenko, p. 530.
45 Kostyrchenko, pp. 516–517.
46 Mitrokhin, p. 405.
47 Vladimir Bolshakov, *Golubaya Zvezda protiv krasnoy: kak sionisty stali mogilshchikami kommunizma*, Moskva: Algoritm, 2014, pp. 336–337.
48 Kostyrchenko, p. 517. On 'kikologist', see Bolshakov, p. 336.
49 Viktor Shnirelman, *Russkoye Rodnoveriye. Neoyazychestvo i natsionalizm v sovremennoi Rossii*, 2012, p. 153.
50 Ibid.
51 Kostyrchenko, p. 539.
52 Ibid.
53 Mitrokhin, p. 404.
54 Kostyrchenko, p. 525.
55 Baruch A. Hazan, *Soviet Propaganda: A Case Study of the Middle East Conflict*, Routledge, 2000 (first published in 1976), p. 49.
56 The *New York Times* reports that this pamphlet was widely publicized' by another Soviet news agency, TASS. Hedrick Smith. 'Soviet Steps Up Criticism of Israeli Life. *New York Times*, 28 January 1972. https://www.nytimes.com/1972/01/28/ archives/soviet-steps-up-criticism-of-israeli-life.html (accessed 17 February 2022).
57 Izabella Tabarovsky, Hijacking History. *Tablet*, 24 December 2020, https:// www.tabletmag.com/sections/history/articles/tabarovsky-leningrad-hijacking -history-soviet-jews (accessed 13 February 2022).
58 Sovetish Heimland Editor Says Trials Secret to Prevent Antisemitic Stirrings. *JTA Daily News Bulletin*, 8 January 1971. http://pdfs.jta.org/1971/1971-01-08 _005.pdf?_ga=2.158240185.288052354.1643188497-111540297.1607076895 (accessed 9 February 2022).

59 WJ Congress Challenges Vergelis' Statement on Soviet Jewry. *JTA Daily News Bulletin*, 12 January 1971. http://pdfs.jta.org/1971/1971-01-12_007.pdf?_ga =2.211822999.288052354.1643188497-111540297.1607076895 (accessed 9 February 2022).

60 *Soviet Jews Reject Zionist Protection: Novosti Press Agency Roundtable, Discussion*, Moscow: Novosti, 5 February 1971. Aron Vergelis. *Letters from Europe (January–March 1971)*, Moscow: Novosti Publishing House, 1972.

61 Spartak Beglov, A Soviet View on Jews. *New York Times*, 23 January 1971. https://www.nytimes.com/1971/01/22/archives/a-soviet-view-on-jews.html?searchResultPosition=1 (accessed 9 February 2022).

62 Kostyrchenko, pp. 492–497.

63 Ronen Bergman, The KGB's Middle East Files: The Fight against Zionism and World Jewry, *Ynet Magazine*. https://www.ynetnews.com/articles/0,7340,L -4886594,00.html (accessed 9 February 2022).

64 Trofim Kichko, *Iudiasm bez prikras*, Lviv: Vidavnitsvo AN USSR, 1963.

65 Boris Morozov, *Documents on Soviet Jewish Immigration*, London: Frank Cass Publishers, 1999, pp. 58–59.

66 Morozov, p. 89–93.

67 Morozov, pp. 125–126, 230.

68 Hyman Lumer, '*Soviet Antisemitism*' a Cold War Myth, New York: Political Affairs Publishers, 1964. https://www.marxists.org/subject/jewish/lumer-soviet -anti-semitism.pdf (accessed 11 February 2022).

69 *Zionism: Is It Racist? Two Statements on the UN Resolution by Dr. Hyman Lumer and Meir Vilner*, New York: Committee for a Just Peace in the Middle East. Hyman's contribution is a republication of his article in *The Daily World Magazine* of 29 November 1975. https://www.marxists.org/subject/jewish/zion-ism-racist.pdf (accessed 11 February 2022).

70 The 1974 collected volume *Against Zionism and Israeli Aggression* included chapter by him titled 'The Reactionary Role of Zionism'. The 1980 volume *Zionism: Truth and Fiction* contained a shortened version of his pamphlet: *Israel Today: War or Peace?*

71 Harvey Klehr, Jon Earl Haynes, Kyrill M. Anderson. *The Soviet World of American Communism*, New Haven: Yale University Press, 1998, Kindle edition, Section: Fifty Years of Soviet Subsidies.

72 Victor Loupan, Pierre Lorrain, *L'argent de Moscou: L'histoire la plus secrete du PCF*, Plon, 1994, pp. 231–234.

73 Martin Deeson, Still flying the red flag. *Independent*, 23 May 2005. https://www .independent.co.uk/news/media/still-flying-the-red-flag-491723.html (accessed 21 February 2022).

74 Loupan, ibid.

75 Deeson, ibid.

76 Klehr et al, ibid.

77 Loupan, Lorrain, p. 212.

78 Beatrice de Graaf, *Evaluating Counterterrorism Performance: A Comparative Study*, Routledge, 2011, Kindle edition. To locate the quote, see footnote 41 and the text it references.

79 Jonathan S. Tobin, Opposing Honors for Angela Davis Isn't Racist. *National Review*, 11 January 2019. https://www.nationalreview.com/2019/01/opposing -honors-for-angela-davis-isnt-racist/ (accessed 22 February, 2022)

80 Scott A. Shay, *Conspiracy U: A Case Study*, Wicked Son, 2021, pp. 45, 81–83.

81 Lucy Fisher, Ex-Communist Who Defended Stalin Will Lead Corbyn's Team. *Times of London*, 16 May 2017. https://www.thetimes.co.uk/article/ex-communist-who-defended-stalin-will-lead-corbyns-team-h5wxqgq0l (accessed 22 February, 2022).

82 Daniel Sugarman, Corbyn Appoints Anti-Israel Activist Andrew Murray as Campaign Chief. *Jewish Chronicle*, 15 May 2017. https://www.thejc.com/news /uk/corbyn-appoints-anti-israel-activist-andrew-murray-as-campaign-chief-1 .438501 (accessed 22 February 2022).

83 Cohen, *That's Funny, You Don't Look Antisemitic*, p. 41.

84 Lukasz Hirszowicz, Soviet Perceptions of Zionism. *Soviet Jewish Affairs*, 9(1), 53–65, 1979.

85 E. L. Solmar, Protocols of the Anti-Zionists. *Soviet Jewish Affairs*, 8(2), 57–66, 1978.

86 Kostyrchenko, p. 525.

87 Baycfsky, p. 72.

88 Quassim Cassam, *Conspiracy Theories*, Cambridge: Polity Press, 2019, p. 89.

89 Randall, p. 210.

90 Umland, p. 164.

91 For example, the deeply antisemitic novel *Tlya* by Ivan Shevtsov was republished in the post-Soviet era with the subtitle: *An Antizionist Novel*. Also see Ivan Shevtsov, *Tlya. Antisionistskii roman*, Moskva: Institut russkoi tsivilizatsii, 2014.

92 ADL, *David Duke in Russia*. https://web.archive.org/web/20131231155744/ http://archive.adl.org/anti_semitism/duke_russia.html#.UsLpe-rP02w (accessed 11 February 2021).

93 It was obvious that the translation was retyped by a non-Russian speaker, because whoever typed it had omitted Cyrillic references in the endnotes. After I linked to the site in one of my articles, the site, and the book, disappeared. I have the book in my personal archive.

94 Elizabeth Grimm Arsenault and Joseph Stabile. Confronting Russia's Role in Transnational White Supremacy Extremism. *Just Security*, 6 February 2020. https://www.justsecurity.org/68420/confronting-russias-role-in-transnational -white-supremacist-extremism/ (accessed 11 February 2022).

95 TOI staff, Corbyn Praised by Former KKK Grand Wizard and Ex-leader of Far-right BNP. *Times of Israel*, 24 August 2018. https://www.timesofisrael.com/ corbyn-praised-by-former-kkk-grand-wizard-and-ex-leader-of-far-right-bnp/ (accessed 11 February 2021). Also see Victor Morton. David Duke Praises Rep. Ilhan Omar. *AP News*, 7 March 2019. https://apnews.com/article/race-and -ethnicity-racial-injustice-david-duke-a97b8b2d48c163c5965c2574ccbbe3d3 (accessed 11 February 2021).

96 Cohen, p. 37.

2

TURNING FULL CIRCLE

From the Anti-Nazi League to Corbynism: how so much of the radical left in the UK abandoned Jews and embraced antisemitism

Philip Spencer

In the late 1970s, the radical left in the UK created a surprisingly successful mass movement, the *Anti-Nazi League* (ANL), to combat the rising force of the far right. Much of the drive for this appeared to come from a commitment to combat antisemitism, and indeed support from the Jewish community was an important factor in winning support for that struggle. Then, the antizionism of some on the radical left was not taken that seriously, either by many in the movement or by the Jewish community. Over time, however, as the hopes of the radical left have been repeatedly disappointed, an antizionism which is fundamentally antisemitic has become increasingly mandatory, effectively substituting itself as a way of thinking about the world for the original radical leftist one. Within this frame of reference, the state of Israel, and the very large majority of Jews who support it, are seen as responsible for all the major evils that afflict the world today and in direct opposition to all the progressive forces seeking to change it. This was not inevitable, although there are certainly some powerful undercurrents that can be traced back to the origins of the left itself, which have pulled it in this destructive, and self-destructive direction.

The radical left

The radical left in the UK (as more generally) may be said to comprise an assortment of groups who have long identified themselves as being further to the left than social democratic parties. Many of the groupings involved share a commitment with Communist parties to the legacy of the Russian Revolution, but for a considerable time they were sharply critical of those parties for having, in their view, betrayed that legacy. Despite these distinctions,

DOI: 10.4324/9781003222477-3

radical leftists have from time to time secretly entered both social democratic and Communist parties, in the hope of winning over some of their
members so that they could then form mass parties themselves, whilst others have attempted (rather more honestly) to create mass parties on their
own. Either way, they have been repeatedly unsuccessful, but this has not
prevented them from exercising sometimes considerable influence over the
rest of the left.

With regard to the struggle against antisemitism, this influence has at
times been exercised for good. However, over the past three decades, this
influence has increasingly been exercised for ill. In that time, there has been
a distinct and alarming shift in the ways that much of the radical left in the
UK has come to relate to Jews. What once could largely have been assumed,
that the radical left would be the first to defend Jews against antisemitic
attacks, is no longer the case. In fact, it is very largely the opposite. Much
(though not all)[1] of the radical left not only does not defend Jews from
attack, but collude with, facilitate and actively participate in and even promote antisemitism itself.

The radical left, anti-imperialism, anti-capitalism and anti-Stalinism

For many decades, the radical left in the UK as elsewhere was dominated
by the Communist Party. The latter never succeeded in establishing itself as
a credible rival to the Labour Party and by the late 1950s had lost much of
even the limited appeal it had, especially to younger people. The crushing
of popular uprisings against Communist rule in East Germany in 1953 and
even more so in Hungary in 1956 led moreover to a significant exodus of
members from the party. In alliance with a heterodox set of other radicals,
these dissidents created what became known as the *New Left*. Broadly
speaking, this *New Left* sought to provide an alternative vision of socialism
both to that of the Communist Party, still tying itself to the Soviet model,
and to the reformist one offered by the Labour Party. Whilst it shared with
Communists an anti-capitalist and anti-imperialist orientation, it was also
resolutely anti-Stalinist. Its anti-imperialism (and this has in the end proven
to be a fatal flaw) was never that easy to distinguish from that of what it
derided as an *Old Left*, since it was also almost exclusively focused only on
Western imperialism, even if the *New Left* saw itself as more determined
and more active in supporting anti-colonial movements, especially in its
mobilisation of opposition to the Vietnam War. Its anti-capitalism, on the
other hand, led the *New Left* to see not only parties of the right but also
social democratic parties, and at times Communist parties too (notably in its
response to the explosive uprising of students and workers in France in May
1968), as objectively upholders of an essentially exploitative order.

The *New Left's* anti-Stalinism was particularly formative, however, as its roots in disgust at the events of 1953 and 1956 were strengthened by reactions to the further repression by the Soviet Union of the attempt to build a 'socialism with a human face' in Czechoslovakia in 1968. For a long time, therefore, it was possible for many radicals to believe quite sincerely that Communist antisemitism had nothing to do with them but was only part and parcel of the deviation from or betrayal of Marxism by Stalin.

There are of course very many problems with this response more generally, which there is no space to go into here. But on the question of antisemitism, it has particular weaknesses, which have come to play a decisive role in how and why the radical left has reversed its position and come not to support Jews but to target them as the main enemy.

Emancipation, antisemitism and the left

At the most fundamental level, these weaknesses may be traced back to the Enlightenment, the intellectual crucible from which the left first emerged in the 17th and 18th centuries.[2] Many (though again not all) Enlightenment thinkers adopted a highly problematic and exclusionary form of universalism which cast Jews as a problem. They thought that antisemitism hitherto had been understandable because Jews, confined to the ghetto and excluded from the 'benefits' of civilisation, had supposedly adopted many bad habits. They then made emancipation conditional on Jews behaving better but many came to believe that Jews had failed this test. Too many Jews (apparently) clung to their own peculiarly backward religion (far worse than Christianity or Islam which, as universalist doctrines, had supposedly rightly superseded Judaism). The new universalism required Jews to abandon their backward beliefs, indeed their Jewish identity as such, and to assimilate wholly and unreservedly to the values, beliefs and norms of the society which was now generously offering them admittance, and adhere to the progressive movements which were trying to realise the promises of the Enlightenment.

Instead, some on the left came to believe that Jews continued without good reason to remain more loyal to each other than to their fellow citizens; to place their own interests over and above those of others; to claim unreasonably that their misfortunes were greater than others; to engage in special pleading that they deserved better treatment than others who were actually in a much worse situation. In these circumstances, some came to think that antisemitism, for which there had been no excuse before Emancipation, might now be understandable, condonable, even legitimate.

In one version of this argument, which emerged on the radical left in the late 19th century, antisemitism was even seen as having some potential for progressive movements. If people might understandably react angrily to Jews continuing to behave 'badly', then they might also then be won over to the progressive cause.[3] This approach was criticised by others at the time who defined antisemitism as the 'socialism of fools', but this was never a wholly satisfactory formulation either because it could be taken to imply that it was still a form of socialism, even if foolish. It has never provided that much of a barrier to a fuller embrace of antisemitism when hopes might appear more terminally frustrated. It could then become all too easy to blame Jews entirely, to see them as fundamentally responsible for things not turning out well, for being in league with the forces of reaction, conspiring with (if not directing) them to block radical change.

Antisemitism more generally always has the potential to attract radicals (right and left) because it offers, as a number of Marxists have rightly pointed out, a superficially attractive explanation for why things keep going wrong.[4] The superficiality lies in the focus on a surface phenomenon in which a small part comes to stand for the whole. To give only three examples, it can be made to appear, from an anti-capitalist perspective, that the problem lies with a few (Jewish) individuals rather than with the capitalist class as a whole; or that it is (Jewish) finance capital (or even, within finance capital, the phenomenon of speculation) that is to blame rather than the accumulation dynamic that is at the heart of the capitalist mode of production; or that it is the malign behaviour of a few individuals (Jews) that causes crises rather than the recurring tendency of the capitalist system itself to generate them. In each of these cases, moreover, there has been a marked tendency to personalise the problem, to identify particular individuals (Jews) as the guilty party, the wicked ones who have to be punished.

In many ways, that has been what has happened on the radical left in recent years. The hopes of those who created the *New Left* have been dashed repeatedly. Radical change did not come about, or, if it did, it came from the right, not the left. Instead of socialist revolutions spreading in the West, as seemed possible at one moment – from France in 1968 to Portugal in 1975 – the forces of reaction took hold, rolling back many of the gains that had been made by working class movements and political parties (albeit oft derided social democratic ones) in the three decades that followed the Second World War.[5] Globally, anti-colonial movements which had succeeded in throwing off the yoke of imperialism often ended with the imposition of home-grown authoritarian and oppressive regimes, from China to Cuba to Algeria to Cambodia to Zimbabwe to Venezuela and Nicaragua (to give only a few examples). Sometimes these regimes became extremely violent and adopted ideologies and self-justifications diametrically opposed to everything that radical leftists originally held dear. Faced with the wreckage of hopes and aspirations, it has been hard for some to resist exactly the temptation identified above – to adopt a superficially radical explanation which blames Jews for things going so very wrong.

This is not, however, inevitable. There has always been another tradition on the radical left, also going back to the Enlightenment, which has not cast Jews as the other of the universal. There has always been another version of universalism, inclusionary not exclusionary, which seeks to include Jews within its compass. Although Marx spoiled his own argument with some appalling language, in his response to a contemporary radical, the left Hegelian Bruno Bauer, he did insist that Jews were as entitled as any other group to their rights and he insisted that they did not have to meet any conditions at all for their full inclusion.[6] Rosa Luxemburg followed Marx in this, distinguishing herself from other Marxists of her generation who absurdly claimed that philosemitism was much more of a danger than antisemitism,[7] a line of argument that has reappeared in antisemitic antizionism. Trotsky, as well as some of the most serious 20th century Marxist thinkers known as the Frankfurt School, came to see that antisemitism posed a threat both to Jews and to humanity. This argument was also made by Hannah Arendt, who, if clearly not a Marxist, understood exactly why an assimilationist universalism had proved such a hopeless response to antisemitism.[8] What they all understood was that a radical left that fails to take antisemitism seriously undermines itself as well as the Jews it abandons. As the experience of Nazism made clear, antisemitism is what Horkheimer and Adorno called a 'central injustice': it shines a searing light on what is wrong both with society and also with movements seeking to make it better, when they condone, collude with or worse still facilitate it.

Antisemitism on the far right and the radical left

It is important to distinguish the left-wing form of antisemitism from that to be found in the modern world on the far right. As far as the latter are concerned, Jews should never have been admitted in the first place. They never belonged and, once mistakenly admitted, have been seen ever since as a source of decomposition and corruption of an order that was either sound and stable or in need of restoration and reconstruction. In the most extreme case, the corrupting threat that Jews supposedly posed meant that they had not only to be expelled but also eliminated entirely, not just from one nation or continent but also from humanity itself, which was the objective of the genocidal form of antisemitism adopted by the Nazis.

At the same time, it is important to see what the antisemitism on the far right and on the radical left have in common. They are, after all, *both* forms of antisemitism, even if they have partially different rationales and justifications. Both forms of antisemitism are implacably hostile to Jewish self-determination in Israel; they are antizionist. It has proven perfectly possible for antisemites on the radical left to pick up tropes and claims that were first developed on the far right and recycle them – wittingly or unwittingly – obviously, or in forms that can be, and are, angrily denied.

Such recycling is not at all unusual in the history of antisemitism. Antisemitism is not an invariant phenomenon, fixed for all times and places, any more than it is eternal. Just as it waxes and wanes, though it rarely disappears entirely, even when there are no Jews present,[9] so it takes different forms, depending on the prevailing discourse or conceptual framework within which it is formulated. Each set of antisemites may make their own distinctive contribution to this history but every new trope, once established, remains available to be picked up and reworked and rearticulated in a different context.

Understanding both this difference and the connection can help us see why the radical left might think, quite genuinely, that it has always been opposed to antisemitism, but also how it can end up generating a form of antisemitism which is different in some respects from that of the far right but not in others.

Again, this is not a wholly new phenomenon and there is an important more recent pre-history to what has unfolded in the UK over the past two decades, which generated two fundamental and ultimately fatal specific weaknesses in the understanding of and response to antisemitism on the radical left.

The radical left and the Holocaust

The first weakness has to do with the Holocaust, and how the radical left responded to the threat posed to Jews by the radical genocidal antisemitism of the Nazis. The certainty of much of the radical left in the UK of its opposition to fascist antisemitism has been mythologised into the narrative of the heroic victory over them at *Cable Street*, in October 1936. The left and the Jewish community mobilised together against Sir Oswald Mosley's Blackshirted British Union of Fascists in the East End of London. This memory was often referred to when Jeremy Corbyn, as leader of the Labour Party, and his supporters were challenged over their record on antisemitism. Those who fought that day in the streets against the fascists were indeed courageous, and they did have a victory, driving the Mosleyites off the streets. But that mobilisation was not that typical of the radical left's response to Nazi antisemitism in general. First, it required Jewish rank and file activists in the Communist Party to pressure the leadership from below into participating in this response. Second, the defence of the streets was organised alongside many others, and with the support of some in the oft-maligned Jewish 'establishment', which funnelled them resources to help them do it.[10] But to its profound shame, less than three years after *Cable Street*, the Communist Party in Britain effectively abandoned its support for the Jews who were threatened by Nazism. It did this because the Soviet Union, which controlled the party in Britain, had signed a non-aggression pact with Nazi Germany. This gave the Nazis control over huge numbers of Polish Jews,[11] as well as control over many thousands of German Jews who had found refuge from them in Poland. As long as the Nazi–Soviet alliance lasted, which it did for almost two whole years, the Nazis were free to ghettoise, enslave and murder Jews. And the British Communist Party, with great nimbleness, pivoted overnight from supporting British war preparations against Nazi Germany to embracing a pacifist line which sought to weaken the British war effort.

As those who side with fascists and mass murderers always do, they found plausible reasons to rehearse at their public meetings and in their press. The key issue, they said, was the survival of the revolution, which was in peril. Everything, in the short term, must be subordinated to the interests of the USSR, because its interests were identical to those of the international working class, and therefore of humanity as a whole. Communists cannot put everything at risk just to save a few rather privileged and mainly reactionary Jews. And in any case, it would be wrong to side with the oppressors of the whole of the British Empire in an ultimately trivial struggle between two old capitalist European powers.

It is of course true that the British Communist Party pivoted back again two years later, when Nazi Germany invaded the Soviet Union (much to its surprise). Suddenly, it was no longer for the defeat of the British Empire, but it was completely in favour of the victory of the British, who were siding with the revolution, and there was a choice to be made between communism and barbarism.

The Red Army eventually freed Eastern Europe from the Nazis, though not without huge support from the United States and Britain. But the rescue or defence of Jews from the Nazis wasn't their priority by any means, neither for European Communists, nor for the USSR. Instead, they systematically downplayed what the Nazis were doing to the Jews. Even when it set up the *Jewish Anti-Fascist Committee (JAC)*, the Soviet Union did so entirely cynically and instrumentally, only in order to win support in the West for what, inside the Soviet Union, was promoted as the Great Patriotic War, which it insisted was not in any way being fought to save Jews.[12] As even those who are most reluctant to explain this indifference in terms of a specifically Soviet antisemitism have noted, 'neither from the Soviet state nor from the Party was there a single appeal to underground organisations or the local population to help Soviet Jews'.[13] Once the war had been won, any effort to highlight and memorialise what had been done to the Jews was swiftly repressed. A detailed record of Nazi violence was put together by two leading figures in the JAC: Vassily Grossman and Ilya Ehrenburg. But *The Black Book: The Nazi Crime against the Jewish People* was withdrawn from publication on the grounds that it contained 'grave political errors'. All copies were destroyed, along with the typeset.[14]

As soon as the war was over, moreover, the Stalin regime moved rapidly to liquidate this committee and to arrest, torture and murder its leaders.[15] This was a prelude to what was then to become a sustained antisemitic onslaught against Jews across the entire Communist bloc, as the Soviet Union developed its own distinctive form of antisemitism in which Jews were cast once again as the enemies of progress disloyal to the Soviet Union, because they were both nationalists (Zionists) and cosmopolitans. In the late 1940s and 1950s, this repertoire was polished, and was presented in a series of show trials throughout Eastern Europe, most infamously in that of Rudolf Slansky in Czechoslovakia, which became a template for many others.[16] By combining apparent opposites, this Soviet antisemitic framework fell into a long tradition in which Jews could be accused of seemingly contradictory crimes. What connected these charges as a new form of the *Jewish Question* was the representation of Jews both as a transnational group with connections and loyalties running across national boundaries, and also as a national group with connections and loyalties to a nation state of their own. Either way, Jews could be treated as enemies of the internationalism supposedly embodied in the Soviet state.[17]

The *New Left's anti-Stalinism* never led it to pay much attention to this aspect of Stalinist history. Neither the Stalinist nor the non-Stalinist currents of the left ever really noticed that the left as a whole had failed to prioritise the question of antisemitism as part of the fight against Nazism. Large parts of the left regarded antisemitism as a secondary question. Many on the left believed that making too much noise about antisemitism would not help them to win support in the working class, that associating itself with support for Jews would prove counterproductive and that it would be better to downplay any specific left-wing concern about antisemitism.[18] In the Communist-led resistance right across Europe during the war itself, what was being done to Jews had not generally been emphasised in propaganda or deed.[19] Even when it was known that millions of Jews had been murdered, there was no serious effort on the left, including on the radical left, to think about why the annihilation of Jews had been such an overriding priority for the Nazis, or why that aim was pursued above all others; why it was prioritised even over the defence of Germany itself against Allied forces; and, above all, why it was significant that the Nazis had built not just concentration but also extermination camps. The Marxist historian Isaac Deutscher, venerated by the *New Left* and whose biography of Trotsky inspired a generation of anti-Stalinists, stands to this day almost alone on the radical left in his confession that he was baffled, *as a Marxist*, at what the Nazis had tried to do.[20] Deutscher's humility, however, was not shared by many others on the radical left and there remains, to this day, no serious history of the Holocaust written from a Marxist perspective.

It is true that Trotsky, uniquely and to his great credit, did at one point (in 1938) suggest that if there was a world war, then the Jews could be annihilated,[21] but none of his followers have, after the fact, followed up his remarkable intuition.[22] No sooner was the Holocaust over than Trotskyists, along with the rest of the radical left, returned to a way of thinking that was essentially unmodified by what had just happened. To give only one example, Ernest Mandel, soon to become by far the pre-eminent figure in the Trotskyist *Fourth International*, argued that what the Nazis had done to the Jews was not that exceptional but that it should be equated with, amongst other crimes of an apparently similar gravity, the post-war expulsion of Sudeten Germans from Czechoslovakia. Guilt for what had been done to the Jews by the Nazis should be shared with those who had just defeated them, who were, apparently, about to commit similar if not worse crimes:

> The death trains have again begun moving but this time in the opposite direction with a different human freight ... if Hitler constructed the trap for the Jews, it was the Anglo-Americans who sprang it ... [T]he massacre of the Jews is borne equally with Nazism ... by all of imperialism.[23]

That Mandel was himself Jewish did not in any way prevent him from making this crass argument immediately after the greatest catastrophe that had ever been inflicted on the Jewish people. It is true that many decades later he modified his argument, acknowledging that 'there can be no greater injustice than Auschwitz' and that the Nazi crimes were 'the worst in history'.[24] Even then, however, he was at pains to emphasise that the dehumanisation and slaughter of the Jews were not unique; the treatment of Roma and Sinti was already identical; and the murder of others deemed subhuman was already being planned. All this was, according to Mandel, the result of a more general phenomenon: the emergence of the biological hyper-racism that accompanied and legitimated imperialist exploitation.

Mandel's desperation not to focus on the particularity of Nazi antisemitism was and still is shared widely on the radical left. To draw attention to the fact that the Nazis wanted to annihilate Jews above all has been felt to constitute a dangerous departure from an overriding commitment to universalism, to the cause not of Jews but of the working class and humanity as a whole.

The problem with this is, at root, precisely the *exclusionary* version of universalism, identified above, which was adopted by many at the beginning of the modern left in the Enlightenment. It is a form of universalism that has a wholly inadequate understanding of antisemitism and that requires Jews to repress their own Jewish identity, to downplay if not ignore antisemitism entirely, and to adopt a universalist commitment which tends to position Jews as *the other* of the universal.

Antizionism after the Holocaust: the persistence of Stalinist antisemitism on the radical left

The second and related weakness has to do with antizionism. Antizionism before the Holocaust meant one thing. Antizionism after the Holocaust has a quite different political meaning.

Before the Holocaust, it was possible to argue that antisemitism was on the way out and that Jews would sooner or later be accepted as fully fledged members of society with the same rights as everyone else. The radical left version of this perspective added that this would happen, but only when the socialist revolution made it possible. After the Holocaust, that hope, that Jewish liberation from antisemitism would be achieved almost automatically through assimilation, completely lost credibility. The conclusion that the overwhelming majority of Jews came to was that a nation state of their own was an existential necessity. Zionism now became what it had not been before – the political commitment of the overwhelming majority of Jews. Having seen that relying on the universal human community to protect them was not necessarily a reliable strategy, most Jews concluded that it would be better to try to put themselves in a position to defend themselves.

The left as a whole accepted this argument, by and large, at least to begin with. Even the Soviet Union itself, and even as it was creating its own, new, distinctive form of antisemitism, initially accepted the ethical case for a Jewish state,[25] although it is likely that it was actually more motivated by the hope that Israel would be its ally than by ethics. But quite quickly its support for Israel melted away. Instead, the Soviet Union devoted considerable energy and resources to promoting a fundamentally antisemitic antizionism, which has come to be accepted as common sense by much of today's radical left.[26]

This antizionism is an ideology[27] in two senses: it is both false and it involves turning things upside down. First, it asserts falsely that Jews, almost uniquely among the world's peoples, are not and never have been a nation. This, it is claimed, is the classic Marxist position, although in fact there have been a whole host of different Marxist approaches to the question of Jewish identity, its roots and its development over time.[28] Second, it follows that Jews are not entitled to a state of their own, even after the Holocaust, as opposed to other nations which have not faced anything like this magnitude of threat to their very existence. Third, by contrast, those who are entitled to their own nation state are the supposedly only indigenous people of the region, the Palestinians, notwithstanding the fact that Jews have in fact lived there for millennia. Fourth, Israel was a creation of the West, it says, although the USSR proposed and voted for its creation at the UN, and even though it was actually the Soviet Union that supplied the Haganah, via Czechoslovakia, with the arms that it could not obtain elsewhere due to the British and American arms embargo; without those Czech-supplied arms, Israel would probably not have survived. Fifth, Israel should be regarded as a tool of the West and as a keystone of its system of domination over the region, even though Western imperialist states were by no means wholly enthusiastic about the creation of the new state. Colonial rule had ended, but this Israel-centred web of power was held to maintain imperialist control without it. Sixth, Zionism, the ideology that underpins the state of Israel, is a form of racism that sees Jews as inherently superior to others, who it treats as less than human, even though this was exactly what was done to Jews themselves. The crime that was perpetrated against them is turned upside down and they are accused of it.

Before the 1967 war, few on the radical left paid much attention to any of this. Antizionism was not a condition of membership of any significant radical left-wing organisation in the West. It was largely an abstract argument, with little purchase on the complex reality of the construction of a safe haven in the Middle East for Jews after the Holocaust and after their expulsion of Jews from the ethnically designated Arab states, which replaced colonial rule and which had no room for Jews in their 'liberated' cities. Those concerned primarily with expanding the influence of the radical left in the UK were not particularly concerned with a small country far away. Those more fixated on the anti-colonial struggle were more exercised by, and infatuated with, what they thought was going on in Cuba, Algeria or Vietnam, to give only three examples of many.

Things began to change after Israel's overwhelming victory in 1967. Now, many on the radical left could no longer think of Israel as vulnerable but only as powerful, and *ipso facto* therefore no longer deserving of or entitled to support, or even indifference from the radical left.[29] Almost immediately there began to be signs of the adoption by some on the radical left of anti-semitic antizionism. This was even true in West Germany,[30] and of course it was also well developed in East Germany. But these were early days, and by and large the exception at the time, and antisemitic antizionism, had little resonance in the UK.

Anti-fascism and antisemitism: the radical left and the Anti-Nazi League

As the 1970s progressed, the left in Britain became more and more aware of a far right political, racist, fascistic threat. In the UK, the anti-fascist commitment of the radical left appeared to entirely override antizionism and to signal, as had seemed to be the case at the time of Cable Street, an unreserved and exemplary commitment to defend Jews. That was certainly what many on the radical left, and very many Jews at the time, believed to be the case. This shared belief was responsible to a significant extent for the remarkable, if short-lived, success of one of the most significant political achievements of the radical left in Britain, the creation of an *Anti-Nazi League*, in the mid-to-late 1970s.[31]

The central role in the creation of this movement was played by what was then the most significant group on the radical left in the UK, the *Socialist Workers Party* (SWP). The SWP's origins lay in a small organisation, the *International Socialists* (IS), who were, it has to be said, because this throws an important light on the revival of Stalinist antisemitism on the radical left in recent years, by far the most overtly anti-Stalinist group on the radical left to emerge after the Second World War.[32] Unlike every other Trotskyist organisation at the time, let alone the still devotedly Stalinist Maoists, IS believed that the Soviet Union had broken irrevocably from any kind of socialism in the late 1920s when Stalin embarked on his huge campaign of collectivisation and the first of his five-year plans to build 'socialism in one country'. IS thought that what had been constructed in the Soviet Union, with great violence directed against the working class itself (along with millions of others of course), had nothing to do with socialism at all but was only another kind of capitalist society, one in which the state operated as a collective capitalist; the state acting as capitalist, they thought, was a phenomenon that had already been seen in the West, under certain conditions. The slogan on the front page of its weekly newspaper, *Socialist Worker*, rejected both the American and Soviet forms of capitalism: 'neither Washington nor Moscow but International Socialism'. At the same time, it rejected the romantic fantasies entertained by many others on the radical left about regimes that had emerged from the anti-colonial struggle (from China to Algeria to Cuba to Vietnam), seeing them too as state capitalist formations because they were not anchored in working-class mobilisations.

The ANL was an unusually successful political project not just for the SWP but also for the radical left more generally. It called for the broadest possible mobilisation against the growing threat from the far right in the UK, now embodied in the form of the National Front (NF). The latter was an openly racist organisation, attacking Black and Asian communities in Britain, whilst also making little effort to hide its admiration for the Nazis, and openly advertising their shared hatred of Jews. The ANL was an entirely non-sectarian initiative: anyone who cared about the threat from the far right was welcome to join. The call for an Anti-Nazi League was explicitly designed to draw on an anti-fascist tradition in the UK, fortified to some extent by Britain's role in the defeat of Nazi Germany.

The attempt to draw on that tradition was the focus of one of the two main criticisms of the ANL from a tiny minority of others on the radical left.

One was that it made a fatal concession to British patriotism, when many Black and Asian communities did not feel at all included in prevailing senses of Britishness. The other criticism (at the time more *sotto voce)* was that in stressing the Nazi 'angle' and harking back to the Second World War, too much was made of antisemitism and not enough attention was being paid to other and contemporary victims of racism in the UK.[33] Both criticisms were fundamentally flawed from the outset, but have come to inform much of the common sense of the radical left in recent years.

The mass mobilisation effected by the ANL was itself a challenge to the very notion that British identity was essentially white; many ANL activists put their bodies on the line to defend Black and Asian communities on the streets from the NF, most strikingly in what became known as the Battle of Lewisham in the summer of 1977, where it was not difficult to see similarities with what had happened in Cable Street in the 1930s.[34] This was by no means the only time that ANL activists risked life and limb to defend Black and Asian communities. At the tail end of the brief history of the ANL in 1979, a major demonstration to prevent the NF marching through the streets of Southall, which had a large Asian population, ended with the killing by British police of an ANL and SWP activist, Blair Peach.[35]

The argument that too much was made of antisemitism was even more seriously wrong. The ANL reached out very effectively to the Jewish community, and the Jewish community responded, as it had done at the time of Cable Street, but neither privileged Jews over others. On the contrary, the fight against the NF's antisemitism was part and parcel of a wider commitment to fighting racism against anyone in the UK.

There was, at the time, perceived to be no contradiction between the recognition of the particularity of antisemitism, and the significance of the Holocaust to Jews, and a universalist commitment to fighting all forms of racism. Many Jews (and not only on the left) themselves succeeded in balancing their particular anxieties about antisemitism with a universalist solidarity with other victims of racism. The much-maligned Board of Deputies, which one might have expected to be only concerned with Jews, argued (much as it had done in the 1930s) that resistance to the far right should primarily be couched in terms of the threat it posed to democracy and toleration. As Joshua Cohen has shown,[36] it had what he calls 'a traditional aversion to special pleading' and already in response to the 'swastika epidemic' of 1959–60 had again appealed to a wider defence of democracy. At the same time, the Board's (actually quite universalist) approach was complemented by that pushed by other Jews, notably in the 62 group (as had their predecessors in the 43 group) and in the Yellow Star Movement (YSM), who were more open in arguing that more priority should be given to attacks on Jews and to the memory and shadow of Holocaust. When the ANL was then set up, a decade or so later, these complementary approaches not only helped mobilise Jews and the left but, especially through the recognition of both the particular and universalist meanings of the Holocaust, also connected anti-fascism and anti-racism. The truth therefore is exactly the opposite of what is now argued in the defective and exclusionary universalism of too many on the radical left. Recognising the particular significance of the Holocaust to Jews was no impediment whatsoever to recognising its universal significance.

Moreover, no one in the SWP or the ANL took either of these criticisms seriously at the time, quite rightly. Nor did there appear to be any reason to fear that the radical left and the SWP in particular would abandon the struggle against antisemitism, as the Communist Party had done in the late 1930s.

From anti-fascism to anti-imperialism: antisemitism returns on the radical left

But abandon the struggle against antisemitism and turn its back on Britain's Jews was exactly what the SWP and many others on the radical left were eventually to do. This did not happen all at once but took place in stages.

In the first stage, the radical left moved its focus away from the ANL, believing (rightly) that the NF had been comprehensively defeated for the time being.

What replaced it as the focus, and indeed for the left more generally, was the threat posed by a resurgent Conservative Party under the leadership of Margaret Thatcher. The Conservative election victory of 1979 turned out to be an epoch changing moment. It was not only the first of four Conservative election victories in a row but it also signalled the definitive end of what the Communist Party historian Eric Hobsbawm called the 'forward march of Labour'.[37] Faced with a sustained onslaught on almost all the gains made by the labour movement as a whole in the post-war period, the radical left weakened if it did not largely disintegrate.

The radical left then faced a new and largely unpredicted problem, which was the collapse of the Soviet Union. The assumption that lay behind anti-Stalinism for much of the radical left was that, in the (not so likely) event that the Stalinist system was overthrown, it would open up a space for a genuinely socialist democratic transformation. No such hope was realised, as a transition to an oft-chaotic free-market system took place right across the former Communist bloc. Even if there was discontent at the widespread corruption and outright theft involved in this transformation, it did not take anything like the form the radical left expected. Radical politics in the former communist states more often took xenophobic, ethnic nationalist and fascistic shapes. Instead of reflecting on what this might mean for the various theories of how and why the Stalinist system had come into being and lasted so long, the radical left's attention turned only to the one remaining superpower, the United States. For the SWP, its cherished slogan 'neither Washington nor Moscow' now made little sense. In its place, the SWP joined up with the rest of the radical left in identifying Western capitalism and imperialism, and the United States in particular, as the only global, systemic enemy.

A crucial effect of this move was that a new variant of anti-imperialism effectively replaced anti-fascism as the hegemonic ideology of the radical left. It might appear on the surface that, rather than replacing it, anti-impe-rialism subsumes anti-fascism. Many on the radical left appear to think this is the case, because they remain in their own eyes resolutely opposed to the far right in the West, especially in the United States, which they regard as completely central to the global system of imperialist power. To the extent that this far right is anti-democratic, racist and embraces an evangelical Christian nationalism, this might appear to have some justification. There are, however, at least three major problems with this approach.

The first is that the United States is obviously not the only imperialist power in the world. If anti-imperialism subsumes anti-fascism, it would have to be opposed to the fascism that lies within other imperialisms, notably in the case of Russia and China, whose regimes are not only racist in their own (Great Russian and Han Chinese) traditions, but are more ferociously anti-democratic than the United States at its worst. It is not just that an anti-imperialism that only focuses on the imperialism of the United States is seriously imbalanced and has proven quite unable to grasp or respond to the extremely grave injustices committed by those other empires, from Tibet to Crimea and beyond. It is also that these regimes exhibit what many would identify as classic fascist tendencies, including one party rule, a monolithic ideology in which a xenophobic and aggressive nationalism plays a key role; the concentration of power in the hands of a single often supreme leader; and the systematic use of terror against those identified as enemies of the nation, near and far.

The second problem that flows from the subsumption of anti-fascism into a new, totalising anti-imperialism is that some of the regimes that grew out of the anti-colonial struggle, which had been so important to the develop-ment of the radical left in the late 1950s and 1960s, have imperialist or sub-imperialist ambitions of their own, and also exhibit similar important fascist characteristics. An anti-imperialism only focused on 'Western imperialism', which does not see and seek to combat fascist tendencies in those regimes is, to put it mildly, not exactly consistently anti-fascist.

But thirdly, and of particular significance here, neither anti-fascism nor anti-imperialism were always opposed to antisemitism. The Soviet Union's anti-fascism, as we have seen, did not prevent it from adopting antisemitic discourse and pursuing virulently antisemitic policies of its own devising.

In doing so, it identified Jews as backward, reactionary, untrustworthy, in league with its enemies, a major barrier to progress.

In the unbalanced and blind anti-imperialism now adopted by the radical left, these tropes were rearticulated above all in relation to Israel, the safe haven for Jews, and to people designated as its supporters. At this point, antisemitism as the 'socialism of fools' was effectively replaced by antisemitism as the 'anti-imperialism of fools'.[38] Now a sensibility began to emerge on much of the radical left – that antisemitism was understandable and explicable. All those who were assumed to have experienced oppression (notably the Palestinians) at the hands of the Jewish state were supposedly being radicalised by this experience. It was understandable if they saw Jews as their oppressors and understandable that anti-imperialist movements (like Hezbollah in Lebanon, and Hamas in Gaza) would see Jews as their main enemy. The self-appointed task for the radical left was to get them to see that it was not only their Jewish oppressors (but still their Jewish oppressors) who were their enemy but the West, and especially the United States. An alliance with these, supposedly inherently and objectively progressive, forces was now the order of the day.

All of this became increasingly clear in the new millennium, first with 9/11, then with the subsequent invasion of Afghanistan by the United States and its allies to overthrow the Taliban, and then in the hugely successful mass mobilisation against the Iraq War, which radicalised new layers of young people.

All of the forces lined up against the West in these cases, from Bin Laden's *Al Qaeda* on 9/11 to the *Taliban* in Afghanistan to the *Ba'athists* in Iraq, were openly and overtly antisemitic. They made no effort at all to hide this commitment but that did not in any way prevent many on the radical left from supporting their cause against the hated West and against Israel. Sometimes it was not clear whether Israel was understood to be the tool of the West or whether the West was thought to be the tool of Israel.

Many on the radical left saw the Iraq War as a re-run of the Vietnam War, which had been so important in the growth of the *New Left*. We may leave aside here the inconvenient difference between Ho Chi Minh and Saddam Hussein, and that the Vietnamese Communist Party, despite its Stalinism, had not carried out one, let alone two genocides as the *Baath* Party had done in Iraq, first against the Kurds then against the Marsh Arabs. What was incontestably different was that antisemitism had no place in the mobilisations against the war in Vietnam, and indeed left-wing Zionists of that era had been quite active in them. Now, however, getting too worked up about the evils of antisemitism would have alienated the radical left from precisely the global actors and the local mobilisations that they saw as their routes to the masses and to 'resistance'.

This required a significant theoretical and political shift for many on the radical left in thinking about fundamentalist Islamist movements.

Originally, the SWP's historic leader and founder, Tony Cliff,[39] had, for example, characterised the *Muslim Brotherhood* as a 'clerical fascist' movement. The Brotherhood was a pioneer, in Egypt in the 1920s, of the fusion of specific kinds of radical, expansionist and anti-Christian politics with anti-feminist, antisemitic and authoritarian reading of Muslim holy texts. In characterising the Brotherhood as clerical fascist, Cliff was referring to this specific kind of political movement, not at all to Islam or Muslims in general.

In an important article,[40] which some have seen as exercising an influence on the radical left far beyond the shores of the UK, Chris Harman rejected the idea that Islamism was always and everywhere reactionary, or to be equated with, for example, Christian fundamentalism, which he did see as an integral element of the far right in the United States. Islamism, he argued, was destabilising capitalism everywhere across the Middle East and mobilising popular bitterness. Again there is no space here to go into this argument in detail, save to note that there is little evidence to support the optimistic prognosis that those first attracted to Islamism would then migrate on to the radical left. What is more important in this context is that the shift in position had major implications for the radical left's view of antisemitism. Alliance with Islamists, locally and globally, could only be forged on the assumption that antisemitism was potentially, if not essentially, 'progressive'.

This was particularly the case with two Islamist movements in the Middle East, both sworn to the destruction of Israel, *Hezbollah* and *Hamas*. In important respects, they can both be seen as fascist parties, which is precisely what Harman denied (and he was by no means alone in this).[41] Both are monolithic political parties with an ideology which brooks no dissent; both have an extensive and greatly feared terror apparatus; both deploy extreme violence against democratic forces near and far, most catastrophically in Syria; and both are openly antisemitic. As Hezbollah's leader Nasrollah notoriously remarked, from their point of view, it was of great benefit that Israel was full of Jews, since 'If all the Jews were gathered in Israel it would be easier to kill them all at the same time'.[42] Hamas, for its part, quite explicitly holds Jews responsible for the French Revolution, the Russian Revolution and both the First and Second World Wars.

Support for these organisations for many on the radical left was open and manifest. After the mass demonstrations against the Iraq War had died down, the SWP along with others on the left helped organise demonstrations, for example, with participants marching through the streets of London in August 2006 chanting 'we are all Hezbollah now'. In relation to Hamas, many on the radical left openly support it in its war against Israel. It is not uncommon to see direct comparisons with and equivalence to the Warsaw Ghetto, as a description of what Israel is supposedly doing to the inhabitants of Gaza.[43] Hamas is often portrayed on the contemporary Western left as a liberation movement.

In the UK, the embracing of antisemites such as Hamas was only one example of what many Jews believed was a long list of associations, cultivated over several years, by the man who was in 2015 to become the new leader of the Labour Party, Jeremy Corbyn.

There is no space here to analyse the whole experience of Corbynism, which culminated in the worst election result the Labour Party had experienced since the 1930s. What is of more immediate relevance here is that among Corbyn's most enthusiastic followers were not just a whole raft of younger people drawn into politics by the anti-Iraq War movement but also a coalition of Stalinists[44] and self-proclaimed Trotskyists. These former bitter antagonists now buried their historic differences in support of a form of politics in which antisemitism, rearticulated within a selectively anti-imperialist frame of reference, played a crucial role.[45]

That form of politics involved a complete reversal of the position the radical left had adopted in the 1970s with the ANL. The latter was *openly* a project initially of the radical left, drawing others to its side. It accepted that its supporters could have different views on a range of questions but that what they shared was what mattered, a commitment to fight antisemitism and all forms of racism (not one or the other). As its name implied, it took the Holocaust seriously and thus gained the support of many Jews, whilst not in any way setting one set of victims of racism against another.

Corbyn's candidature, by contrast, opened the way to a sustained effort to *take over* an existing political party by those whose beliefs ran counter in crucial respects to those of the large majority of its existing members, and of its traditional voters. Where a whole raft of younger people had been drawn to the ANL to join with others in fighting racism and antisemitism, some of the new members now were mobilised in support of a campaign to drive out those who objected to clear evidence of a rising tide of antisemitism inside the party itself.[46]

This development was no accident. For antisemitism in its post-Holocaust antizionist form was central to the anti-imperialist worldview of Corbyn and his supporters, which rearticulated key antisemitic tropes which had first appeared in the Enlightenment in relation to Emancipation. Now it was claimed not just that Western imperialism was the main enemy but also that Israel, and the vast majority of Jews who supported it, played the central role in maintaining the radically unjust world the West had created in the first place. In this rearticulated version, Israel was either a tool of Western imperialism to secure its control of the region or even the other way around. Israel was said to be a wholly and uniquely illegitimate nation state, because Jews did not and never could constitute a nation but had settled and colonised a region, using systematic violence to displace, evict and exploit the indigenous people, the Palestinians. The ideology underpinning the inherently oppressive state Jews had set up, Zionism, which prioritised loyalty among Jews to each other over everything else, was seen as racist to the core. It supposedly justified and underpinned the creation of an apartheid system, placing Jews over others, worse even that constructed by white South Africa, but also other crimes against humanity which the Jewish state committed, and even genocide, which effectively made it the worst state in the world, since these constitute the gravest crimes of all.[47] None of this, they insisted, had anything to do with antisemitism or, if it did (since in some cases it was quite impossible to deny it), it was understandable, condonable and indeed potentially progressive. In a further elaboration of the idea that antisemitism could even have a rational kernel, the struggle to liberate Palestine from Jewish control was now claimed to be central to all progressive movements across the globe.

Corbyn himself could not, his supporters argued, be antisemitic because his mother had been at Cable Street. Moreover, some of his most prominent supporters were Jews themselves, though the vast majority of their fellow Jews viewed them (rightly) with disdain and contempt, knowing fully well that there could always be a tiny minority of Jews eager (as in the heyday of Stalinism) to demonstrate their loyalty to the cause of an exclusionary universalism. When Israel and its supporters used the charge of antisemitism against their critics, according to Corbyn and his supporters, they did so dishonestly and for malign purposes. They invented antisemitism where it did not exist, or grossly exaggerated it. They engaged moreover in special pleading, especially through invoking the Holocaust, both to insulate themselves from wholly legitimate criticism and to advance their own interests at the expense of others who, in the unjust world constructed by the racist West, are the real victims. In fact, Jews had, supposedly, become white themselves, not only in Israel but also in the West. There is no space here to consider this preposterous assertion in any detail,[48] save to note that it has also led to the disgraceful[49] assertion that Jews, the victims of the most radical genocide (to date[50]), have become not just any perpetrators but Nazis.

These charges are entirely ideological. They construct the reality they seek to explain and turn things on their head. But many of them are also quite contradictory, not for the first time in the long history of antisemitism. The Nazis argued that Jews were both superhuman and subhuman, responsible for both capitalism and communism. The Stalinists argued that Jews were both nationalists (Zionists) and cosmopolitans. On the radical left today, the definition of Jews as white has led to the assertion that the Holocaust is only a 'white on white' problem, which presumably means it has no wider significance for the 'real' victims of white racism. If nothing else, this would seem to contradict the exclusionary universalist argument that the Holocaust is only of universal significance and that far too much is made (by Jews of course) of Jewish suffering and other victims are ignored.

It is no accident that the Holocaust came to play an important role in this rearticulation of antisemitic tropes. The failure to understand, respond to and reflect on the Holocaust had long been a crucial weakness of the radical left, alongside the confusion of fighting fascism with fighting antisemitism. Now, despite or perhaps because of this weakness, it became necessary for Corbyn and his supporters to wage a bitter battle with the Jewish community over the greatest crime ever committed against Jews. In the summer of 2019 Corbyn and his supporters stubbornly resisted the effort by the International Holocaust Remembrance Alliance (IHRA) to provide a definition of antisemitism. Again, there is no space here to cover this debate in any detail, but what lay at the heart of it was Corbyn's refusal to accept the argument that it is antisemitic to claim that a state of Israel is *per se* a racist endeavour. This was far more than an objection to the policies of any Israeli government at any moment in time. It was an objection to the idea that there should ever be such a state.

The state of course came into being, and its existence was viewed as an existential necessity by the vast majority of Jews everywhere, because of the Holocaust. The refusal to accept this is, however, not only to repeat the failings of the past. In rejecting the demand to ground the fight today against antisemitism in a better understanding of the greatest crime committed against Jews, too many on the radical left have ended up blaming Jews once again for antisemitism. Within the framework of the anti-imperialism of fools, if there is any antisemitism now (when it is not being denied outright), then it can only be *because* of Israel and because of the way Jews themselves behave. If they did not continue to behave so badly, then there would be little or no antisemitism, in the UK or anywhere else in the modern world.

This assertion was, as we noted at the beginning, a key conclusion of the set of antisemitic tropes first developed in the Enlightenment, now rearticulated to 'explain' why the radical left's hopes had yet again been frustrated. Once again, antisemitism has been found to be a superficially attractive explanation for why things have gone wrong. Once again, it has been the behaviour of Jews which is to blame. Once again (as in the harassment of prominent Jewish MPs) it has been desirable to personalise the problem by identifying particular individuals (Jews) as the guilty party, the wicked ones who have to be punished.

Conclusion

The rearticulation of these tropes means that the radical left has come full circle. Undermined by its inability to reflect seriously on its own past, abandoning its anti-fascism for the anti-imperialism of fools, it became what it had originally fought. This is not, of course, the first time in history that a progressive moment has turned into its opposite. Marx and Engels themselves suggested long ago that if a revolutionary movement took power before the objective conditions were ripe, then it would be forced to behave as the regime it sought to overthrow.[51] The Russian Revolution ended up under Stalin as a tyranny as bad if not worse than the one it replaced, and arguably even more murderous towards those it suspected as enemies of the state.[52]

It is possible of course to argue that radical leftism itself is a kind of original sin,[53] that it is doomed to fail and that only a more moderate form of socialism (or not even that) can take antisemitism seriously. There is no space here to consider this argument, save to note (as we have alluded to here briefly) that less-radical forms of leftism have not always covered themselves in glory in this respect.

The collapse into antisemitism by too much of the radical left, however, was not and is not inevitable. If there have been serious weaknesses in how the radical left has at times responded to antisemitism, they can be thought about and addressed in both theory and in practice. There have always been those on the radical left prepared to do this thinking, although certainly the Holocaust was the greatest test and required the most fundamental rethinking (though it has also to be said that the radical left has been by no means alone in failing this challenge).[54] But there have also been those on the radical left who, as the ANL showed, *have* taken antisemitism seriously in practice and led the struggle against it with courage and determination. If both these traditions, intellectual *and* practical, have been obscured by the disastrous capitulation to antisemitism of the past three decades, it may still not be too late to reverse course and repair the damage it has inflicted, both to the radical left and to Jews.

Notes

1 In the UK, one Trotskyist organisation in particular, the Alliance for Workers Liberty (AWL) has to its considerable credit, resisted this general trend. See, amongst other publications, Sean Matgamna, *Marxism and the Jewish Question in Israel–Palestine: Two Nations, Two States, Alliance for Workers Liberty*, London, 2001, pp. 19–22.

2 For a more detailed discussion of these weaknesses, see Robert Fine and Philip Spencer, *Antisemitism and the Left: On the Return of the Jewish Question*, Manchester: Manchester University Press, 2017.

3 This approach repeatedly tempts some on the radical left. To give only one other example, in the 1920s, the German Communist Party leader Ruth Fischer adopted it when she told workers that they were quite right to attack Jewish capitalists but should then realise that it was not only Jewish capitalists who were the problem.

4 To give only three examples, one could consult any of the following. Moishe Postone's seminal essay: History and Helplessness: Mass Mobilization and Contemporary Forms of Anticapitalism. *Public Culture*, 8(1),93–110, 2006; Lars Rensmann, *The Politics of Unreason: The Frankfurt School and the Origins of Modern Antisemitism*, Albany, NY: SUNY Press, 2018; or Werner Bonefeld, Critical Theory and the Critique of Antisemitism: On Society as Economic Object. *Journal of Social Justice*, 9, 2019.

5 See the reflections on this trajectory by a key figure in the events of May 1968 in France, Henri Weber, who was for many years one of the leaders of by far the most intelligent Trotskyist organisation, the Ligue Communiste Revolutionnaire (LCR). Henri Weber, *Rebelle Jeunesse*, Paris: Robert Laffont, 2018.
6 In his 'Essay on the Jewish Question', in *Karl Marx: Early Writings* edited by Lucio Colletti, Harmondsworth: Penguin, 1973. For a careful discussion of what Marx was trying to do, see Robert Fine, Rereading Marx on the 'Jewish Question': Marx as a Critic of Antisemitism. In: Marcel Stoetzler, ed., *Antisemitism and the Constitution of Sociology*, Lincoln, NE and London: University of Nebraska Press, 2014, pp. 137–159.
7 See Lars Fischer's extremely important analysis of how far too many Marxists, but not Rosa Luxemburg, actually followed Bauer not Marx! Lars Fischer, *The Socialist Response to Antisemitism in Imperial Germany*, Cambridge: Cambridge University Press, 2007.
8 On Trotsky's recognition of the danger posed by antisemitism, see Alan Johnson, *Leon Trotsky's Long War against Antisemitism*. https://fathomjournal.org/the-fathom-long-read-leon-trotskys-long-war-against-antisemitism/#_edn1, 2019. On the Frankfurt School, see Rensmann, *Politics*; on Arendt (and Trotsky and the Frankfurt School), see Fine and Spencer, *Antisemitism and the Left*.
9 As in England, from where Jews were excluded for centuries. See Anthony Julius, *Trials of the Diaspora: A History of Anti-Semitism in England*, Oxford: Oxford University Press, 2010.
10 For detailed account of this episode, see Daniel Tilles, *British Fascist Antisemitism and Jewish Responses, 1932–40*, London: Bloomsbury, 2020.
11 This extraordinary development, which disoriented some on the left (though not enough), is covered in some detail by Roger Moorhouse in *The Devils' Alliance: Hitler's Pact with Stalin, 1939–1941*, New York: Basic Books, 2014.
12 As one Military Council leader put it in 1943, explicitly citing Stalin, 'some comrades of Jewish descent believe that this war is being fought to save the Jewish nation. These Jews are mistaken. We fight the Great Patriotic War for the salvation, the freedom and the independence of our homeland led by the Great Russian people'. Cited in Arno Lustiger, Stalin and the Jews, *The Red Book: The Tragedy of the Jewish Anti-Fascist Committee and the Soviet Jews*, New York: Enigma, 2003, p. 108.
13 Harvey Asher, The Soviet Union, the Holocaust and Auschwitz. In: Michael David-Fox, Peter Holquist and Alexander M. Martin, eds., *The Holocaust in the East: Local Perpetrators and Soviet Responses*, Pittsburg: University of Pittsburg Press, 2014, p. 44.
   Asher. *Soviet Union*, 44.
14 See Zvi Gitelman, Politics and the Historiography of the Holocaust in the Soviet Union. In: Zvi Gitelman, ed., *Bitter Legacy: Confronting the Holocaust in the USSR*, Bloomington: Indiana University Press, 1997.
15 Joshua Rubenstein and Vladimir P. Naumov, *Stalin's Secret Pogrom: The Postwar Inquisition of the Jewish Anti-Fascist Committee*, New Haven: Yale University Press, 2001.
16 Of the 14 defendants singled out in the Slansky trial, the largest of all the purge trials held in this period, at least 11 were Jews. See Tomas Snigeon, Vanished History: *The Holocaust in Czech and Slovak Political Culture*, Oxford; Berghahn, 2014, p. 61. Antisemitism had also been a feature of the Moscow trials of the late 1930s, where it formed a crucial 'subtext', and even before, in the context of actions taken against Trotsky in the 1920s. See Vadim Rogovin, *1937: Stalin's Year of Terror*, Sheffield: Mehring, 1998, p. 154. On the antisemitic aspect of the campaign against Trotsky in the 1920s, see Bernard Wasserstein,

On the Eve: The Jews of Europe Before the Second World War, New York: Simon and Schuster, 2012, 64.

17 See, for example, Orlando Figes, *The Whisperers: Private life in Stalin's Russia*, London; New York: Allen Lane Books 2007, p. 454; Frank Gruner, 'Russia's Battle against the Foreign': The Anti-Cosmopolitanism Paradigm in Russian and Soviet Ideology.In: Michael L. Miller and Scott Ury, eds., *Cosmopolitanism, Nationalism and the Jews of East Central Europe*, London: Routledge, pp. 109–136.

18 The Social Democrats produced little propaganda to challenge the antisemitic arguments of the Nazis in the last years of the Weimar Republic. Once the Nazis came to power, the underground was instructed not to prioritise the issue on the grounds that antisemitism was more popular than originally estimated and that it would make the work of the resistance more difficult. Klaus Mann, though not a member of the party, spoke for many on the non-Communist left when he argued in 1941 that 'antisemitism has already played too predominant a part in our propaganda ... it is a dangerous mistake to overemphasise this one particular angle'. David Bankier, *German Social Democrats and the Jewish Question in Probing the Depths of German Anti-Semitism: German Society and the Persecution of the Jews 1933–1941*, Oxford: Berghahn, 2000, p. 521. In the Communist underground no significant efforts were made to confront antisemitism and it was not until *Kristallnacht* that the party's paper *Die Rote Fahne* finally gave the issue any prominence. See Jeffrey Herf, German Communism, the Discourse of 'anti-Fascist' Resistance and the Jewish Catastrophe. In: Michael Geyer and John W. Boyer, eds., *Resistance in the Third Reich*, Chicago: Chicago University Press, 1994, pp. 257–294.

19 On France, see Daniel Blatman and Renée Poznanski, Jews and Their Social Environment: Perspectives from the Underground Press in Poland and France. In: Beata Kosmala and Georgi Verbeeck, eds., *Facing the Catastrophe: Jews and Non-Jews in Europe during World War Two*, Oxford: Berg, 2011, pp. 159–228.

20 As he put it, 'I wonder whether even in a thousand years people will understand Hitler, Auschwitz, Majdanek and Treblinka better than we do now ... [O]n the contrary, posterity may understand it all even less than we do ... [T]he fury of Nazism, which was bent on the unconditional extermination of every Jewish man, woman, and child within its reach, passes the comprehension of a historian ... [W]e are confronted here by a huge and ominous mystery of the degeneration of the human character that will forever baffle and terrify mankind' (1981: 1634). Deutscher's biography of Stalin, however, was a much more flawed work, in that making an analogy between Stalin and Napoleon, it made Stalinism appear not only as inevitable in some ways but as progressive in the overall scheme of things.

21 Trotsky's 1938 prediction can be found in a collection of his writings, *On the Jewish Question*, New York Pathfinder Press, 1970, p. 29. It is discussed in some detail by Norman Geras in his brilliant essay: Marxists before the Holocaust. In: *The Contract of Mutual Indifference*, London: Verso, 1998.

22 One initially promising exception to this was Enzo Traverso's set of essays, *Understanding the Nazi Genocide: Marxism after Auschwitz*, London: Pluto Press, 1999. Sadly, this promise has not been fulfilled – quite the opposite. In his earlier work, *Marxists and the Jewish Question*, New Jersey: Humanities Press, 1994, Traverso had argued convincingly that Marxists had repeatedly failed to take antisemitism seriously. Sadly, he himself has repeated exactly these failings in his recent work, *The End of Jewish Modernity*, London: Pluto Press 2016, where he now defends the position that antisemitism is no longer a problem or, if it is, it is only a response to the bad behaviour of Jews.

23 Ernest Mandel, The Jewish Question since World War Two. *Fourth International*, 8(4), 09–113, 1947.

24 Mandel 1999: 2002.

25 In a now entirely and wilfully forgotten speech made when the UN was debating whether or not to recognise the state of Israel, the Soviet foreign minister Gromyko made this entirely clear. 'The delegation of the USSR maintains that the decision to partition Palestine is in keeping with the high principles and aims of the United Nations. It is in keeping with the principle of the national self-determination of peoples …. The solution of the Palestine problem based on a partition of Palestine into two separate states will be of *profound historical significance, because this decision will meet the legitimate demands of the Jewish people, hundreds of thousands of whom, as you know, are still without a country, without homes, having found temporary shelter only in special camps in some western European countries. I shall not speak of the conditions in which these people are living; these conditions are well known*' (my emphasis). https://www.jewishvirtuallibrary.org/united-nations-debate-on-partition-november-1947 (accessed 26 June 2022).

26 See Izabella Tabarovsky's chapter in this book; also see Izabella Tabarovsky, Soviet Anti-Zionism and Contemporary Left Antisemitism, *Fathom, May 2019*. http://fathomjournal.org/soviet-anti-zionism-and-contemporary-left-antisemitism/ (accessed 27 February 2023).

27 More generally on antizionism as an ideology, see David Seymour, Continuity and Discontinuity: From Antisemitism to Antizionism and the Reconfiguration of the Jewish Question. *Journal of Contemporary Antisemitism* 2(2), 11–24, 2019. https://www.degruyter.com/document/doi/10.26613/jca/2.2.30/html?fbclid=IwAR3_hRZpON8dozf8yUvoZdTVYdylPDiKfH-ah8CXH-9cznSpIo-EFNp5eTi8 (accessed 17 October 2021).

28 As Enzo Traverso made quite clear in his classic book on the question. See note 25.

29 See Colin Schindler, *Israel and the European Left: Between Solidarity and Delegitimization*, London: Bloomsbury, 2012.

30 In 1969, a section of the German anti-fascist left, determined to expose what it saw as the continuity between the Nazi state and the liberal democratic Federal Republic, decided that Jews were complicit in Western imperialism and attempted to bomb a synagogue. Only a few years later, members of the Baader-Meinhof group separated Jews out on a plane that they had hijacked and flown to Entebbe. Others on the radical turn resisted this turn, coming to see that anti-fascism was not a sufficient barrier to the re-emergence of antisemitism on the radical left. See Hans Kundnani, *Utopia or Auschwitz: Germany's 1968 Generation and the Holocaust*, New York: Columbia University Press, 2009.

31 One version of the history of this organisation can be found in David Renton, *Never Again: Rock Against Racism and the Anti-Nazi League 1976–1982*, London: Routledge, 2018.

32 A selection of some key pieces outlining this distinctive position can be found in *The Origins of the International Socialists*, London: Pluto Press, 1971 Full disclosure – the author was a member of this organization for many years.

33 The most sophisticated version of this criticism can be found in Paul Gilroy's '*There Ain't No Black in the Union Jack': The Cultural Politics of Race and Nation*, Chicago: Chicago University Press, 1987.

34 See Mark Townsend, How the Battle of Lewisham Helped to Halt the Rise of Britain's Far Right. *The Guardian*, 13 August 2017. https://www.theguardian.com/uk-news/2017/aug/13/battle-of-lewisham-national-front-1977-far-right-london-police (accessed 25 February 2023).

35 https://www.theguardian.com/uk/2010/apr/27/blair-peach-killed-police-met-report. Again, a personal disclosure: the author and his partner were only a few hundred yards ahead of Blair Peach on that demonstration and were very

fortunate to escape being attacked by the police, thanks to the quick thinking of locals who pointed us down an alleyway.

36 Joshua Cohen, 'Somehow Getting Their Own Back on Hitler': British Antifascism and the Holocaust, 1960–1967 in Fascism. *Journal of Comparative Fascist Studies*, 9(1–2), 121–145.

37 Eric Hobsbawm, *The Forward March of Labour Halted?*, London: Verso, 1981.

38 See, for example, Paul Berman's short piece with this very title, in *Dissent*, Winter 1987, and Camila Bassi, The Anti-Imperialism of Fools: A Cautionary Story on the Revolutionary Socialist Vanguard of England's Post-9/11 Anti-war Movement. *ACME: An International Journal for Critical Geographies*, 9 (2), 113–137, 2015. The most sophisticated critique of this approach was produced by the late Moishe Postone in History and Helplessness.

39 He used this definition, for example, in 'A New British Provocation in Palestine'. *Fourth International*, September 1946.

40 Chris Harman, 'The Prophet and the Proletariat'. *International Socialism Journal*, 2(64), Autumn 1994. Jean Birnbaum refers to this article extensively in his critique of a similar shift on the radical left in France, *Un Silence Religieux: la gauche face au djihadisme*, Paris: Seuil, 2016.

41 For an argument that the term fascism is not helpful in relation to Hezbollah, see Joseph Daher, *Hezbollah:The Political Economy of Lebanon's Party of God*, London, Pluto Press, 2016. For the contrary view (taken here) and also applied to Hezbollah's sponsor Iran, see Stephan Grigat, Antisemitic Anti-Zionism: Muslim Brotherhood, Iran, and Hezbollah. In: Armin Lange, Kerstin Mayerhofer, Dina Porat, & Lawrence H. Schiffman, eds., *Confronting Antisemitism in Modern Media, the Legal and Political Worlds*, De Gruyter, 2021. Grigat argues that use of the term Islamic fascism is virtually unavoidable when it comes to dealing with authoritarian antisemitic mass movements with a leader cult and martyrdom ideology, that wage permanent campaigns against groups deemed threatening to the unity of the umma, use unrestrained brute force against political opponents, and advocate a '"third way" between capitalism and socialism East and West'. His reservation, which is significant in this context, is that too much focus on fascism risks obscuring the centrality of antisemitism.

42 Quoted in Ruth Gledhill, Anti Semitism Now at Second World War High, Argues Mandela's Former Counsel. *The Times*, 15 February 2009. https://www .thetimes.co.uk/article/anti-semitism-now-at-second-world-war-high-argues -mandelas-former-counsel-dqtgsrq9xjv (accessed 26 February 2023).

43 A devastating critique of this analogy by Eve Garrard can be found here: https:// normblog.typepad.com/normblog/2007/08/the-warsaw-ghet.html

44 It is absolutely no accident that Seamus Milne should have been Corbyn's closest aide.

45 For a substantial Marxist critique of Corbynism, see Matt Bolton and Frederick Harry Pitts, *Corbynism: A Critical Approach*, Bingley: Emerald Publishing, 2018.

46 Among the MPs driven out were Luciana Berger, chair of the Jewish Labour Movement and the veteran Louise Ellman. See, for example, https://www .newstatesman.com/politics/2019/10/luciana-berger-on-antisemitism-misogyny -and-the-labour-party-trigger-ballots. https://www.timesofisrael.com/jewish-uk -lawmaker-quits-labour-over-anti-semitism-after-55-years-in-the-party/.

47 Genocide and crimes against humanity have been clearly identified as the gravest crimes of all in international law, in, for example, Articles 6 and 7 of the statute of the International Criminal Court. https://www.icc-cpi.int/sites/default/files/ RS-Eng.pdf.

48 There are fortunately a growing number of compelling critiques of this absurd assertion. See especially Balázs Berkovits, Critical Whiteness Studies and the 'Jewish Problem'. *Zeitschrift für kritische Sozialtheorie und Philosophie*, 5(1),

86–102, 2018; and David Schraub, White Jews: An Intersectional Approach. *AJS Review*, 43, 379–407, 2019.

49 It is disgraceful because it effectively inverts the meaning of Holocaust, turning victims into perpetrators. For more on this, see Lesley Klaff, Holocaust Inversion Israel Studies, 24(2), 73–90, 2019.

50 This is of course not to say that such a radical genocide could not happen again. As Hannah Arendt long ago argued (in Eichmann in Jerusalem), 'it is in the very nature of things human that every act that has once made its appearance and has been recorded in the history of mankind stays with mankind as a potentiality long after its actuality has become a thing of the past. No punishment has ever possessed enough power of deterrence to prevent the commission of crimes'. Although there have been a large number of genocides committed since the crime was defined in the Genocide Convention (which itself recognised that genocide has long been 'an odious scourge' which has 'inflicted great losses on humanity'), it does not appear that any yet have been motivated by the global ambition of the Nazis to wipe the Jews off the face of the earth. This is not in any way to privilege the suffering of Jews, which, as the late Norman Geras explained, would be quite 'morally odious'. It is rather to identify what was so radical in the Nazis' genocidal project. Readers concerned by the recurrence of genocide since the Convention could look at my own *Genocide since 1948*, London: Routledge, 2012.

51 Most famously in chapter 6 of Engels' Peasant Wars in Germany, where he argued that 'the worst thing that can befall a leader of an extreme party is to be compelled to take over a government in an epoch when the movement is not yet ripe …. What he *can* do is in contrast to all his actions as hitherto practised, to all his principles and to the present interests of his party; what he *ought* to do cannot be achieved … Whoever puts himself in this awkward position is irrevocably lost'. *Collected Works of Karl Marx and Frederick Engels*, vol. 10, New York: International Publishers, 1978, pp. 397–482.

52 In her memoirs, Maria Joffe, who was the daughter of one of Trotsky's closest comrades and spent decades in the Gulag, explicitly contrasted the number of death sentences meted out by the Tsars with the rates of capital punishment imposed by Stalin. The difference is startling.

53 Rather than rejecting such an argument outright, it might be better for radical leftists to remind themselves of Victor Serge's rejoinder. 'It is often said that "the germ of all Stalinism was in Bolshevism at its beginning". Well, I have no objection. Only, Bolshevism also contained many other germs, a mass of other germs, and those who lived through the enthusiasm of the first years of the first victorious socialist revolution ought not to forget it. To judge the living man by the death germs which the autopsy reveals in the corpse – and which he may have carried in him since his birth – is that very sensible?' *From Lenin to Stalin*, New York: Pathfinder Press,1973.

54 As Jacob Katz long ago pointed out, in a discussion of what was anticipated anywhere by intellectuals before the Holocaust, there was an almost universal failure by other social theorists to predict what was to happen. Jacob Katz, Was the Holocaust Predictable? In: Yehuda Bauer and Nathan Rotenstreich, eds., *The Holocaust as Historical Experience*, New York: Holmes and Meier, 1981, pp. 23–41. It should though be conceded that Marxists may be perhaps particularly vulnerable on this score, because they have long tended to claim that they have a deeper grasp of history and social reality than those they deride as bourgeois ideologists.

3

DURBAN ANTIZIONISM[1]

David Hirsh and Hilary Miller

Introduction[2]

In her 'Durban Diary', Joëlle Fiss describes her impression of the Durban conference:

> Wherever you turn, Israel is compared to Nazi Germany. Posters associate Israel with the former South African regime and its apartheid policies. Everywhere, there are images of suffering Palestinian children. Arab women display photos of their "martyred" husbands, killed during the Second Intifada.

She describes how the Protocols of the Elders of Zion is on sale from the stand of the Arab Lawyers Union. 'Caricatures are hung up', she says:

> Caricatures are hung up. One of them depicts a rabbi with The Protocols of the Elders of Zion under his arm and an Israeli army cap on his head. Another poster describes how the Jews make their bread: with the blood of Muslims.

Durban was a super-spreader event for a new variant of the antisemitism virus. This new variant was especially well-adapted to thrive in populations which were thought to have already been vaccinated against racism and other bigotries. It had been assumed that the experience of the Holocaust had functioned like a vaccine, achieving effective herd immunity to antisemitism in human populations. It turns out that existing vaccines fail to inhibit the new variant. In fact, the new variant has evolved a mechanism

DOI: 10.4324/9781003222477-4

that specifically makes use of the complacency caused by the existing vaccination programmes to make its way around the natural defences of populations that believe themselves to be immune to racism.[3]

Perhaps this 2021 reconfiguration of the virus metaphor for antisemitism helps us to think about the significance of Durban even if we have to overlook, for the moment, the well-rehearsed shortcomings of the analogy. Should one judge that Durban was not especially significant because the antisemitism that erupted there was little more than a continuation of what was always present? Or should Durban be thought of as a moment of creation, of what was at the time named the 'new antisemitism'?[4] The superspreader metaphor positions Durban as a significant step-change, but not as an innovator of something completely new.

The conference was attended by people from all over the world who were influential, or who would become influential: in government and civil society, in non-governmental organisations (NGOs), as well as in left-wing, anti-racist and feminist movements and their associated scholarly spaces. The worldview that was consolidated at Durban was to become influential in academia as well as in human rights and international humanitarian law circles, in teaching, journalism and the arts, in practical and activist politics and in more scholarly and theoretical thinking.

Key people from each of those milieus had already been finding their ways, by different paths, to similar worldviews that put Israel and Zionism at their centre. There was no conspiracy. There was no genius who decided that Durban was the moment to entrench Israel hatred and antisemitism as the new radical common sense, and who had the political talent to make it happen. Rather, these key people were already infected by the new variant of antisemitism before September 2001. At the conference, they created such a huge viral load in such a small and intense space that a significant proportion of participants took it home and infected, in turn, other influential people in many countries and in distinct social, political and intellectual milieus.

Over the next 20 years many layers of people were indeed influenced. A call for an academic boycott of Israel was made in Britain in 2002[5] and has continued to gain legitimacy and traction around the world, to the present day. It functioned as a targeted campaign for the exclusion of Israelis, and nobody else, from the global academic community. More general campaigns for 'boycott, divestment and sanctions' (BDS) followed, which functioned as campaigns to exclude Israelis, and nobody else, from the global community of humankind. The boycott campaigns were built on ideological foundations that were taken into the 2001 conference by diverse streams of leading activists and delegates, who succeeded in transforming them into truisms for wider groups of participants.

Campuses around the world were especially affected. The delegitimisation of Israel and Zionism, and the acceptance of Israel and Zionism as being materially, symbolically and globally significant, have come to be seen as more and more normal over the two decades since Durban. David Miller, for example, defined his aim as the ending of Zionism 'as the functioning ideology of the world'.[6] These new common-sense notions are only enthusiastically embraced by a minority on campus, but that minority has succeeded in forcing much wider layers of people to recognise them as important and legitimate positions in a wide range of debates. The description of Israel as nothing more than a manifestation of European and American imperialism, and as symbolic of colonialism, racism, ethnic cleansing, genocide and apartheid,[7] closely mirrors the language mobilised by students at the Durban youth summit, by justice activists at the Durban NGO Forum, by diplomats at the government conference and by thousands of protesters in and around the bustling cricket stadium in which the conference was held.

The final arguments over the wording of the official declarations at the Durban conference were scheduled for Saturday 8 September. Because it was Shabbat, many Jewish delegates were excluded, although some attended. In the end, business went on into the evening and observant Jews were then able to join for the end of proceedings. The following Tuesday was 9/11, the day of the attacks on the World Trade Centre in New York and on the Pentagon, and the thwarted attempt to destroy the White House.

Durban was influential in the ways the left, broadly conceived, came to think about the world. In both symbolic and also material ways, Durban can be seen with hindsight to be associated with the 21st century re-emergence of a way of thinking which centres Jews in its understanding of universal problems. 9/11 was perpetrated by a movement that embraced antisemitism and antizionism, without finding the distinction between the two significant. 9/11 saw radical totalitarian politics, which defined itself in relation to its own re-interpretation of the texts and symbols of Islam, come to global prominence. The parts of the left that were especially vulnerable to antizionism had significant commonalities and points of contact with the factions that defined themselves by these 20th century political interpretations of Islam. They both understood the world as being fundamentally divided between what might be called 'imperialism', 'capitalism', 'modernity', 'Judeo-Christianity' or 'the West' on the one hand, and victims of that formidable, global system of domination on the other. Many were ready to overlook the potential for disagreement around issues like democracy, human rights, women's rights, LGBT+ equality, freedom of speech and pluralism. The left seems largely to have forgotten the experience of going into coalition with fellow 'anti-imperialists' in Iran during the 1979 revolution. There, much of the left had helped Khomeini consolidate his power before it was then murderously suppressed and defeated by the new regime.

This chapter starts by looking at the ways in which Jews at the Durban conference were themselves alienated from a social space in which they had felt they belonged, by the acceptance of the idea that Zionism was the key racism in the world and that Zionists were oppressors. They looked for solidarity against the antisemitism they felt they were experiencing and they found little.

The chapter goes on to focus on the relationship between this Durban antizionism and other, older anti-Jewish ideologies. It finds a route through some of the debates about the alleged historical essentialism of Nirenberg's anti-Judaism on the one hand and the Arendtian focus on geographical, temporal and social specificities of each distinct anti-Jewish movement on the other. This leads to a consideration of agency and responsibility for a form of antisemitism which is angrily denied by those who appear to embrace and carry it. This question of agency is one of the key problems with the metaphor of antisemitism as a virus. The chapter tentatively suggests ways in which we might think of antisemitism in a functionalist way and ways in which we might draw from the vocabulary of evolution and adaptation to specific environments.

As a case study, the chapter traces an antizionist thread from the UN women's conferences, starting in 1975, through the time of the peace process, and into Durban. It suggests that one might look at a number of other threads which similarly connected Durban back to the UN 'Zionism is racism' culture of the 1970s. Although antizionism was not dominant on the left in the 1980s and the 1990s, it was kept alive in a number of specific social spaces by committed supporters. That is one reason it was able so ferociously to re-emerge at the Durban conference.

Durban as a traumatic event for Jewish participants

One of the characteristic impacts of antisemitism is to exclude Jews from places where they feel a genuine sense of belonging. Antisemitism alienates Jewish members of any community where it is tolerated. It constructs Jews as alien, accusing them of simulating loyalty, while really betraying their ostensible community to their actual Jewish interests. Jews in 15th century Spain were forced to convert or were driven out of the country. Alfred Dreyfus was accused of using his position as an officer in the French army to spy for Germany. The Rothschilds were accused of fomenting the First World War and financing the war effort of every belligerent state against the others. 'Jewish finance' was accused of pushing the British Empire into the Boer War in the interests of its gold and diamond investments.[8] German Jews were stripped of their citizenship by the National Socialist movement and were later stripped of all other remaining rights. Prominent universities in the United States put racial quotas on Jews in the 1930s, which remained, for example at Yale, until the 1960s. The 'America First' movement argued that Jews were trying to draw the US into the war against the Nazis against its own interests. In 2007, John Mearsheimer and Stephen Walt published an ostensibly respectable academic thesis that the 'Israel Lobby' had been decisive in sending the USA to war against Iraq against its own interests.[9] Jewish feminists in the 1980s were accused of betraying their Palestinian sisters on account of their 'Zionism', and were excluded from the Spare Rib collective, amongst other feminist spaces. Jewish academics who opposed boycotts of Israeli colleagues were treated in their trade unions as disloyal to the principles of solidarity and in their universities as unscholarly. Jewish Labour Party members in Britain were accused of disloyalty when they spoke out against the antisemitism of the Jeremy Corbyn faction. Jewish lesbians were excluded from the Chicago Dyke Marches due to their alleged failures of intersectional solidarity. Antisemitic replacement fantasists on the right seek to warn white people that Jews are bringing in non-whites to replace them and on the left they seek to warn non-white people that Jews are bringing in white colonists to replace them.[10]

Antisemites have not always held state power and alienation from spaces in which Jews felt they were at home has not always ended in death. But the act of constructing Jews as disloyal to their nation, their class, their sex, their sexuality, their community of scholarship, their fellow trade unionists; the act of constructing Jews as disloyal to humankind as a whole, is a familiar one. It is traumatic to be constructed as disloyal and dishonest by one's own community. To feel at home is to feel that people around you accept you as one of them, to feel that they value you as you value them and to feel that you share basic notions of what is important. It is to feel that people will stand with you if you are threatened and to promise that you will stand with them if they are threatened.

Many Jewish participants at Durban experienced a sudden and complete alienation from the global community of anti-racism, from the social space of which they had felt themselves to be a part. Their anti-racism was not transactional, it was not offered in exchange for reciprocation against antisemitism. But when solidarity was appropriate and urgent, it did not materialise from those who purported to stand against 'racism, xenophobia, discrimination and *all* forms of hatred'. The conference was a concentrated and intense event. Jews in the anti-racist world had experienced antizionism before but what was new to many at Durban was the experience of antizionism as a hegemonic ideology and as something which their anti-racist colleagues either embraced with enthusiasm or feared to oppose. Criticism of Israel, antisemitic tropes, Jew-hating crowds, the centring of Zionism as a key global enemy and the singling out of Jewish delegates as representative of it, swirled one into the other, around the meetings, the streets and the spirit of the conference.

Some of the Jews who were present at Durban, and who we interviewed, report that the 9/11 attacks felt entirely in keeping with the atmosphere of fear and unreality which still enveloped them on Tuesday morning. Others report that 9/11 made Durban feel like it had never happened, and an ordinary kind of rational, political and emotional processing of what had happened was abruptly cut off by the enormity of the new event. Many report that Durban changed their lives and many of them have devoted the two decades since to resisting and critiquing what they experienced as exclusionary antisemitism which has the potential to cause significant harm.

Durban antizionism in relation to previous anti-Jewish ideologies

Left-wing antisemitism was not new at Durban. For as long as there has been a left, there have been authentically left-wing currents tempted by antisemitic shortcuts to making sense of the world, and tempted by shortcuts to liberation. There have always also been other left currents which recognised and resisted antisemitism. Moshe Postone writes that antisemitism can appear to be anti-hegemonic: 'to be the expression of a movement of the little people against an intangible, global form of domination'.[11]

Left antisemitism was not new at Durban, but neither, even, was the anti-Jewish ideology or worldview of *antizionism*. There has been anti-Zionism since the 1890s. There had been Jewish opposition to Herzl's call for Jews to migrate to Palestine and build a nation state there. There was debate amongst Jews about how to best deal with the antisemitism that they faced. But after the Holocaust and after 1948, anti-zionism appeared in a world which had been wholly, materially transformed for Jews since those old-time debates about Jewish strategy. Antizionism now presented itself as the innocent inheritor of those older movements; but the pre-war arguments had not been won or lost, the arguers had been obliterated. Socialists, Zionists, Bundists, assimilationists and traditionalists were murdered together by the Nazis. What could opposition to Zionism possibly mean now, in a world where Jews had been driven out of Europe anyway, where Jews lived under Stalin's totalitarian terror and where life in the Middle East was being transformed by ethnic Arab nationalist movements throwing off the old European empires? And in a world where Jews in Israel had prevented themselves from going the way of Jews in Europe?

The new antizionism was not a critique of an idea, it was an ideology which designated the Israel that now existed as being racist in its very essence. The antizionism that was to erupt at Durban had been pioneered by the antisemitic and totalitarian propagandists of the Soviet Union, after the Jewish world had been radically and materially transformed in the 20th century, but long before 2001.[12]

Jews were targeted by antizionism as early as 1951. Rudolf Slánský, the leader of the Communist state in Czechoslovakia was 'found guilty' of 'bourgeois Jewish nationalism', and hanged, together with his mostly Jewish comrades. In 1968, Jews who had been loyal to the Communist regimes in Poland and East Germany were purged from positions of power and influence after being accused of 'Zionism'.

'Tel Aviv and Pretoria are akin, just as Apartheid in the South African Republic and Zionism in Israel are simply different brands of racialism',[13] wrote N Oleynikov in 1977, for TASS, the official propaganda organ of the USSR. Soviet antizionism was not 'criticism of Israel', nor was it related to the local conflict between the Palestinians and the Israelis, it was a universal ideology of Jewish evil influence. From the newspaper *Izvestia*, 'The Criminal Handwriting of Zionism' in 1975:

> Israeli aggression, which maintains the entire Middle East, as well as the whole world, in a state of tension, has for many years been 'substantiated' by Zionist ideology. Zionism has taken to extremes Judaism's assertion that the Jewish people is 'God-chosen' and 'exclusive' and is superior to other peoples.[14]

Antizionism was here positioning everything bad in the world to be caused by Zionism and the evil of Zionism to be a direct outcome of the essential evil of Judaism.

Antizionism had also become a common thread in left-wing, Arab nationalist and Islamist understandings of their shared enemy, whether named 'imperialism', 'the west' or 'modernity'. Campaigns to construct Zionism as a form of racism and apartheid had already been raging in the 1970s.

In Israel's early years there had also been much left-wing warmth towards it. Zionism was thought of as the movement of the 'oppressed' from Europe and Russia. Zionism's role as a movement of the oppressed Jews from the Middle East and Africa was less well understood. Israel was thought of as a pioneer of socialist and 'progressive' institutions and cultures, as a motor for economic development and as an enemy of British imperialism. In the 1980s and 1990s, at least within mainstream democratic left and liberal opinion, the demonising narratives of Israel had been kept marginal by the widely shared hope that peace would soon be realised between Israel and its neighbours. Israel was not thought of as an evil to be eradicated but as a potential constituent of a new, peaceful, democratic and liberated Middle East.

When the peace process began to collapse and the *Second Intifada* raged, the barriers confining antizionism to the margins of left and liberal opinion began to collapse too. For some, this happened as early as 1995, when Israeli Prime Minister Yitzhak Rabin was murdered by a Jewish Israeli opponent of Palestinian independence. So even the post-peace process resurgence of antizionism predated Durban by up to six years. Many on the left gave up on the peace process during Benjamin Netanyahu's premiership from 1996 to 1999, which they interpreted as indicating the end of Israeli support for a Palestinian state. Ehud Barak was elected with an Israeli mandate to make the deal, but within a year the *Second Intifada* had erupted and Yasser Arafat appeared to be unambiguously re-committed to the destruction of Israel and to the rejection of a Palestinian state alongside Israel.

At the Durban conference, an ostensibly coherent and specifically antise-mitic way of seeing and understanding Israel was pushed hard. Contrary to appearances, antisemitism is never really about Jews, and antizionism is not really about Israel. Both are ways of projecting all that is bad in the whole world onto an 'other'. At the 'World Conference against Racism' the evil that needed explaining was racism.

Hannah Arendt wrote that antisemitism makes Jews into the keys of history. She meant that for the antisemite, history can only be understood via the role of Jews in it. Everything that happens in the world seems to make sense to those who believe that the Jews are the real root cause of it. Antisemitism is conspiracy fantasy. In architecture, a keystone is the single wedge-shaped block at the top of an arch without which the arch would fall. Durban antizionism was a worldview which made Israel into the keystone of a global, interlinked and coherent system of oppression.

In his huge work of history, David Nirenberg shows what each anti-Jew-ish movement has in common with the others. He tells a single story of the development of 'Anti-Judaism' over 30 centuries.[15] Yet in her equally impressive 'Origins of Totalitarianism', Arendt warns us not to essentialise antisemitism as a single determining fact of human history.[16] She emphasises the aspects of antisemitism which are specific to the particular antisemites who mobilise them, and to their particular purposes. She pays attention to the different times, places and societies in which antisemitism finds new forms even if the new forms borrow, but re-construct, emotionally powerful language and tropes from previous ones.

In the spirit of Nirenberg's understanding, we can see that Durban pro-jected racism, the thing which is most hated and feared in 21st century society, especially amongst the left and liberals, onto Israel. Previous anti-semitisms had projected their own conceptions of pure evil onto 'the Jews': the rejection and murder of the universal God, a murder ritually re-enacted on children; the rejection of progress and modernity; the clinging to reac-tionary tradition; betraying their community be it nation, class, people, or humanity. Both those who hated 'socialism' and those who hated 'capital-ism', which had been re-christened 'neoliberalism' by the time of Durban, gave what they hated Jewish faces so everyone could grasp the depth of the evil in their hearts and in their bones.

In the spirit of Arendt's understanding, Durban antizionism, and the way it resonated and caught on, tells us something about our own society in the 21st century. This anti-Jewish ideology is not just the latest head of an eternal monster, which grows anew each time the old one is cut off. Durban tells us nothing about Jews or Israel but plenty about the particular society in which people pick up old bits and pieces of discarded antisemitism and use them to build their own way of dealing with what they find unbearable. Antisemitism and antizionism are not only effects of 'society', they are also ideologies which specific human beings construct and use for their own purposes.

Agency for an antisemitism that its proponents disavow

> However when I tried to air some of these problems in conversation with UCU activists I encountered a sense of honest bewilderment that I could possibly have any objection to Ken Loach. The idea was unthinkable...
>
> *Sarah Annes Brown*[17]

Sarah Annes Brown writes of the 'honest bewilderment' she observed when union activists were told that one of their socialist heroes had a record of engaging in antisemitic rhetoric. The question of human agency is challenging in this context because the people who pushed antisemitism at Durban thought of themselves as good people seeking justice, and as people who stood firmly *against* antisemitism. In general, the denial seems genuine, even if its shrillness and certainty may sometimes point in the direction of unacknowledgeable doubt. The denials are also characteristically followed by aggressive counter-accusations that the very suggestion of antisemitism itself could only be understood as evidence of Jewish dishonesty and double-dealing.[18]

It is often said that Israel's bad behaviour is the cause of the 'new antisemitism' variant but, in truth, the antisemitism is caused by the ways in which people make sense of Israel's behaviour, as they describe and imagine it. Antisemites are responsible for the antisemitic things they say and do. They are responsible for their own ignorance and for their own mechanisms of denial.

The somewhat clichéd metaphor of antisemitism as a virus rather sides with the ahistorical Nirenberg picture of antisemitism. It also seems to absolve antisemites of agency. Those who attended Durban were not passively infected by antisemitism. They decided to embrace it. Many who did not go so far as to embrace antisemitism either denied or trivialised it. Participants were offered an ostensibly coherent worldview which resonated emotionally and powerfully, albeit perhaps for reasons of which they were not fully aware. Because, as Karin Stögner argues, antisemitism is itself a quintessentially intersectional ideology, it is well suited to function as a unifying framework for people embedded in different religious and political traditions, as well as people situated in different parts of complex global power structures.[19] But they wanted to be unified and they valued the unity that it brought.

So we insist that antisemites, that is people who embrace and who legitimise antisemitic worldviews, have agency and that they are politically and morally responsible for what they do. But we also observe that they are often clear about their own subjective opposition to antisemitism. They insist on their own innocence. We also observe that some at Durban appeared fully conscious and rather relaxed at the prospect that their antizionism could, and would, be instrumentalised for the advancement of openly antisemitic purposes. At Durban, they could see the antisemitism quite clearly, around them. But still they chose not to notice it, not to understand it, to disavow it or simply to downplay its importance or significance. Was not the antisemitism, which did not exist, caused by Israel?

Antizionists had fought hard for Israel and Zionism to be at the top of the agenda of the 'World Conference against Racism' long before anyone arrived in South Africa. One of the planning conferences was held in Tehran. The Iranian government did not grant visas to Israeli passport holders or to people associated with Jewish non-governmental organisations. They were thus barred from contributing to the writing of the Durban Declaration and Program of Action which would be adopted months later at the government conference. This was a clear violation of the rules and norms of the UN, but one which was allowed by other delegates to stand. The draft text, proposed by the Organization of the Islamic Conference (OIC), and adopted at the Tehran conference, referred to Israel as 'a new kind of apartheid', and a 'crime against humanity', while it designated 'Zionism' as a 'form of genocide'. At the follow-up Geneva conference, the OIC delegates also sought to dilute any mention of 'Holocaust' to 'holocausts' in an apparent effort to normalise the Nazi genocide of the Jews in Europe.

Agency and responsibility for antisemitism are difficult to pin down but it is clear that there were many at Durban, such as the Iranian government delegation, who endowed no significance to nice distinctions between hostility to Jews, to Zionism and to Israel, which are held by subjectively anti-racist antizionists to be of crucial significance. There were many at the conference who were quite prepared to work alongside antisemites in the construction of declarations against racism and more still who were prepared to downplay the significance of antisemitism. The minority which stood up against antisemitism during the process was marginalised, delegitimised and was itself denounced as racist. This was allowed to happen by the mainstream of the global anti-racist movement.

A functionalist way of understanding antizionism?

The fact that a variant of antisemitism is so well suited to the purpose of unifying disparate individuals and movements in picturing evil as having a Jewish face is not accidental, nor is it a product of conspiracy, nor simply is it a given fact of human history. The antisemitic notion of 'the Jews' has evolved through the profoundly changing ecosystems of human history into a nest of emotions, ideas and images that are perfectly adapted to symbolise the nightmares of the collective subconscious. Antisemitism survived because it could be adapted by social agents to their specific needs in each new context. The remnants of previous variants of antisemitism retained enough emotional potency to make it worthwhile recycling them rather than building from scratch. But, as David Seymour writes, they do not do so without some shame. They disavow the old before they employ it in building the new:

> A common characteristic between "classic" and "new" antisemitic ideology is that each begins with a disavowal and a distinction. Both iterations will often begin by acknowledging and lamenting prior forms of anti-Jewish hostility. This opening gambit of disavowal is followed immediately by a distinction between these disavowed ideologies and the writer's own "novel" contribution.[20]

Perhaps, in Darwinian terms, anti-democratic movements that embrace antisemitism thrive compared to the ones that do not embrace antisemitism. This makes sense when one recalls that antisemitism has evolved in ways that are specifically adapted to thrive in the specific conditions of a succession of historical anti-democratic environments. This idea of antisemitism having evolved to be well adapted in particular environments might lead us to try thinking of antisemitism in functionalist terms, not as a virus but as a resource and as a source of power.

Antisemitism is especially attractive when the evil which it is mobilised to explain is too painful to address rationally. What is more profoundly dreaded in America than racism? Is America founded on human equality or is it corrupt in its heart because of its original sin of slavery? In Britain, the partly addressed nightmare is colonialism. Britain was the colonial power and the Israelis overthrew the mandate but now there is a British temptation to project its own partly resolved past onto Israel's present. Today's Europe is founded on the narrative that antisemitism and racism have been transcended and overcome. Europe was often tempted to project its own unacknowledged horrors onto 'the Jews' in its midst and onto other 'races' outside. Now Europeans can project their own disavowed racism onto Jews who are no longer European; even if about half of Israelis were never European at all and the other half are hardly 'not European' in any relevant sense simply on the basis that they were given the choice of death or trying to escape.[21] It is Europeans who accuse Israelis of failing to learn the lessons of Auschwitz and then of re-importing racism back into the now clean again Europe, in the form of Islamophobia. In South Africa, the global and nation-founding triumph over apartheid can feel like a token victory as hopelessness, violence and inequality persist under a state that appears dysfunctional and quite unable to make life better.[22] The temptation to re-focus anger and despair onto an emotionally satisfying symbolic target is irresistible to some. The spirit of Durban, then, was to portray racism, apartheid, imperialism, state violence and the negation of human rights as having an Israeli face.

Recently, we have seen the appearance of the slogan 'Globalize the Intifdada'.[23] It cements a fantasy of Israel as being symbolic of all evil and it raises a fantasy of the Palestinian struggle as a universal symbol of the innocence and courage of all those who suffer. 'Globalize the Intifada' reconstitutes the passion plays of old Europe, by which good people could identify with the divine, and with the ultimate justice which would be theirs. The meek shall inherit the earth. And they shall do so by defeating Zionism.

During the 2021 conflict in Gaza, academics were passing around statements pressuring each other to affirm that the substance of the antizionism that was spread from Durban was integral to their scholarship and to their personal morality.[24] Students too, some of whom were not yet born in 2001, are socialised into a culture in which it is common to believe that justice cannot prevail around the world until Israel is destroyed; that racist cops in Minnesota were taught by Zionists how to murder African American men;[25] and that it is legitimate to exclude feminists from asserting pride in their identities, which they locate at the intersection of their lesbianism and their Jewishness, by flying a rainbow flag with a *Magen David* on it. These are examples of elements of an accepted political culture which make one's attitude towards Israel into a universal test of one's human value. They constitute antisemitic loyalty tests that exclude Jews.

Case study: antizionism at the UN women's conferences

Durban antizionism was not authored or organised by a single actor and it was not the product of a secret conspiracy. It happened because of a confluence of factors: a coming together of distinct trajectories into something nearing a perfect storm.

One example of a current which fed antisemitism into Durban was the UN women's movement. There was a series of world conferences on women, starting in 1975, which embraced a deepening antizionism throughout the period when most of the broad left had embraced the 'two state solution' that the peace movement was working towards. The women's conferences constituted one unbroken thread connecting the radical antizionism of the 1970s to the 2001 Durban conference. There were others.

UN General Assembly Resolution 3379, adopted in November 1975, declared formally that 'Zionism is a form of racism and racial discrimination'.[26] But this kind of language in official UN documents had itself already been pioneered at the first UN 'World Conference on Women' in Mexico City earlier in the year. Delegates there voted to adopt a text that repeatedly listed Zionism among every other 'scourge' to be eliminated, such as colonialism, neo-colonialism, foreign occupation, apartheid and racial discrimination. The 'Declaration on the Equality of Women', which ought to have been remembered because it was a historic step forward for the global women's movement, was also innovative as one of the first international documents to label Zionism as a form of racism. The Declaration singles out Israel, and only Israel, by calling on the UN body for women's rights to devote specific assistance to the campaign to realise self-determination for Palestinian women in 'their struggle against zionism' and 'alien domination'. It may be remembered how many other nations were fighting 'alien domination' at that time, for example within the Soviet Union itself, but of course much more widely too. Cambodian women, Lithuanian women, Polish women, Bosnian and Croatian women, Kurdish and Tibetan women, Tamil women, Tutsi women, women in Indonesia and East Timor, Algeria and Equatorial Guinea, in Argentina and Uganda, to name but a few, were not mentioned in the Declaration.

In 1963, Betty Friedan had written of one of the founding texts of Second Wave Feminism, 'The Feminine Mystique'[27]. In 1966, she was the founding president of the National Organisation of Women, the key institution of the women's movement in the United States. Friedan led a delegation of American feminists to Mexico City for the 1975 conference in the hope of helping to 'advance the worldwide movement of women to equality'.[28]

Born in 1921 Bettye Naomi Goldstein, Friedan was Jewish. She was 20 years old at the time the Holocaust began and 28 when Israel declared its independence. Leah Rabin, the wife of Yitzchak Rabin, who was serving his first term as the Prime Minister of Israel, was also at the Mexico City gathering. When she rose to address the plenary, many delegates booed and walked out. 'We shall wait until the exodus is over', Rabin said, with faux patience as more than half of the room poured out of the conference hall at the Mexican Foreign Ministry building.[29]

Friedan recalls feeling shocked by the anti-Americanism, antisemitism and antizionism that was pulsing through the conference. She felt they served to divert attention away from the goal of the conference, which was to promote the causes of women's rights and women's equality.[30]

Delegates from states which defined themselves constitutionally as 'Arab' or 'Communist' moved to link the Ten-Year Plan of Action for Women to the abolition of 'racism, apartheid and Zionism'. The New Zealand delegation head, Whetu Tirikatene-Sullivan, who was of both Maori and Jewish descent, said in response: 'If Zionism is to be included in the declaration, we cannot understand why sexism was not included'.[31] This followed some wrangling over the claim that the word 'sexism' was a 'nasty North American neologism'.[32]

At the parallel NGO conference, Jewish feminists faced an equally hostile environment. Many were harassed and intimidated. Friedan herself received anonymous letters warning her not to speak or she would be denounced 'first as an American and then as a Jew'.[33] At key moments microphones were muted and speakers were silenced. Jewish feminists left the conference feeling demoralised: the assault on them as 'Zionists' was entirely inappropriate in the context of what they had assumed would be a shared endeavour to advance the feminism shared by women around the world. The follow-up conference in Copenhagen in 1980 again adopted a resolution that defined Zionism as a form of racism and it went further, constructing Zionism as an obstacle to the full enjoyment of universal women's rights. The centring of Zionism as a universal obstacle to all liberation was antisemitic because it put Jewish evil, real, imagined and exaggerated, at the centre of all evils.

The rhetorical attacks on Israel at the UN women's conferences, led by the OIC and by the Soviet Bloc, were part of a concerted effort to make Israel into an international pariah in the way that apartheid South Africa had been.

At the 2001 conference, held in a South Africa still glowing from the victory over officially sanctioned racism there, it must have been clear that there would be a particular opportunity to leverage the portrayal of Israel as apartheid.

Other threads linking 1970s antizionism to Durban

Parallel campaigns can be traced through the anti-racism conferences, too. These efforts to construct Israel as a unique and symbolic evil in the world also made significant progress at the UN world racism conferences in 1978 and 1983 in Geneva. Apart from the UN women's and the racism conferences, there were other routes to the 2001 Durban event for this same focus on the evils of Israel. They were neither entirely independent of each other nor were they part of a single, organised campaign.

There had been analogous trajectories, for example, in the related UN, activist and academic worlds of human rights, and international humanitarian and human rights law. Apartheid, for example, was abstracted from the context of South Africa and transformed into an ostensibly universal violation of specific human rights principles, and into a crime in international humanitarian law. But rhetoric of universality sometimes functions in the interest of specific particularisms. This danger was realised when the universal standards of humankind were forged into specific traps for the Jewish state, and for its allied Jewish ideology, 'Zionism'. There were also analogous trajectories within some of the internal political cultures of some of the increasingly influential and vocal non-governmental organisations.

Although they saw themselves as taking responsibility for the implementation and monitoring of universal standards, they were similarly not immune to the temptations of a similarly eccentric and particularistic focus on Israel.

Leading tendencies in the left more generally were open to the Durban focus on Zionism. The 1968 'new left' had mushroomed as a response to Stalinism but it had tended to replicate some of Stalinism's key features: in particular its devaluing of Enlightenment democratic values as 'bourgeois', and its raising of a rhetoric of anti-imperialism to an absolute principle, above all other left-wing and democratic principles. Class, with its arguably inherent universalism, a structure both of exploitation and of potential liberation, was often de-centred and replaced by 'race' and then by a rainbow of other 'intersecting' 'oppressions'. With the decline of labour movements in the democratic states and with the collapse of 'actually existing socialism', there was movement on the left away from the material politics of making the world better towards performative and symbolic substitutes.

These developments in left-wing thinking and practice were diverse and they led in many directions. But one possibility that they opened up was an intellectual and emotional openness to the kind of antizionism which felt to so many who were at Durban to be radical, exciting and new. People concerned with anti-racism, women's liberation, human rights and international humanitarian law and global justice found a way in which they could feel united and confident. The left had lost the possibility of associating itself with powerful 'socialist' states and the programme of harnessing the power of organised labour to realise its restructuring of society was also feeling increasingly utopian to many.

Some heads on the left were turning with interest towards the power of states which ruled in the name of the struggle against imperialism, and towards religious and nationalist political movements which seemed, from afar, to know how to mobilise the oppressed. If the plan was to manoeuvre close to these new sources of power, values such as women's rights, democracy, the rule of law, liberty and freedom of speech would need to be firmly subordinated to the overriding principle of opposing imperialism, which was a rhetoric in which these governments and movements were fluent.

One possible short cut to left and liberal unity, related to these political temptations, was antisemitism. It marked the abandonment of the common project of making the world better and it traded measurable progress for symbolic and emotionally satisfying explanations of why the world was so essentially compromised. What remained for those who gave up the positive project of changing the world was the business of assigning responsibility for the injustices which could not be addressed, and in particular for making sure that they themselves were seen to be not. The danger of a 'not in my name' approach to injustice is that concern for one's own moral and political cleanliness may come to seem more important than the seemingly impossible aspiration to make things better. As some social justice movements withdraw from the material world, they tended to rely more and more on moral statements of their own innocence and on a performative politics of resistance, which did not aspire, in practical terms, to positive change. The temptation of conspiracy fantasy is always there, together with the temptation to reach for ways of designating others as responsible for, and as symbolic of, that which cannot be addressed. Those held responsible for the state of the world must be formidable, to explain our inability to overcome them, and cunning, to explain why they are able to create such unjust structures, but camouflage them with the appearance of fairness and liberty.

Conclusion

This chapter has tried to weave together a number of questions, and tentative answers, relating to the antizionism of Durban and its impact on the first 20 years of the century.

We see Durban neither as a moment of creation of something completely new nor as an indistinguishable part of a fundamentally eternal antisemitism. We have described it as a significant moment of crystallisation of an antizionist antisemitism which had roots in the past and continuities with the past, but which also formed something which would be recognisable, important and influential, into the future. The rewards potentially available for recycling the shapes and emotions of old antisemitic movements into the 21st century were significant. But if people for whom positioning on the anti-racist left was important were to profit from them, they would have to formulate their worldview such that it did not remind them either too much, or too little, of other anti-Jewish worldviews.

We have raised questions about antisemitism and human agency. Antisemitism is more than a reservoir of emotionally significant tropes which overflow onto, or which infect, unsuspecting people and movements.[34] Antisemitism is the act itself of picking up these old poisons, reconfiguring them for one's own specific purposes, and those actions successfully constructing significant shared meanings amongst communities of people. We have also used the metaphor of evolution. Antisemitism has evolved in distinct environments in human history to be well-adapted to live in symbiosis with anti-democratic movements. Durban antisemites angrily deny their antisemitism. While we might accept some of these denials as honest reporting of their own inner subjective feelings, they are not thereby absolved of political or moral responsibility. The contention that antisemitism is caused by the bad behaviour of Jews is hardly unusual in relation to ideologies of illegitimate and unjust structural power. Every racism and bigotry contends that the racist or the bigot is innocent while the object of the hatred is actually dangerous and threatening to the happiness of 'the people'.

The defenders of Durban antizionism endow great importance to the distinction between antizionism as an anti-racist movement of the oppressed, and antisemitism as a racist movement of the oppressors. The 'Jerusalem Declaration on Antisemitism' takes the key elements of antizionist rhetoric and insists that they are not 'in and of themselves' antisemitic.[35] But we should be concerned with those key elements as they appear in the world, not as they appear in the defensive imagination of the Declarationists. The antizionism which erupted at Durban, the antizionism which constitutes a worldview, the antizionism which constructs an ideology around an invented caricature of Israel and the antizionism which depicts racism and imperialism with an Israeli face – this antizionism fits comfortably into a series of historical phenomena: Christian, anti-capitalist, anti-communist, nationalist, anti-nationalist and totalitarian antisemitisms.

Perhaps, in a sense, the questions of when antizionism becomes antisemitic, or whether antizionism is antisemitism, are redundant. Antizionism in the 21st century, as it was crystallised at Durban, is a movement that puts Jews at the symbolic and material centre of all that is most feared and hated in the world. The tools of organising and understanding that Durban offered have been significantly and progressively picked up and honed in the following years. The normalisation of antizionism is not yet catastrophic, neither is it unopposed; yet it advances slowly and relentlessly. It clouds scholarly and academic attempts to understand the world; it perverts emancipatory movements; it mis-educates people who grow to become educators, opinion-formers and lawmakers.

Why is this happening now? Perhaps people are always attracted to the notion that they live in the end of times, that this moment in history, the now, is the key turning point. This is an especially present zeitgeist in the 21st century. Democracy feels to so many as fragile and discredited as it did to so many of their great grandparents in the 1930s. Humanity is confronted by climate change, Covid, the rise of illegitimate power and the decline of clarity about legitimacy itself. These all constitute fertile ground for an ideology with the characteristics of Durban antizionism.

Populism is a framework that simplifies social life into a homogenous and fundamentally innocent 'people' that is held down and lied to by an elite, which pretends to be democratic and liberal but which really only acts to increase its own money and power.[36] In populist rhetoric, this elite is responsible for conditions of significant exploitation and subjugation, but it disguises the situation with illusions of democracy, freedom of information, the rule of law, free markets and international co-operation. Insofar as populism is conspiracy fantasy, antizionism is a system of thought that is in keeping with the spirit of contemporary populism. Antizionism makes Zionism symbolic of these powerful and dishonest global elites. Insofar as antizionism disables rational, democratic and anti-racist movements, it also weakens political forces which might be expected to oppose populism.

We are aware of the irony that as we critique the notion that the Jews are at the centre of all that is most to be feared in the world, we ourselves are open to criticism that we do the same: that we say that *antizionism* is in danger of becoming a phenomenon that is central to all that is to be genuinely feared in the world. But then, if we are right, that the practice of putting Jews at the centre of the world might become globally significant, then we are right to treat that as globally threatening.

Notes

1 This chapter was originally published as David Hirsh and Hilary Miller, Durban Antizionism: Its Sources, Its Impact, and Its Relation to Older Anti-Jewish Ideologies. *JCA*, 5:1, 2022. https://doi.org/10.26613/jca/5.1.98 (accessed 26 February 2023). It is reproduced with the permission of the journal.
This chapter is dedicated to the memory of Suzette Bronkhorst, who we interviewed during our research, and to her partner Ronald Eissens. They attended the Durban conference, representing the anti-racism NGO that they had built together in Amsterdam. Suzette, the daughter of an Auschwitz survivor, told us that as Jews they literally feared for their lives in the streets of Durban in September 2001. She told us: 'I promised myself I would refuse to let Durban define my life in the way that Auschwitz defined my father's'. This was shocking, how could she refer to Auschwitz and Durban in the same sentence? Our research task is to understand why she did that. They were friends and colleagues to many of us and lovers and comrades to each other. Suzette died in October 2021, Ronald in January 2021.
2 We would like to acknowledge the input of David Seymour, whose wide reading and thoughtful understanding on the topic of antisemitism has contributed to the development of some of the ideas in this chapter. He has set out his account of the relationship between antisemitism and antizionism in David Seymour, Continuity and Discontinuity: From Antisemitism to Antizionism and the Reconfiguration of the Jewish Question. *Journal of Contemporary Antisemitism*, 2(2), 11–24, 2019. https://doi.org/10.26613/jca/2.2.30 (accessed 17 October 2021). His chapter in this volume is relevant too.
3 The metaphor of Durban as a super-spreader event was first used by David Hirsh on Twitter and Facebook on 17 August 2021. See: David Hirsh. 'The 2001 Durban...' Twitter, 17 August 2021. https://twitter.com/DavidHirsh/status/1427592079451070467. See also: David Hirsh. "The 2001 Durban..."' Facebook.com, 17 August 2021. https://www.facebook.com/dhirsh1/posts/10158024613955918.) It was also, independently, used by Kenneth Marcus on 19 September 2021. *Fight Racism, Not Jews: The UN and the Durban Deceit Conference* held on 19 September 2021. https://brandeiscenter.com/resources/videos/. The transcript was published as follows: Kenneth Marcus. *We Must Call for an End to Durbanism*. JNS.org, 20 September 2021. https://www.jns.org/opinion/we-must-call-for-an-end-to-durbanism/.
4 Phyllis Chesler, *The New Anti-Semitism*, San Francisco: Jossey-Bass, 2003.
5 Letters: More Pressure for Mid East Peace. *The Guardian*, 5 April 2002. https://www.theguardian.com/world/2002/apr/06/israel.guardianletters. Also see S. Rose and H. Rose, The Choice Is to Do Nothing or Try to Bring About Change. *The Guardian*, 15 July 2002. https://www.theguardian.com/world/2002/jul/15/comment.stevenrose.
6 David Miller, Miller's Contribution to 'the Enemy We Face Here Is Zionism'. *YouTube*, 15 February 2021. https://www.youtube.com/watch?v=zrAlJl73NCQ (accessed 17 October 2021).

7 See, for example, the statement formally endorsed by 168 Gender Studies departments and centres in May 2021. Gender Studies Departments in Solidarity with
   Palestinian Feminist Collective. . http://genderstudiespalestinesolidarity.weebly
   .com/ (accessed 17 October 2021).
8 Claire Hirshfield, The Anglo-Boer War and the Issue of Jewish Culpability.
   Journal of Contemporary History, 15(4), 619–631, 1980.
9 John Mearsheimer and Stephen Walt. *The Israel Lobby and US Foreign Policy*,
   London: Penguin Books, 2008.
10 Joel Finkelstein et al., NCRI – Antisemitic Disinformation: A Study of the Online
   Dissemination of Anti-Jewish Conspiracy Theories. Network for Contagion
   Research Institute. https://networkcontagion.us/reports/antisemitic-disinfor-
   mation-a-study-of-the-online-dissemination-of-anti-jewish-conspiracy-theo-
   ries/?fbclid=IwAR1Iz8n1xn_dr9lT20VP-cbnS9mvLC6eWBPpkyzHP9S7qMhT
   ZBY1I9uINVc (accessed 19 October 2021).
11 Moishe Postone, History and Helplessness: Mass Mobilization and Contemporary
   Forms of Anticapitalism. *Public Culture* 18, 1, 2006.
12 The pre-war movements are written with a hyphen because they were movements in opposition to a Zionism which really existed as a political movement.
   Post Holocaust and post 1948 antizionism are written without a hyphen because
   the Zionism in opposition to which they define themselves, which is symbolic
   of racism and all else that is evil, comes from their own imaginations. This
   'Zionism' is analogous to the ways that older antisemitisms set themselves up in
   opposition to their own imagined concept of 'the Jews', which they designated as
   being symbolic of everything bad in the world.
13 N Oleynikov, TASS in Russian for Abroad and in English, 23.8.1977. In: *Soviet
   Antisemitic Propaganda*,London: Institute of Jewish Affairs, 1978.
14 V. Kudryavtsev, The Criminal Handwriting of Zionism, Izvestia, 2.12.1975. In:
   Soviet Antisemitic Propaganda,London: Institute of Jewish Affairs, 1978.
15 David Nirenberg, *Anti-Judaism: The Western Tradition*, New York: W.W.
   Nortan & Company, 2014.
16 Hannah Arendt, *The Origins of Totalitarianism*, New York: Harcourt Brace
   Jovanovich, 1973.
17 Sarah Annes Brown, Distinguishing Criticism from Antisemitism: Contradictory
   Experiences in Activism, Scholarship and Teaching. In: David Hirsh, ed.,
   *The Rebirth of Left-Wing Antisemitism in the 21st Century: From the
   Academic Boycott Campaign into the Mainstream*, London: Routledge, 2022
   (forthcoming).
18 David Hirsh, 'How Raising the Issue of Antisemitism Puts You Outside the
   Community of the Progressive: The Livingstone Formulation. In: Eunice G.
   Pollack, ed., *Anti-Zionism and Antisemitism: Past & Present*, Boston: Academic
   Studies Press, 2016. https://engageonline.wordpress.com/2016/04/29/the-living-
   stone-formulation-david-hirsh-2/ (accessed 18 September 2021).
19 Karin Stögner, Intersectionality and Antisemitism: A New Approach. *Fathom*,
   May 2020, https://fathomjournal.org/intersectionality-and-antisemitism-a-new
   -approach/.
20 David Seymour, Disavowal, Distinction and Repetition: Alain Badiou and the
   Radical Tradition of Antisemitism. In: J. G. Campbell and L. D. Klaff, eds.,
   *Unity and Diversity in Contemporary Antisemitism: The Bristol-Sheffield
   Colloquium on Contemporary Antisemitism*, Boston: Academic Studies Press,
   2019, pp. 203–218.
21 See Robert Fine, Fighting with Phantoms: A Contribution to the Debate on
   Antisemitism in Europe. *Patterns of Prejudice*, 43(5), 459–479, 2009.
22 Linda Givetash, After Deadly Riots in South Africa, Army of Volunteers Leads
   Defense, Cleanup Efforts. *NBC News*, 19 July 2021 (accessed 7 November 2021).

23 See, for example, this argument from 2011: Jamal Juma. *The Global Intifada: Stop the Wall*, October 16, 2011. https://stopthewall.org/2011/10/16/global-intifada/ (accessed 19 September 2021). See also this news report of a demonstration: Jeremy Sharon, Protestors in New York Cry 'Globalize the Intifada' at Demonstration. *The Jerusalem Post*, 2021. https://www.jpost.com/israel-news/protestors-in-new-york-cry-globalize-the-intifada-at-demonstration-675520.

24 Gender Studies Departments in Solidarity with Palestinian Feminist Collective. *Gender Studies Palestine Solidarity*. http://genderstudiespalestinesolidarity.weebly.com/. Also see: Scholars for Palestine Freedom. *Palestine and Praxis.* https://palestineandpraxis.weebly.com/?fbclid=IwAR3aoOn_GADFt-PTn ALePjIaoSqtCz4TerRPwNrHfH9uKc0KKyeOc4MrZlI. Bonnie Honig. I Am an Academic and I Call for a Free Palestine and an End to the Israeli State's Apartheid. This Is Integral to Both My Moral World View and My Scholarship. Pass It On. *Twitter*, 16 May 2021. https://twitter.com/bonnie_honig/status /1393935707081740300?lang=en-gb.

25 See, for example, this piece in the British Communist newspaper the *Morning Star*: *Minnesota Cops Trained by Israeli Forces*, June 2020. https://morning-staronline.co.uk/article/minnesota-cops-trained-israeli-forces-restraint-tech-niques. See also this fact check from *Channel 4 News*: Georgina Lee. FactCheck: Did Israeli Secret Service Teach Floyd Police to Kneel on Neck? 26 June 2020, https://www.channel4.com/news/factcheck/factcheck-did-israeli-secret-service -teach-floyd-police-to-kneel-on-neck. See also Eve Garrard's explanation of why this claim is antisemitic: What John McDonnell Still Does Not Understand. *Fathom*, July 2020. https://fathomjournal.org/fathom-opinion-john-mcdonnell -man-of-principle/.

26 United Nations, General Assembly Resolution 3379, *Elimination of All Forms of Racial Discrimination*, 10 November 1975.

27 Betty Friedan, *The Feminine Mystique*, New York: Norton, 1963.

28 For the outlines of this story, we are indebted to Gil Troy's book: *Moynihan's Moment: America's Fight against Zionism as Racism*, New York: Oxford University Press, 2013, p. 83.

29 Many Exit as Mrs. Rabin Speaks at Conference. *New York Times*, 26 June 1975, p. 2. https://www.nytimes.com/1975/06/26/archives/many-exit-as-mrs-rabin -speaks-at-conference.html.

30 Troy, *Moynihan's Moment*.

31 Ibid.

32 Jocelyn Olcott. 'We Are Our Sister's Keeper': US Feminists at the 1975 International Women's Year Conference, *UN History Project*, June 2017. https://www.histe-con.magd.cam.ac.uk/unhist/image-of-the_month/image_of_the_month_June17 .html

33 Troy, *Moynihan's Moment*.

34 Ben Gidley, Brendan McGeever and David Feldman, Labour and Antisemitism: A Crisis Misunderstood. *Political Quarterly* 91(2), 413–421, 2020.

35 The Jerusalem Declaration on Antisemitism. *JDA*, 6 May 2021. https://jerusal emdeclaration.org/.

36 Hirsh, David, "Brexit and Corbynism Could Lead to a Crisis of UK Democracy – UK in a Changing Europe." UK in a changing Europe, September 18, 2018. https://ukandeu.ac.uk/brexit-and-corbynism-could-lead-to-a-crisis-of-uk -democracy/.

4

DEMYSTIFYING ANTISEMITISM

A return to critical theory

David Seymour

Introduction

Robert Fine and Philip Spencer articulate the importance of recognising what the Jewish Question is, appropriately contextualised,

> not only in its emphatically antisemitic form as 'the final solution' but also its less lethal forms *within* Enlightenment, *within* emancipation struggles, *within* revolutionary Marxism, *within* critical theories, *within* solidarity movements, and *within* the contemporary left.[1]

This chapter addresses an identifiable trend within the study of antisemitism that can best be captured by its *mystification*. Although present within many traditional or orthodox accounts,[2] this mystification has now crossed over to more 'critical' accounts. This point becomes clear when we review and compare the trajectory of critical theories with its progenitors of critics of antisemitism over the past two centuries. After 1945, a radical change appears. We see a shift from understanding antisemitism as a *social* phenomenon – that is, as emerging from and embedded within modern society – to its location outside or beyond the social world when antisemitism is presented as a *legacy* or an aftermath of a trauma that can only be felt in lingering waves and ripples or as latent rather than a matter of actually-existing social relations.

This shift in understanding antisemitism brings with it a shift in the understanding of its social and political nature. It implies that if the social conditions for antisemitism are lacking, then a contemporary antisemitism is impossible, and that since the *Shoah* these conditions have been resolved.

DOI: 10.4324/9781003222477-5

To phrase the matter differently, it implies that the 'Jewish Question', that has haunted the social world since the dawn of the modern age, has been resolved. Two points follow from this observation. First, it is an ironic inversion of the National Socialists' claim to have offered a 'final solution' to the Jewish Question; and second, its resolution implies the full emancipation of Jews and Jewish life within contemporary society. In short, it implies that the social order of things that gave rise to the 'real' antisemitism that emerged in the 18th century and continued until, if not culminated in the events of 1933–1945, is now over.[3] However, as we will see, this presumption may be premature.

In the discussion that follows, I offer a comparison between pre- and post-*Shoah* critical accounts of antisemitism. I argue that the most relevant dividing line between them is the removal and relocation of antisemitism from an understanding that recognises its embeddedness *within* society to one that places it in a supposedly 'extra-social' realm. It is this removal and relocation that accounts for what I have termed *the mystification of antisemitism*.

In approaching the issue in this way, we immediately confront a problem, if not *the* problem besetting attempts to understand and oppose antisemitism. Unlike most, but by no means all social phenomena, antisemitism is both 'true' and 'false' at the same time. It is 'false' in the sense that it lacks *any* explanatory value of the society which it attempts to explain. It is 'true', however, in the sense that it is produced from within the nature of contemporary society. Perhaps the best way to capture this reality of antisemitism is through recourse to Adorno's aphorism that, in essence, 'even a lie tells a truth about society'. As we will see, it is this contradiction that is at the root of so much confusion surrounding the understanding of antisemitism.

The springboard for this discussion is Gidley et al.'s recent essay, 'Labour and Antisemitism: A Crisis Misunderstood'.[4] I argue that despite some important insights, their essay reproduces rather than challenges antisemitism's mystification. I argue that they treat antisemitism as if it is detached from the world of social relations retaining only a spectral presence which haunts the modern world at various times.

Questioning Gidley et al.'s work in this way brings the study of antisemitism closer to understandings of other forms of racism. Rather than some sort of spectral latency or legacy of the past, anti-Black racism and Islamophobia are likewise best comprehended as arising from very real social inequalities, social conflicts and the 'othering' that flows from them. Indeed, as will become apparent, it is questionable whether the social conflicts can be separated from their racist manifestations. Perhaps the clearest example here is the issue of policing in much of the United States where a real social conflict involving Black Americans is inseparable from its negative racist presentations. This intertwining of real social conflict and its mystifications arises when we note the connection between antisemitism and other forms of racism, which turn, ultimately, on the continued existence of a society that falls short of its realisation of its emancipatory promise. It is this context that frames the following discussion of antisemitism.

Antisemitism as reservoir

The central theme of *Labour and Antisemitism* is Gidley et al.'s rejection of the common metaphor of antisemitism as a 'virus'. They replace it with the metaphor of a 'reservoir'. They note correctly that at the core of the 'virus' metaphor is the notion of a 'strange disease which erupts in different times and places, creating antisemites'.[5] The 'antisemite', in turn, is characterised as 'someone who displays a thoroughgoing and ideologically inflected negativity against Jews'.[6] They review the available data on contemporary Labour antisemitism and they reject the 'virus' metaphor, because they see too great a disjuncture between the small number of what they call 'real' antisemites and the larger phenomenon beyond that core, amongst a periphery of 'uninfected' people who may nonetheless embrace antisemitism. They look beyond the 'virus' metaphor to explain 'why antisemitism that exists within the Labour Party rises to the surface'.[7]

Gidley et al. define a 'reservoir' as a pool of 'negative attitudes', 'myths' and 'tropes' about Jews that 'can be drawn from wittingly or unwittingly by those who lack an ideological commitment to an antisemitic worldview'[8] and which, in turn, accounts for the presence of antisemitism 'in the absence of recognizable antisemites'.[9]

It is with this description of the 'reservoir' and its implicit separation from the messiness of social relations that Gidley et al.'s work can be located within the broader tradition of critical post-Holocaust accounts of antisemitism. For example, Zygmunt Bauman treats modern antisemitism as something which is *imposed upon* society by an external alliance of 'power and knowledge' or 'legislators and interpreters',[10] while Giorgio Agamben dissolves it, through a radical reading of Carl Schmitt, into a more universal 'state of exception'.[11] Likewise, Jean-Francois Lyotard displaces antisemitism away from the social realm within what he terms the 'latency' of 'Europe's unconscious'.[12] Correspondingly, the idea of antisemitism as a cumulative and condensed legacy of the past that can find its way into the present can also be found in authors as politically diverse as Steve Cohen[13] and David Nirenberg,[14] who present antisemitism as an overarching 'meta-concept'. Each of these theories in its own way traces the origins of contemporary antisemitism to the early days of Christianity, if not before. Having done so, they then follow the differing *forms* it adopts as it moves from era to era until it changes so radically in the mid-20th century. Despite their different emphases, each explains modern and contemporary antisemitism as the *secularisation* of a pre-existing (and seemingly complete) pre-modern theology of anti-Jewish *praxis*.

Of course, there is no question that using the word in its most abstract meaning, 'antisemitism', has existed from the Classical World, if not before. There is also no doubt that some, but by no means all, of the content of pre-modern antisemitism has fed into contemporary imaginings in a manner that offers some credence to the notion of a 'reservoir' that can be felt today.

It is in this sense that Gidley et al.'s definition of antisemitism as a reservoir is entirely accurate. There is no question that, understood in this sense, the content of contemporary antisemitism contains the sediments of centuries of anti-Jewish hostility and prejudices, while at the same time still capable of subsuming novel imaginings. Indeed, this metaphor of a reservoir captures something important about the concept of antisemitism; as a concept, antisemitism is simply incapable of development, theoretical or historical. It is premised on the one simple idea that 'the Jews' are the cause of all the ills that one wants to attribute to them and that some solution needs to be found to counter their malevolence. It is this key characteristic of antisemitism that gives some truth to the oft-used and oft-criticised phrases 'eternal antisemitism' or 'the longest hatred'.[15] It is, likewise, because antisemitism is little more than an *Idée fixe* that genealogy, rather than history, is the appropriate method for understanding its content.

Yet, the key problem with these accounts is their tendency to remove antisemitism from the mundane world and to understand it as existing outside the realm of social relations. They relocate antisemitism elsewhere, *beyond* the social. Thus, Gidley et al.'s reservoir metaphor explains antisemitism as comprising 'diffuse antisemitic attitudes that exist *latently*, 'negative and stereotypical idea[s] about Jews which have accumulated over *centuries* and are *deeply embedded in our culture*'[16] and, 'one in which is replenished over time and from which people can draw with ease'.[17]

Gidley et al.'s presumption that the reservoir is detached from actually existing social relations requires a two-step procedure. First, one must frame a social conflict (that may or may not include Jews) and, second, reframe it as a 'Jewish issue'. In other words, one must fail to adopt a rational understanding of a given conflict and then, as a kind of *afterthought*, treat Jews, or rather 'the Jews', as the explanatory factor. This second or later step appears to be grounded not *within* contemporary society, but from a cumulation of *historical* imagery that is not only abstracted and detached from the actuality of the past, but is also perceived as *latent* and so becomes detached also from the present. Perhaps the clearest example of this perception is Hannah Arendt's explanation of antisemitism as *ideology* in which conflicts between Jews and non-Jews come to be captured within an ideological framework that no longer remains tied to the world.[18]

From this central problem, others emerge, both substantive and methodological.

The first is the tendency for these understandings of antisemitism to mirror many of the characteristics of the phenomenon it is investigating. For example, the idea of the *latency* of antisemitism reproduces the myth of the *latency* of an ever-present Jewish malevolence that, at any given moment, can erupt or spill over into the social world. Correspondingly, there is the danger that the image of a 'reservoir' may reproduce some of the problems with what has been termed 'eternal antisemitism'. If contemporary antisemitism is presented as having 'accumulat[ed] over centuries' and as 'embedded deeply within our culture', there is a danger that it can take on the aura of a permanent 'law of nature'.

The second, related, observation is the problem of 'antisemitism without antisemites'; of an account of antisemitism that lacks human agency. This point arises in the idea, again implicitly, that antisemitism operates, so to speak, behind the backs of those who 'wittingly or unwittingly' draw on it. This raises a key issue relating to contemporary antisemitism where it appears typically to be articulated by people unaware of their own antisemitism and who often think of themselves as its opponents. Concepts such as 'institutional racism' or cultural, political or discursive antisemitism might help here. Be that as it may, the important questions still remain: why, when and how do social agents access the contents of a latent 'reservoir'?

A final observation turns on the question of methodology. The substantive relocation of antisemitism away from society is intimately connected to a post-*Shoah* methodological retreat of the social sciences, critical or otherwise, from understanding the *Shoah* using their own disciplinary tools and methods. There are two reasons for this disengagement and disenchantment.

The first reason is illustrated by the idea of what we can term a 'negative implication' if not 'collaboration'. Again, Bauman and Lyotard are exemplary in this regard, but it is not entirely absent from Gidley et al.'s essay. This idea points to the belief that the modern, 'rational' disciplines were complicit in modern antisemitism, both in its genocidal and non-genocidal manifestations. Secondly, there is an assumption that the Holocaust brought with it an unprecedented trauma that has resulted in a corresponding trauma within social and critical theory. Both of these notions have led to a feeling that if social theory and the social practices it seeks to reflect upon are implicated in the conception and execution of antisemitism and the Holocaust, then attempts to utilise these disciplines as explanatory frameworks are discredited and appear as little more than a tautology.

Taken together, it is the failure, on the one hand, to locate antisemitism within the social realm and, on the other hand, to reject social science as an explanatory framework for understanding it that gives rise to the mystification of antisemitism. One potential way in which we can avoid this problem is to revisit the progenitors of critical thought, most notably Hegel, Marx Nietzsche and Adorno. Although a thorough discussion of each individual thinker is beyond the scope of this chapter, we can nonetheless identify several commonalities between them relevant to the present discussion.

The social origins of antisemitism

In revisiting the work of the early progenitors of critical theory, two points regarding their understanding of the antisemitism of their day come into view.

First, it is noteworthy that their confrontation with antisemitism served as a *foil* against which they offered their critical understanding of the rationality of the modern state, civil society, private property, rights and the rule of law. Thus, the 'system' Hegel produced in *Elements of the Philosophy of Right* can be read in a critical relationship against the antisemitic, populist 'practical philosophy' of his contemporary Jacob Fries.[19] Likewise, Marx's pro-emancipation critique of the connection of rights and private property in *On the Jewish Question* was written against Bruno Bauer's anti-Jewish emancipation abstract 'humanism'.[20] For Nietzsche, his thinking was to counter the antisemitism of his time expressed through Richard Wagner and the pan-Germanist racism of his own sister and her husband.[21] Adorno's work was written in an attempt to account for the corresponding failure of socialism and the rise of Nazism.[22]

In making this observation, and this is the second point, it is important to note that common to all these thinkers (along with those of an earlier age)[23] is the recognition of antisemitism as a thoroughly contemporary problem, one whose origins lay precisely in the contours of the society they were investigating. There is no suggestion of antisemitism as something 'latent' or as something that had emerged from beyond the confines of the social world.

Given the importance of these critical approaches, it is perhaps paradoxical that having identified the social presence of contemporary anti-Jewish hostility they may have missed something important. Despite recognising the dialectic between the 'rationality' of the modern state' and the 'irrationality of antisemitism', they appeared to assume that rationality would overcome irrationality.[24] It is for this reason that one can detect within these works the sense of the transience of (the irrationality) of antisemitism when confronted with the institutional crystallisation of the modern state.

Perhaps the idea of antisemitism as 'latent' follows from this lack of foresight in these early accounts of modern antisemitism. The modern disciplines to which these works gave birth focused their attention on the rationality of the modern era. Viewing the world through a rational lens, the irrational disappeared from view. The later idea that antisemitism was seemingly absent from the social world,[25] therefore, could be seen as a consequence of these disciplines' own assumptions, rather than an absence of the phenomenon itself. In other words, despite the critical nature of many of these disciplines, or what came to be known as the 'social sciences' and practices (i.e. Marxism), they all shared the belief that the world *really had* become rational. The consequence of this belief was that antisemitism (irrationality) was excluded as an object of reflection. It was this exclusion that came to be confused with its absence and, in turn, gave the ground for the notion of 'latency'. Arendt captures this ambivalent location of antisemitism when she writes,

> Moreover, what is true for the history of antisemitism, that it fell into the hands of non-Jewish crackpots and Jewish apologetics, and was carefully avoided by reputable historians, is true, *mutatis mutandis*, for nearly all elements that later crystallised in the new totalitarian movement; they had hardly been noticed by either learned or public opinion because they belonged to a subterranean stream of European history where, hidden from the light of the public and the attention of enlightened men, they had been able to gather an unexpected virulence.[26]

However, more recently and especially in the wake of Jeremy Corbyn's election to leadership of the Labour Party and the move of antisemitism from the margins of left thought into the mainstream, we see a reconnection being made between contemporary understandings of antisemitism and earlier ones that reject its mystifications and reframe it as an inherently *social* phenomenon. This move towards demystification is important not only in understanding and opposing antisemitism but, equally important, it also aids in our understanding of the nature of contemporary society. This critique questions the optimistic assumption that, although an ethereal reservoir of antisemitic imagery exists latent and deeply embedded in cultural life, the social conflicts and contradictions that give rise to antisemitism in the first place (i.e. the question *why* anyone would think of accessing the reservoir in the first place in the face of such conflicts and contradictions) have been overcome. It challenges the idea of the presentation of contemporary antisemitism as little more than an anachronism. In doing so it illustrates that in misrecognising antisemitism in this way, it misrecognises not only the society of which it is a part, but also the threats to that same society it poses.

These points come to the fore in Robert Fine and Philip Spencer's book, *Antisemitism and the Left: On the Return of the Jewish Question.*[27] In this work, antisemitism is firmly located within the dialectic between the Jewish *emancipation* and the Jewish *question*. In framing the matter in this way, Fine and Spencer question the implicit assumption within mystifications of antisemitism that the social conditions that produced this dialectic have been resolved or at the least no longer exist in a socially meaningful way.

Fine and Spencer articulate this strand of their thinking by reflecting on the nature of modern and contemporary antisemitism. They begin their account by correctly identifying what they term 'the equivocations of Enlightenment'. These equivocations point to the dialectic of Jewish emancipation and the Jewish question which,

> indicate the presence of an internal struggle within Enlightenment thought: it was both immersed in the muddy waters of the Jewish question and it opened up the space for emancipatory ways of thinking that were fiercely critical of the [then] status quo.[28]

It is within this dialectic that the Jewish question gains its meaning as 'the classic term for the representation of Jews as harmful to humanity as a whole',

> The fundamental questions it asks are about the nature of the harm Jews supposedly inflict on humanity, the reasons why the Jews are so harmful, and what is to be done to remedy this harm.'[29]

For present purposes, the point to be foregrounded and which connects with the earlier thinking is the continuation of the dialectic of the rationality of the State and of the irrationality of the Jewish question. It is this aspect of their thinking that shows that antisemitism threatens not only Jews but also the universalism of the modern state (a universalism that, following Hegel, does not deny or erase Jews', or any other groups', particularity). The Jewish question captures and recasts the entire social world as a conflict between Jews and the apparent 'opponents of Jews'. In other words, the ascendancy of the Jewish question over and above that of Jewish emancipation reduces all social conflicts to that of 'antisemite and Jew'. Fine and Spencer allude to this radical nature of modern antisemitism when they write,

> The Jewish question signifies an asymmetric relation of Jews to others, It is an expression of the distorted face of universalism, a question that never was a question in the first place, a question whose answers are the pre-given conditions of the question itself. And yet we find that the Jewish question keeps re-appearing in different shapes and different times, in different places. *It is like a ghost* how other sees Jews and sometimes how Jews see themselves, *It interpellates social relations between Jews and non-Jews, Judaism and Christianity, Judaism and Islam, the Jewish state and other nations, Jewish ideas and other ideas, etc.* as if *they were conflicts of a metaphysical kind between the abstract forces of inclusive universalism on one side and exclusive particularism on the other.*[30]

Despite appearing 'like a ghost' and despite its ability to reappear in different contexts, Fine and Spencer recognise and are emphatic about recognising that the Jewish question is imbricated within the mundane world of social relations; that the Jewish question and the antisemitism inherent within it is, like the emancipation of which it remains a part, entwined one with the other and cannot be separated. Thus, while Fine and Spencer acknowledge that abstract 'anti-Judaic ideas certainly go back to a distant past' (i.e. a reservoir of negative images and tropes), they add immediately that 'there is also a sense in which the Jewish question is a creature of the modern age',

> To speak of the *modernity* of the Jewish question is to suggest that it is not a natural or 'eternal' question, second, *that it is reproduced and reconfigured by the conditions of modern life even at times when we least expect it*, and, third, that it is open to contestation and rarely goes uncontested.[31]

It is the two points highlighted here, the radical nature of antisemitism in its reframing of social conflicts through the prism of the Jewish question, and its location deep within social relations, that challenge the notion of the reservoir. By so doing, the pool of antisemitic imagery is integrated into the confines of contemporary society.

Despite the cumulative nature of its imagery, antisemitism cannot exist without some connection with the concerns and conflicts of the actually existing social world. Without this connection, the idea of an ontological Jewish negativity, the Jewish question would simply not have the traction to convince population after population. The continuing existence and temptation of the Jewish question is its power to reframe social conflicts through the lens of its antisemitism. In this way social complexities and contradictions, some of which involve Jews specifically, suffer malevolent distortion when caught within the pernicious framework of the destructive simplicity of a word reduced to the conflict between its conceptual schema of 'the Jews' and 'the opponents of Jews'. In other words, the 'reservoir' can not only be found within and entwined within modern society and modern social relations, but, although comprised of historically accumulated content, reshapes that content in keeping with the contemporary social conflicts it claims to capture and recast.

Labour's antisemitism crisis: if first you kneel, then you will pray

> The absence of good reasons to boycott Israeli academic institutions has led to ever more wild and hyperbolic depictions of Israel itself. Pascal once said: if first you kneel, then you will pray. Marx translated this aphorism into the notion that being determines consciousness. In this case,

those who call for an academic boycott of Israel end up offering increasingly Manichean images of Israel's evil essence in order to justify their practice... The existence of these projections of course preceded the boycott, but the boycott encourages us to search everywhere for evidence of Israel's criminality that will then justify the boycott itself.[32]

In this quote, Robert Fine references the idea that one first takes a position on any given issue and only after does one find the content that validates adopting that position in the first place. As we will see, this approach not only questions the explanatory power of antisemitism as a 'reservoir', but also offers a critical reflection on the distinction made by Gidley et al. between 'real antisemites' and those who 'wittingly or unwittingly' draw from this pool. Equally importantly, it offers a critical explanation, lacking in many accounts discussed in the first section of this chapter of how a *socially-situated individual* accesses the reservoir. This latter point brings to the fore the problem of mediation between society and what is said to be latent within it. 'Labour and Antisemitism' provides the point of departure.

In this context, the first point to note is that the question of Labour's antisemitism did not reach 'crisis' point solely because of members who, in discussions of Israel and/or finance, adopted views implicit in the Jewish question. As Gidley et al. suggest, utilisation of antisemitism is far from unique either to specific sections of the party or to the left in general.[33] Rather, the real crisis emerged when the antisemitism that had been present in the margins of the Party moved into the centre with the election of Jeremy Corbyn as leader. Yet, even here we have to be careful. It is probably more accurate to say that the crisis reached its climax when Corbyn's own history, along with others close to him, came to be challenged on the grounds of antisemitism. It is precisely at this point that Pascal's aphorism gains relevance.

My argument is that for many, if not the vast majority of those involved, the initial impetus was no more than to defend Corbyn on both a personal level and as Party leader. Yet, as became obvious, it was only *after* adopting this position did the defence against antisemitism come to include antisemitic *content*. However, this recourse to antisemitic content, if not belief, is less a question of cultural osmosis or of imbibing from a 'latent', 'deeply embedded cultural' reservoir of 'negative tropes and images', but is more a question of the contemporary and continued presence of a socially-situated Jewish question (in this instance, the view of Jews as harmful to the Corbyn project and, from there, to 'the British people').

In hindsight, we can see that this crisis of antisemitism follows the contours of the Jewish question. From almost the very beginning of this 'crisis' therefore, the issue of the Labour party's antisemitism and the conflicts that arose from it were captured within the frame of the Jewish question and reproduced by reference to its binary worldview. From the point of view of the Labour leadership and its defenders, the crisis of antisemitism turned from a problem of *antisemitism* to a problem *of 'the Jews'*. Captured within the confines of the Jewish question, it is little wonder that those who kneeled in defence of Jeremy Corbyn slowly adopted its framework and worldview. Although the accusations levelled at the Jews may have been drawn from a reservoir, at least in their imagery (but even here, we must be cautious in precisely noting which images were 'drawn'), neither the content nor the existence of the reservoir was 'latent' or buried deep within the cultural terrain. They were as socially present as the emancipatory arguments of which anti-antisemitism is a part.

We can trace this capture, along with the Jewish question's distortive reductions of it, by following the trajectory of the crisis as it unfolded in the three or four years following Corbyn's election. For the purposes of this chapter, however, it is unnecessary to enter too great a detail but, rather, to present the timeline in broad strokes.

The scene was set early. Almost immediately, the response to any concern about Corbyn's past comments and their potential antisemitism was that they were little more than a 'smear'. Two reasons were given for this accusation. Both, however, were articulations of the Jewish question. First, was that 'the Jews' were fearful of Corbyn's advocacy of 'socialism', a view that came on the heels of former Labour MP and Mayor of London Ken Livingstone's telling the Jewish Leadership Council that Jews no longer voted Labour because they were 'rich'. Secondly, and not necessarily unrelated, 'the Jews' were recast as 'Zionists' who were said to oppose Corbyn because of his support for the Palestinians. This initial response of a 'smear' is of course, a familiar element of the Jewish question with the antisemitic implementation that the claims being made are not simply 'wrong', but that those raising concerns, *know* it is wrong and so are acting in a spirit of deceit and dishonesty.

As the crisis gained traction and refused to go away, not least because of Corbyn's evasions and prevarications, so did putative defences take on an even more antisemitic hue. Before long, there were overt claims of press bias, often articulated as 'Jewish' or 'Zionist influence' at work in the 'mainstream media' and that behind the whole affair one could detect the malevolent operations of the Jewish/Zionist/Israel Lobby. There were claims that these 'unwarranted, dishonest attacks' on Corbyn and the leadership in general originated from or were being coordinated by the Israel embassy and, by implication, by Israel itself. This particular strand of antisemitism reached its climax with the online circulation, borrowed from a far-right website for which permission was asked and granted, of an alien bloodsucking creature with a Star of David on its back smothering the Statue of Liberty. (This image, in turn, was held not to be antisemitic by the party.) Likewise, memes of quotes falsely attributed to Voltaire as well as antisemitic parodies of

Jewish jokes, again originating with the far-right, were circulated online by the Party's defenders.

At a slightly later date, antisemitic myths concerning 'the Rothschilds' began to appear online. Emphasis was placed on their supposed domination and control of the global banking system and, through that domination, of almost all the states of the world and, in particular, its role in the creation of the state of Israel. This development is particularly noteworthy in the light of its relative (but not complete) absence from the left and elsewhere during the banking crash a few years earlier and the debilitating and cruel policies of 'austerity' that followed. Yet, less than ten years later, when the 'antisemitism crisis' was in full flow (and, again noteworthy, is its detachment from economic developments),[34] this staple of the Jewish question appeared again and again.

At first sight there is nothing in these developments that could not be answered by reference to the metaphor of the 'reservoir'. However, to answer in this way, or to believe the matter settled in such a way would be an error. The core of the error is the failure to draw a distinction that is all too often overlooked for both an understanding of antisemitism and the means of opposing it. *This distinction is between the ways in which the* Jewish Question *is articulated (i.e. its forms) and the* social relations and contradictions *that give rise to antisemitism which, in turn, come to be articulated in those forms.*

There is little doubt that it may be plausible to argue that the *forms* antisemitism take – i.e. belief in an omnipotent Jewish or Zionist or Israel Lobby, or the power of the Rothschilds (or 'Soros', for that matter), or that 'the Jews 'cry antisemitism' to silence those who only wish to speak 'truth to power' – are, as the metaphor of the reservoir mentioned above would indicate, culturally embedded, 'latent', 'negative tropes and images accumulated over centuries' that can be 'drawn on with ease'; but that tells us little of *why* people would think of accessing them *in the first place*?

I believe that the answer to this question is that the conflict within the Labour Party comes to be reframed within the contours and confines of the Jewish question and which, as we have seen, restructures the social world and social relations around the figure of 'the Jews'. Far from 'latent', antisemitism, its modes of articulation and its inherent (mis)understandings of the social world are the consequence of *ongoing social conflicts and contradictions* including that of the unfinished business of the dialectic of Jewish emancipation and Jewish question.

Once understood in this way, even the plausibility of the idea that the *forms* in which the Jewish question appears (i.e. the negative tropes, etc.) are outside or beyond the realm of mundane social relations can be called into question. Here, one need only refer to the publication of Walt and Mearsheimer's *The Israel Lobby* (2008), in which the complex reasons for why the United States chose to go to war against Iraq was reduced to a personalised collusion of like-minded individuals who, comprising a 'Lobby', were able to manipulate the world's most powerful states that not only acted against its own interests, but also did so for the interests of Israel. Likewise, it is also to be recalled that the book, published by a leading publisher, garnered wide media and public note receiving reviews in numerous prestigious papers and journals. The point here, of course, is that the forms in which antisemitism is articulated – the 'reservoir' – is as much *part* of and product of society as the Jewish question itself.

Conclusion

Using Gidley et al.'s metaphor of the reservoir as my point of departure, this chapter has questioned the separation between society and antisemitism that has gained predominance mainly after the *Shoah*. It has argued that this separation implies that while antisemitism remains a problem, whatever connections it may have had with the social realm and social relations have been lost. To the extent this is true, the understanding of antisemitism takes on an idealist and mystificatory hue. In offering this critique, I have sought to demystify antisemitism by relocating it within the confines and contradictions of modern and contemporary society and by reconnecting it with the traditions of critical theory. In this context, lying at the heart of these contradictions is what Fine and Spencer refer to as the 'equivocations of Enlightenment'. These equivocations turn on the dialectic of Jewish emancipation and the Jewish question, a dialectic which, to this day, remains unresolved.

Notes

1 Robert Fine and Philip Spencer, *Antisemitism and the Left: On the Return of the Jewish Question*, Manchester University Press, 2017; p.3.
2 H. Arendt, *The Origins of Antisemitism*, Shocken Books, New York, 2004. Although, as we will see, despite these accounts being subject to harsh criticism, most notably under Arendt's labelling of them as 'eternal antisemitism', they are not without value.
3 "The elements of this new "critical theory" – emphatic historicisation of antisemitism, dissociation of racism and antisemitism, particularisation of the Holocaust commemoration, a cynical reading of resistance to antisemitism – demonstrate that while it claims to oppose antisemitism in the name of a universalistic ethos, its conviction is that antisemitism is a problem of the past, that to focus on it in the present is an anachronism, that the priority of contemporary antiracism should lie with other racisms, that opposition to antisemitism has been consumed by a damaging particularism and that a conspiratorial agenda lies behind the charge of antisemitism". Fine and Spencer, *supra*, pp.102–103. See also Seymour, D. M., Continuity and Discontinuity: From Antisemitism to Antizionism and the Reconfiguration of the Jewish Question. *Journal of Contemporary Antisemitism*, 2(2), 11–23, 2017.
4 Gidley, McGeever and Feldman, *The Political Quarterly*, 91(2), 413–421, 2020.

5 *Supra*; p. 416.
6 *Supra*; p. 414.
7 Supra; p. 415.
8 Supra; 416.
9 Supra; p. 416.
10 Z. Bauman, *Modernity and the Holocaust*, London: Polity Press, 1991; *Legislators and Interpeters*, London: Polity Press, 1991.
11 G. Agamben, *Homo Sacer*, Stanford: Stanford University Press, 1998; *State of Exception*, Chicago: University of Chicago Press, 2005.
12 J.-F. Lyorard, *Heidegger and the Jews*, Minnesota: University of Minnesota Press, 1990. For a discussion of these thinkers, see, D. M. Seymour, *Law, Antisemitism and the Holocaust*, London: Routledge, , Chapter 2.
13 *That's Funny, You Don't Look Antisemitic: An Anti-racist Analysis of Left Antisemitism*, 3rd ed., London: No Pasaran Media Ltd, 2019.
14 *Anti-Judaism*, London: Norton, 2018.
15 R. Wistrich, *Anti-Semitism: The Longest Hatred*, London: Methuen, 1991.
16 Surpa, p. 415.
17 Supra, p. 416.
18 Supra, Seymour, Continuities and Discontinuities.
19 Preface, *Elements of the Philosophy of Right*, Cambridge: CUP, 1991.
20 *Early Works*, London: Penguin, 1991.
21 *On the Genealogy of Morals*, London: Vintage, 1990; *The Case of Wagner*, Random House, 1967. See also, supra, Seymour, *Law, Antisemitism and the Holocaust*, Chapter 5.
22 Adorno and Horkheimer, *Dialectic of Enlightenment*, London: Verso, 2016.
23 The idea of the threat to the emancipatory ideals of the modern state haunts those of other texts to; see Locke's *Two Treatises*, and Montesque's, *Spirits of the Law*.
24 But see, e.g., Marx's '18th Brumaire' and his discussion of the rise of the (anti-) political mob.
25 This point is, of course, different from the idea of the complicity of modern disciplines with antisemitism and the Holocaust discussed above.
26 Supra, Arendt, p. 8 Arendt's reference to 'subterrain' should not be confused with the idea of a 'reservoir', but rather that the social causes for antisemitism and totalitarianism were a product of the contemporary world, but remained undiscussed within the 'public realm'.
27 Supra.
28 Ibid, p. 21.
29 Ibid, p. 2.
30 Ibid, p. 3 (emphasis added).
31 Ibid, p. 4 (emphasis added).
32 Robert Fine debates the boycotters in Leeds. *Engage*, 21 March 2014. https://engageonline.wordpress.com/2014/03/21/robert-fine-debates-the-boycotters-in-leeds/ (accessed 25 February 2023).
33 This finding is not surprising considering that, as we have seen, one of the consequences of the 'Jewish question' is to dissolve the divisions inherent in the modern rational state and restructure them around the figure of 'the Jews'.
34 This importance of this particular point should not be overstated. It throws into doubt the 'orthodoxy' in which antisemitism is linked, if not explained, by reference to economic shocks and crisis.

5

IS PALESTINE A FEMINIST ISSUE?

Intersectionality and its discontents

Karin Stögner

The concept of intersectionality has steadily gained influence since the 1990s and functions as a basis for global solidarity in many Western feminist and antiracist movements and organisations in the sense that feminists ought not turn a blind eye to other forms of oppression. An intersectional view recognises that in modern society different forms of oppression and discrimination occur simultaneously rather than separately, that they are mutually entangled and that social categories like gender, race and class must be analysed as multifaceted and dynamic social processes that intermingle and intertwine. Not so obvious, however, is which forms of oppression find entry into the intersectionality framework. Most often, the spectrum is tied back to the classical triad race, class and gender, and more recently age, ability or religion, whereas antisemitism is rarely considered. One reason for such omission is that antisemitism is often simply subsumed under racism, which hides the specificity of antisemitic ideology and thus makes it undetectable. In addition, however, antizionist political agendas become effective here. In recent years the concept of intersectionality has therefore increasingly been contested since it does not only commonly exclude antisemitism as a specific form of oppression and ideology from its analytical framework, but sometimes even serves as an ideological background for proliferating an antisemitism that is related to a thorough delegitimisation of Israel. In an ideological antizionism, which has become a cultural code in the mainstream of antiracist intersectionality, activists apply double standards when they defame women's and LGBTIQ* rights in Israel as 'pinkwashing' and 'homonationalism'. Intersectional antiracist and feminist initiatives and platforms such as Women's March on Washington, Chicago Dyke March and Black Lives Matter repeatedly exclude Jewish experience with global

DOI: 10.4324/9781003222477-6

antisemitism. Hence, the question arises to what extent a gender-sensitive and feminist critique of antisemitism can rightfully and reasonably refer to intersectionality.

This chapter begins with a discussion of the strange connections between certain currents of global feminism and Israel-related antisemitism. I call these lines of connection strange because feminism is emancipatory in its basic understanding, while antisemitism is the epitome of anti-emancipatory reaction and rebellion. So how do these two moments intertwine? It will turn out that those intersectional currents that I criticise here understand something different by emancipation than is usual in the critical tradition from Hegel to Marx to the Critical Theory of the Frankfurt School; and that, on the other hand, these same currents often do not even recognise Israel-related antisemitism or sometimes even attest to it an oppositional force against global elites and against imperialism and exploitation of the Global South. Israel-related antisemitism thus turns out to be specifically attractive and dangerous to the left because it poses as oppositional and resistant to global relations of domination. But it is not a critique of domination; rather, it offers a simplistic and Manichean explanation of oppression in the face of complex global relations of domination.

I start from certain constrictions of intersectional feminism that become manifest notably in Queer BDS, that is, in a global alliance between the Queer International and the Boycott, Divestment, Sanctions campaign.[1] I will take note of the current problematics – how specific forms of intersectional feminism, while ignoring global antisemitism, themselves knowingly or unknowingly set in motion an Israel-related antisemitism and thereby also disregard the rights of Palestinian queers – and offer an interpretation of these processes. Finally, I will propose some theoretical and practical reflections on how this development can be countered and how the concept of intersectionality can reasonably be applied to the critique of antisemitism.

Intersectionality's theoretical and practical pitfalls

From the outset in the 1970s intersectionality has been associated with political activism in the wake of the Civil Rights Movement, the Second Women's Movement and Black Feminism in the United States.[2] The term was originally coined by the Combahee River Collective in 1978,[3] followed by Kimberlé Crenshaw's seminal essays.[4] Both the Combahee River Collective and Crenshaw advocated for identity politics based on the experience of complex oppression and discrimination as Black (lesbian) women. The intention, however, was to think concretely, starting from their own particularity, of a common interest in liberation that goes beyond that particularity. So, the focus of the early writings in intersectionality was on a critique of supra-personal power relations and of the structures of domination in modern societies. Thus, if we read in 'A Black Feminist Statement': 'Above all else, our politics initially sprang from the shared belief that black women are inherently valuable, that our liberation is a necessity not as an adjunct to somebody else's but because of our need as human persons for autonomy'[5] – the liberation of Black lesbian women is grounded on the universal category of humanity, or, as Hannah Arendt put it, 'the right, to have rights, or the right of every individual to belong to humanity'.[6]

In recent years, however, a shift in intersectional identity politics can be observed in which domination is personalised and seen primarily as the oppression of one group by another, often leading to hierarchies of victimisation. In contrast, the objective relations of society based on domination and the way different forms of discrimination intertwine are increasingly lost from view. Thus, the demand for empowerment on the part of marginalised groups has led to more and more talk about cultural, religious etc. identities and less and less about the structures of domination and power that are effective in society as a whole, thus also within marginalised groups. As a result, the issue of power and domination within marginalised groups is increasingly hidden, which eventually leads to a form of anti-intersectionality. The objective relations between different forms of oppression and discrimination, for example, how antisemitism operates with moments of sexism or how sexism can be structured by moments of racism and in what way these entanglements are produced by the antagonistic society itself, not only by culturally, racially or economically opposed groups within society – this structural perspective on the objective conditions of social processes is less and less put into the foreground. This manifests a growing unwillingness to even think of society as a dialectical context of function and entanglement. Instead, society disintegrates into homogeneously conceived groups that are set against each other, which results in an almost tribalistic understanding of social conflicts.

This has led to a discursive fragmentation of the social whole of oppression into seemingly unrelated fragments, accompanied by a loss of a common goal and interest beyond the immediate experience of being a member of a marginalised social group. This development must be understood as a reaction to the neoliberal trend to dissolve the social context into atomised and abstract self-responsible individuals[7] to which intersectional feminists increasingly respond by strengthening collectives and cultural and religious communities. Neoliberal abstract individualism and intersectional collectivism seem to be two corresponding sides of the same coin. While the recognition of cultural and religious dignity of communities is brought to the fore, the idea of equality of individuals and the idea of individual rights that need to be protected against and within cultural and religious communities is increasingly relegated to the background and even considered an example of the 'tyranny of the universal'.[8] Counteracting neoliberal abstract individualism, on the other hand, requires not an indiscriminate anti-individualism and collectivism, but rather strengthening individuals' awareness that their individualisation arises in a field of tension between difference and equality, i.e. that they are not completely independent of communities, but neither do they merge into them.

The anti-queerness of Queer BDS: it is not about queers in Queer BDS

To give an example for how this breaking down of the dialectics of society and the individual, or in other words of the universal and the particular, affects intersectionality and how this can be instrumentalised in an antizionist and eventually antisemitic drift, I would like to refer to Angela Davis, who in a talk that she gave in December 2012 in a panel on 'Queer Visions' at the *World Social Forum: Free Palestine* in Porto Alegre, Brazil, mentioned that it would be 'refreshing to be out of the USA where we don't always have to challenge the constant individualisation that happens especially under the impact of neoliberal ideologies. We talk about collectivities and communities'.[9] Davis utilises an indiscriminate bashing of individualism and in connection to this the implicit neglect of the individual towards and within collectives and communities to legitimise Queer BDS, as becomes clear in the same talk:

> This is to say that queers for BDS not only directs its message at people who identify into LGBTQ communities, and it's important to direct our messages in that direction.[10]

But she also argues that the message must be directed outwards too and that it is not only a question of advocating for queer people in Palestine:

> in fact it's clear about not wanting support from those who refuse to see that cynicism and that contemptuousness behind Israel's pro-gay image, but rather it directs its message at anyone who is a potential supporter of BDS.[11]

That Queer BDS is not about the protection of queer Palestinians against any form of homophobia, that they do not matter as individuals with rights to sexual self-determination, but are rather turned into abstract images, tokens in antizionist activism, or 'bodies' as they are called in this jargon, is also confirmed by Jasbir Puar: 'Palestinian Queers for BDS members point out that it is irrelevant whether Palestinian society is homophobic or not, and that the question of homophobia within Palestinian society has nothing to do with the fact that the occupation must end'.[12] The Israel question overrides the sexuality and gender questions, the latter clearly considered secondary. With this move Davis and Puar try to bridge the obvious strangeness of a coalition between LGBTIQ* activism and the Boycott, Divestment and Sanctions campaign.

The instrumentalisation of intersectionality for delegitimating Israel, of promoting antizionism and the BDS campaign has become paradigmatic in recent years on an international level in broad areas of feminism and academic gender studies, as has shown a campaign by the *Palestine Feminist Collective*, a 'US-based network of Palestinian and Arab women and feminists'[13] in 2021, demanding that

> a truly intersectional and decolonial feminist vision for the United States, Palestine and our world [...] upholds the legacies of solidarity between Palestinian, Black, Indigenous, Third World feminist working class, and queer communities

and

> stands in contrast to liberal feminist traditions in the U.S. that continue to weaponize feminist discourses against Palestinians and other marginalized communities by failing to confront the structural forms of gendered and sexual violence inherent to settler/colonialism, imperialist wars, racial capitalism, and global white supremacy.[14]

Thus, the Palestine Feminist Collective pledges that 'Palestine is a Feminist Issue',[15] but, however, this is a mere slogan just as the demanded confrontation of structural forms of gendered and sexual violence remains completely vague since it does not include a critique of the Palestinian authorities, Hamas, Islamic Jihad or of patriarchal social relations in Palestinian society constantly denying women and LGBTIQ* persons their individual rights of sexual self-determination, as one would expect from a feminist perspective even if critical of liberal feminist traditions. Rather, it is about a fight for the national self-determination of Palestine as such, whereas no critical thought is spent on the obvious question of how a future Palestinian nation state would treat its female and LGBTIQ* citizens and what the position of the Palestinian Authority, Islamic Jihad and Hamas is towards gender equality and sexual self-determination. But if the issue is regarded from a truly intersectional lens, one must also admit that national liberation does not by and in itself lead to sexual liberation.

Even to ask this question is sometimes considered colonialist and implicitly racist. Starting from a comparatively secure Western position regarding their own rights to sexual self-determination, some Western postcolonial star writers like Joseph Massad and Jasbir Puar claim that scrutinising Arab and Palestinian homophobia would impose on the Muslim Other (whom they themselves conceptualise as completely abstract) homonormative and homonationalist principles of the so-called 'Gay International which produces homosexuals, as well as gays and lesbians, where they do not exist'.[16] In this perspective, homosexuality as a sexual identity with demands to self-determination and individual rights is something alien to the Muslim and Arab world, where, according to Massad and Puar, sexuality is not composed into an identity but is rather conceived of as a cultural composition of practices and desires that stay non-identical, in other words: unnamed and clandestine. In that manner, the argument goes on, homosexuality would always have been practiced in the Arab countries, albeit not named.[17] Arabs would just not embrace homosexuality openly and build an identity of it, since this is considered as Western and thus non-Islamic. Eventually, gay rights themselves are considered Western and alien, yet hostile to the Muslim world and their introduction in Arab countries a neo-colonialist act. Similarly, the women's rights discourse is considered 'antirevolutionary, as it relies too much on notions of tolerance, equality, and normality', as the Palestinian activist Haineen Maikey suggests.[18] But even if we scrutinise and criticise the notion of normality, Nikita Dhawan rightfully insists that 'one cannot *not* want rights'.[19]

The postcolonial charge against the so-called Gay International is that in a new imperialism and colonialism, the white queer/gay wants to save the brown queer from the brown homophobic man. This criticism of homonationalism wants to rescue the *idea* of an authentic Arabic sexuality from Westernisation and thus identification as gay or queer, without much caring about the actual lives, problems and experiences of LGBTIQ* persons in Arab countries. Hence, the image of a pure, non-Western Arab sexuality is the product of Western neo-orientalism – and a projection screen for Western longings for authenticity.[20] This happens in order to turn the supposedly authentic Arabic sexuality against the purportedly artificial and individualistic gay and queer sexuality in Israel, whose intention would be to denigrate the Arabic Other as homophobic and antifeminist. Thus, the Arab authenticity is needed to fight off Israeli artificiality. The dichotomy constructed here between Western and Arab sexuality supports the narrative of the incompatibility of Arab/Muslim and queer identities – a dichotomy that serves as the projection screen for the allegations of homonationalism and pinkwashing. The term pinkwashing, used in this context, assumes that the gay-friendly image of, and LGBTIQ* rights in, Israel were mere hypocrisy, cynicism and a neoliberal mask providing ideological cover for a racist and apartheid-like system.[21] This is itself an entirely Western view that is hardly compatible with the struggle of queer Palestinians, who see themselves stripped of the possibility to be whoever they want to be and of demanding the protection of their individual rights of sexual self-determination. To the contrary, the order with which they are urged to comply is to remain authentically Arab.

Being queer, they are told, would be treason against the common Palestinian cause. Samira Saraya from the Palestinian queer feminist group *Aswat* criticises this as an 'abuse of the occupation as an excuse for not supporting our fight'. She goes on asking:

> Does it mean that this idea doesn't move around like other ideas? Cultures don't exist in isolation from each other; there is always mobility of ideas, concepts, and terms across cultures.[22]

For her, this way of arguing in terms of a purported authentic sexuality works to delegitimise the struggle as Palestinian LGBTIQ*:

> It harms our struggle against homophobia. [...] For those of us who are worried about the negative impacts of the imperial West on Arabic culture I say, too late. Arab queers are already here. So you can stop worrying.[23]

In view of queer activists worldwide seeing themselves increasingly instrumentalised for a cause that is not actually theirs and feeling an enormous pressure being exerted on them to bow to the single issue policy of BDS and antizionism, even the Palestinian theorist and queer activist Sa'ed Atshan, who, just like Samira Saraya, is definitely not suspected of being pro-Israel, is fundamentally criticising pinkwashing allegations that blind out the real situation of queers:

> Just as it is a form of epistemic coercion to attempt to impose queer discourses on particular individuals, it is also presumptuous to assume that such individuals must forgo queer politics in the name of anti-imperialism. I am weary when the latter impulse elides the cry for the amelioration of queer suffering. Such neglect contributes to the normalization of structural homophobia and the bolstering of the social and political pressures of heteronormativity.[24]

Muslim homophobia is not only an attribution of the West, but also a means used by the non-West to distinguish itself from the West. Addressing this would mean, not least, taking non-Western actors seriously. Thus, Palestinian LGBTIQ* activists see themselves threatened in the West Bank. In 2019, the queer-feminist group *alQaws for Gender and Sexual Diversity in Palestinian Society* was banned by the Palestinian Authority. AlQaws responded to the police statement: 'The police claimed it goes against "traditional Palestinian values" accusing us as "foreign agents". The statement went further, calling on citizens to complain about any "suspicious" activities and for the persecution of alQaws staff and activists'. The response goes on stating that 'This recent backlash is in direct response to the dismantling of societal denial regarding the existence of LGBTQ Palestinians!'[25] The group has now moved its activities to Haifa, where it is still relatively safe for Palestinian queers, while they face severe restrictions, discrimination and oppression in the West Bank.

These and many other criticisms from the part of queer Palestinians shall not be misinterpreted as a pro-Zionist or pro-Western attitude. To the contrary, these activists are extremely critical of Israeli politics and often they support the BDS agenda. Still, they see themselves being viewed as traitors to the Palestinian cause. Accordingly, their critical voices are mostly ignored by Queer BDS, one of the loudest forms of current international queer discourse that regularly hijacks social movements all over the world for its antisemitic agenda. To accuse Israel of pinkwashing and homonationalism, the measure of letting the homophobic Palestinian communities and authorities off the hook is considered right and cheap. The intention of the ethnicising homonationalism and pinkwashing allegations is to single out Israel from all other nation states by applying double standards. This, however, is a colonial practice par excellence. In that sense, the resistance against gay rights in non-Western countries is said to be less homophobic in the classical sense than 'grounded in communitarian claims of difference, specificity, cultural authenticity, and history'.[26] These claims, in turn, 'are grounded in the language of rights of self-determination of a people',[27] hence their premise is the idea of homogeneity and sovereignty of a nation while blinding out real conflicts within the national community. But as Max Horkheimer once wrote, 'the sovereignty of a nation is something different from the freedom of those who live in it'.[28]

Is Palestine a feminist issue?

Against that background, the slogan 'Palestine is a feminist issue', when stripped of any critique of the antifeminism, sexism and homophobia deeply entrenched in Palestinian society and exerted on a daily basis by the Palestinian authorities, is a pure manifestation of an antizionism that turns feminism on its head.

So, the problem goes deep and reveals the structural antisemitism that permeates the whole argumentation: the idea of Palestine is completely void of any concrete political and historical content, is held pure of any contradictory conflict within and is designed and personalised as the epitome of a victim of universal evil in the form of imperialism, capitalism, racism and sexism. This universal evil is explicitly identified with Israel. In this perspective, a liberated Palestine would eventually amount to a liberated humanity. As the PFC puts it:

We are re-imagining and recreating a world free from systems of gendered, racial and economic exploitation that commodify human life and land.

Ours is a vision for a radically different future based on life-affirming interconnectedness, empowering the working classes, and love for each other, land, life and the planet itself. For these reasons, we pledge, today and everyday, to recognize Palestine as a Feminist issue and to uphold this commitment in our daily lives and organizing praxis.[29]

The fight against Israel is connected to a worldwide fight against capitalism and commodification in which the 'planet itself' is at stake. Victory over Israel would imply a 'radically different future' not only for Palestinians, but for the whole world. This argumentation corresponds to the classic antisemitic ideology that the Jews would embody all the world's misfortunes and goes even further by implying that the world can only be freed from its evils by destroying Israel. This interpretation is supported by the fact that the Palestinian Feminist Collective does not make clear whether the demanded 'decolonization' refers to the Palestinian areas within the 1967 borders or some broader geographical area that includes existing Israeli territory, whether they are calling for a two-state solution or the destruction of Israel. It comes near the latter interpretation when we read of the state of Israel as a 'settler state' that drives Palestinians from their homes and denies them 'the right to return home'.[30] This is in accordance with key actors in the Palestinian conflict advocating a Palestine 'from the River to the Sea', which means the destruction of Israel as a Jewish state and so the end of Israel as a possible safe haven for Jews worldwide. This aim is also on the agenda of the BDS campaign whose founder Omar Barghouti[31] has stated:

Definitely, most definitely we oppose a Jewish state in any part of Palestine. No Palestinian, rational Palestinian, not a sell-out Palestinian, will ever accept a Jewish state in Palestine.[32]

One might not be too disturbed by the Palestinian Feminist Collective if it weren't for more than 250 Women Studies programmes and other organisations (and more than 4,000 individuals) in the United States but also elsewhere to endorse this 'Pledge that Palestine is a Feminist Issue' in 2021. This pledge was sent on the occasion of the Gaza War in May 2021, and only addresses the destruction of Palestinian homes in Sheikh Jarrah, whereas the thousands of rockets that the Hamas and Islamic Jihad, provided mainly by the Iranian regime, fired from the Gaza strip targeting Israel were not mentioned at all.

The one-sided PFC pledge that 'Palestine is a Feminist Issue' is not an isolated phenomenon but a manifestation of a broad tendency. Instances of intersectional activism excluding Jews, downplaying antisemitism and promoting radical antizionism are numerous. One of the most notorious cases of antisemitism in intersectional framings is Women's March on

Washington, a large-scale, intersectional feminist campaign against racism, xenophobia, homophobia and antifeminism that was formed in the fall of 2016 after Donald Trump was elected president of the United States. Three of the campaign chairs at the time, who have since resigned – Linda Sarsour, Tamika Mallory and Carmen Perez came under criticism for trivialising or even promoting antisemitism. Linda Sarsour, supporter of BDS, defended Islamic Sharia law[33] because it forbids interest taking, called Israel an apartheid state, and declared that feminism and Zionism were mutually exclusive because Zionism was racist and made solidarity with Palestinian women impossible. When asked if there was room for Zionist feminists in the Women's March, she replied:

> It just doesn't make any sense for someone to say, 'Is there room for people who support the state of Israel and do not criticize it in the movement?' There can't be in feminism. You either stand up for the rights of all women, including Palestinians, or none. There's just no way around it.[34]

Like many other activists, also Linda Sarsour relates the oppression of Palestinian women solely to the Israeli occupation, while the patriarchal structures of the Palestinian authorities and of the Islamic tradition with its terror of virtue are not criticised as misogynistic and antifeminist, but even legitimised in the form of Sharia law. Equally limited is the image of Zionism, which is perceived as an ideology of oppression and equated to racism. While Sarsour, as well as other activists and defenders of Sharia, insists that Islam should not be reduced to one side, but that the lived diversity of Islam among Muslims should be considered (and thereby are prone to conceal the oppressive aspects within Islam), the same activists do not concede such diversity to Zionism. In contrast, many Jewish activists who adhere to feminism as well as Zionism, like Emily Shire, who was harshly attacked by Linda Sarsour, point out that they understand Zionism in terms of the right to Jewish self-determination, but that this does not prevent them from advocating a two-state solution and standing up for the rights of Palestinian women.[35] So in fact Zionism is not in contradiction to feminism and antiracism. An antizionism that does not take that into account is mere ideology and has as little to do with Zionism as antisemitism has to do with Jews.[36]

Another example of tying back intersectionality to an antizionist, if not to say antisemitic agenda, is the lesbian 'Chicago Dyke March' in June 2017, in which two women were denied participation because they carried rainbow flags with a Star of David. The organisers considered this flag a symbol of Zionism that would make other participants feel unsafe. Jewish activists would be welcome at the march if they professed antizionism, the organisers demanded. No other group was required to take an explicit stand on any nation state, positive or negative, and no other specific form of national identification was explicitly excluded. This reminds of the compulsion to convert in Christian antisemitism, according to which Jews could supposedly escape institutional exclusion or persecution if they renounced their Jewish identity and Judaism or made 'apologies' for their sins.[37] In the aftermath, Dyke March organisers explained their actions by equating Zionism with racism and white supremacy.

In such intersectional practices, Jews are regularly denied the right to express their own intersectional identity. While the Star of David was banned and reduced to a political sign of Zionism, the Muslim headscarf was actively adopted as a symbol of resistance: the official poster of the Women's March, 'We The People Are Greater Than Fear' by Shepard Fairey, shows a woman wearing the American flag as a headscarf.[38]

Angela Davis and the 'Intersectionality of Struggles'

One of the most prominent protagonists of antizionist intersectionality is Angela Davis, who in her concept of an 'intersectionality of struggles' shifts from a historically informed analysis of power relations to a delegitimisation of Israel:

> We are still faced with the challenge of understanding the complex ways race, class, gender, sexuality, nation, and ability are intertwined – but also how we move beyond these categories to understand the interrelationships of ideas and processes that seem to be separate and unrelated. Insisting on the connections between struggles and racism in the US and struggles against the Israeli repression of Palestinians is a feminist process.[39]

This passage, which links the Israeli-Palestinian conflict with the Civil Rights Movement and Black, intersectional feminism in the United States, turns the Middle East conflict into a racial conflict between whites and People of Colour (which, incidentally, only makes sense if Israeli Arabs are not considered truly to be Israelis and the very existence of Black Jewish Israelis is denied).

Once Jewish Israelis have been defined as representatives of 'white hegemony', it becomes logical to deny them the special interests of a minority deserving support. Then antisemitism can be viewed as an intra-white problem and the Shoah even as 'little family quarrels between Europeans'.[40] Antisemitism and the Shoah thereby fall outside the range of intersectional relevance because they cannot be interpreted in terms of the *colour line*.[41]

The refusal to acknowledge Jewish special interests as well as Israeli diversity is a recurrent feature with Angela Davis, for example when, in order to defend *Black Lives Matter*, she produces a long list of significant special interests and lives that does not include Jewish lives.[42] That she screens out or at least keeps quiet about Jewish lives is therefore striking, since from the beginning Black Lives Matter was a very diverse movement, in which Jews too played a leading role in advocating civil rights.[43] For Davis, however, Jewish lives seem to belong to the 'all lives', i.e. to the universal that is marked as white, middle class and male. Since Jews are considered white, there is no need to make room for considering antisemitism within the intersectionality framework.

Davis makes clear, though, that the creation of a broad alliance against Israel such as Queer BDS necessitates a new perspective on intersectionality in the sense of moving away from identity politics. The intersectional fragmentation of identities and special interests that is at the heart of identity politics needs to be overcome in order to achieve an unconditional solidarity with Palestine from the part of international feminist and queer organisations and individuals. Because to accept the slogan that Palestine was a feminist issue turning solely against Israel and concealing gender apartheid and homophobia in Palestine necessitates putting the common goal of destroying Israel above their own special interests and experiences as queer feminists.

Instrumentalising intersectionality for single issue antizionism, Angela Davis constructs an ideological bundling that in the end even departs from the intersectional holy trinity of race, class and gender:

> The more we try to complicate ideas of struggle using concepts of race, class, gender, sexuality, nation, ability etc., it seems that we move from broad categories to more restrictive ones. It seems that we are constantly narrowing our focus.[44]

Gender and sexuality, even identity, otherwise sanctified in intersectionality of late, become subordinate.

In order to restore the idea of a universal antizionism in the face of intersectional fragmentation, Davis calls for the focus to be broadened through an 'intersectionality of struggles.'[45] However, the selection of struggles which she links together intersectionally follows not an inner logic but her antizionist agenda and leads to the proclamation 'From Ferguson to Palestine': 'Insisting on the connections between struggles and racism in the US and struggles against the Israeli repression of Palestinians is a feminist process'.[46]. As evidence that these two struggles are actually intertwined in an intersectionality of struggles, Davis introduces the fact that BDS had reached out to the Ferguson protesters[47] and to the fact that tear gas (manufactured by the US firm Combined Systems) was used in both cases and that the US police units had been trained by Israeli units.[48]

No other historical, political or religious connections are mentioned that might make this particular intersectionality of struggles plausible. As Cary Nelson convincingly points out, the intersectionality paradigm initially 'proposes that injustices and systems of discrimination, oppression and domination intersect within a society'.[49] He argues that this view indeed helps us to understand the relationships between race, class and gender, as well as other social categories, and 'it is a useful way to compare how those forms of social differentiation and discrimination compare and contrast in different societies'. But, he says, the Ferguson-to-Palestine extension of that logic requires a similar intersectionality to hold even if the distinct oppressions

> occur in different parts of the world in different contexts under different political systems. Then the intersection often occurs only in the mind of the beholder or in a political manifesto, and it begins to function like a conspiracy theory.[50]

Davis turns intersectionality into an ideological cement that yokes together a series of historically, culturally and socially unrelated political events in order to build alliances. This produces the opposite of what intersectionality should stand for: the complexity of the real situation is reduced to a homogeneous schema of good and evil; the multi-layered links between discrimination, oppression and domination are contracted to a single issue – Israel imagined as an 'artificial foreign body' inside the allegedly authentic 'lands of historic Palestine'. As Seyla Benhabib notes, this dichotomy is characterised by a highly reductive view of power relations, in which the Palestinian resistance movement is presented as guiltless and irreproachably anti-colonialist. However, Benhabib observes, ostensibly anti-colonial movements are not always emancipatory and policies pursued in the name of the oppressed can themselves lead to and reproduce oppression (Benhabib, 2013, 157).[51] Such complexities, however, are blinded out in the BDS campaign's Manichaean worldview.

Nevertheless, the intersectionality of struggles could indeed be a suitable approach to adequately analyse the diverse and contradictory concerns within the Palestinian population and thus do justice to the Palestinian reality. However, Angela Davis reduces the intersectionality of struggles to struggles for self-empowerment between minorities and the majority, leaving out those within the minorities. This is precisely anti-intersectional. An intersectional analysis of struggles would name the different, interlocking levels of struggle: against racism and sexism at the same time, against oppression from the majority as well as oppression within the minority. A true intersectionality of struggles would mediate the struggle for national self-determination against Israel with the struggle for sexual self-determination against the Palestinian Authority, Hamas and Islamic Jihad. In this way, certainties are confused. With Davis, however, cultures freeze into homogeneous blocs and critique becomes abstract.

Reclaiming intersectionality for the critique of antisemitism

In the light of such political misuse, many antisemitism researchers today view intersectionality as an essentially political slogan that should not be used. In contrast, I argue for a critical reclaiming of the idea.

I do this because intersectionality has become so important in feminist academic and political discourses that one cannot avoid positioning oneself in this field. And here it is good to develop an understanding of intersectionality that not only avoids the pitfalls described above with regard to antisemitism, but also actively works against them and reconceptualises intersectionality as a tool to analyse ideologies and not identities. For a critical analysis of antisemitism itself opens up the view of its own intersectional structure. Thus, even if antisemitism is left out of many intersectional political practices and discourses, and sometimes, as illustrated, antisemitism is even propagated under the guise of intersectional antiracism and feminism, there are ways of fruitfully thinking together intersectionality and the critique of antisemitism.

It is interesting, though so far unnoticed, that the Critical Theory of the Frankfurt School already in the 1940s presented an analysis of antisemitism that problematised its intersections with other ideologies and thus in some ways anticipated later conceptions of intersectionality.[52] The broad empirical studies *Authoritarian Personality*, conducted in the 1940s in the United States with the aim of surveying the authoritarian-fascist potential across the American population, concluded that ideologies such as antisemitism, racism, sexism, homophobia, ethnocentrism, nationalism and class bias rarely occur isolated from each other but develop within a broader framework – the authoritarian ideological attitudinal syndrome.[53] Within this larger framework ideologies dynamically buttress, mutually overlap and strengthen one another, taking on a specific interpenetrative and interblending form from which they derive their tough and flexible effectiveness. Following this seminal insight, ideologies are indeed intersectional: they interpenetrate and reinforce each other, constantly reforming and reactivating themselves in this process. Moreover, depending on political expediency, one ideology may come to the fore while the others continue to operate in the background and can be recalled at any time. This makes evident that ideologies are mobile and processual social phenomena.

How does antisemitism operate with sexist, racist and nationalist moments? How do antisemitic motifs shine through in antifeminism? How does nationalism or antigenderism (as a specific form of antifeminism) mask latent antisemitism? Along such questions, I have developed the concept of intersectionality of ideologies.[54]

However, this does not mean interchangeability or equation of ideologies. Rather, following Oskar Negt, in the critique of ideologies, discernment as well as a sense of relationality must be developed. Then it becomes recognisable that ideologies gain their specificity precisely from the interplay with other ideologies. Such an approach has implications for insight into the socio-historical structure and function not only of antisemitism but also of antifeminism, sexism, racism and nationalism. This entails an important change of perspective in intersectionality research: from the level of identity formation, which is often in the foreground today, to the level of the ideological concealment of social contradictions.

Antisemitism stands out here as a thoroughly intersectional ideology, i.e. it integrates and operates through moments that may not in themselves appear antisemitic, but sexist, homophobe, racist, nationalist and so on. Thus, in antisemitism, we find innumerable images of deficient physicality that are meant to express a lack of masculinity and even effeminacy in male Jews and a lack of femininity in female Jews – insinuating that Jews undermine the ruling heteronormative gender order.[55] Such overlaps between antisemitism and sexism also make it possible for antisemitism to be overlaid with a form of antigenderism in circumstances where the socio-political structure has made antisemitism a taboo. In these cases, feminism and women's emancipation are still viewed as a Jewish machination against the non-Jewish communities.[56] Moreover, overlaps with racism are also clear in antisemitism[57] and the same goes for nationalism, in the figure of the 'anti-national' Jew who threatens the national principle.[58] Similarly, antizionism as a specific form of anti-nationalism may conceal antisemitism. On top of all this, antisemitism provides a distorted reflection of the class antagonism, often masking itself as a critique of capitalism and imperialism while viewing Jews as representing both Bolshevism and capitalism at one and the same time. The fact that the guilt for capitalist exploitation is thrown onto the Jews and that they are identified with the abstract side of the capital relation, that of free-floating finance capital, is a further permanent component of the antisemitic ideology.[59] Via this multi-layered fusion with other ideologies, antisemitism represents a comprehensive and solidified worldview. It achieves this feat by integrating intersectional moments of other ideologies.[60] This specific assemblage of ideological clichés gives antisemitism its potency as a comprehensive worldview that conceals the real conflicts and antagonisms, given which I consider antisemitism to be the quintessential intersectional ideology.

One of the most important questions for critical antisemitism research is why and how antisemitism can persist through social change, i.e. how and why antisemitism is so flexible and adaptable to changing conditions. Through the use of an intersectional approach, it becomes clear that this may be attributable to the special ideological structure of antisemitism: it is a flexible ideology that interacts and blends with other ideologies. It may also be obscured by other ideologies that show a structural affinity.

At the same time a focus on ideology, particularly antisemitism, requires from intersectional theory an additional dimension of self-awareness, in order to counteract clear signs of terminological and conceptual stagnation and identity-political contractions. An intersectional approach must not allow itself to be restricted to the insight that society is constructed through definite categories, but must expose, in a radical critique of power, the social grounds and conditions of these categories, just as the perennial process of categorising of people in society and the underlying identity logic must be criticised. The intersectionality of ideologies approach proposed here is therefore critical towards other intersectional approaches that support an identitarian and culturally relativistic discourse and, under cover of antiracism and intersectional feminism, can give rise to antisemitic and homophobic practises.

I think we need to constantly point out these ideological intersections in order to prevent the current trend of fragmentation, desolidarisation and repressive particularism. Viviane Teitelbaum, co-founder of the Feminist Observatory of Violence against Women, has pointedly called these trends an 'identity house arrest'.[61] We need to reopen the perspective and see intersectionality for what it can be: a framework for analysing the larger contexts that constitute our society without reducing its real complexity. A framework that makes a certain universality and in that sense solidarity possible in the first place and thus is able to break through the narrowness of selective empathy and restrictive identity politics. An intersectional analysis of ideologies can also advance the practice of coalition building, so that antiracism and the struggle against antisemitism are no longer regarded as opposites but recognised to be a common struggle. For this to happen, however, it is necessary to address and critique the sometimes latent, sometimes quite overt antisemitism in some intersectional contexts.

The critique of intersectionality presented in this chapter is intended as a rescue operation aimed at making the approach available for a feminist dialectical theory and an emancipatory practice that does not exclude Jews and that is mindful of global antisemitism. From this point of view, intersectionality too can be seen as an attempt to experience and think plurality, without denying the general in the sense of the connecting and the shared.

Notes

1 Schulman, Sarah, *Israel/Palestine and the Queer International*, Durham, NC: Duke University Press, 2012.
2 Crenshaw, Kimberle, Mapping the Margins: Intersectionality, Identity Politics, and Violence against Women of Color. *Stanford Law Review*, 43(6), 1241–1299, 1991; Davis, Angela, *Women, Race, and Class*, New York: Vintage Books, 1983;

Hill Collins, Patricia, Intersectionality's Definitional Dilemmas. *Annual Review of Sociology.*, 41(1), 1–20, 2015.

3 The Combahee River Collective, A Black Feminist Statement. *WSQ*, 42(3-4), 271–280, 2014.

4 Crenshaw, Kimberle, Demarginalizing the Intersection of Race and Sex: A Black Feminist Critique of Antidiscrimination Doctrine, Feminist Theory and Antiracist Politics. *University of Chicago Legal Forum*, 1, 139–167, 1989; Crenshaw, Kimberle, Mapping the Margins.

5 The Combahee River Collective, A Black Feminist Statement. *WSQ*, 42(3–4), 273, 2014.

6 Arendt, Hannah, *The Origins of Totalitarianism*, New York, Orlando: Harcourt Brace Jovanovich, 1979; [*A Harvest Book*], p. 298; cf. also Benhabib, Seyla, Another Universalism: On the Unity and Diversity of Human Rights. *Proceedings and Addresses of the American Philosophical Association*, 81(2), 7–32, 2007.

7 Brown, Wendy, Neoliberalism's Frankenstein. Authoritarian Freedom in Twenty-First Century 'Democracies'. In: Wendy Brown, Peter E. Gordon and Max Pensky, eds., *Authoritarianism: Three Inquiries in Critical Theory*, Chicago, London: The University of Chicago Press, 2018; [*Trios*], pp. 7–44.

8 Davis, Angela Y., *Freedom Is a Constant Struggle: Ferguson, Palestine, and the Foundations of a Movement*, Chicago, IL: Haymarket Books, 2016, p. 87. For a critique on such homogenising trends with regard to cultural groups, see Benhabib, Seyla, and Drucilla Cornell, Introduction: Beyond the Politics of Gender. In: Seyla Benhabib and Drucilla Cornell, eds., *Feminism as Critique: Essays on the Politics of Gender in Late-capitalist Societies*, Cambridge: Polity, 1987; [*Feminist Perspectives*], pp. 1–15.

9 Davis, Angela, *What Is Queer BDS? Pinkwashing, Intersections, Struggles, Politics*, 2018. https://vimeo.com/55886232 (accessed 3 March 2022).

10 Ibid.

11 Ibid.

12 Puar, Jasbir K., The Golden Handcuffs of Gay Rights: How Pinkwashing Distorts both LGBTIQ and Anti-Occupation Activism. *Jadaliyya*, 7 February 2012.

13 Palestinian Feminist Collective, *Pledge that Palestine Is a Feminist Issue*, 2021. https://actionnetwork.org/petitions/pledge-declaring-palestine-is-a-feminist-issue?fbclid=IwAR1SufztPhUMv0tTy9zlQRnYUtH_FNcjLR5Sx5oPpG4gVA9 1zfZ0oZKfGZc (accessed 5 January 2022).

14 Ibid.

15 Ibid.

16 Massad, Joseph, *Desiring Arabs*, Chicago: University of Chicago Press, 2007. Cited in Dhawan, Nikita, Homonationalism and State-phobia: The Postcolonial Predicament of Queering Modernities. In: María A. Viteri and Manuela Lavinas Picq, eds., *Queering Paradigms V*, 2015, p. 58. See also Puar, Jasbir K., *Terrorist Assemblages: Homonationalism in Queer Times*, Durham: Duke University Press, 2007; [*Next Wave*], p. 57.

17 Dhawan, Nikita, Homonationalism and State-phobia: The Postcolonial Predicament of Queering Modernities. In: María A. Viteri and Manuela Lavinas Picq, *Queering Paradigms V*, 2015, pp. 51–68.

18 Hochberg, G. Z. et al., No Pride in Occupation: A Roundtable Discussion. *GLQ: A Journal of Lesbian and Gay Studies*, 16(4), 609, 2010. See also Laura Eigenmann, *Zur Kritik der Homonationalismus-Kritik: Eine Analyse der Leerstellen und Machteffekte der Homonationalismus-Kritik anhand ihrer Rezeption durch libanesische und palästinensische Queer-und LGBT-Aktivist_innen* (2013).

19 Dhawan, Nikita, p. 61.
20 Kerner, Ina, Provinzialismus und Semi-Intersektionalität: Fallstricke des Feminismus in postkolonialen Zeiten. *Feministische Studien*, 38(1), 76–93, 2020.
21 Puar, Jasbir K., and Maya Mikdashi, Pinkwatching and Pinkwashing: Interpenetration and Its Discontents. *Jadaliyya*, 9 August 2012; Schotten, Heike and Haneen Maikey, Queers Resisting Zionism: On Authority and Accountability beyond Homonationalism. *Jadaliyya*, 10 October 2012. For a criticism of the pinkwashing allegation, see Blackmer, Corinne E., Pinkwashing. *Israel Studies*, 24(2), 171–181, 2019.
22 Hochberg, G. Z. et al., No Pride in Occupation, p. 606.
23 Ibid.
24 Atshan, Sa'ed, *Queer Palestine and the Empire of Critique*, Redwood City: Stanford University Press, 2020, p. 213.
25 AlQaws Response to the PA Police Statement. http://alqaws.org/articles/AlQaws-response-to-the-PA-police-statment?category_id=0 (accessed 9 April 2023).
26 Stychin, Carl F., Same-sex Sexualities and the Globalization of Human Rights Discourse. *McGill Law Journal. Revue de droit de McGill*, 49(4), 957, 2004.
27 Ibid.
28 Horkheimer, Max, Letter to Hans Dollinger, 3.11.1960. In: Horkheimer, Max, *Briefwechsel 1949–1973*, *Gesammelte Schriften* 18, Frankfurt a.M., 1996, p. 491.
29 Palestinian Feminist Collective, *Pledge that Palestine Is a Feminist Issue* (2021).
30 Ibid.
31 For an alternative view of BDS as a product not of Palestinian activists, but of British intellectuals, who popularized the boycott idea and exported it to the Palestinian territories, see Hirsh, David, *Contemporary Left Antisemitism*, New York, NY: Routledge, 2018, p. 100.
32 Barghouti, Omar, *Strategies for Change* (2014). https://vimeo.com/75201955 (accessed 2 March 2022).
33 Linda Sarsour, If Only My Fellow Liberals Understood What Sharia Law Actually Is. Smh. #ScaliaLaw. *Twitter*. https://twitter.com/lsarsour/status/484513285921046529?ref_src=twsrc%5Etfw (accessed 2 March 2022).
34 Linda Sarsour cited in Meyerson, Collier, Can You Be a Zionist Feminist? Linda Sarsour Says No. *The Nation*, 13 March 2007.
35 Shire, Emily, Does Feminism Have Room for Zionists? *The New York Times*, 7 March 2017.
36 Seymour, David, Continuity and Discontinuity: From Antisemitism to Antizionism and the Reconfiguration of the Jewish Question. *Journal of Contemporary Antisemitism*, 2(2), 11–24, 2019.
37 Rensmann, Lars, Israelbezogener Antisemitismus, *Bundeszentrale für politische Bildung*, 11 February 2021.
38 See https://www.artsy.net/artwork/shepard-fairey-we-the-people-are-greater-than-fear.
39 Davis, Angela, *Freedom Is a Constant Struggle*, p. 4.
40 Frantz Fanon cited in Cousin, Glynis, and Robert Fine, A Common Cause: Reconnecting the Study of Racism and Antisemitism. *European Societies*, 14(2), 172, 2012.
41 Stögner, Karin, Intersectionality and Antisemitism. A New Approach. *Fathom*, May 2020. https://fathomjournal.org/intersectionality-and-antisemitism-a-new-approach/

42 "If indeed all lives mattered we would not need to emphatically proclaim that 'Black Lives Matter'. Or, as we discover on the BLM website: Black Women Matter, Black Girls Matter, Black Gay Lives Matter, Black Bi Lives Matter, Black Boys Matter, Black Queer Lives Matter, Black Men Matter, Black Lesbians Matter, Black Trans Lives Matter, Black Immigrants Matter, Black Incarcerated Lives Matter. Black Differently Abled Lives Matter. Yes, Black Lives Matter, Latino/ Asian American/ Native American/ Muslim/ Poor and Working-Class White People's Lives Matter. There are many more specific instances we would have to name before we can ethically and comfortably claim that All Lives Matter." Angela Y. Davis, *Freedom Is a Constant Struggle*, p. 87.

43 Isaacs, Anna, How the Black Lives Matter & Palestinian Movements Converged, *Moments Magazine*, March/April 2016, pp. 44–67.

44 Davis, Angela, *What Is Queer BDS? Pinkwashing, Intersections, Struggles, Politics* (2018). https://vimeo.com/55886232 (accessed 3 March 2022).

45 Davis, *Freedom Is a Constant Struggle*, p. 16.

46 Ibid., p. 4.

47 Davis, Angela, Gayatri C. Spivak, and Nikita Dhawan, Planetary Utopias: Angela Davis and Gayatri Chakravorty Spivak in Conversation with Nikita Dhawan. *Radical Philosophy*, 2(5), 72–73, 2019.

48 Davis, *Freedom Is a Constant Struggle*, p. 140.

49 Nelson, Cary, *The Intersectionality Muddle* (2015). https://www.insidehighered.com/views/2016/02/15/concept-intersectionality-mutating-and-becoming-corrupted-essay (accessed 14 January 2022).

50 Nelson, Cary, *The Intersectionality Muddle* (2015). https://www.insidehighered.com/views/2016/02/15/concept-intersectionality-mutating-and-becoming-corrupted-essay (accessed 14 January 2022).

51 Benhabib, Seyla, Ethics Without Normativity and Politics Without Historicity. On Judith Butler's Parting Ways. Jewishness and the Critique of Zionism. *Constellations*, 20(1), 150–163, 2013.

52 Horkheimer, Max, Theodor W. Adorno, *Dialectics of Enlightenment. Philosophical Fragments*, Stanford: Standford University Press 2002, pp. 192–234.

53 Adorno, Theodor et al., *The Authoritarian Personality*, Verso, 2019.

54 Stögner, Karin, *Antisemitismus und Sexismus: Historisch-gesellschaftliche Konstellationen*, 1st ed., Baden-Baden: Nomos 2014, volume 3; Interdisziplinäre Antisemitismusforschung/*Interdisciplinary Studies on Antisemitism*; Stögner, Karin, Nature and Anti-nature: Constellations of Antisemitism and Sexism. In: Ulrike Brunotte, Jürgen Mohn and Christina Späti, *Internal Outsiders: Imagined Orientals?: Antisemitism, Colonialism and Modern Constructions of Jewish Identity*, Würzburg: Ergon Verlag, 2017; Stögner, Karin, Antisemitism and Intersectional Feminism: Strange Alliances. In: Armin Lange, Dina Porat and Lawrence Schiffman, *An End to Antisemitism: Theoretical Approaches and Practical Challenges*, Berlin: De Gruyter, 2021, pp. 69–87.

55 Gilman, Sander L., Freud, Race and Gender. *American Imago*, 49(2), 155–183, 1992; Stögner, Karin, *Antisemitismus und Sexismus: Historisch-gesellschaftliche Konstellationen*.

56 Stögner, Karin, Fear of the 'New Human Being': On the Intersection of Antisemitism, Antifeminism and Nationalism in the Austrian Freedom Party. In: Cornelia Möser, Jennifer Ramme, Judit Takács, *Paradoxical Right-Wing Sexual Politics in Europe*, Cham: Palgrave Macmillan 2022, pp. 145-172.

57 Cousin, Glynis, and Robert Fine, pp. 166–185.

58 Holz, Klaus, *Nationaler Antisemitismus: Wissenssoziologie einer Weltanschauung*, 1st ed., Hamburg: Hamburger Edition HIS Verl.-Ges, 2001.

59 Grigat, Stephan, Adorno and Iran: Critical Theory and Islamic Antisemitism, *Fathom. For a Deeper Understanding of Israel and the Region*, 2020; Postone, Moishe, Anti-Semitism and National Socialism: Notes on the German Reaction to 'Holocaust'. *New German Critique*, 19, 97–115, 1980.
60 Stögner, Karin, *Antisemitismus und Sexismus: Historisch-gesellschaftliche Konstellationen*; Stögner, Karin, Nature and Anti-nature: Constellations of Antisemitism and Sexism.
61 European Jewish Congress, *Antisemitism and Sexism: Points of Intersection*, 8 March 2021. https://eu rojewcong.org/ejc-in-action/events-meetings/le-cje -vous-invite-a-la-conference- antisemitisme-et-sexisme-points-dintersection/.

6

CANCELLING ISRAEL AND DISPLACING PALESTINE

Narratives of a boycott

John Strawson

The campaign for the academic boycott of Israel is based on politics of no-normalisation with the Jewish state. This draws on a long Western tradition of questioning the identity of the Jewish people. Since 1948 this has come to encompass Israel. Arab politics assimilated these positions as Arab nationalism established itself from the middle of the 19th century. In this account, Israel is not a normal state because the Jewish people are not a normal people. I will argue that the centrality given to Israel by the academic boycott as part of the Boycott Disinvestment and Sanctions campaign (BDS)[1] has, perhaps surprisingly, contributed to the marginalisation of Palestine. By the 2020's, the Palestinian cause in North America and Europe was held hostage by a narrow sectarian movement obsessed by Israel. Instead of a broad democratic movement supporting Palestinian self-determination, there are fringe groups imbued with sectarian and sometimes antisemitic politics. This chapter will explore the paradox of how the boycott movement has become more concerned with cancelling Israel than with the emancipation of Palestine. I will first draw on my experience of the boycott and then reflect on the tradition and politics of no-normalisation with Jews and Israel.

The issue of the academic boycott of Israel was a rude interruption to my work on the Palestinian–Israeli conflict. At the time I was regularly in Palestine as part of a visiting professor scheme supporting the teaching of the MA in law at Birzeit University. The European Consortium supporting the Birzeit Law Centre (later Institute)[2] was formed in the mid-1990s comprising of academics from Birzeit, Belgium, Netherlands and the UK and funded the international development ministry of the Flemish regional government. It was very much a post-Oslo project. The plan to begin law teaching at Birzeit with a master's course had the ambitious aims

DOI: 10.4324/9781003222477-7

of evaluating what legal system would suit a Palestinian state and to create a cadre of Palestinian legal academics and practitioners to staff it.[3] I was assigned to teach part of a legal history course that dealt with the British Mandate period. Assessing the legal narrative of Palestine was seen as part of the process of liberating Palestine from its long period of Imperial rule. As part of this project, the Law Centre worked to assemble all laws in force at the end of each period of occupation, Ottoman, British, Jordanian, Egyptian and Israeli. This took the form of the first legal database in Arabic – *al muqtafi*.[4]

Events

The campaign to boycott Israeli universities became a real issue for me in 2006 while attending two international academic conferences, one in Berlin and the other in Amman. In Berlin, the Law and Society Association conference had a number of panels on Palestinian themes. Some of the Palestinian scholars were participating in a project I had put together on Palestinian state building funded by a British Academy grant.[5] At the first panel after the presentations, an Israeli participant began to ask a question and was immediately interrupted and asked to denounce the occupation. The singling out of an Israeli stuck me as particularly problematic given that at the time in Iraq the US and British forces were attempting to quell a rising against its occupation. I did not hear anyone questioning American or British participants on their attitude to the occupation of Iraq. Despite presenting a paper, charring a session and making many interventions, certainly no one asked me. It underlined the way in which the BDS project works by turning on Israeli citizens and holding them to account in a way that other nationalities are not.

In Amman it was the occasion of the second World Congress of Middle East Studies. It brought together Middle East studies associations, universities, research centres and scholars working in the area.[6] Of the 2,000 participants were perhaps some 20 Israeli scholars, who had ignored the Israeli Ministry of Foreign Affairs' advice not to attend for security reasons.[7] Their presence was to create a crisis for the Congress as BDS supporters termed the participation of individual Israeli scholars as normalisation with Israel. I was part of a discrete stream on law reform in the Arab world coordinated by Birzeit University. My colleagues from the university met to decide whether to continue participation or not. Pragmatically, they decided they would as there were no Israeli scholars in our stream. However, the Jordanian Bar took a very harsh position and declared that any member taking part in the Congress would be disbarred. Several distinguished Jordanian jurists were forced to withdraw their papers. This position was all the more problematic given that since 1994 Jordan had full diplomatic relations with Israel.[8] No doubt lawyers, members of the same Jordanian Bar, had been involved in drafting the treaty to normalise relations with Israel.

At the same time enormous pressure was applied on film directors from around the Arab world to withdraw their films from the associated film festival. Threats were made that if they allowed their films to be shown they would find it difficult to work or raise funds for future work. The film festival collapsed. In these two instances, BDS operated in a coercive manner against Arab jurists and filmmakers as well as against Israeli scholars.

The disciplining of Arab intellectuals was instructive and demonstrated a wider problem for research and thinking about Israel and Jewish identity in Arab universities. The no-normalisation policy curtails free discussion of the Palestinian–Israeli conflict and thus deprives Arab societies and policymakers from considering how to resolve it in practice. It is an irony that Arab states that have recognised Israel since 2020 have done so unconditionally as far as the Palestinians are concerned.[9] In other words, no-normalisation has shut down discussion on the very issue that it was meant to address, Palestinian self-determination.

In 2007, I found myself the subject of boycott for attending an academic conference marking 40 years of the Israeli occupation after the 1967 war. It took place at the Hebrew University of Jerusalem and Tel Aviv University.[10] The conference was sponsored by the International Committee of the Red Cross and the Konrad Adenauer Foundation and attended by many leading international lawyers. Perhaps because of its high profile it became a focus for boycott campaigners. Arab and Palestinian scholars were put under immense pressure not to attend and very few did. My contribution entitled 'Occupation and colonial footprints of international law' argued that the prolonged occupation had become a form of colonialism and how Palestine has been constructed within international legal discourse.[11] It was seen as a pro-Palestinian paper and had been roundly denounced by the late Professor Ruth Lapidoth for this stance. The overall argument had already appeared in the Palestinian Yearbook of International Law and been generally well received, with one author writing

> The ground has been well described by John Strawson in Volume XII of the *Palestinian Yearbook of International Law* where he identified Palestine as a "particular victim" of the heritage of its "international law as rooted in its colonial origins".[12]

Despite such approval for the views expressed in a publication associated with Birzeit University, the same university cancelled a workshop I had planned to take place there shortly after the conference. I received an email from the then director of the Institute of Law saying that I would not be welcome. From that moment a ten-year association with Birzeit came to an end.

The reason was evidently not the views that I had expressed but the place where I had expressed them.

Boycott narratives

As can be seen from these events, any hint that Israel is a normal state with normal citizens is resisted by the boycott movement as undermining the Palestinian position. This necessarily raises the question of how BDS construct the 'Palestinian position'.

Since 1993 the Palestine Liberation Organization (PLO) has recognised the State of Israel, in the exchange of letters between Israel and the PLO that accompany the Oslo Accords. In the letter from the Chair of the PLO, Yasser Arafat writes, the 'PLO recognizes the right of the State of Israel to exist in peace and security'. The letter continues to accept United Nations Security Council resolutions 242 and 338, both of which guarantee the security of all Middle Eastern states. This commitment is underlined through an affirmation that 'those articles of the Palestinian Covenant which deny Israel's right to exist ... are now inoperative and no longer valid'.[13] The PLO has never reversed this position and has been engaged in negotiations with Israel on that basis. In the West Bank, the Palestinian Authority, composed of PLO members, has worked with Israel on security coordination since 1994. In 2002, Arab League's peace initiative effectively rejected no-normalisation and proposed the recognition of Israel once a Palestinian state had been created, the West Bank and Gaza.[14] This position has regularly been re-affirmed by the Arab League.

These developments within Palestinian and Arab politics are studiously ignored by the boycott movement. This is problematic from a movement that talks about self-determination but implies that the PLO does not have the right to adopt policies on behalf of the people it represents. Recognising Israel was seen in the interest of Palestinians, and for the PLO negotiations were a step towards achieving self-determination. At the level of the Arab League, the Peace Initiative is also a reflection that the recognition of Israel is linked to the creation of a Palestinian state. It is not just that this position is ignored by the boycott movement but it also appears that it denies the agency of the Palestinians and the Arab world to make these decisions.

Of course, over the past 30 years there have been other developments in Palestinian politics, in particular the emergence: of Hamas as a major actor.[15] Hamas (or the Islamic Resistance Movement) is attached to the oldest established Islamist movement, the Muslim Brotherhood.[16] Hamas reflects its general politics but applied to Palestine where it rejects Israel's right to exist on the grounds that Palestine is part of the *Dar al Islam* – the territory of Islam.[17] It came to prominence in the first intifada (1987–1993) and became a rival of Fatah, the main component of the PLO. Initially, it rejected the Oslo Agreements which it denounced as betrayal as it involved recognising Israel. As a result, it did not participate in the first Palestinian elections in 1996. However, it changed its policy and in 2006 won the Legislative Council elections albeit with a minority of the vote (44.5%). The vote was not so much in favour of its Islamist politics as a rejection of the PLO's corruption and lack of progress in the negotiations. However, the organisation squandered its opportunity for power and retreated to Gaza (its birthplace) in 2007. None the less, Hamas as part of the Muslim Brotherhood, together with Iran, has been able to form a significant rejectionist front internationally. The Israel–Gaza conflicts in 2008–2009, 2014 and 2021 have placed Hamas in the spotlight for some in Europe and North America and have turned the organisation into a symbol of resistance. However, while technically still occupied, Israel withdrew all its armed forces and settlers from Gaza in 2005, and Hamas's military has since aimed attacks againt Israel itself. Hamas's political aims are clear, which are not to end the occupation of Palestinian territory but to destroy the State of Israel. In effect, it appears that BDS politics has aligned with this view and has become for the organisation the 'Palestinian position'.

We therefore need to establish what the BDS 'Palestinian position' is. The call for the academic boycott is posed in the following terms, 'Israeli academic institutions are a key part of Israel's regime of occupation, settler colonialism and apartheid'.[18] As can be noted, the 'complicity' of the Israeli universities is not only with the occupation but also with settler colonialism and apartheid. If you click on the hyperlink under the three terms, the reader will find a fuller explanation. In its account of the creation of the Jewish state we find the following.

> Israel was formed in 1948 through the brutal displacement of 800,000 Palestinians and the destruction of more than 530 towns and villages. This pre-meditated ethnic cleansing is known as al-Nakba, the catastrophe. Since then, Israel has implemented a regime of settler colonialism, apartheid and occupation over the Palestinian people.[19]

It goes on to claim that from the beginning, Israel has sought to control ever more 'historic' 'Palestinian land' and to drive 'indigenous Palestinians off their land'.

> Israel's oppression involves settler colonialism: Zionism seeks to establish a distinct new society, take control of the land and resources and forcibly remove the Palestinians.[20]

This potted history is seriously misleading as the creation of the Jewish state as part of the partition of Palestine was a decision of the United Nations,[21] supported by the two big powers the United States and the USSR. The United Nations' plan provided for the creation of two states, Jewish and Arab, and an international zone for Jerusalem and Bethlehem within an economic union. The plan guaranteed that all inhabitants would remain in their homes and provided for each state to protect the rights of minorities.[22] This plan was rejected by the then Palestinian leadership and the Arab League declared war on Israel when it was created in May 1948. As a result, the war in Israel was created on 78% of the area of British Mandate Palestine, larger than that allocated under the partition plan. The rest of the territory was occupied by Jordan and Egypt which counties would not countenance the creation of a Palestine state. Although such a state could easily have been established and its capital would have been east Jerusalem. The rejection of the partition plan, on the grounds that it created a Jewish state, effectively meant that Palestinian self-determination that the plan also provided for was sacrificed. In 2011, Palestinian President Mahmoud Abbas told an interviewer that 'it was our mistake, it was an Arab mistake as a whole'.[23] The reader of the BDS website will learn nothing of this actual history.

The text of the call for the boycott is so ahistorical that it is forced to advance largely invented history in which Jews are constructed as shadowy invaders conspiring to steal the land of others. There is no hint that the international community recognised the historical connection of both Jews and Arabs to Palestine in 1947 and set out to address the right of both peoples to self-determination. Nor would you understand from the boycott account that the political left in the late 1940s saw the creation of Israel as progressive.[24] Nor would you know that many internationalists and Marxists such as Isaac Deutscher, although not Zionists, were strongly in support of the creation of the Jewish state.[25] The erasure of this history is an essential element of the claim that Israel from its creation was a 'regime of occupation, settler colonialism and apartheid'.

This position is enlightening when trying to determine the way in which the 'Palestinian position' is understood by BDS. While not couched in the Islamist language of the Hamas Covenant, the politics has much in common. Perhaps most significant is the way in which the term occupation is used. Many opponents of the current Israeli occupation of Palestinian territory might be drawn to the idea that an academic boycott might put pressure on the Israeli government to withdraw from the territories conquered in the 1967 war. However, the occupation that BDS is referring to is the creation of the State of Israel in 1948. According to BDS, since then Israel has 'implemented a regime of settler colonialism, apartheid and occupation'. This formulation is somewhat perplexing as it says that a regime 'implemented' settler colonialism, apartheid and occupation. This implies that the regime was not a product of these phenomena but made a choice to adopt them. The statement is silent on the political or sociological character of this regime. This issue is not explained. However, the statement does tell its readers, 'You don't need to be an expert in history to understand what's happening in Palestine'.[26] This cynical remark presumably licenses the authors of the guidelines to present inaccurate historical 'facts' such as the 'majority of Palestinians are the 7.25 million who have been forced from their homes to make way for Jewish Israelis'.[27] This figure one assumes is an estimate of the descendants of Palestinians displaced in 1948, but it is presented as if 7.25 million were displaced rather than the United Nations' figure of 726,000.[28] The guidelines present as a fact that there was 'pre-meditated ethnic cleansing' of Palestinians in 1948. In his authoritative study of the issue, Benny Morris concludes that most Palestinian Arabs fled as a result of the war although there were instances of forced removal of populations from towns and villages.[29] There is no evidence of a 'pre-meditated' plan.[30] Ironically, when Morris revisits his study in 2004, he argues that there should have been such a plan.[31]

At the hands of these authors history is bent to serve an ideological purpose. This is achieved through a variety of devices. Sometimes historical facts are taken from their context and thus appear distorted. At other times the silences and omissions on the course of history misleads the unwary. In this account Jews appear as rapacious colonial settlers out to seize the land and resources. The creation of Israel consolidates this truth. The dispossession of the Palestinians is the proof. We can agree that Israel was created, and the Palestinians were dispossessed. However, how both came about and what the connection between the two is, is only explained as one long pre-meditated plan. The complexities of 1947 and 1948 are ignored. There is no discussion of the UN plan, and there is no discussion of Arab and Palestinian politics of the period and the consequences. The 1948 war launched by the Arab League States was defeated by Israel not acting as a pawn of Imperialism but as a state armed in part by the Soviet Union's efforts. The Soviet Union almost alone of all UN members in 1947 and 1948 made the connection between the creation of the Jewish state and Holocaust. There is nothing in the boycott account that suggests that Jews had a long history of discrimination and oppression of which the Holocaust was the last chapter. Indeed, the way Jews are constructed in this narrative portrays them almost as irrational colonial interlopers who arrived for no reason but to take the land. It is a worrying image which is redolent of conspiracy theory.

Having created this lens through which we are asked to look at the situation, we are then presented with its logic. That is, the removal of occupation, colonial settlers and apartheid, which means necessarily the elimination of Israel. Only once it has been removed from the scene will order have been restored. However, what is important to grasp is that for the BDS the only way to achieve this is by accepting that the analysis characterises Israel in this way. The reason for no-normalisation is because no one should deal with a regime that implements occupation, settler colonialism and apartheid. Thus, to be pro-Palestinian it is necessary to accept the politics of no-normalisation.

Any analysis that fails to refer to this mantra is seen as undermining the Palestinian cause. Thus, supporting the end of the 1967 occupation, Palestinian self-determination and the recognition of a Palestinian state is not regarded as sufficient. This explains the silence over Oslo and the Arab Peace Initiative. It also explains the rage over the Abraham Accords[32] and the participation of Mansour Abbas's Ra'am party in the Israeli government formed by Bennet and Lapid in June 2021.

This attitude extends to the academic world. My own work on the conflict which as we have seen was highly commended in the Palestinian Yearbook of International Law has subsequently been reconstructed as anti-Palestinian. An analysis of an article I had written on whether Israel was a colonial state[33] is framed as follows: 'John Strawson castigates the pro-Palestinian discourse that calls Zionism "colonialism" as he writes that "the use of the term colonialism by BDS supporters is not historiography but political rhetoric"'.[34] The author does not discuss the merits of the argument but asserts that contesting the analysis that Israel is the result of colonialism necessarily means that I am 'castigating the pro-Palestinian discourse'. In other words, deviation from a particular analysis is seen as betrayal of the Palestinian cause. BDS thus tries to exercise coercive control over theory.

This highlights the challenges that face scholars who are working in the field. BDS operates as a vetting service. It gives an imprimatur to views that it supports and issues anathemas for those that it does not. As in my case it is quite possible to have the imprimatur removed.

Once I had publicly opposed the academic boycott my work became suspicious.[35] In a recent article my comment that 'It was ironic therefore that just at the moment the United Nations recognized the Arab people of Palestine's right to self-determination, their representatives were to reject it'[36] is said to be 'disingenuous'.[37] It is noteworthy how a disagreement about such a commonplace view should be denounced as in some way unreliable or dishonest. It is troubling to see an academic view portrayed in this way. The use of such terms is also problematic in the context of discussing a conflict involving Jews.[38]

The Palestinian–Israeli conflict and the academic boycott

The academic boycott was launched as the Second Intifada was at its height. The years 2001 and 2002 were indeed miserable ones in Palestine. The Oslo peace process was unravelling and the optimism that surrounded the signing of the 1993 Accords had dissipated. At Camp David in August 2000, neither Barak nor Arafat was strong enough to make a deal. The provocative visit of the then opposition leader Ariel Sharon to Temple Mount/Haram al Sharif in September re-ignited violence and the Israeli government embarked on a military campaign to retake many of the areas that Israel had left in early 1996 under the Interim Agreement. Arafat's Ramallah headquarters the Maqata was surrounded by Israeli forces and most Palestinian police stations were destroyed by air strikes. Palestinian civilians felt abandoned by the international community as they struggled to maintain daily life against the background of violent clashes between Palestinian militias and the Israel Defence Force (IDF) and frequent military incursions into cities and towns by the latter. Living standards plummeted, unemployment rose and services were disrupted, leading to plummeting morale and a loss of confidence in the peace process. Many children were traumatised by scenes they witnessed for themselves and by watching television coverage of the events. The failures of the political leadership at Camp David had drastic consequences for Palestinians. It is against this background that the Oslo values of cooperation and negotiations faded. In their place an older Palestinian and Arab narrative re-asserted itself.

The Oslo peace process had attempted to create a framework of negotiations between Palestinian and Israelis on key questions: Israeli settlements, Jerusalem, refugees, relations with neighbours and borders. Having signed the Declaration of Principles in 1993, the parties then negotiated the withdrawal of the IDF from 68% of Gaza and the Jericho area in the West Bank and created the Palestinian Authority in May 1994. The following year the Interim Agreement paved the way for further IDF redeployment from the main Palestinian cities and the holding of the first Palestinian elections. However, before the Interim Agreement could be implemented, Israeli Prime Minister Yitzhak Rabin was assassinated. This deprived the peace process of the courageous and steady hand that Rabin exercised over the negotiations. It also destroyed the relationship that Rabin had built with Arafat.[39] Shimon Peres, his successor, did implement the agreement and the IDF left the key cities in December 1995. Presidential and Legislative elections – the freest in the Arab world – were held in January 1996. In February, Baruch Goldstein carried out the Hebron Massacre, killing 29 and wounding 125 Palestinian praying in the Mosque at the Tomb of the Patriarchs. On the same day, Hamas, which opposed the accords, began a sustained attack on Israeli civilians using suicide bombers. Nearly 50 Israelis were killed in four attacks in a seven-day period. This allowed the opposition leader Binyamin Netanyahu to argue that Oslo was making terrorism worse. In the May elections Netanyahu scored a victory over Peres and formed a right-wing government that was committed to lowering Palestinian expectations.[40] He slowed the negotiations but did remove troops from some key areas. In 1998, he lost the next election to Ehud Barak, who squandered the opportunity to reinvigorate the negotiations with the Palestinians through a forlorn attempt to reach an agreement with Syria first. By the time he arrived at Camp David in 2000, he was facing new elections, having lost a vote of confidence in the Knesset. Barak lost the elections to Ariel Sharon in early 2001. By this time the Second Intifada and the Israeli response to it was well underway.

I reflect on this history as it leads quite directly to a new course in Palestinian politics. It needs to be understood that the Oslo peace process had a contradictory impact on Palestinian society. It re-established a Palestinian political and legal order,[41] but at the same time it introduced different zones to the West Bank, which was to make life more difficult for Palestinians. The 1995 Interim Agreement divided the West Bank into area A under exclusive Palestinian control, area B under Palestinian civilian control but under Israeli security control and area C under full Israeli control.[42] In implementing these zones, a complex system of check points was created, which meant movement between them was difficult in calm times and almost impossible during periods of conflict. The areas are not continuous but fragmentary, which means that simple journeys such as going to work, taking children to school or seeing friends and relatives often become a major challenge. They are also unpredictable and sometimes close apparently randomly or make people wait for long periods. Equally being able to cross the Green Line into Israel itself has also been curtailed. Before the First Intifada (1987–1992) Palestinians could generally move freely across the West Bank and Gaza, but also in Israel. So, while the peace process created a new national dispensation, life for many Palestinians became more difficult. This meant the confidence in the peace process was tenuous. Such deprivations might have been acceptable if movement towards a Palestinian state seemed on the agenda. Once Netanyahu stalled the negotiations and then Barak showed more eagerness to suppress the second intifada than negotiate a deal with Yasser Arafat, confidence in the process slumped.

It was at this point that Palestinian political discourse began to draw on the politics that had framed the conflict from the 1940s onwards. Israel was not a genuinely legitimate state, and Jewish historic connections with the region were challenged. Palestinian intellectuals in the 1940s, 1950s and 1960s expended great energy trying to prove that Jews were either not connected to the land or that if ancient Jews existed contemporary, Jews were unrelated to them.[43] These arguments had been used extensively by the Arab states in the debates on Palestine in the United Nations in 1947.[44]

However, in the 21st century, these positions were to return within a new context. Amongst some Palestinian intellectuals there was a sense that the Palestinian national project had been defeated. Or perhaps it should be said that three Palestinian national projects had been defeated. First, in 1947–1949 the failure to prevent the creation of the Jewish state. After this setback the Palestinian national movement still retained its position that Israel was a fictitious and illegitimate state and would fail or could be easily erased and replaced by a Palestinian state. From 1949 to 1967 in the second phase of this project, it has to be pointed out that Jordan and Egypt suppressed Palestinian nationalism in the West Bank and Jordan, which they controlled as a consequence of Palestinian nationalism that focused on eliminating Israel. The creation of the PLO in 1964 was to a large extent part of an Arab League policy to manage Palestinian nationalism. After the 1967 Israel–Arab War, the PLO was to emerge with greater independence, especially when Yasser Arafat gained the leadership of the organisation in 1969. In this second project, rejection of Israel and the projection of the 'Democratic Secular State' for all British Mandate Palestine was the policy. Originally, the PLO's position was that Jews who had immigrated since 1948 would be expelled from this entity. However, this project failed too. In 1979, the Egyptians signed the Camp David treaty with Israel, which included a Palestinian protocol providing for self-rule in the West Bank and Gaza which would lead tol discussions on the eventual status of the territory.[45] Then, in 1988, after a long and sometimes violent internal struggle, the PLO issued its 'Declaration of Independence,[46] which included the policy to create a Palestinian state on any liberated area. Then, as a result of the secret Oslo negotiations came the Declaration of Principles with the third project of a state in the West Bank and Gaza with its capital in East Jerusalem. This position of the PLO was never accepted by Israel and the term Palestinian state does not appear in any of the Oslo documents. Indeed, the fact that the permanent status talks would include discussing who should control Jerusalem underlines the tenuous character of this position. Whereas the Palestinians in 1979 had denounced Egypt for its betrayal of Palestine, they now accepted the same formula, self-rule and further discussions.[47]

The Oslo process, and its implication of a Palestinian state in the occupied territories, was embraced empirically rather than ideologically. What I mean by this is that there was never an acceptance of the legitimacy of a Jewish state but rather a pragmatic realisation that Israel was unlikely to disappear and that any Palestinian state would be better than none. Not all Palestinians were to agree. This was brought home to me by an exchange at Birzeit University at the time. In September 1993, I asked a professor what he thought of the Oslo document, and he replied that he would 'rather have all of Palestine in his imagination than part of Palestine in reality'.[48] So Oslo was seen as being born of defeat and weakness. For it to succeed it would have needed real momentum and significant changes on the ground. In the event as we have seen the reverse was to be the case. In retreat the Palestinian national movement reverted the politics of the pre-Oslo era, although without the prospect of removing Israel. The rise of the campaign for the academic boycott needs to be seen in this context.

This has seen the political drift towards some problematic positions. The reconstruction of the old discourse has taken place in the distinctly less favourable conditions of an Israel with a dynamic economy, stable institutions and strategic superiority. This flies in the face of the original assumptions from the 1940s that Israel would collapse as it was in some way a fake state based on non-existent national identity. However, the latter position remains strong and is the Achilles' heel of the Palestinian national movement. Its inability to recognise the right of Jews to self-determination is what prevented Palestinians from exercising their right to self-determination in 1948. It is this position that academic boycott reinforces.

In the process there has been a move towards a de facto one-state position. Israel and Palestinian-Occupied Territory is seen as one regime, and the demand is therefore for the inclusion of the population of both territories in a common political system.[49] This has also been associated with the designation of Israel as an apartheid state and therefore recasting the conflict into a struggle for democratic rights along the lines of the political struggle in South Africa since 1912.[50] However, the conflict has from the beginning been between two national movements and its resolution requires addressing how to reconcile the aspirations of both peoples. In failing to deal with that issue, the one-state policy is also anti-democratic in that the wishes of the Palestinian people are ignored. Israelis have a state and so have a polity in which such a proposition could at least be discussed – however outlandish that would be in practice. Palestinians remain under occupation, and thus do not have the same rights as Israelis. The one-state theories and those who treat Israel and Palestinian-Occupied Territory as one regime such as Amnesty International[51] obliterate the Green Line and its significance and this at the same time undermines the Palestinian emancipation. Amnesty has drunk from the BDS poisoned well as has the academic boycott. The International Court of Justice made clear in its advisory opinion in 2004 that there were two legal regimes separated by the Green Line: Israel and Palestinian-Occupied Territory.[52] Maintaining this position is vital for the protection of Palestinian aspirations. However, in this discourse the main issue is to attack Israeli legitimacy in any way rather than advancing Palestinian liberation.

The origins on no-normalisation

Arab nationalism developed in the late 19th century at a time when the Arab world was part of the Ottoman Empire. The movement drew its inspiration from the philosophy of the European Enlightenment and projected the nation as freedom.[53] However, the European Enlightenment comes with an element of antisemitism. This can be seen in the writing of Nagib Azoury, who was much concerned with the 'universal Jewish peril'.[54] However, it would be wrong to suggest that Arab nationalism was itself antisemitic. What it did draw from Enlightenment thinkers was problematic views of the Jews. Indeed, the Enlightenment constructed the 'Jewish question' and much attention was given to trying to solve it. The Jews were seen as a hangover from a different age who clung to their traditions, culture and religion which seemed at odds with modernity. As Steven Smith has observed

> Liberalism has typically offered full and equal membership of the pol-ity to the extent that we are prepared to forgo any claims to exclusivity and loyalty to particular tradition. The very terms of Jewish emancipa-tion have meant assimilation and abandonment of an ancient identity. For Jews seeking to retain some sense of their own identity but also desiring the benefits of emancipation liberalism has been both a problem and an opportunity.[55]

This was also a theme in Marx whose work *On the Jewish Question*[56] is riddled with antisemitic comments.[57] Robert Fine and Phillip Spencer mount an elegant but unconvincing defence of Marx,[58] but cannot really obscure his position that 'the emancipation of the Jews is, in the final significance, the emancipation of mankind from Judaism'.[59] Nor can we pretend that Marx's use of the Y word and the N word are merely theoretical banter. Marx stands in the wake of Montesquieu and Voltaire, who saw the Jews as variously barbarous, crude, dishonest, antisocial and often the source of the wrongs of the world.[60] What also emerges from the Enlightenment is the way in which Jews identity slips between a race to a religious group. As with Marx's position above, Judaism informs the identity of the Jew and Judaism is seen as inimical to modernity. This ambivalent position on the Jew in the-ory was of course lost on the anti-Semites, who launched pogroms against Jews in the Russian Empire and elsewhere. It was not just religious symbols that were attacked but also Jewish homes and businesses – in other words, the targets were Jews, whatever their religiosity. Theodore Herzl understood that the issue that had to be addressed was Jewish national identity.[61] The development of modern Zionism went against the grain of the main streams of Western thought.

The boycott movement draws on this intellectual history that has been woven into Arab nationalist politics. It simply does not take Jewish iden-tity seriously. In this account, Jews have no right to self-determination simply because they are not given the attributes of a people. Thus, the state that was created in 1948 was illegitimate from the beginning. What the boycott seeks to do is to sanitise the academia by not interacting with Israeli universities. The BDS website dealing with the academic boycott is regularly campaigning against such contact. Exchanges of views between academics and students will contaminate the atmosphere. There is nothing to discuss but the elimination of Israel. In this sense, the boycott movement does not see a genuine conflict as Israelis (and the Jews) have no legitimate standing.

As I pointed out at the beginning of this chapter, the contradictory aspect of this focus on proving the illegitimacy of Israel is to displace Palestinians. The opposition to intellectual relationships between the two peoples is part of the process of preventing negotiations. The BDS programme therefore is a roadblock to any notion of peace and reconciliation. Reconciliation is impossible with the colonial apartheid state based on ethnic cleansing. As a result, the BDS programme is a programme for a conflict without end. And in this situation Palestinian self-determination becomes unobtainable. The refusal to recognise the national character of the conflict necessarily means that no solution will be found. This plays into the hands of the Israeli right and as the second Netanyahu government (2009–2021) showed, how it was possible to manage the conflict, expand Israeli settlements and increase the number of Arab states recognising Israel. Over these years Palestine became ever more isolated from the international community and from the Arab world. It also ceased to be an international priority.

As we have seen, the boycott also undermines research on the conflict, especially within the Arab world. Even in the rest of the world the pressure of the boycott has a coercive effect. In 2006, when I publicly opposed the boycott, I was removed from a journal's editorial board and I heard from my publisher that he was being pressed not to publish a book I was working on. He also advised me against speaking at a public meeting on the boycott 'as I was not Palestinian'. I did speak at the meeting and the book was published, but this experience demonstrates how the boycott movement attempts to close down academic debate. It is ironic that many of the boycott supporters oppose the International Holocaust Remembrance Alliance (IHRA) definition of antisemitism on the erroneous grounds that it prevents academic work on Israel and Palestine.[62] What I have witnessed in both Britain and the Middle East leads me to conclude the boot is on the other foot.

The appeal of the boycott is often posed in terms of the need to act due to the latest crisis in the conflict. However, it is remarkable how this has always been a consistent theme of the boycott narrative for decades. In explaining the justification for that boycott policy in 1966, Marwan Iskander writes, 'Arab states have a perfect right to exercise an economic boycott of Israel. Actions by Israel in overt violations of international agreements left no scope for constructive progress towards peace'.[63] At the time, the West Bank, including East Jerusalem and Gaza, were administered by Jordan and Egypt, respectively. This demonstrates if nothing else the consistency of boycott politics.

Conclusions

The Israeli occupation of Palestinian territory since 1967 has created an intolerable situation for Palestinians. The victory in the Six-Day War gave Israel the opportunity to implement the partition plan to which the state is committed in the Declaration of Independence. However, after the war the PLO and the Arab League's rejectionist position made that difficult. The Oslo peace process opened a new opportunity but that has been lost through default of leadership on both sides. Israel has studiously avoided responding to the 2002 Arab Peace Initiative. The Palestinian leadership walked away from promising talks with Ehud Olmert in 2008.[64] These are tragedies for both peoples. What they underline is the need for more contact between Israelis and Palestinians at every level. The role that academics can play can be invaluable in critically thinking through the roots of the conflict, its history and the politics of the negotiations. Both Israel and Palestine have built fine universities and have produced talented scholars. These can be resources for conflict resolution. They can assist in changing the atmosphere between the parties and be a source of innovative thinking of how to reconcile the rights of two peoples to self-determination. The academic boycott movement wants to turn universities into a front line of confrontation. Far from being a movement that projects non-violence, it provides the oxygen for perpetual conflict. The price will be borne not by Israel but by the Palestinians.

Notes

1 See https://bdsmovement.net/academic-boycott (accessed 13 February 2022).
2 See   https://www.birzeit.edu/en/community-affairs/institutes-centers/institute-law (accessed 13 February 2022).
3 Anne Bourlomd, *Teaching Law in Palestine: Strategies and Challenges*, Bir Zeit: Birzeit Legal Encounters, Birzet University, 1997. http://lawcenter.birzeit.edu/lawcenter/attachments/article/1509/TEACHING%20LAW%20IN%20PALESTINE.pdf (accessed 13 February 2022).
4 See http://muqtafi.birzeit.edu/en/ (accessed 10 August 2021).
5 *Legal Reform in Periods of Transition and State-building: The Case of Palestine, British Academy* 2005–6. https://www.thebritishacademy.ac.uk/funding/ba-leverhulme-small-research-grants/past-awards/2005-06/ (accessed 13 February 2022).
6 See the appeal to attend the congress at: https://davo1.de/tagungen/wocmes2.htm (accessed 6 October 2021)
7 On 9 November 2005, there were three suicide bombings in three hotels in central Amman, killing 57 people.
8 Treaty of Peace between the State of Israel and the Hashemite Kingdom of Jordan, 26 October 1994; see https://mfa.gov.il/mfa/foreignpolicy/peace/guide/pages/israel-jordan%20peace%20treaty.aspx (accessed 6 October 2021).
9 See Joel Singer, The Abraham Accords: Normalization Agreements Signed by U.A.E., Bahrain, Sudan and Morocco. *International Legal Materials*, 60(3), 448–463, 2021.

10 *The Role and Limits of Legal Discourse on Occupation in the Palestinian–Israeli Conflict*. Hebrew University of Jerusalem and Tel Aviv University, 5–7 June 1967, at: http://lawcenter.birzeit.edu/lawcenter/attachments/article/1509/TEACHING%20LAW%20IN%20PALESTINE.pdf (accessed 13 February 2022).
11 It flowed from an earlier publication: John Strawson, British (and International) Legal Foundations for the Israeli Wall: International Law and Multi-colonialism. *Palestine Yearbook of International Law*, XIII, 1–26, 2004/2005.
12 Adi Imseis, Third World Approaches to International Law and the Persistence of the Question of Palestine. *The Palestine Yearbook of International Law*, XV, 1–5, 3, 2008.
13 See https://mfa.gov.il/mfa/foreignpolicy/mfadocuments/yearbook9/pages/107%20israel-plo%20mutual%20recognition-%20letters%20and%20spe.aspx (accessed 17 February 2022).
14 See https://www.kas.de/c/document_library/get_file?uuid=a5dab26d-a2fe-dc66-8910-a13730828279&groupId=268421 (accessed 17 February 2022).
15 See Shaul Mishal and Avraham Sela, *The Palestinian Hamas: Vision, Violence and Co-existence*, New York: Columbia University Press, 2006.
16 The organisation was founded in Egypt in 1928 and now has chapters in many countries. See Richard P Mitchell, *The Society of the Muslim Brothers*, Oxford and New York: Oxford University Press, 1993.
17 Covenant of the Islamic Resistance Movement, at: https://avalon.law.yale.edu/20th_century/hamas.asp (accessed 17 February 2022).
18 PACBI, *Guidelines for the Academic Boycott*. https://bdsmovement.net/academic-boycott#guidelines (accessed 18 February 2022).
19 Ibid. https://bdsmovement.net/colonialism-and-apartheid/summary (accessed 18 February 2022).
20 Ibid. https://bdsmovement.net/colonialism-and-apartheid/summary (accessed 18 February 2022).
21 United Nations General Assembly Resolution 181(II), 29 November 1947.
22 John Strawson, *Partitioning Palestine: Legal Fundamentalism in the Palestinian–Israeli Conflict*, London and New York: Pluto Press, 2010, pp. 71–102.
23 Reuters, *Abbas Faults Arab Refusal of 1947 U.N. Palestine Plan*, 28 October 2011. https://www.reuters.com/article/us-palestinians-israel-abbas-idUSTRE79R64320111028 (accessed 18 February 2022).
24 On the position of the Communist Party of Great Britain at the time, see John Strawson, Communists for the Jewish State: British Communists and the Daily Workers in 1948. *Fathom*, September 2020. https://fathomjournal.org/communists-for-the-jewish-state-british-communists-and-the-daily-worker-in-1948/ (accessed 14 February 2022). On the Labour left and Israel, see James Vaughan, Keep Left for Israel: Tribune, Israel and the Middle East. *British Contemporary History*, 27(1), 1–21, 2013.
25 Isaac Deutscher, *The Non-Jewish Jew and Other Essays*, London and New York: Verso, 2017.
26 Pacbi Guidelines.
27 Ibid.
28 For a discussion of this issue, see Benny Morris, *The Birth of the Palestinian Refugee Problem 1947–1949*, Cambridge: Cambridge University Press, 1987.
29 It needs to be stressed that Jews were also subject to massacres and forced removal from their areas. The Etzion massacre of 129 Jews on 13 May 1948 is an example of the former and the expulsion of Jews from the Jewish Quarter of Jerusalem in 1948, on the latter. See Maoz Araryahu and Arnon Golan, Photography, Memory and Ethnic Cleansing: The Fate of the Jewish Quarter of Jerusalem 1948 – Pictorial Record. *Israel Studies* 17(2), , 62–76, 2012.

30 See John Strawson, *Partitioning Palestine*, pp. 137–151.
31 Benny Morris, *The Birth of the Palestinian Refugee Problem Revisited*, Cambridge: Cambridge University Press, 2004. This re-assessment seems to have been a result of his reaction to the Second Intifada (2000–2005). See Benny Morris, Camp David and After: An Exchange (an interview with Ehud Barak). *New York Review of Books*, 49(10), 2002.
32 See, for example, the way a boycott of Emirate Airline literary festival was posed at: https://bdsmovement.net/news/boycott-emirates-airline-festival-literature -2022 (accessed 1 March 2022).
33 John Strawson, Colonialism. *Israel Studies*, 24(2), 33–44, 2019.
34 Michael R. Fischbach, What Color Are Israeli Jews: Intersectionality, Israel Advocacy and the Changing Discourse of Color and Indigeneity. In: Uri Dorchin and Gabriella Djerrahian, *Blackness in Israel: Rethinking Racial Boundaries*, London and New York: Routledge, 2021. 236.
35 John Strawson, Why I am against the Boycott. *Engage*, 18 May 2005. https:// engageonline.wordpress.com/2005/05/05/why-i-am-against-the-boycott-by -john-strawson-18-may-2005/ (accessed October 23 2021.
36 Strawson, *Partitioning Palestine*, p. 102.
37 Ardi Imseis, The United Nations Plan for Partition of Palestine Revisited: On the Origins of Palestine's International Legal Subalternity. *Stanford Journal of International Law*, 57(1), 1–54, 2021.
38 I did have an email exchange with Imseis asking him to withdraw this accusation but to date this has not happened (emails retained by the author).
39 Jonathan Freeland has described this as the most successful assassination in history. See Jonathan Freeland, The Most Successful Assassination in History. *BBC Radio 4*, 2 November 2020, 20 h.
40 See John Strawson, Netanyahu's Oslo: Peace in the Slow Lane. *Soundings*, 8, 49–60, 1998.
41 See Nathan Brown, *Palestinian Politics after the Oslo Accords: Resuming Arab Palestine*, Berkley, Los Angeles and London: University of California Press, 2003.
42 See Geoffrey R. Watson, *The Oslo Accords: International Law and the Israeli– Palestinian Peace Agreements*, Oxford and New York: Oxford University Press, 2000, pp. 107–110.
43 See, for example, Sami Hadawi, *Bitter Harvest: Palestine 1914–1979*, Delmar NY: Caravan Books, 1979.
44 See John Strawson, *Partitioning Palestine*, pp. 110–117.
45 This was rejected by the PLO and all Arab states with the exception of Egypt. See Fayez A. Sayegh, The Camp David Agreement and the Palestine Problem. *Journal of Palestinian Studies*, 8(2), , 3–40, 1979.
46 See the English original text at https://ecf.org.il/media_items/845 (accessed 26 February 2022).
47 See Yehuda Z. Blum, From Camp David to Oslo. *Israel Law Review*, 28(2–3), 211–235, 1994.
48 Note retained by the author.
49 See, for example, Virginia Tilley, *The One-state Solution: A Breakthrough for Peace in the Israeli–Palestinian Deadlock*, Manchester: Manchester University Press, 2005.
50 The date of the creation of the African National Congress, although under a different name.
51 Amnesty International, *Israel's Apartheid against Palestinian: Cruel System of Domination and Crime against Humanity*, 1 February 2022. https://www .amnesty.org/en/documents/mde15/5141/2022/en/ (accessed 3 February 2022).

52 Legal Consequences of the Construction of a Wall in Occupied Palestinian Territory. *ICJ Reports* 2004, p. 136. https://www.icj-cij.org/public/files/case -related/131/131-20040709-ADV-01-00-EN.pdf (accessed 4 February 2022), note paragraphs 66–78 on this issue. The Court is insistent on making a distinction between the 'territory of Israel itself' and occupied land, see in particular paragraph 67.

53 See George Antonious, *The Arab Awakening: The Story of the Arab National Movement*, London: Hamish Hamilton, 1938.

54 See Negib Azoury, *Le Réveil De La Nation Arabe 1905*, Whitefish: Kessinger Publishing, 2010.

55 Steven B. Smith, Hegel and the Jewish Question: In between Ttradition and Modernity. *History of Political Thought*, 12(1), 87–106, 1991.

56 See Karl Marx, *On the Jewish Question* (1844). https://www.icj-cij.org/public/ files/case-related/131/131-20040709-ADV-01-00-EN.pdf (accessed 29 October 2021).

57 For an incisive critique, see Solomon F. Bloom, Karl Marx and the Jews. *Jewish Social Studies*, 4(1), , 3–16, 1942.

58 See Robert Fine and Philip Spencer, *Antisemitism and the Left: On the Return of the Jewish Question*, Manchester: Manchester University Press, 2017, especially pp. 31–43.

59 Karl Marx, *On the Jewish Question*.

60 See Arthur Herzenberg, *The French Enlightenment and the Jews*, New York: Columbia University Press, 1968.

61 See Theodore Herzl, *Die Judenstaat*, Leipzig und Vien: M Breitenstein Verlas-Buchhandling, 1896.

62 See David Hirsh, *Contemporary Left Antisemitism*, London and New York: Routledge, 2018, pp. 135–153.

63 Marwan Iskander, *The Arab Boycott of Israel*, Beirut: Palestine Liberation Organization Research Centre, 1966, p. 55.

64 Josef Federman, Abbas admits he rejected 2008 peace offer from Olmert. *The Times of Israel*, 15 November 2015.

7

THE LEGAL CONSTRUCTION OF JEWISH IDENTITY AS A 'PROTECTED CHARACTERISTIC' THROUGH AN EXAMINATION OF *FRASER V UCU* (2013), *PARKER V SHEFFIELD HALLAM UNIVERSITY* (2016) AND THE REPORT OF THE EHRC INTO ANTISEMITISM IN THE LABOUR PARTY (2020)[1]

Lesley Klaff

What is Jewish identity in English law?

The question of Jewish identity has preoccupied people for centuries. Are Jews a race, a religion, an ethnic minority or all three? It may surprise readers to learn that the question of Jewish identity was settled in English law as early as 1983 in the case of *Mandla v Dowell Lee*.[2] This case decided that Jews are defined as both a 'racial' and an 'ethnic group', as well as a religious group, for the purposes of the Race Relations Act 1976.[3] This Act provided protection from direct and indirect discrimination in education, employment, training, housing and the provision of goods, facilities and services to members of a 'racial group' but excluded religious groups from its protection as a matter of deliberate legislative policy.[4] This meant that someone claiming protection from discrimination under the Act had to be classed as a member of a 'racial group' to get the law's protection. The Act defined 'racial group' in section 3 (1) as 'a group of persons defined by reference to colour, race, nationality or ethnic or national origins'. The main issue in the *Mandla* case was whether Sikhs were protected by the Race Relations Act as a 'racial group', and it was in seeking to determine the question of Sikh identity for the purposes of the Act that both the Court of Appeal and the House of Lords said that Jews constituted a 'racial group' for the purposes of section 3 (1) of the Act. This was because Jews could be 'defined by reference to their ethnic origins'.[5]

DOI: 10.4324/9781003222477-8

Although the Court of Appeal and the House of Lords came to the same conclusion about the nature of Jewish identity in English law, they did so for different reasons. For Lord Denning in the Court of Appeal, Jews were 'defined by reference to their ethnic origins' for the purposes of the statutory definition of 'racial group' because they were to be distinguished from non-Jews by a 'common racial characteristic'. The 'common racial characteristic' that Jews shared was descent, however remotely, from a Jewish ancestor. This also made Jews members of an 'ethnic group'. He reasoned:

> Why are 'the Jews' given as the best-known example of 'ethnic grouping'? What is their special characteristic which distinguishes them from non-Jews? To my mind, it is a racial characteristic ... When it is said of the Jews that they are an 'ethnic group', it means that the group as a whole share a common characteristic which is a racial characteristic. It is that they are descended, however remotely, from a Jewish ancestor ... There is nothing in their culture of language or literature to mark out Jews in England from others. The Jews in England share all of these characteristics equally with the rest of us. Apart from religion, the one characteristic which is different is a racial characteristic.[6]

The House of Lords, on the other hand, did not require a racial characteristic to determine whether a group of people constitute an 'ethnic group' for the purposes of the Race Relations Act. Instead, the law lords unanimously laid down a test which placed emphasis on the socially determined historical identity of the group, and on the group's own belief in its historical antecedents. Lord Fraser enunciated the criteria for 'ethnic group' according to several characteristics, two of which were 'essential': (1) a long-shared history of which the group is conscious as distinguishing it from other groups and the memory of which keeps it alive; and (2) a cultural tradition of its own, including family and social customs and manners, often but not necessarily associated with religious observance.[7] Other relevant features of ethnicity, according to Lord Fraser, included a common geographical origin, a common language, a common literature, a common religion and being a minority within a larger community.[8] In enunciating this test for 'ethnic group', Lord Fraser quoted with approval the test laid down in the New Zealand case of *King-Ansell v Police* (1979), which ruled that Jews constitute an 'ethnic' group for the purposes of the New Zealand Race Relations Act 1971:[9]

> a group is identifiable in terms of its ethnic origins if it is a segment of the population distinguished from others by sufficient combination of shared customs, beliefs, traditions and characteristics derived from a common or presumed common past, even if not drawn from what in biological

terms is a common racial stock. It is that combination which gives them an historically determined social identity in their own eyes and in the eyes of those outside the group. They have a distinct social identity based not simply on group cohesion and solidarity but also on their belief as to their historical antecedents... *the real test is whether the individual or the group regard themselves and are regarded by others in the community as having a particular historical identity in terms of their colour or their racial, national, or ethnic origins.* (emphasis added)[10]

In declaring New Zealand Jews an ethnic group, Woodhouse J. explicitly recognised Jewish peoplehood. He said that there was a

depth of Jewish history and the unbroken adherence of Jews to culture, traditions, and a mutually intelligible language, as well as a religion, *so that they have maintained a distinct and continuous identity as a people for longer perhaps than any other than the Egyptians* ... undoubtedly Jews in New Zealand are a group of persons with ethnic origins of the clearest kind. (emphasis added)[11]

It is notable that both the Court of Appeal and the House of Lords thought that 'ethnic origins' had been included by Parliament in the statutory definition of 'racial group' to protect Jews from antisemitism. Noting that '[W]hen Hitler and the Nazis so fiendishly exterminated "the Jews" it was because of their racial characteristics and not because of their religion'[12] Lord Denning went on to say:

I have no doubt that, in using the words "ethnic origins", Parliament had in mind primarily the Jews. There must be no discrimination against the Jews in England. Anti-Semitism must not be allowed. It has produced great evils elsewhere. It must not be allowed here.[13]

Likewise, Lord Fraser noted, 'it is inconceivable that Parliament would have legislated against racial discrimination intending that the protection should not apply ... (above all) to Jews'.[14]

Over the years, *Mandla v Dowell Lee* and *King-Ansell v Police* have been consistently cited as authority for the definition of 'ethnic group', and for the recognition that Jews are legally classified as a 'racial' and an 'ethnic group', as well as a religious group, for the purposes of English anti-discrimination law.

Why does Jewish identity in English law matter?

The legal construction of Jewish identity is important because it determines the legal protection that Jews are given if they are the victims of antisemitism. With respect to the offence of incitement under the Public Order Act

1986, for example, a higher degree of protection is given to those who are legally defined as a 'racial group' as opposed to those merely defined as a 'religious group'. This is because the Act criminalises acts intended *or* likely to stir up hatred against a 'racial group' and provides no freedom of expression defence to racial hatred.[15] On the other hand, the Act only criminalises acts *intended* to stir up religious hatred.[16] Intentional incitement is more difficult to prove than the lower 'likelihood' standard and a freedom of expression defence is available for the expression of religious hatred to allow for discussion, criticism, antipathy, dislike, ridicule, insult etc. of a particular religion and its adherents. Incitement against Jews can be prosecuted as either racial hatred or as religious hatred, depending on the facts of the case.

With respect to the Equality Act 2010, which provides protection from discrimination, harassment and victimisation in the public sector – schools, universities, hospitals, local councils, transport providers, government departments, trade unions and political parties, for instance – the legal construction of Jewish identity as a 'protected characteristic' is important for deciding harassment claims brought by Jewish individuals or groups occasioned by antizionist antisemitism. This is because of the way that the unlawful harassment section, section 26, of the Equality Act is defined. As discussed in the following sections of this chapter, antizionist antisemitism will only be found to constitute unlawful harassment of someone who identifies as Jewish under section 26 of the Equality Act, where the decision-maker, whether it be a court, a tribunal or a statutory body, finds that the antizionist antisemitism engages their 'protected characteristic'. Before considering this point in more detail through a discussion of *Fraser v University and College Union, Parker v Sheffield Hallam University* and the Report of the Equality and Human Rights Commission into Antisemitism in the Labour Party, it is necessary to explain the meaning of three key terms that will be used in the discussion. These are 'antizionist antisemitism', 'protected characteristic' and 'unlawful harassment' under section 26 Equality Act 2010. A brief explanation of the free speech implications of a claim for unlawful antisemitic harassment under section 26 will also be provided.

What is meant by 'antizionist antisemitism'?

Antizionist antisemitism is the chief mode of today's antisemitism. It is an expression that purports to be criticism of Israel and Zionism, but which in fact goes beyond legitimate criticism and crosses the line into demonisation and delegitimisation. A good guide to the types of expression that can constitute antizionist antisemitism, depending on context, are to be found in the examples relating to Israel in the working definition of antisemitism published by the International Holocaust Remembrance Alliance (IHRA) in 2016. These include comparing contemporary Israeli policy to that of the Nazis, applying the images and symbols of traditional antisemitism (e.g. the blood libel) to Israel, denying the Jewish people the right to self-determination, applying double standards by expecting a behaviour of Israel that is not expected of any other state and holding Jews collectively responsible for the actions of the State of Israel.[17] Philip Spencer's chapter in this book discusses and elucidates antizionist antisemitism in detail.

'Protected characteristic' under the Equality Act 2010

The Equality Act 2010 was passed to replace and bring together all existing anti-discrimination legislation, including the Race Relations Act 1976, into one statute, and to strengthen the existing law on equality. The Act gives people legal protection from discrimination, harassment and victimisation in the workplace and wider society in relation to nine personal characteristics. These are age, disability, gender reassignment, marriage and civil partnership, pregnancy and maternity, race, religion or belief, sex and sexual orientation. These nine personal characteristics are known under the Act as 'protected characteristics'. Jews are protected under the Act as both a 'race' and a 'religion or belief', following the decision in *Mandla v Dowell Lee*. Section 9 of the Equality Act defines 'racial group' in exactly the same way as section 3 of the Relations Act 1976 did, as 'a group of persons defined by reference to colour, race, nationality or ethnic or national origins'.

'Unlawful harassment' under section 26 Equality Act 2010

Harassment occurs where someone experiences behaviour that makes them feel intimidated, humiliated or degraded, or that creates a hostile environment for them. Section 26 Equality Act defines 'harassment' as 'unwanted conduct related to a relevant protected characteristic'. To qualify as 'harassment', the conduct must 'violate the victim's dignity or create an intimidating, hostile, degrading, or offensive environment' for them. In deciding whether the conduct has had that effect, the decision-maker must take into account the victim's perception under section 26 (4) (a). This is a subjective test which focuses on the victim's realm of experience. The decision-maker must then take into account all the other circumstances of the case under section 26 (4) (b) and consider whether it was reasonable for the conduct to have had that effect under section 26 (4) (c). This is an objective test which requires the decision-maker to consider whether the victim's perception is reasonable given all the circumstances. A claim under section 26 is frequently referred to as a claim for 'hostile environment harassment'.

Unlawful harassment and free speech implications

In any claim for unlawful antisemitic harassment under section 26 Equality Act 2010, the decision-maker must consider the free speech implications of the claim. The right to freedom of expression is protected by Article 10 of the European Convention on Human Rights (ECHR) and section 3 of the Human Rights Act 1998, which brings the ECHR directly into UK domestic law. In general, conduct or speech should not be regarded as harassment and no action should be taken on it if this would breach the Article 10 right to freedom of expression of the person whose conduct or speech is in question. In making this kind of decision, the right to freedom of expression must be weighed against any harmful effects of the conduct or speech, given the context in which the conduct or speech occurred. Only if the decision-maker is satisfied that the harmful effects of the conduct or speech in that specific context outweigh the freedom of expression right of the person concerned, can the conduct or speech be found to constitute harassment. However, even where conduct or speech is within the scope of the right to freedom of expression in Article 10, it may still be sanctioned or restricted where it is proportionate to do so. This is by virtue of Article 10 (2) which provides that the right to freedom of expression under Article 10 may, since it carries with it duties and responsibilities, be subject to such formalities, conditions, restrictions, or penalties as are prescribed by law and are necessary in a democratic society for the protection of the rights of others. Accordingly, in the case of harassment, conduct or speech may be regarded as unlawful, and action may be taken on it, where this is proportionate to protect the rights of others not to have their dignity violated or to be exposed to an intimidatory, hostile, degrading, humiliating or offensive environment.

The following discussion of *Fraser v The University and College Union* (2013), *Parker v Sheffield Hallam University* (2016) and the EHRC Report into Antisemitism in the Labour Party 2020 will focus on the statutory definition of 'harassment' and the legal construction of Jewish identity as a 'protected characteristic'. These three cases have been chosen because they are the only available examples to date of a tribunal and two statutory bodies deciding the question of whether antizionist antisemitism can unlawfully harass a Jewish complainant under section 26 Equality Act. As such, they demonstrate three stages in the development of the legal construction of Jewish identity as a 'protected characteristic'.

Jewish identity as a 'protected characteristic': *Fraser v The University & College Union* (2013)

This case, which was decided by the Central London Employment Tribunal in 2013, took a step back from the judicial recognition in *Mandla v Dowell Lee* that there is an ethnic and national dimension to Jewish identity. The employment tribunal constructed the 'protected characteristic', that is, the 'race' 'religion or belief' of the Jewish complainant under section 26 Equality Act to deny any attachment to Israel and the Zionist project.

The complainant, Ronnie Fraser, was a retired mathematics lecturer and a member of the University and College Union (UCU). In August 2011, he filed a claim against the union alleging 'hostile environment harassment' under the harassment provision of the Equality Act, section 26, and under section 57, which provides that a trade association such as the UCU must not harass a member. Fraser alleged that the union had harassed him as a Jewish member by engaging in a course of 'unwanted' antisemitic 'conduct' that manifested itself in acts and omissions informed by hostility to Israel and the Zionist project, in other words, by antizionist antisemitism. The ten grounds of his complaint were: (1) annual boycott resolutions against Israel and no other country in the world; (2) the conduct of debates at which these resolutions were discussed; (3) the moderating of the activists' lists and the penalising of anti-boycott activists; (4) the failure to engage with members who raised concerns about antisemitism and the failure to address resignations citing antisemitism as the reason; (5) the dismissive response to the 2006 *Report of the All Party Parliamentary Inquiry into Anti-Semitism*; (6) the failure to meet the Organisation for Security and Co-operation in Europe's special representative on antisemitism; (7) the hosting of South African trade unionist, Bongani Masuku, after he had been found guilty of antisemitic hate speech by the South African Human Rights Commission; (8) the dismissive attitude towards the Equality and Human Rights Commission; (9) the repudiation of the European Monitoring Centre on Racism and Xenophobia's (EUMC) working definition of antisemitism; and (10) the response to Fraser's 'letter before action'. In March 2013, the Employment Tribunal unanimously dismissed all ten grounds of Fraser's complaint as unfounded and mostly time barred.[18]

For Fraser to have been successful in his complaint against the UCU, the tribunal would have needed to recognise that Israel and Zionism are aspects of contemporary Jewish identity through its construction of 'protected characteristic' in section 26 Equality Act. This is because of the way that 'harassment' is defined in section 26 as 'unwanted conduct *related to* a protected characteristic, which has the purpose or effect of violating a person's dignity' etc. In other words, there must be a nexus between the 'unwanted conduct' complained of and the complainant's 'protected characteristic'.

Given the judicial dicta in *Mandla v Dowell Lee* as to why Jews are defined as members of a 'racial group' for the purposes of anti-discrimination law, one would expect the connection between being Jewish and the Jewish ancestral homeland, Israel, to be self-evident to the employment tribunal. Among the determining criteria for membership in a 'racial group' enunciated by the House of Lords were 'a long-shared history', 'a cultural tradition which includes religious observance' and '*a common geographical origin*, or descent from a small number of common ancestors' (emphasis added).[19] Moreover, the test enunciated in the New Zealand case of *Kings-Ansell v Police*, and repeated with approval in the House of Lords, was whether the individual or the group *regard themselves and are regarded by others in the community as having a particular historical identity* in terms of their colour or their racial, national, or ethnic origins (emphasis added).[20] Fraser's lawyer, Anthony Julius, explained Jewish identity to the tribunal as follows:

> The complainant has a strong attachment to Israel. This attachment is a non-contingent and a rationally intelligible aspect of his Jewish identity. It is an aspect that is of his race, and or religion or belief ... The fact that not all Jewish people have the same views does not prevent it from being an aspect of the protected characteristic. A significant proportion of Jewish people have an attachment to Israel which is an aspect of their self-understanding as Jews, or Jewish identity.
>
> *(para. 18)*

The tribunal accepted that the 'related to' test in section 26 denotes a 'loose associative' connection between the behaviour under consideration and the protected characteristic, and that it does not require a 'causative' connection. This means that the 'unwanted conduct' does not need to be 'because of' the 'protected characteristic' but 'broadly related to' it. Acknowledging the wide interpretation Parliament intended by using the words 'related to' in the statutory section, the Tribunal declared that '[I]t seems to us that the practise of repeatedly criticising the actions and policies of the United States could certainly be seen as "related to" race' (para. 35).

Nevertheless, the tribunal went on to conclude that '[I]t seems to us that a belief in the Zionist project or an attachment to Israel ... is not intrinsically a part of Jewishness' (para. 150). In other words, the tribunal refused to find any 'loose associative connection' between Israel and Zionism and being Jewish. This amounted to a construction of 'protected characteristic' for the purposes of the Equality Act that denied the racial, ethnic and even the religious dimensions of being Jewish that had been recognised in *Mandla v Dowell Lee* and the New Zealand case of *Kings-Ansell v Police*. Indeed, dicta by Woodhouse J in the *Kings-Ansell* case had explicitly acknowledged Jewish peoplehood.[21]

The tribunal's conclusion that there was no nexus between Zionism and Israel, and Fraser's Jewish religious and racial status, was based on its characterisation of 'Zionism' and 'antizionism' as mere 'political' ideologies which are unrelated to, and independent of, a person's race or religion. Such characterisation amounted to a wholesale acceptance of the argument advanced by the UCU that many different positions are taken on the Israel–Palestine conflict, and specifically on the academic boycott of Israel, and that these are political positions that tend to be associated with distinct groups. As Jews are represented in many such groups, it therefore follows that any disagreements between the groups are political and do not touch on any 'protected characteristic', that is, on any religious or racial identity under the Equality Act (para. 54).

The tribunal's acceptance of the UCU's position was because some of the pro-boycott witnesses called by the UCU were Jewish, while some of the anti-boycott witnesses called by Fraser were Christian, Muslim or some other faith. Referring to a pro-boycott member of the UCU as Jewish (para. 130), the tribunal said:

> The Claimant's main contention is that the conduct of which he complains was inherently discriminatory in that it consisted of acts and omissions concerning the conflict between Israel and Palestine and so related to *his* (although of course not every Jew's) Jewish identity and, as such, *his* Jewish race and/or religion or belief.
>
> *(para. 49, emphasis in original)*

It was then a short step for the tribunal to conclude that 'a belief in the Zionist project and an attachment to Israel is not intrinsically a part of Jewishness' (para. 150).

In coming to this conclusion, the tribunal ignored Julius's argument that hostility to Israel engages Fraser's protected characteristic. Julius explained to the tribunal that the majority of British Jews have an affinity with Israel and the Zionist project because they regard Israel as their ancestral homeland and assume an obligation to support it and to ensure its survival. This affinity does not equate to unconditional or unstinting support for the government of Israel or its policies, but rather amounts to a sense of connection with, or an affiliation with, Israel and a sense of its importance in the context of Jewish history and the persecution of the Jewish people. It is for this reason that hostility to Israel engages Jews not only in conventional political terms, but also because Israel is an aspect of their identity. It is in this way, Julius argued, that hostility to Israel engages Fraser's protected characteristic.[22]

The tribunal further ignored Julius's argument that the fact that a range of views on Israel exist within the body of Anglo-Jewry does not override the argument that Fraser's protected characteristic is engaged when Israel is demonised. Julius countered the UCU's 'range of views' argument by explaining that the existence of a group of Jews who are hostile to Israel and Zionism is not evidence for the proposition that an attachment to Israel is not an aspect of contemporary Jewish identity. These Jews are either marginal or non-normative, or the form their protected characteristic takes is in their hostility to Israel or Zionism.[23]

In rejecting Julius's argument that Fraser's protected characteristic is engaged when Israel is demonised because an attachment to Israel is an aspect of Jewish identity, the tribunal said it could find no authority for the proposition that legal protection also attaches to 'a particular affinity or sentiment not inherent in the protected characteristic but said to be commonly held by members of the protected group' (para. 18). There was no relevant authority because the Fraser case was the first of its kind under section 26 Equality Act 2010. It was within the power of the tribunal to stipulate that an 'affinity or sentiment' fell within the scope of the protected characteristic because of the ample evidence that Jews regard themselves as having a particular historical identity that connects them to the land of Israel. Moreover, this is the reason the law defines Jews as a 'racial group' following the test laid down in *Mandla v Dowell Lee*.

It can only be assumed that the tribunal's unwillingness to find the required nexus, or 'loose associative connection', between Israel and Fraser's Jewish religious and racial status arose because of its strong dislike of Fraser's claim. It characterised the claim as a dishonest attempt to play the 'antisemitism card' to abrogate free political speech in the union for the sole purpose of shielding Israel from criticism. In ruling against Fraser, the tribunal said, '[W]e greatly regret that the case was ever brought. At heart, it represents an *impermissible attempt to achieve a political end by litigious means*. It would be very unfortunate if an exercise of this sort were ever repeated' (para. 178, emphasis added), and '[W]e are troubled by the implications of the claim because underlying it we sense a worrying disregard for pluralism, tolerance and freedom of expression' (para. 179). Evidence of the tribunal's dislike of Fraser's claim is elaborated in the section on *Parker v Sheffield Hallam University*, below.

In sum, by ruling that Zionism is a political ideology or movement that is unconnected to race or religion, and that Israel is not intrinsically a part of Jewishness, the tribunal gave permission to antizionists to characterise Zionism as a uniquely racist ideology, and Israel as a uniquely evil state which ought not to exist, while denying Jews the prospect of a successful claim for antisemitic harassment under section 26 Equality Act. Fortunately, the decision did not set a precedent because the tribunal was only a trial court, and the case was never appealed.

Jewish identity as a 'protected characteristic': *Parker v Sheffield Hallam University* (2016)

The Office of the Independent Adjudicator for Higher Education (OIA) was the next body to address the issue of Jewish identity through the construction of 'protected characteristic' in the Equality Act 2010. The OIA is a statutory body that was set up under the Higher Education Act 2004 to review the handling of student complaints by universities. It conducts such reviews in accordance with the law and relevant sector guidance but does not act as a court. The case was thus not a court case but a case involving a student complaint that was pursued within Sheffield Hallam University and then appealed to the OIA.

As with *Fraser v UCU*, the complaint was brought under section 26 Equality Act 2010 for antisemitic 'hostile environment harassment' of a Jewish student occasioned by anti-Israel activity on campus. This case therefore raised the issue of whether disproportionate hostility to Israel, or antizionist antisemitism, can constitute the harassment of someone who identifies as Jewish under section 26 Equality Act 2010.

The complaint, which was brought in May 2015 by a Jewish student named Parker, alleged that Sheffield Hallam University tolerated anti-Israel activity on campus that crossed the line from legitimate criticism of Israel into antisemitism and harassment. It listed Facebook posts and tweets by the University's Student Palestine Society (PalSoc) that, Parker argued, went beyond the right to free speech and created a hostile environment for him. These posts accused Israel and Israelis of genocide, deliberately killing Palestinian children, deliberately killing other Palestinian civilians, war crimes, atrocities, using chemical weapons, ethnic cleansing, inhumanity, cruelty, behaving like Nazis, sexual and other abuse of Palestinian children (including abduction and human trafficking), stealing Palestinian organs, being racists and fascists and rejoicing in Palestinian deaths.[24] For example, one specific social media post listed in the complaint was:

> One of the most sophisticated, nuclear powered, technological (sic) advance (sic) armies in the world is committing monstrous atrocities; it has dropped bombs on disability shelters killing those seeking safety within, it has made targeted airstrikes on family homes killing entire families in cold blood, it is slaughtering children who are arriving to hospital "in bits".
>
> *(C. para. 68)*

Parker complained that these posts contributed to 'an intimidating campus climate' (C. para. 47) and, inter alia, that he felt 'intimidated and afraid to mention Israel on campus or to wear my Star of David or my skull cap for fear of being picked on' (C. para. 188).

However, despite an evidence file spanning 154 pages, Sheffield Hallam University dismissed Parker's complaint in February 2016.[25] The University found that evidence of antisemitism from Parker's complaint was 'not conclusive' and suggested that Parker was conflating criticism of Israel with anti-Jewish prejudice (C. R. para. 16). The University categorised all PalSoc's social media output as merely 'controversial and provocative' and as 'offensive to some people, in particular, those who have strong opposing views about the issues involved' (C.R. para. 18).

Parker appealed to the OIA in May 2016, and it handed down its decision in October 2016 in a document known as the OIA Complaint Outcome. The OIA decided that it was not satisfied that the University engaged adequately with Parker's complaint that certain tweets and posts by PalSoc had led him to feel harassed and intimidated, and upheld this part of his appeal as 'Justified'.[26]

The decision of the OIA marked a welcome step forward in the development of the legal construction of Jewish identity to include an attachment to Israel. It did this without explicitly discussing the 'related to' requirement in the definition of 'harassment' in section 26 Equality Act. In other words, there was no explicit discussion of the connection between Israel and Jewish religious or racial status. The nexus was simply assumed to exist.

In coming to its finding that it was reasonable for certain expressions of hostility to Israel to engage the 'protected characteristic' of a student who identifies as Jewish, the OIA discussed three issues. These were free speech, the Macpherson principle and the definition of antisemitism. As we shall see, the reasoning of the OIA was very different to that of the *Fraser* tribunal.

Free speech

On the issue of free speech, the OIA noted that special legal status applies to the promotion of free speech and freedom of enquiry within universities and colleges under the Education (No. 2) Act 1986 and the Education Reform Act 1998. This, said the OIA, requires universities to be tolerant of the expression of a wide range of views, and this includes the students' right to criticise a particular political regime or to express views on a contentious topic. But, noted the OIA, this duty to do all that is reasonably practicable to ensure freedom of speech within the law has to be balanced against the universities' responsibility to ensure that staff, students and visitors to the university are protected from discrimination, harassment and victimisation and to foster good relations by having due regard to the need to tackle prejudice and promote understanding. This is by virtue of section 149 Equality Act 2010.

While the OIA recognised that there were competing rights, such as the right of the Jewish student complainant not to be harassed, that had to be balanced against the right to freedom of speech, the Fraser tribunal had done no such thing. On the contrary, it had implicitly characterised Fraser's case as one of Jewish particularism versus the universal right to freedom of expression and concluded that 'the narrow interests of [Fraser] must give way to the *wider public interest* in ensuring that freedom of expression is safeguarded' (para. 156, emphasis added). This reasoning suggests that freedom of expression cases will, and indeed should, always work against the Jewish complainant. This approach contradicts the spirit of anti-discrimination law, whose broad definition of 'racial group' was designed to cast the net of protection as widely as possible to protect those in society who are vulnerable to discrimination.[27] This must include Jews. As noted by Lord Denning and Lord Fraser in *Mandla v Dowell Lee,* it is inconceivable that Parliament did not intend to protect Jews from antisemitism. It is fortunate that the Fraser tribunal's decision had no precedent value and that the OIA did not feel compelled to follow it.

The Macpherson principle

Further, unlike the Fraser tribunal, the OIA stressed the importance of the Macpherson principle in relation to the subjective test in the statutory definition of 'harassment' in section 26 Equality Act. The subjective test relates to section 26 (4) (a), which provides that the court must take into account the victim's perception in deciding whether the unwanted conduct has violated the victim's dignity etc., so as to qualify as unlawful harassment. The Macpherson principle is highly relevant to the subjective test for harassment as it states that a racist incident should be defined by the victim.[28] This means that when a person reports an experience of racism, their perception of the experience is an important consideration. They should be listened to carefully, and assumed to be right, until an informed judgment can be made. As the OIA stated, 'When deciding whether harassment has occurred, the perception of the person who is the recipient of the behaviour is of particular importance' (OIA para. 35). In addition, the OIA noted that Sheffield Hallam University's definition of 'harassment' in its anti-harassment policy echoed the definition in section 26 Equality Act, and that the University's procedure highlighted the importance of the recipient's perception of the behaviour, whether the harassment was intended by the perpetrator or not (OIA para. 36).

The OIA accordingly paid particular attention to the impact of PalSoc's social media activity on Parker. He had stated in his complaint that he felt intimidated and afraid to mention Israel on campus or to wear his skull cap for fear of being picked on, and that he could not be open about his Jewish identity. He had also felt unable to attend lectures during Israel Apartheid Week in 2013 and 2014 because of a flare up of a health condition caused by stress and anxiety. The OIA quoted from Parker's complaint:

Hate speech is recognised by the fear which it generates, and I feel threatened by the campaigning of PalSoc and in particular its output on Facebook and Twitter, which are based on lies and half-truths about Jews, invoking blood-libel motifs, stereotypes and defamations on campus and online, creating a threatening mob mentality... The nature of the behaviour that PalSoc engaged in ... has been threatening, abusive, and insulting and contributes to an intimidating campus climate where students feel they cannot speak their mind.

(OIA para. 37)

The OIA then said,

[I]n our view, the above statements required the University to give careful consideration to whether, *as a student identifying as Jewish*, PalSoc's activities had caused harassment to Mr Parker by violating his dignity, or creating an intimidating, hostile, degrading, humiliating, or offensive environment for him.

(OIA para. 38, emphasis added)

Further, in addressing the University's finding that Parker's complaint conflated antisemitism with antizionism, and that PalSoc's activities were merely 'controversial and provocative', the OIA said:

We accept that there is often a fine line between provocative or emotive material which some people might find offensive, and material which might reasonably cause a person to feel harassed. We also accept that none of the tweets or Facebook posts highlighted by Mr Parker in his evidence file was directed at him personally; nor does any appear overtly to refer to Jews or the Jewish faith ... We are not satisfied, however, that the University properly turned its mind to the question of whether Mr Parker *as a student identifying as Jewish was likely to have felt harassed as a result of some of the material.*

(OIA para. 40, emphasis added)

In contrast, the employment tribunal denied Fraser's subjective experience of antisemitism within the UCU. When focusing on his experience as required by the subjective test in section 26 (4) (a), the tribunal gave the statutory language a strict, narrow construction, and declared that an effect amounting to 'harassment' had not been made out by Fraser, who used words such as 'upsetting', 'disappointment' 'troubled' 'hurt', 'saddened and amazed' to describe the effect the union's conduct had on him.[29] The tribunal thought that these words indicated 'minor upsets' caused by 'trivial acts' rather than antisemitic harassment.[30] Further, the Fraser tribunal did not consider the application of the Macpherson principle at all. The only reference made to Macpherson was when the tribunal dismissed as 'glib' and 'unhelpful' the evidence given by parliamentarian Denis MacShane, who had been called as a witness for Fraser. The tribunal remarked, 'For Dr MacShane, it seemed that all answers lay in the *Macpherson Report* (the effect of which he appeared to misunderstand)'.[31] Disregarding the application of the Macpherson principle makes it unlikely that an effect amounting to harassment will be made out where a Jewish complainant complains about antizionist antisemitism and was consistent with the tribunal's refusal to find a connection between Israel and Jewish identity.

The definition of antisemitism

Finally, on the issue of antisemitism, the OIA noted that one of the outcomes that Parker had sought as a result of his complaint was Sheffield Hallam University's adoption of the European Union Monitoring Centre on Racism & Xenophobia's (EUMC) working definition of antisemitism, as a means to identify antisemitism on campus.[32] The University had dismissed Parker's request as a 'policy matter' which was beyond the scope of his complaint. The OIA decided that the University ought reasonably to have engaged with the EUMC definition in its consideration of Parker's complaint because

> [i]t was, in our view, relevant to the question of whether material which purportedly was criticising the (alleged) actions of the Israeli state 'crossed the line' from being merely offensive or inflammatory to Mr Parker, to amounting or potentially amounting to material which might reasonably be perceived to be antisemitic and likely to cause Mr Parker, as a student identifying as Jewish, to experience harassment.
>
> *(OIA para. 42)*

This reasoning amounts to an explicit endorsement by the OIA of a definition of antisemitism that recognises that hostility to Israel can, depending on the context, be antisemitic. This implicitly recognises Israel as an aspect of contemporary Jewish identity.

The Fraser tribunal, on the other hand, refused to rule on a meaning or definition of antisemitism on the grounds that there were legitimately held differences of opinion on what constitutes antisemitism. The tribunal reasoned that the range of views presented to the tribunal, including where the line should be drawn in relation to when criticism of Israel becomes antisemitic, is the 'stuff of political debate'.[33] The tribunal's refusal to settle on a definition of antisemitism was curious given the fact that Fraser's claim was a claim for unlawful *antisemitic* harassment. As the House of Commons Home Affairs Committee reported, '[I]t is extremely difficult to examine the issue of antisemitism without considering what sorts of actions, language and discourse are captured by the term'.[34] Given the Tribunal's attitude to Fraser's case, one might conclude that its refusal to rule on a definition of antisemitism, and in particular on the EUMC Definition which Fraser urged on it, amounted to a denial of Israel-related antisemitism. This again was consistent with the tribunal's refusal to find a connection between Israel and Jewish identity.

Jewish identity as a 'protected characteristic': the report of the Equality and Human Rights Commission into antisemitism in the Labour Party 2020

The Equality and Human Rights Commission's (EHRC) legal construction of Jewish identity as a 'protected characteristic' gave explicit recognition to Jewish peoplehood in a way that was denied by the Fraser tribunal and only implicitly acknowledged by the OIA. The EHRC is a statutory body with powers granted by the Equality Act 2006 to enforce compliance with the Equality Act 2010.

The Commission carried out an investigation into the Labour Party under section 20 (1) (a) of the 2006 Act following complaints made to it about antisemitism in the Labour Party by Campaign Against Antisemitism and the Jewish Labour Movement. The purpose of the investigation, which was launched in May 2019, was to decide whether the Labour Party had committed unlawful acts of discrimination, victimisation or harassment against its Jewish members under the Equality Act 2010. The Commission reported on October 29, 2020, that the Labour Party had unlawfully harassed its members contrary to section 101 (4) (a) of the Equality Act related to race (Jewish ethnicity) through the acts of its agents (p. 102).[35] The EHRC also found that the Labour Party had unlawfully indirectly discriminated against its Jewish members related to the Party's policy or practice of political interference in antisemitism complaints and of failing to provide adequate training for those handling complaints of antisemitism (p. 102). However, this discussion will focus solely on the Commission's finding of harassment to consider the legal construction of Jewish identity.

As with the OIA in the Parker appeal, the EHRC did not discuss the 'related to' requirement in the definition of 'harassment' in section 26 Equality Act and did not explicitly consider the connection between Israel and Jewish religious or racial status. The nexus between Israel and Jewish racial status, or ethnicity, was simply taken for granted. The Commission said, '[O]ur investigation focused on whether the Labour Party committed unlawful acts of discrimination or victimisation relating to race or religion, or *harassment relating to race*' (p. 21, emphasis added). There was no explanation for the Commission's distinction between race and religion, but it implicitly treated Jewish people as an ethnic or national group and Judaism as a religion, as was confirmed when the Commission stated, 'Protected racial characteristic means Jewish ethnicity. Protected religion or belief characteristic means

Judaism' (p. 21). This permitted the Commission to focus only on the racial dimension of being Jewish for the purpose of considering 'harassment' under section 26 Equality Act. It accordingly defined harassment as 'unwanted conduct *related to race*, which has the purpose or effect of violating a person's dignity, or creates an intimidating, hostile, degrading, or offensive environment for them' (p. 21, emphasis added).

Through its construction of 'protected characteristic' as Jewish 'race' or 'ethnicity' for the purposes of 'harassment' under section 26, the Commission was able to recognise antisemitic harassment occasioned by expressions of hostility to Israel, or antizionist antisemitism. In so doing, it addressed the question of free speech, the Macpherson principle and the definition of antisemitism.

Free speech

Having explained the law on freedom of expression under Article 10 of the European Convention on Human Rights and section 3 of the Human Rights Act 1998, the Commission went on to note that while speech does not lose the protection of Article 10 just because it is offensive, provocative or insulting, the ECHR does not protect racist speech. This is because such speech negates, or is incompatible with, the fundamental values of tolerance, social peace and non-discrimination guaranteed by Article 17 of the ECHR. The Commission noted that racist speech may include antisemitic speech and Holocaust denial because of certain decisions of the European Court of Human Rights (p. 26). It was within this context that the Commission stated that

> Article 10 ECHR will protect Labour Party members who, for example, make legitimate criticisms of the Israeli government … It does not protect criticism of Israel that is antisemitic. Where we refer to legitimate criticism of Israel throughout the report we mean criticism that is not antisemitic.
>
> *(p. 27)*

The Commission gave examples of criticism of Israel which, it said, did not warrant the free speech protection of Article 10 because they went beyond legitimate criticism of Israel and were therefore antisemitic. These included comments by MP Naz Shah in 2015 that Israel should be relocated to the United States, and her social media post likening Israeli policies to those of Hitler and Ken Livingstone's support for those comments (pp. 29–30). Significantly, the Commission also found that responding to complaints of antisemitism by labelling them as 'fakes' or 'smears' was a denial of antisemitism, which amounted to the unlawful harassment of Jewish members (p. 28). This denialist narrative, known as the Livingstone Formulation, is frequently related to Israel and has become a contemporary antisemitic trope.[36]

The Livingstone Formulation does not, therefore, attract free speech protection under Article 10 ECHR.

Other types of antisemitic conduct that the Commission found to amount to the unlawful harassment of Jewish members of the Labour Party included the allegation that Jews are part of a wider conspiracy, that Jews control others, that Jews manipulate the political process, including the Labour Party, and referring to Jews as a 'fifth column', diminishing the significance of the Holocaust and expressing support for Hitler and the Nazis (p. 28). While these are classic antisemitic tropes not directly related to Israel, they have become part and parcel of the broader antizionist narrative and are often included alongside illegitimate criticism of Israel.

The Commission also discussed the antisemitic conduct on social media by ordinary members of the Labour Party for whom the Labour Party could not be responsible under the Equality Act because they did not hold any office or role within the Labour Party. These included claiming that complaints of antisemitism had been manufactured by the 'Israel lobby', blaming Jews for the actions of the State of Israel, accusing British Jews of greater loyalty to Israel than to Britain, using the term 'Zio' to refer to Jews and accusing Jews of crying antisemitism in bad faith to prevent Israel from being criticised (p. 31). These were examples of Israel-related antisemitism which did not warrant the free speech protection of Article 10.

The Commission's finding that the antisemitic tropes listed amount to the unlawful harassment of Jews means that these tropes do not attract free speech protection. It is a clear indicator that these tropes amount to racist speech rather than speech that is merely provocative, offensive or controversial, as was claimed by both the Fraser tribunal and Sheffield Hallam University.

The Macpherson principle

The Commission endorsed the Labour Party's compliance with the Macpherson principle in assessing antisemitic conduct and in deciding how to deal with it and was critical of the Party for not having adopted it until 2018 (p. 35). Taking the point of view of the victim as the starting point for recording and investigating complaints of antisemitism allows for the possibility that an attack on Israel can amount to unlawful antisemitic harassment and implicitly acknowledges Israel as an aspect of contemporary Jewish identity for the purposes of the construction of 'protected characteristic' under section 26 Equality Act. The Commission's discussion of the Macpherson principle, by which all complaints of racism should, in the first instance, be recorded and investigated as such when they are perceived by the complainant, or a third party, as an act of racism, is consistent with the Commission's recognition that antisemitism is often an Israel-related phenomenon.

EHRC and the definition of antisemitism

The Commission's discussion of the range and volume of antisemitic conduct across the compliant sample provides clear cut examples of antisemitism under the IHRA definition. Indeed, the Commission stated that its findings were consistent with IHRA (p. 26); that it 'may have regard to the IHRA's working definition of antisemitism and associated examples' (p. 125); and that the unwanted conduct meets the definition of 'harassment' and would also meet the IHRA definition and examples (p. 116). The Commission clearly understood and recognised that antisemitism is frequently an Israel-related phenomenon and treated Jewish people as an ethnic or national group for the purposes of 'harassment' under section 26 Equality Act. This allows for the possibility that an attack on Israel can amount to the unlawful harassment of a Jewish person because it engages his Jewish ethnic identity. This decision is surely in line with the dicta in *Mandla v Dowell Lee* about the nature of Jewish identity.

Conclusion

While the EHRC gives recognition to Israel as an aspect of Jewish identity through its construction of 'protected characteristic' for the purposes of section 26 of the Equality Act, we should exercise caution in claiming that this construction amounts to a general principle of law. This is because the Commission's decision does not set a binding precedent. It is merely persuasive as it is the decision of a statutory body rather than an appeal court. Nevertheless, what these three cases demonstrate is the gradual willingness in antisemitic harassment claims to recognise the broader ethnic and national dimension to Jewish identity, as first identified in *Mandla v Dowell Lee* in 1982. This opens the door to the possibility of successful claims for unlawful harassment under section 26 Equality Act occasioned by antisemitic antizionist expression.

Notes

1 An earlier version of this chapter was published as 'What is an English Jew?: The legal construction of Jewish identity under the UK Equality Act of 2010' in the *Indiana Journal of Law and Social Equality* 11 Ind. J. L. & Soc. Equal. 208 (2023).
2 *Mandla v. Dowell Lee* [1983] 2 AC 584 House of Lords per Lord Fraser.
3 Ibid.
4 *Mandla v. Dowell Lee* [1982] 3 All ER 1108, p. 1109.
5 *Mandla v. Dowell Lee* [1982] 3 All ER 1108 Court of Appeal per Lord Denning; *Mandla v. Dowell Lee* [1983] 2 AC 584 House of Lords per Lord Fraser.
6 *Mandla v. Dowell Lee* [1982] 3 All ER 1108, pp. 1112–13.
7 *Mandla v. Dowell Lee* [1983] 2 AC 548, p. 562.
8 Ibid., p. 562.
9 *King-Ansell v. Police* [1979] NZLR 531.
10 *King-Ansell*, 543, quoted by Lord Fraser.

11 Ibid. 535–536, 539.
12 *Mandla v Dowell Lee* [1982] 3 All ER 1108, pp. 1112–1113
13 Ibid.
14 *Mandla v Dowell Lee* [1983] 2 AC 548, 561.
15 Part III of the Public Order Act 1986.
16 Section 29B of the Public Order Act 1986.
17 IHRA Working Definition of Antisemitism (2016)., https://www.holocaustre membrance.com/working-definition-antisemitism (accessed 17 January 2022).
18 *Mr R Fraser-v-University & College Union*, Courts and Tribunals Judiciary, 25 March 2013, http://www.judiciary.gov.uk/media/judgments/2013/fraser-uni -college-union (accessed 17 January 2022). Throughout this section, quotations from the judgment are referred to by paragraph number.
19 *Mandla v Dowell Lee* [1983] 2 AC 548, p. 562.
20 Kings-Ansell v Police, 543, quoted by Lord Fraser.
21 *Kings-Ansell*, 535–6.
22 Julius's Written Opening Speech for the Claimant, para. 3.
23 Ibid., para. 3.1
24 Complaint submitted to the OIA May 2016. This is an internal document and is not available to the reader. Throughout this section, quotations taken from this document are referred to by 'C.' followed by paragraph number.
25 Sheffield Hallam University Complaint Response, February 2016. This is an internal document and is not available to the reader. Throughout this section, quotations taken from this document are referred to by 'C.R.' followed by paragraph number.
26 OIA Complaint Outcome. This is an internal document and is not available to the reader. Throughout this section, quotations taken from this document are referred to by 'OIA' followed by the paragraph number.
27 An early history of British race relations legislation – House of Commons Library, https://commonslibrary.parliament.uk/research-briefings/cbp-8360/ (accessed 20 January 2022).
28 William Macpherson, *Report of the Stephen Lawrence Inquiry*, London: Home Office, 1999. http://www.archive.official-documents.co.uk/document/cm42 /4262/sli-o6.htm (accessed 20 January 2022).
29 Fraser judgment, para. 158.
30 Ibid., para. 38.
31 Ibid., para. 148.
32 This was adopted by the International Holocaust Remembrance Alliance (IHRA) in 2016 and is now known as the IHRA Definition of Antisemitism.
33 Fraser judgment, para. 53.
34 House of Commons Home Affairs Committee, Antisemitism in the UK. Tenth Report of Session 2016–2017, para. 12. https://www.publications.parliament.uk /pa/cm201617/cmse-lect/cmhaff/136/136/pdf (accessed 23 January 2022).
35 EHRC Report into Antisemitism in the Labour Party, 29 October 29 2020. https://www.equalityhumanrights.com/en/publication-download/investigation -antisemitism-labour-party (accessed 25 January 2022).
   Throughout this section, quotations from the report will be referred to by page number.
36 David Hirsh. How Raising the Issue of Antisemitism Puts You Outside the Community of the Progressive: The Livingstone Formulation. Eunice G. Pollack, ed., *Anti-Zionism and Antisemitism: Past & Present*, Boston: Academic Studies Press, 2016. https://engageonline.wordpress.com/2016/04/29/the-livingstone -formulation-david-hirsh-2/ (accessed 26 February 2023).

8

SEVEN JEWISH CHILDREN AND DEFINITIONS OF ANTISEMITISM

Sarah Annes Brown

As a teacher of English literature, I relish the process of identifying and wrestling with ambiguities in literary texts.[1] I often use the duck–rabbit illusion, made famous by Ludwig Wittgenstein in *Philosophical Investigations* (1953), to illustrate the way in which a text – perhaps just a single word – can simultaneously hold two quite different, often contradictory, meanings (Figure 8.1). *King Lear*, for example, has been seen as a godless and despairing play, but also as one suffused with religious sensibility.[2] It has been co-opted by both conservatives and Marxists.[3] Milton's *Paradise Lost* is another famous example of a text which polarises critics, particularly in their responses to God and Satan.[4] Students of English literature – and of course of many other disciplines – don't have to be entirely even-handed or impartial, but they are routinely encouraged in their essays to explore different sides to such debates.

This openness to different perspectives can seem conspicuous by its absence within debates about Israel/Palestine – even though many of the most zealous activists come from academia. In this chapter, I will first analyse my experience of teaching Caryl Churchill's *Seven Jewish Children* (2009), and the slightly disorienting convergence of my (usually distinct) activist and academic identities. My focus will be on ambiguities within both the play itself and its critical reception.[5] The play divided opinion sharply, and I will explore some of the reasons why it seems so difficult to see a different point of view, acknowledge that a duck might also be a rabbit, once Israel or antisemitism enters the equation. I will then reflect on how activism is impoverished by a failure to acknowledge nuance and complexity, and tentatively indicate some ways in which the different 'sides' in debates over academic boycotts and definitions of antisemitism might begin to find a little more common ground.

DOI: 10.4324/9781003222477-9

FIGURE 8.1 Duck–Rabbit illusion.

Source: Retouched picture, public domain, via Wikimedia Commons

In 2009, I chose to include Churchill's short play on a module for students taking an English Literature MA, largely because of its topicality and clear ability to provoke discussion. It offers seven vignettes, beginning with pogroms and the Holocaust, moving quite quickly to Israel, and ending with a scene which appears to comment on Operation Cast Lead. All these brief sketches revolve around parents discussing how to deal with painful or difficult topics when talking to their children. At this point I had already participated in online debates about the play and was squarely on the side of its more hostile readers. Here are a few of the most important objections raised at the time of its first performance: its distorted, selective and telescoped version of Jewish history creates a perversely simplistic dynamic of causation and symmetry between the Holocaust and Operation Cast Lead;[6] Churchill ignores the convention that plays focused on a specific minority should be written by a member of that group;[7] the play tapped into the 'blood libel' trope, casting Jews as child killers, as well as invoking the idea of the Jews as 'chosen people' in a damaging way;[8] it also emphasised deceit and prevarication in the way Jewish parents raise their children.[9] However, at the same time I found the play, from a literary point of view, effective and thought-provoking, and agreed with John Nathan's verdict that it was 'an impressively distilled piece of writing'.[10]

A key element of its power, for me, lay in the ambiguities caused by the decision not to attribute lines to specific characters. When teaching the play I was reminded of a similar ambiguity in one episode of Edmund Spenser's epic poem *The Faerie Queene* (1590). Here the Red Cross Knight, protagonist of Book One, is tempted to suicide by Despair, one of his many evil antagonists. As their dialogue develops, it becomes increasingly unclear how the lines are divided between the characters;[11] speech markers are missing or ambiguous, and a statement which could be read as an affirmation of Christian resignation to God's will might as easily be a specious justification of sinful suicide:

> Is not his deed, what ever thing is donne
> In heaven and earth? did not he all create
> To die againe?[12]

Rather than seeing this as a problem with a definite answer, it may be more rewarding to see this ambiguity as a reflection of Red Cross's susceptibility to Despair. In Spenser's allegorical poem, although 'Despair' functions like a distinct character, he is also an aspect of Red Cross's personality, an inner voice urging him to the sin of suicide. The fact that those lines could be attributed to either character reflects the complexities of the debate, the traps that even the most devout can fall into, and a dangerous alignment of Red Cross's views with Despair's as their dialogue develops. The passage's ambiguities draw the reader in and provoke debate.

The ambiguities in *Seven Jewish Children* have a different function but I found the process of reflecting on the range of contradictory effects which could be generated similarly absorbing. For example, who says 'tell her she's a special girl'?[13] Is it a voice associated with the softer remarks or the more assertive, angry lines? To frame the same question a different way – is it a generic remark which any adult might say of a child to cheer her up or does it, more disturbingly, invoke the idea of Jews as a chosen people, a phrase often used within antisemitic discourse to imply Jewish arrogance or ruthlessness? The play's shifting patterns promote uncertainty. We get used to the 'tell hers' sometimes being used to preface things which are not true, or not wholly true. So by the time we get to the description of the Six-Day War, the impact of a true statement – 'tell her how big their armies were' – might be interpreted as a falsehood.[14] If the same person who delivers this line also says 'tell her this wasn't their home'[15] (a reference to the Nakba in which many Palestinians were displaced), that could have a subconscious impact upon an audience's reaction, implying a pervasive pattern of parental deceit.

The absence of speaker attribution means that these two short and apparently simple lines can be interpreted in quite different ways.

> Tell her we kill far more of them
> Don't tell her that[16]

We could interpret the brief disagreement as a triumphalist being chided by a gentler voice or as a left-wing activist, perhaps someone who refused to take part in national service, being corrected by a more conservative family member. A similar process can be identified here:

> Tell her we're entitled
> Tell her they don't understand anything except violence
> Tell her we want peace[17]

The first two lines are clearly cold and unsympathetic, particularly the second. But the third is trickier to evaluate. Is it spoken by a similar voice or a different voice? Is it genuine, or a rather sinister lie? We are faced with the same kind of choice when confronted with one of the details which horrified some through its apparent resonance with the blood libel.

> Don't tell her about the family of dead girls
> Tell her you can't believe what you see on television
> Tell her we killed the babies by mistake[18]

We move from deception to implicit deception to – what? The final line could easily be given to the same speaker who insisted Israel wants peace. Both lines can be as readily interpreted *in bono* as *in malo*. The speaker could be compassionate – honest, in not wanting to hide the truth from a child, but (whether for or against this particular war) upset by the babies' deaths. Or the speaker could be differentiated from others only in being more subtle, more conspiratorial, a reading which emerges clearly in this critique by Howard Jacobson:

> Thus lie follows lie, omission follows omission, until, in the tenth and final minute, we have a stage populated by monsters who kill babies by design – 'Tell her we killed the babies by mistake,' one says, meaning don't tell her what we really did[.].[19]

A similar point was made by John Nathan: 'Churchill's Jews are no longer victims but perpetrators of atrocity, who no longer protect their children from truths but conspire to distort them'.[20]

When *Seven Jewish Children* was first published, I gained a strong sense of two different approaches to the play. Its admirers were likely to insist that it contained a range of Israeli voices, many quite sympathetic; its detractors, by contrast, tended to interpret ambiguous lines in the least positive available way. Sometimes this was because of a heightened awareness of antisemitic tropes, such as the blood libel, sometimes because a greater knowledge of Jewish/Israeli history made them more sensitive to gaps and errors in the

FIGURE 8.2 Hans Holbein the Younger's painting, *The Ambassadors* (1533).
Source: National Gallery, faithful photographic reproduction, public domain

compressed narrative. I can understand why some readers were baffled by this hostile response to the play, why, although they accepted that it was critical of Israel's actions, they hotly denied that it demonised all Israelis, or all Jews.

When teaching, I've sometimes invoked Hans Holbein the Younger's painting *The Ambassadors* (1533) to demonstrate that if we change our perspective, our interpretive lens, we may see a literary text in a completely different light (Figure 8.2).[21] Viewed conventionally, the anamorphic image in the foreground is just a strange blur. Viewed from the side it is clearly a skull. For me, the antisemitism I see in the play resembles the skull in that many readers honestly don't spot it. In order to see it they need to shift their perspective, acknowledge that those who can spot it are not deluded. (Conversely, I think readers who are more attuned to issues such as the blood libel need to recognise that those who fail at first to detect problems in the play may be neither dishonest nor malign.) The painting's hidden skull, its intimation of mortality, reminds me of the image used by Mark Gardner and Dave Rich in their powerful, but measured, condemnation of the play:

> The virus of antisemitism is easily transmitted by those who are not aware they are carrying it. Churchill almost certainly does not intend it, but her play culminates in powerful antisemitic resonances. The Guardian's online production further amplifies them.[22]

That 'almost certainly' is interesting. After drafting this chapter, it was pointed out to me that Holbein's placement of the skull is utterly deliberate, which makes it an inappropriate parallel if I want to imply that Churchill had no intention of writing an antisemitic play. But she did at least appear to have anticipated that some would find it antisemitic, even if she claimed their accusations were dishonest. A letter she wrote to the *Independent* in response to Howard Jacobson's critical piece opens: 'Howard Jacobson writes as if there's something new about describing critics of Israel as anti-Semitic. But it's the usual tactic'.[23] Stephen Greenblatt notes that the skull's shadow falls in a different direction from those of the ambassadors, meaning that its presence – like racism in the play – 'is at once affirmed and denied'.[24]

Rich and Gardner's warning about 'the virus of antisemitism' seemed particularly prescient when I revisited the play in 2021, trying to catch up with a decade's worth of academic criticism as well as more informal commentaries. A number of articles ignored anxieties about antisemitism, or invoked them briefly and dismissively. For example, Sian Adiseshiah describes its critics as 'censorious' – I return to her analysis below – and Miriam Felton-Dansky refers to their 'self-righteous fury'.[25] However, some acknowledged the play's more problematic elements and explored them with sensitivity. Although academic criticism tends to be tempered with more nuance and restraint than social media discussions, I felt I could still trace the contours of the original debates – Churchill's fans denied any hints of antisemitism; others acknowledged at least a *prima facie* case.

However, I also encountered a third and more troubling set of voices, one which I don't remember coming across in 2009. To illustrate this, here are four statements about the play.

1. 'Churchill forcefully challenges Jews by revealing their paradoxical situation as victims of long persecution in Europe who morally fail to condemn Israel's latest vicious actions.'
2. 'In addition, the play's detractors ignore that this violent outburst [the controversial monologue near the end of play] is followed immediately

by the voice of reason: "Don't tell her that/ Tell her we love her/ Don't frighten her"' (Churchill, 2009).

3. 'Although *Seven Jewish Children* certainly condemns the practices of the state of Israel, there is no suggestion that this should be taken as a critique of all Jewish people. It is possible to find fault with the actions of Israel without being anti-Semitic .'

4. 'Churchill stands up to the Jews, who were liable to broadened maltreatment in Europe, revealing their ethical inability to censure recent Israeli practices.'

If read in isolation, I'd identify statements 1 and 4 as antisemitic, and guess that statements 2 and 3 were written from a pro-Churchillian perspective, by someone anxious to exonerate the play from charges of antisemitism. They are however all taken from the same 2020 article by A. A. Aziz, published in the *International Journal of Language and Literary Studies*.[26] Although I think statements 2 and 3 are flawed, I would normally accept them as good faith interventions. However, in combination with the statements which they apparently contradict, the article offers a strange replication of the ambiguous polyphony of the play itself: those final lines from the play, cited in statement 2, can be read as an Israeli voice of reason or as a conspiratorial whisper, complicit with the views, if not the tone, of the ranting monologist. In the context of the article as a whole, the ostensible 'voice of reason' offered by statement 3 rings similarly hollow. There's something particularly disorienting in reading a sentence by Aziz, which opens with a point which might have been made by one of Churchill's fiercer critics – 'The six-page drama goes past ordinary criticism of Israel' – which is then revealed to be a note of praise rather than censure. The sentence concludes: 'articulating to the Jews of the world its unbending dissent against Israel's current actions'.[27] Those on polar opposite sides of the debate – like Red Cross and Despair – can sound remarkably similar.

It could reasonably be argued that this is an obscure article which never seems to have been cited (until now). However, it is possible to find equally troubling moments in far more mainstream sources. Amelia Howe Kritzer is the editor of Churchill's plays. In an article for *Theatre Journal*, she wrote:

> *Seven Jewish Children* addressed its uncompromising protest against Israeli militarism to Jews around the world. Churchill boldly confronts Jews with a non-Jewish perspective on their suffering as victims of persecution in Europe, their pride in Israel's persecution and development, and their failure to condemn recent Israeli actions.[28]

This might at first look like part of a sarcastic critique of Churchill, not an enthusiastic endorsement. It captures much of what I found disquieting in Aziz's article. When teaching the play, I acknowledged that some of the hostile readings I offered – not as definitive, but as plausible, available interpretations – could be seen as perverse. (I'm referring here to my tendency to interpret the 'nicer' lines as freighted with some more sinister agenda, discussed above.) However, I failed to dream up any interpretation as lurid as the argument put forward by another academic critic, Reem Ahmed El Bardisy. He claims that the Jewish characters in the opening scenes invoke the Holocaust in order to 'divert the children's attention away from their ancestors' shameful history, which is full of massacres and atrocities'.[29] Churchill responded plaintively to Howard Jacobson's own bleak perspective on her play: 'Jacobson seems to see the play from a very particular perspective so that everything is twisted ... I don't recognise the play from [his] description'.[30] And yet it is perhaps her admirers rather than her detractors who, disturbingly, have managed to tease out the most antisemitic meanings from her ambiguous script.

To conclude this section, it seems that my sense of there being broadly two perspectives on the play – it is antisemitic and thus dangerous or it is not antisemitic at all – was inadequate. Some admirers of the play see the play as antisemitic *and admire it and want to spread its message for that reason* (even if they would not own the word 'antisemitic'). It is important for advocates of the play to acknowledge this evidence that Gardner and Rich's warnings that the play contains a hidden virus were correct – and we might acknowledge too that for most people in this category views such as those I've just cited are about as welcome and congenial as Tommy Robinson at a march in support of Israel.

When I mentioned on an online forum back in 2009 that I was going to teach *Seven Jewish Children*, a friend cautioned that I too might be in danger of spreading the virus. That unwelcome warning stuck in my mind as I began to grapple with the dissonances between activism and teaching. As I introduced the play to my students, I experienced a conflict between different impulses. I wanted to encourage students to consider the full range of responses to the play and feel comfortable articulating their own feelings about the debates. But whereas I routinely give credit to well-evidenced arguments that I don't personally agree with, I found it much more challenging to do so with this very recent text whose political and ethical implications are so charged. I also found it much more difficult to be open about my own response – my agreement with those who found it antisemitic – and affected a far more uncertain and ambivalent stance than I really held (whether more for my own sake or for the benefit of students with a different perspective I'm now not sure). I referred earlier to my appreciation of the play's ambiguities, my ability to take pleasure in teasing them out. However, Churchill's play is not a remote 16th century text, and aesthetic appreciation began to seem morally dubious when negotiating Churchill's slippery lines in a seminar. So the next year I exchanged it for a different text and didn't return to it until working on this chapter.

Memories from teaching returned to me when I read Sian Adiseshiah's article 'Political returns on the twenty-first century stage: Caryl Churchill's *Far Away, Drunk Enough to Say I Love You?* and *Seven Jewish Children*'. Here is her take on attempts to prevent the play from being performed: 'This censorious response to *Seven Jewish Children* demonstrates the degree to which the play as an event created space to articulate what is not permitted to be said'.[31] The logic of this point is superficially clear. However, it raises further questions. Attempts to stop the play from being performed were unsuccessful. Criticism of Israel is commonplace – in universities and newspapers, and of course on social media where it is easy to find material much more obviously offensive than Churchill's play. 'What is not permitted to be said' is a category which could include both courageous dissent and offensive racism. Adiseshiah's account allows little space for this latter option to be considered. If another form of racism were in question, would she dismiss attempts to close the play as merely 'censorious'? From an activist perspective there are many occasions when opposition to what I consider to be antisemitic – not the antisemitism itself – has felt like 'what is not permitted to be said'. I've often been torn between feeling an imperative to voice concerns about academic boycotts of Israel, or to speak out against manifestations of antisemitism (particularly on the left), and experiencing an anxiety about being associated with an unpopular position. In complete contrast to Adiseshiah's perception, for me it was forums such as Engage,[32] or the experience of coming together with other witnesses in the Ronnie Fraser trial, which represented a 'space to articulate what is not permitted to be said'.

I've suggested that Sian Adiseshiah's perception of what is unsayable – or not easily sayable – directly clashes with my own experiences, as an academic and trade unionist, in discussions relating to Israel and antisemitism. Debates about definitions of antisemitism have been almost as much of a flashpoint as those around academic boycotts. These have proved particularly toxic within the University and College Union (UCU) – in relation to both the recent International Holocaust Remembrance Alliance (IHRA) definition and its earlier European Monitoring Centre on Racism and Xenophobia (EUMC) incarnation. Here there is little acknowledgement of the complexity and sensitivity of this issue. Too often, to borrow a phrase from Jeremy Corbyn, there seems to be a 'subliminal nastiness' at work, a cold refusal to empathise with sincere concerns about racism.[33] This was notoriously apparent in the motion passed at UCU's 2011 Congress repudiating and outlawing any use of the EUMC definition of antisemitism.[34] Ten years on, motions put forward to UCU's 2021 Congress demonstrated a similar lack of sensitivity. Higher Education Motion 23 (proposed by the

UCU Higher Education Committee) condemned 'unfounded accusations of antisemitism against academic staff' as well as what it described as a 'scurrilous attack on Ken Loach'.[35] (The motion was not debated or voted on due to lack of time.) In November 2021, a motion passed by Sheffield Hallam in opposition to the sacking of Professor David Miller from the University of Bristol described the charges of antisemitism against him as 'malicious'.[36]

Those drafting or supporting these motions don't seem to have made the slightest attempt to engage with just *why* people might have objected to Ken Loach's invitation to an event at Oxford University or have felt concerned by some of David Miller's statements.[37] The words 'scurrilous' and 'malicious' imply extreme bad faith on the part of those bringing the accusations. When, in conversation with UCU activists, I tried to explain in detail why many found statements made by Ken Loach problematic, I encountered a sense of honest bewilderment that I could possibly have any objection to a film maker with such impeccable left-wing credentials. The very idea was unthinkable – the problems apparently as elusive, as difficult to identify, as Holbein's anamorphic skull.

Free speech is a complex and multi-faceted issue. Which kinds of speech do we want to ban outright, which do we just want to bar from certain platforms or contexts, and which we do we merely want to censure or vigorously oppose? There are inconsistencies within the UCU on issues of freedom of thought and expression. Different causes, different minorities, attract different levels of support. Two contrasting motions from the Congress held online in June 2021 reveal inconsistencies between what might be termed the union's normative response to anxieties about Islamophobia, on the one hand, and antisemitism on the other. One motion, number 18, called for solidarity with the Muslim community following a ban on face coverings in Switzerland. There seemed good reasons to support this motion. The Swiss far right has long agitated against Islam, campaigning (successfully) for a ban on minarets in 2009. The Swiss People's Party (SVP) gained notoriety in 2007 for its use of posters depicting a white sheep on a Swiss flag triumphantly kicking a black sheep off its land.[38] However, there was some potential complexity here – it wasn't simply a case of freedom versus fascism. For example, the Swiss-Yemeni academic Elham Manea, from a reformist Muslim perspective, supported the ban while utterly disassociating herself from the SVP.[39] She is a minority voice within the Muslim community, articulating a feminist position which might seem well aligned with the principles of a left-wing trade union. A loose parallel might tentatively be made with the position of non-Zionist Jews who have often been the most passionate promoters of Israel boycotts and opposition to those definitions of antisemitism supported by Jewish communal organisations. Both could be said to articulate liberal or left-wing positions based on a concern for human rights. But the agendas of both are vulnerable to contamination by, or confusion with, far right or racist positions. No one spoke against the Swiss motion. I voted for it, while believing that Manea's concerns, those of a minority within a minority, were a legitimate part of the debate.

By contrast, in a string of other motions the views of that other minority within a minority (Jewish anti-Zionists) were strongly supported. I shall say more below about a cluster of motions which proposed opposition to the IHRA definition and support for the Jerusalem Declaration. Here I will pause briefly on one detail from another successful motion passed into policy by UCU's 2021 Congress. This was Motion 12, 'Adopting a better definition of antisemitism', brought forward by the University of Exeter; once again, it reveals an apparent inconsistency in the treatment of antisemitism. It proposed that 'descriptions of the discriminatory nature and acts of Israel should not be treated eo ipso as anti-Semitic, without independent evidence of anti-Jewish intention'. This insistence on the need to demonstrate an antisemitic intention sets the bar for racist/discriminatory rhetoric very high, and can be seen as an example of the phenomenon described in David Baddiel's *Jews Don't Count*[40] – an inability to engage meaningfully with all but the most serious and unambiguous examples of antisemitism. This goes against the ways in which racism is usually discussed and theorised on the left; here we expect an alertness to institutional racism, microaggressions and unconscious bias.

Some motions opposing the IHRA definition sought to promote the Jerusalem Declaration as an alternative.[41] The Jerusalem Declaration contains some unexceptionable clauses. For example, it offers a useful explanation of how coded statements (such as references to the Rothschilds) can mask antisemitism. However, there are two main problems with the definition – its omissions and its insistence that certain kinds of discourse or action targeting Israel should not be seen 'in and of themselves' as antisemitic. The key omission is perhaps its failure to recognise and condemn the prominent use of analogies between Israel and the Nazis in contemporary antisemitism. Another gap is its failure to acknowledge how the word 'Zionists' is used as a synonym for Jews in antisemitic discourse. Even when there is an implicit acknowledgement that not all Jews are Zionists, if Zionism is evoked as an unambiguously malign and racist ideology, such a position – through lumping together Meretz supporters and Kahanists – might surely be viewed as antisemitic.

Dave Rich notes an irony in the enthusiasm for the Jerusalem Declaration from many academics. Whereas the IHRA definition is more tentative, acknowledging grey areas in its use of words such as 'might', 'may' and 'could', the Jerusalem Declaration, Rich reminds us, sees only a binary – things either 'are' or 'are not' antisemitic.

One of the most curious aspects of the academic enthusiasm for the Jerusalem Declaration over the IHRA definition is this desire for something that removes the need to think about the complexities of antisemitic manifestations, or to consider the context and impact of each individual example.[42]

This of course chimes closely with my own frustrations about both much of the academic discussion of *Seven Jewish Children* and the discourse around antisemitism within academic trade union activism. There seems a failure of intellectual curiosity about the motives of those who support the IHRA definition which in turn suppresses generosity, even civility. But is there any corresponding lack of generosity or curiosity on the part of those whose views are more aligned with the contributors to this volume – supporters of the IHRA definition and opponents of academic boycotts? With that question in mind, I have set out to explore where I might be able to find some common ground with my antagonists in these debates.

The way the Conservative government tried to apply pressure on universities to adopt the IHRA definition in 2019 can reasonably be seen as counterproductive and heavy-handed. The threat contained in Universities Minister Gavin Williamson's letter that funding might be withdrawn from those who didn't comply, in particular, inevitably alienated many who didn't otherwise have strong feelings about the issue.[43] (Conversely, it is entirely understandable that many individuals and organisations welcomed the government's intervention with relief.)

It is also possible to see why some clauses of the IHRA definition should be perceived to inhibit – potentially – some legitimate as well as antisemitic criticisms of Israel. Perhaps the most contentious clause is that which refers to the founding of Israel.

> Denying the Jewish people their right to self-determination, e.g., by claiming that the existence of a State of Israel is a racist endeavor.[44]

Even if one concludes that the definition allows space to criticise Israel robustly and bars no legitimate debate, it should at least be possible to understand why a Palestinian, faced with the clause relating to the founding of Israel, might feel inhibited from discussing their family's traumatic experience of displacement, exile and occupation. Many have sought to defend and explain this clause, noting that each part of the definition is caveated through a reminder of the need to consider the context, and the use of the word 'may'. Some supporters of the IHRA definition emphasise the significance of the indefinite article in this clause. David Hirsh writes:

> [I]t is clear that the IHRA definition is inviting us to consider, as a possible example of antisemitism, after taking context into account, the claim

that any possible state of Israel would necessarily be a racist endeavour. And that would be an extraordinary claim to make.[45]

Presumably, however, most supporters of the IHRA definition would wish to identify some charges of racism against the – as opposed to a – state of Israel as antisemitic. However, I don't believe there's an easy consensus over where the line should be drawn when it comes to determining which accusations of racism against Israeli governments or organisations are antisemitic.

I have criticised the Jerusalem Declaration's failure to say enough about what *is* antisemitic. Perhaps it would also help if those who prefer the IHRA definition could be more explicit, more capacious, in explaining what kinds of criticisms of Israel they do *not* find antisemitic. Like many, I have developed a cynical response to yet another reassurance that x person or organisation is utterly opposed to antisemitism (and all other forms of racism of course). It seems possible that those on the other side of this particular debate have a similar response to assurances that, naturally, legitimate criticisms of Israel are not antisemitic.

As a brief case study to help supply some specific examples of criticisms of Israel which are not – I think – antisemitic, I have turned to a UCU report of a visit to Palestine.[46] The report is 50 pages long and describes in considerable detail a visit made by UCU officials to Palestine in 2018. It charts meetings with trade unionists and educationalists, and visits to contested sites such as Sheikh Jarrah and Hebron. It highlights the difficulties caused by the occupation for Palestinians: delays at checkpoints; new roads and settlements creating access problems in the West Bank; farmers and villagers unable to access their olive trees or springs; difficulties faced by Palestinians in Area C who want to build or develop; and by students who wish to travel.[47] The punishment of protestors is another significant theme. Although it could certainly be described as one-sided, it does acknowledge, inter alia, problems with the internal politics of Gaza, PA corruption, PA restrictions on electricity to Gaza and Egypt's control of one of the Gaza borders[48] – in other words, it doesn't claim that Israel is solely to blame for all problems in the region. A distinction is drawn between land captured in 1967 and that 'recognised by the UN as part of Israel'.[49] The language is factual and generally quite calm – Israelis are not demonised. There is one reference to land being zoned 'in an apartheid-like fashion'.[50] Gaza is likened to an 'open-air prison' – but certainly not to the Warsaw ghetto.[51]

I didn't find any element of this report antisemitic although I did think it would have strengthened the document to have engaged a little more with Israeli perspectives. For example, there is a reference to the 'Palestinian curriculum' in schools, and the much-discussed problems of antisemitism in Palestinian education could have been described alongside difficulties teaching the Nakba to Palestinian children.[52] Such absent presences are distracting – if acknowledged, the reader may be better prepared to engage with the very real difficulties faced by Palestinians due to both government and settler actions. It was positive to explain that Israel stopped fuel deliveries to Gaza 'due to the violence at the fence',[53] and to acknowledge the anxieties of Israelis living near the border with Gaza.[54] The report helpfully explained that many settlers had been driven by economic not ideological incentives – thus discouraging demonisation not just of Jews, or Israelis, but of settlers too.[55] There is discussion of Israel as a 'settler colonial' project, but this is a view ascribed to one particular Palestinian interlocutor.[56] A reference to Ajamai as 'in effect, a ghetto' (in 1948) did make me wince – and thus had the effect of distracting from its emphasis on very real injustices against Palestinians.[57] Both in some of its details and taken in the round the report is unlikely to be fully congenial to those more in sympathy with the book you are reading and its contributors. I can't of course myself know how others would respond to this report – some might think it crossed a line. However, I would be very surprised if it attracted the same degree of disapprobation as, say, *Seven Jewish Children*. There are many obvious differences between the play (a work of dramatic fiction) and the fact-filled documentary report. One important difference is in the space each gives to Palestinian voices. Palestinians are voiceless in Churchill's play – victims with no agency, ciphers conjured up by the Jewish/Israeli voices who can't agree on what their children should be told about them. Although most of Churchill's critics have focused on her treatment of Jews, Kate Leader explains why her play does no great service to Palestinians either:

> Churchill's decision to speak for Jews exclusively and to give no voice to the Palestinians arguably perpetuates the dichotomous relationship of perpetrator and victim. As seen in the above, this leads to language that is at times stereotyped and also to a degree 'others' the Palestinians who are unseen and unheard victims, an uncomfortable positioning that carries the traces of colonialism.[58]

If Churchill had chosen to focus on Palestinian voices, she would have been forced to confront the complexities and tensions in that community, articulate viewpoints which are uncomfortable as well as sympathetic, present us with debates over strategy, morality, history and religion. But instead, she focuses solely on Jews/Israelis – and implicitly (because of the flattened narrative trajectory) only on Ashkenazis; there is no hint of the distinctive experiences of Mizrahi Israelis. In the UCU report, by welcome contrast, many Palestinians are given a voice. They have a degree of agency, and disagreements between different Palestinian individuals and groupings emerge clearly as well as, of course, clashes between Palestinians and Israelis.

I have deliberately paused on this UCU report, highlighting several different elements to be weighed in the balance when evaluating the overall context of how it frames its criticism of Israel. I have done this because it sometimes seems hard to pin down exactly what criticisms of Israel are likely to be perceived as antisemitic. In a rather similar spirit, I've recently engaged with several of the online productions of *Seven Jewish Children*. Here I was spurred on by critic Kate Leader, who writes with great sensitivity about several of the problematic aspects of the play, and yet ends up acknowledging a more universal, more sympathetic side to the play when seen in production.

> Indeed, while it may be easy to highlight difficulties with this piece in close textual examination, paying attention to non-text-based signs yields a richer interpretation. At its most affective, *Seven Jewish Children* is about the constant desire for – and absence of – home and safety.[59]

I couldn't banish my preconceptions about the play, so was almost certainly more alert to details which unsettled me rather than the 'richer' possibilities identified by Leader. The Grit TV reading gave the same speaker both these lines:

> Tell her they don't understand anything except violence
> Tell her we want peace[60]

This could be said to contribute to a more cynical effect, although the attribution of the line 'tell her we killed the babies by mistake' to an actor with a gentler persona acted as something of a counterbalance.[61] Perhaps the most disturbing element of this production was the decision to give the violent and hateful monologue to an older female actor who had seemed a rather calm and measured voice in earlier scenes. The fact that the brief response to this monologue was given to the same actor who spoke the two lines quoted above undercut the sincerity of his response, bringing out a more conspiratorial atmosphere. The dramatically effective use of a whispered chorus of indistinct Tell her/Don't tell her injunctions between scenes in a Warwick student production created a similar effect – although I fully acknowledge that this is unlikely to have been the intention. In a production at the Abbey Theatre for Palfest in 2015, one of the most memorable decisions related to the line 'Tell her maybe we can share'.[62] The response – 'don't tell her that' – was spoken by every other cast member in unison, turning their disapproving gaze on the lone dissenting voice, and sparking audible sniggers from the audience. These productions tended to reinforce my existing feelings of antipathy towards the play. Even a performance such as the ROOMS Gallery production (2009), which seemed to offer a clearer rejection of that final violent monologue, left a troubling impression of evasion and dissimulation, of an overarching collusion which overwrote local wrangles over details.

Kate Leader's useful cautionary note about any individual performance might be applied to the – any – playtext itself:

> Let me be clear: it is not the job of the performance scholar to make a pronunciation on the definitive 'meaning' of a live performance. As many prominent writers have argued at length, trying to pin down the 'intention' of a performance ignores the complexity of signifiers and the equally important role of reception involved in meaning-making.[63]

This play, in particular, is hard to pin down to one fixed meaning. Certainly – to borrow that useful distinction between 'a' and 'the' from debates around the IHRA definition – I can identify *a* benign and thoughtful *Seven Jewish Children* within a dramatic multiverse of countless real and hypothetical performances. But the context(s) within which it operates – the ways in which it can be read, performed, discussed and received – offer even more scope than I realised back in 2009 to connect with and amplify antisemitic patterns of thought.

With Rich and Gardner's warning about the 'virus of antisemitism' in mind, I will conclude with some thoughts about a single line which had seemed straightforward when I first encountered the play in 2009, but on rereading seemed fraught with a disturbing ambiguity. The line 'don't tell her what they did' is repeated twice in scene 2.[64] I had previously assumed that 'they' was a reference to the Nazis. But it struck me for the first time, as I revisited the play in 2021 in the light of Bardisy's article (discussed above), how easily 'they' could be attached to the Holocaust victims. Because it is such a tricky shifting signifier, that 'they' could be said to enable or justify Bardisy's disturbing victim-blaming reading of the play, instantiating in a single ambiguous word the antisemitic trope whereby Jews are conflated with Nazis. 'They' here is less Wittgenstein's duck–rabbit than another animal hybrid, Aesop's master of plausible deniability, the bat who claims to be a mouse when faced with a bird-hunting predator, only to switch identities when a new danger threatens. Those who wish to combat antisemitism – no matter which definition they favour – need to engage with the damage which such ambiguities can cause, independent of the author's intention.

Notes

1 There are of course many different kinds of ambiguity, as the title of William Empson's famous study, *Seven Types of Ambiguity* (1930), indicates. There are local ambiguities – puns or syntactical uncertainties. There are wider patterns of ambiguity – perhaps created by an unreliable narrator or inconclusive ending. Some ambiguities – such as a clever play on words – may be under the

full control of the writer, there for the reader to decode if they are able. But in other cases the intentions of the author are unknowable, or overtaken by the power of the text to generate irreconcilable interpretations in the minds of later readers.

2 Sean Lawrence offers a helpful introduction to the critical debates on this issue. Sean Lawrence, 'Gods that We Adore': The Divine in *King Lear. Renascence: Essays on Values in Literature*, 56(3), 143–159, 2004.

3 See Chris J. Fitter, 'The Art of Known and Feeling Sorrows': Rethinking Capitalist Transition, and the Performance of Class Politics, in Shakespeare's *King Lear. Early Modern Literary Studies*, 19(1), 2016, for an overview of different interpretations.

4 See, for example, William Kolbrener, 'Reception', in: Louis Schwartz, ed., *The Cambridge Companion to Paradise Lost*, Cambridge: Cambridge University Press, 2014, pp. 195–210.

5 See, for example, Miriam Felton-Dansky, 'Clamorous Voices: *Seven Jewish Children* and Its Proliferating Publics'. *TDR/The Drama Review*, 55(3), 156–164, 2011.

6 Stef Craps, Holocaust Memory and the Critique of Violence in Caryl Churchill's *Seven Jewish Children: A Play for Gaza*. In: Jane Kilby and Antony Rowland, eds., *The Future of Testimony: Interdisciplinary Perspectives on Witnessing*, Abingdon: Routledge, 2014, 179–192.

7 John Nathan, *Review: Seven Jewish Children: The Jewish Chronicle* (Thejc .com, 12 February 2009). https://www.thejc.com/news/all/review-seven-jewish -children-1.7642 (accessed 25 February 2023).

8 Howard Jacobson, Let's See the 'Criticism' of Israel for What It Really Is. *Independent*, 18 February 2009. https://www.independent.co.uk/voices/com-mentators/howard-jacobson/howard-jacobson-let-rsquo-s-see-the-criticism-of -israel-for-what-it-really-is-1624827.html (accessed 29 May 2022). Anthony Julius, *Trials of the Diaspora: A History of Anti-Semitism in England*, Oxford: Oxford University Press, 2010, p. 241.

9 Ibid.

10 John Nathan, ibid.

11 This ambiguity is discussed by Paul J. Alpers in *The Poetry of the Faerie Queene*, Princeton: Princeton University Press, 1967, pp. 354–355.

12 Edmund Spenser, *The Faerie Queene*, edited by A. C. Hamilton, London and New York: Longman, 1980, 1.ix.42.

13 Caryl Churchill, *Seven Jewish Children: A Play for Gaza*, London: Nick Hern books, 2009, p. 3.

14 Churchill, p. 5.

15 Churchill, p. 4.

16 Churchill, p. 2.

17 Churchill, p. 6.

18 Churchill, p. 7.

19 Jacobson, 2009. See also Julius, 2009, pp. 240–241.

20 John Nathan, Review: Seven Jewish Children. *The Jewish Chronicle* (Thejc.co m, 12 February 2009). https://www.thejc.com/news/all/review-seven-jewish -children-1.7642 (accessed 25 February 2023).

21 For a subtle and extended discussion of the painting, see Stephen Greenblatt, *Renaissance Self-fashioning: From More to Shakespeare*, Chicago and London: University of Chicago Press, 1980, 2005, pp. 18–27.

22 Dave Rich and Mark Gardner, The Blood Libel Brought Up to Date. *Guardian*, 1 May 2009.

23 Caryl Churchill, My Play Is Not Anti-Semitic. *Independent*, 21 February 2009.

24 Greenblatt, p. 19.
25 Sian Adiseshiah, Political Returns on the Twenty-First Century Stage. Caryl Churchill's *Far Away, Drunk Enough to Say I Love You?* and *Seven Jewish Children*. *C21 Literature: Journal of 21st-Century Writings*, 1(1), 103–121, 2012; Miriam Felton-Dansky, Clamorous Voices: *Seven Jewish Children* and Its Proliferating Public. *TDR*, 55(3), 156–164, 2011.
26 A. A. Aziz, The Politics and Poetics of Oppression in Caryl Churchill's *Seven Jewish Children*. *International Journal of Language & Literary Studies*, 2(1), 116–123, 2020. The numbered quotations can be found on pages 118, 121, 121 and 122.
27 Aziz, 117.
28 Amelia Howe Kritzer, Enough! Women Playwrights Confront the Israeli–Palestinian Conflict. *Theatre Journal*, 62(4), 611–626, 2010.
29 Reem Ahmed A. El Bardisy, Re-dramatizing the Palestinian–Israeli Conflict: Representations of Trauma and Postmemory in Caryl Churchill's *Seven Jewish Children: A Play for Gaza* (2009). الجزء الأول 28, 95–130, 2020.
30 Churchill, 21 February 2009.
31 Adiseshiah, p. 117.
32 See David Hirsh's introduction in this book.
33 Jeremy Corbyn referred to the 'utterly disgusting subliminal nastiness' of an article by journalist Jonathan Freedland in a 2016 fly-on-the-wall documentary. Jonathan Freedland, What Did Corbyn Mean When He Insulted Me? *The Jewish Chronicle*, 22 January 2020.
34 Marilyn Stowe, Is the UCU anti Semitic? *The Times*, 3 June 2011. https://www.thetimes.co.uk/article/is-the-ucu-anti-semitic-xwnzx7ql2x5 (accessed 28 December 2021)
35 https://www.ucu.org.uk/media/11530/UCU1089/pdf/UCU1089.pdf
36 David Hirsh, Sheffield Hallam UCU says David Miller was a victim of 'malicious and unfounded allegations' of antisemitism. *Engage*, 17 November 2021. https://engageonline.wordpress.com/2021/11/17/sheffield-hallam-ucu-says-david-miller-was-a-victim-of-malicious-and-unfounded-allegations-of-antisemitism/ (accessed 28 December 2021).
37 On Ken Loach and antisemitism, see, inter alia, Dave Rich, Loach, Livingstone and the Holocaust. *The Jewish Chronicle*, 27 September 2017. https://www.thejc.com/comment/comment/loach-livingstone-and-the-holocaust-a-study-in-slander-1.445044 (accessed 25 February 2023); Abigail Howe, Students, Societies and Colleges Respond to Ken Loach Event. *Cherwell*, 9 February 2021. https://cherwell.org/2021/02/09/ken-loach-responses/ (accessed 29 December 2021). For an overview of concerns about Professor David Miller, see Dave Rich, Why 'Academic Freedom' Is No Defence of the Bristol University Professor David Miller. *The New Statesman*, 23 March 2021. https://www.newstatesman.com/politics/2021/03/why-academic-freedom-no-defence-bristol-university-professor-david-miller (accessed 29 December 2021).
38 Helena Bachmann, Bye-Bye, Black Sheep. *Time*, 21 September 2007. http://content.time.com/time/world/article/0,8599,1664269,00.html (accessed 29 December 2021).
39 Tunku Varadarajan, The Swiss Won't Miss the Burqa. *Wall Street Journal*, 9 March 2021, https://www.wsj.com/articles/the-swiss-wont-miss-the-burqa-11615332345 (accessed 29 December 2021).
40 David Baddiel, *Jews Don't Count*, London: TLS Books, 2022.
41 The full text of the Jerusalem Declaration can be found at https://jerusalemdeclaration.org/

42 Dave Rich, Read It Again. Read Better. Dave Rich on Derek Penslar's serial misrepresentations of the IHRA, *Fathom*, May 2021. https://fathomjournal.org /read-it-again-read-better-dave-rich-on-derek-penslars-serial-misrepresentations -of-the-ihra/ (accessed 29 December 2021).

43 Alison Busby, Universities may face cuts if they reject definition of antisemitism, says education minister. *Independent*, 9 October 2020.

44 The full text of the IHRA definition can be found at https://www.holocaustre membrance.com/resources/working-definitions-charters/working-definition -antisemitism

45 David Hirsh, It Was the New Phenomenon of Israel-focused Antisemitism that Required the New Definition. David Hirsh Responds to a Recent 'Call to Reject' the IHRA. *Fathom*, January 2021.

46 Douglas Chalmers, Palestinian Diary Report of UCU Trip to Palestine. *UCU*, 2018. https://ucu.org.uk/media/10242/Palestinian-Diary-report-of-a-UCU-trip -to-Palestine-Douglas-Chalmers/pdf/ucu_chalmers-palestine-visit-2018-report .pdf (accessed 29 December 2021).

47 Chalmers, pp. 4, 5–6, 15, 12.

48 Chalmers, pp. 7, 13, 12.

49 Chalmers, p. 3.

50 Chalmers, p. 6.

51 Chalmers, p. 12.

52 Chalmers, pp. 7, 20. Report on Palestinian textbooks. https://researchbriefings .files.parliament.uk/documents/CDP-2021-0105/CDP-2021-0105.pdf

53 Chalmers, p. 13.

54 Chalmers, p. 14.

55 Chalmers, p. 16.

56 Chalmers, p. 22.

57 Chalmers, p. 23.

58 Kate Leader, 'Tell Her to Be Careful:' Caryl Churchill's *Seven Jewish Children: A Play for Gaza* at the Royal Court Theatre. *Platform*, 4(1), 132–136, 2009.

59 Leader, p. 135.

60 Churchill, p. 6.

61 Churchill, p. 7.

62 Churchill, p. 4.

63 Leader, p. 135.

64 Churchill, p. 2.

9

LEARNING AND TEACHING ABOUT ANTISEMITISM

Mira Vogel

Introduction

After the 2018 massacre by a white supremacist at the Tree of Life Synagogue in Pittsburgh, USA, a group of academics undertook to integrate teaching about antisemitism into their Modern Public Affairs university curriculum. Jamie Levine Daniel and colleagues searched for guidance to get started but found none:

> We met with a librarian; we assigned a research assistant to do literature searches; we asked our friends in other fields. The absence of research on how to teach about antisemitism feels like gaslighting. Is this not a pressing issue? Does anyone else notice its absence? Why hasn't someone else already done this work?[1]

This chapter aims to lay some groundwork to help us understand why antisemitism may be difficult to learn about, and through that analysis to identify promising approaches for teaching about it. The chapter is divided into three main parts. The first part provides context in the form of a timeline of Jewish students' experiences in British universities, experiences which are frequently unaddressed in institutional strategies promoting inclusivity. Jews tend to be small minorities where they study and are particularly exposed to the kinds of antisemitism discussed in this book. The second part responds to this context by introducing some concepts important to understanding contemporary antisemitism. Here I want to flag a distinction between the *concepts* on the one hand, and the *characteristics* which make them hard to learn about, on the other. The *concepts* I discuss here are not directly concerned with the traditional four libels of blood, conspiracy, economic

DOI: 10.4324/9781003222477-10

injustice and racial pollution which we are used to analysing in classical antisemitism. Instead, I will introduce the interrelated concepts of structural racism, whiteness, intersectionality and Jewishness, and argue that their *characteristics* make them examples of what Meyer and Land term 'threshold concepts'. These are transformative ways of thinking about phenomena which are pivotal to learning about a subject but which are also likely to be experienced as troublesome, counterintuitive and confronting because they disturb adjoining concepts. I describe how I think threshold concepts theory sheds light on resistance to understanding antisemitism. In the final section, I draw out some of the implications for education about antisemitism in a British university setting. Since one of the consequences of the under-theorisation of teaching about antisemitism is a scarcity of published empirical work to discover which strategies and practices are effective, these suggestions will be speculative and tentative but they will raise possibilities for future work.

Background: Jewish students in UK universities

According to a HESA[2,3] survey, in 2019–2020, there were 10,485 Jewish students in UK higher education. This is 0.4% of the total student population, the smallest number in the listed categories – the next smallest group, Sikh, is almost twice the size. It is also a likely underestimation since identification with 'Jewishness' distinct from Judaism is not recorded – even though both identities are protected by the 2010 Equality Act. Half of all recorded Jewish students attend just eight universities, which may indicate 'the degree to which they seek one another out, or desire this sense of familiarity'.[4] Some universities and some degree courses within universities[5] have very small numbers of Jewish students.

Jewish students have an awarding gap, according to HESA data:[6] they are the group most likely to progress and qualify, and most likely to achieve a first class or upper second degree. Although data is not collected for staff,[7] we might expect the academic success of Jewish students to convert into a larger presence in the academic workforce too. Indeed, many Jewish scholars are household names, suggesting that even if some Jewish students experience the transition into university as 'the bursting of their Jewish bubble that has surrounded them their entire life',[8] they may feel less out of place in academic settings than some other minoritised groups.

So, on the surface, Jewish students seem to be thriving in higher education, and undeserving of anti-racist attention. Although there is arguably a high level of awareness of classical antisemitism in wider society, through Holocaust remembrance and the use of Nazism as the gold standard of evil, Jews are largely absent from anti-racist consideration in universities. This is partly due to the imperative to minimise awarding gaps which do not affect

Jewish students. It is also partly that universities – particularly pre-92 and Russell Group institutions – are facing a reckoning with their role in the historic injustices of colonialism and eugenics, and demands that they repair their legacies of harm. These necessary, overdue anti-racist measures are not, on the surface of it, consonant with prevalent ways of viewing and responding to contemporary antisemitism though, as I will try to demonstrate, they could be.

The need to respond to antisemitism in the higher education setting exists because of another apparent contradiction; the tiny Jewish minority in higher education has a visibility that is wildly out of proportion to their very low numbers, due to the prevailing rhetoric around Israel.

Antisemitism experienced by Jewish students

Against a background of political debate about migration, sovereignty, religious extremism, terrorism and global conflict, there has been an increase in hate incidents in general, and against Jews in particular. Although most Jewish students are not the direct targets of antisemitism during their time at university, the incidents are sustained and numerous enough to create a negative atmosphere. Deep hostility to Israel and the ongoing campaign to boycott it are often indistinguishable from long-standing expressions of antisemitism. The following timeline is indicative.

In 2006, a report of the All-Party Inquiry into Antisemitism[9] included a chapter on campus antisemitism which noted that while the 'student body is united in its condemnation of the far right', it was not so alive to anti-Jewish themes in some pro-Palestinian discourse, leaving Jewish students isolated or in conflict.

In 2011, the Institute of Jewish Policy Research (IJPR) touched on the separate but related topics of Israel and antisemitism when it reported the first (and still most recent) National Jewish Student Survey.[10] About 42% of the respondents said they had witnessed or been subjected to antisemitism in the seven months prior to the survey, and most of the incidents had taken place among students. Nearly all the respondents had visited Israel, most felt positive towards the country, and for many support for Israel was an important part of being Jewish. Here the report noted a contradiction: Jewish students were aware of tensions around Israel at their university, and were more likely than the wider student population to feel that Israel was treated unfairly, but on the whole, they were not very worried about anti-Israel sentiment and tended to think the debates could be side-stepped.

In 2011, research by the Equality Challenge Unit (now Advance HE)[11] found that Jewish student survey respondents were by far the most likely to feel discriminated against or harassed because of their religion or belief (27%). Among staff, Jewish respondents were the second most likely after

Muslims. Cautious about sampling issues, the authors drew attention to implications at a population level. Also in 2011, a National Union of Students report[12] found that 31% of Jewish students stated they had been victims of a religiously prejudiced incident, by far the highest proportion in this category.

In 2016, the IJPR published a study of 65 Jewish undergraduates in five UK cities,[13] which describes several incidents related to antisemitism. The report's introduction notes that in the run-up to publication, a university Labour Club chair had resigned saying that many in the club had a problem with Jews, and the National Union of Students elected as president someone who its own inquiry had previously censured for a speech it described as 'antisemitic and therefore in breach of the NUS Code of Conduct'. The report picked up signs that the nature of political debate about Israel had created a situation for Jewish students on campus

> that feels uncomfortable, unpleasant, threatening and even, on rare occasions, dangerous. Importantly this does not only happen within closed environments for those choosing to enter the political fray; on the contrary, it is apparent that Jewish students with no particular interest in political engagement have also experienced these feelings simply by walking across the university campus and encountering a protest or demonstration, or even in the context of university lectures.

Although the negative atmosphere for Jews in universities seemed to be intensifying, the report did not refer to these phenomena as antisemitic, but instead as examples of 'anti-Israel sentiment' or 'prejudice'. It did not try to link the singular intensity of this threatening, occasionally dangerous, sentiment with the growing phenomenon of antisemitic rhetoric, damage, abuse and violence in wider society.

Also in 2016, the ombud ordered Sheffield Hallam University to pay a Jewish student £3,000 after dismissing his complaints about antisemitic forms of pro-Palestine campaigning without giving them due consideration.[14]

In 2017, three Jewish students and a non-Jewish academic reported in-depth interviews with 26 Jewish students across UCL in a podcast series called JewCL.[15] In 'Talking about Israel', they discuss their participants' complex and deeply emotional relationship with the country, and say that disclosing a Jewish identity or being outwardly Jewish on campus increased the likelihood of hostile and interrogatory conversations about Israel, political tests where 'a certain response was expected' or the opposite – deliberate omission from those conversations. In 'Talking about the Holocaust', they recount one lecturer's remarks that 'We only care so much about the Holocaust because it's about white people', and an ensuing discussion about the historical and current status of Jews with respect to whiteness. This event caused one participant weeks of examination about why they found this so disturbing, by which time the moment had passed to challenge it.

The same theme is picked up in 'Jewniversity', which records the hesitance of participants to call on support from their Student Union to counter antisemitism, and a perception that this would take time away from other minorities experiencing more acute forms of racism. The podcasters diplomatically reported that the Student Union was perceived to be unsympathetic and said there may be nobody there who would recognise antisemitism as a structural problem.

In 2020, the School of Oriental and African Studies refunded the fees of a pro-Israel Jewish student who abandoned his studies there because a 'toxic antisemitic environment' exacerbated his anxiety and poor mental health. He described seeing antisemitic symbols and graffiti and said he had been called a 'white supremacist Nazi' by fellow students. Despite this, SOAS did not act on its panel's recommendation to initiate an investigation into institutional antisemitism.[16]

In 2021, the Community Security Trust (CST) was sufficiently concerned about antisemitism in universities to publish a report covering 2018–2020.[17] Most of the 163 incidents were categorised as abusive behaviour, with others including assaults, threats or damage. Some bore the hallmarks of the political right, others of the left, and still others were of uncertain provenance. Supporters of Jeremy Corbyn physically assaulted students protesting antisemitism. Somebody drew a swastika on a Jewish student's car, an act of Holocaust inversion.[18] A lecturer introduced the Holocaust and accusations of Labour antisemitism as examples of fake news and propaganda, and asked Jewish students to identify themselves. A lecturer on Israel and Palestine told students to treat allegations of Labour antisemitism as Israeli propaganda. A Student Union BME officer told a Jewish student to 'Be like Israel and cease to exist'. In one university as many as 240 students voted against the establishment of a Jewish Society, and a lecturer there who referred to it as a Zionist society was later found to have circulated antisemitic conspiracy theories about the 2015 Paris terror attacks. The report noted that opposing antisemitism comes with risks for Jewish students and their societies. They are often blamed for antisemitism and have learned to expect reprisals for drawing attention to it. For example, one student was briefly subjected to a disciplinary investigation after whistle-blowing about antisemitism from a lecturer who then retaliated with a vexatious (and ultimately unsuccessful) counter-complaint of bullying and harassment.

The report focused the attention of the employers' organisation Universities UK, which in 2021 published practical guidance on tackling antisemitism in UK universities.[19] This supplemented its broader advice on tackling racial harassment with steps specific to antisemitism. It attributed poor institutional response to inadequate definitions of antisemitism, which in turn led to misrecognition of the way antisemitic conspiracy beliefs and political disagreements about the Middle East could tip over into antisemitism. The guidance was brief and high level, and would require a lot of careful thinking to implement on the ground.

In 2021, over two years after an initial complaint, the University of Bristol terminated the employment of a professor who had publicly called for the 'end of Zionism as a [or possibly the] functioning ideology of the world'.[20] He also referred to Jewish students in classically antisemitic terms as political pawns ('Israel's assets in the UK'[21]), and described the Union of Jewish Students as a threat to the safety of Arab and Muslim students. Jewish scholars with differing views about how to define antisemitism[22] had united in condemnation of his conspiratorial writing about Zionists and power.

For Jewish students, the kind of antisemitism summarised here is largely overlooked in the Race Equality Charter resources. Consequently, antisemitism remains a peripheral consideration in universities today, eclipsed[23,24] by other kinds of prejudice and discrimination which affect greater numbers of students and which show up as awarding differentials. This low status in the hierarchy of concern is decades old. For example, Harvard law professor Derek Bell described Jews as advantaged 'White ethnics' and philosopher Alain Badiou asserted that to protest the antisemitism that exists within much anti-Zionist activity is to align with 'imperialists against occupied and mistreated peoples'.[25] More recently, Conservative government interventions in favour of the adoption of definitions of antisemitism and free speech guarantees within higher education[26] have further politicised the issue. Along with other individual cases of antisemitism in academic spaces,[27] they have been cited to support the perception of more favourable treatment for Jews and have undermined advocacy against antisemitism.[28] Led by Boris Johnson, the UK government embraced racial differentiation, 'the way in which dominant society racialises and prioritises different minoritised groups at different times to suit hegemonic arguments of racial superiority and inferiority',[29] constructing Jews (and other groups) as model minorities and further separating antisemitism out from other campus anti-racist work. This is not new on the political right. Keith Kahn-Harris describes[30] how injunctions to integrate tend to be at the heart of right-wing philosemitism: 'The corollary of this is the selection for praise of those "model minorities", whose impeccable integration stands as a reproach to those who are obstinately retaining their threatening otherness'.

Meanwhile, antisemitism in wider society from all sources continues to rise steadily[31] at levels proportionally higher than any other group.[32] In the first half of 2021 there were 2 incidents of extreme violence, 87 of assault, 1,073 of abusive behaviour, 85 of threat and 56 of damage or desecration. These figures are likely to be an underestimation.

The trouble with learning about antisemitism

Around the time the boycott campaign was taking root in UK universities, Jan Meyer and Ray Land were working on a government-funded project at the University of Durham, exploring students' conceptual frameworks and conceptual change in five academic disciplines. Their starting point was David Perkins'[33] research into ways knowledge can be 'troublesome'. Perkins distinguished four different kinds of trouble and set out how they can interfere with the kind of conceptual change through learning that teachers hope for. Knowledge can be *inert* – the kinds of routine and isolated facts 'in the mind's attic', which the knower may easily be able to declare in a pub quiz, but which they may fail to connect with actual problems in their world. One example is the answer to the question, 'Who set up the Anti-Nazi League?' *Ritual* knowledge is another type - common sense knowledge or conceptual rules that are taken for granted but rarely examined and not readily transferred into new contexts. For example, a belief that antisemitism is tucked away in the past except for some marginal far right groups would make it difficult to recognise antisemitism in the kind of pro-Palestine campaigning that characterises Zionism as the primary cause of all conflict in the Middle East. Ratifying the IHRA Working Definition of Antisemitism without applying it to specific incidents in the world would be another example of inert knowledge. A third type is *conceptually difficult* knowledge, which is often bewildering. For example, what does it mean when a black Jewish journalist who challenged Wiley's antisemitic rant is told by Wiley that she is not black while at the same time her blackness is insulted by a section of Wiley's opponents?[34] Finally, *foreign or alien* knowledge is knowledge which conflicts with students' existing perceptions or strongly held beliefs. The idea that racism was invented in 1222 with the Synod of Oxford, rather than in 1492 with the first European colony, may have challenging implications, as may the idea that pale-skinned Jews are only conditionally white.[35] Another example is a realisation that an accusation of antisemitism can be received as more incendiary than antisemitism itself, causing the perpetrators of antisemitism 'to respond as victims of those who they think utilise such an evil and destructive weapon'.[36]

Meyer and Land identified a fifth type of trouble, *tacit* knowledge that is known or practised confidently and intuitively without a clear, reflective conception of what, how or why. They flag the possibility of tacit knowledge passing beneath learners' notice like a 'conceptual submarine' because the ideas are presumed by teachers but not articulated, and are withheld as 'expert blind spots'[37] which cannot easily be detected by learners. Without having an idea of where learners are – what they know and can do, in all their diversity – it is even harder to teach about something as complex, counterintuitive and potentially confronting as antisemitism.

One final thing to note about troublesome knowledge is that where it risks exposure or discomfort, it is often resisted. As George Orwell observed:[38]

> What vitiates nearly all that is written about antisemitism is the assumption in the writer's mind that he himself is immune to it. 'Since I know that antisemitism is irrational,' he argues, 'it follows that I do not share it.' He thus fails to start his investigation in the one place where he could get hold of some reliable evidence – that is, in his own mind.

When faced with troublesome knowledge, Land, Cousin and Meyer[39] observe that some learners experience a sense of loss 'as they lose the security of a previously held conceptual stance to enter less certain terrain', and may become stuck, oscillating on the threshold of letting go of old knowledge, but unable to pass into a liminal state of learning.

These types of troublesome knowledge – ritual, inert, conceptually difficult, alien, tacit – became part of Meyer and Land's inquiry into conceptual change in learning. This work eventually yielded a framework for recognising the kinds of profoundly transformative knowledge which they term 'threshold concepts'.

Introducing threshold concepts

We can think of concepts as ideas, expressed as words or terms, which represent phenomena in the world. Concepts function as 'categorisers'[40] which help us to sort things, and so reveal the world to us. Religions such as Islam, Sikhism and Judaism function as categorisers, as do ethnicities such as Caribbean, Irish traveller, Sikh, Jewish and political positions such as Zionist, non-Zionist anti-Zionist. Possession of different concepts allows people to distinguish between the different things which concern us, and make connections between them. Some people contest Zionism, and where Zionism intersects with Judaism and Jewishness, they may need to work harder to make appropriate distinctions and comparisons. Together the concepts we learn and the connections we draw between them become our personal model for making sense of the world. We use these clusters to enquire, analyse and predict – in other words, they become ways of knowing, or 'ontologies'.

A threshold concept is not the same as a *core* concept, such as genocide, Zionism or Judaism. A threshold concept 'acts on the learner's (partially) acquired body of knowledge as a restructuring tool during the learning process'.[41] Meyer and Land present threshold concepts as a way to understand powerfully transformative points during learning and recognise how, in restructuring a view of an academic discipline or even the world, they can be profoundly unsettling and may be resisted. This is their often-quoted definition:

> A threshold concept can be considered as akin to a portal, opening up a new and previously inaccessible way of thinking about something. It represents a transformed way of understanding, or interpreting, or viewing something without which the learner cannot progress. As a consequence of comprehending a threshold concept there may thus be a transformed internal view of subject matter, subject landscape, or even world view. This transformation may be sudden or it may be protracted over a considerable period of time, with the transition to understanding proving troublesome.[42]

Before attempting to apply threshold concepts theory to learning about antisemitism, it is worth establishing some preliminaries. Since threshold concepts themselves are personal and elude being definitively pinned down, it is best to think of the framework as a heuristic, a practical method not guaranteed to be perfect or even optimal, but helpful for people bringing their own experiences to making sense of phenomena. As such, the theory can throw light on why some concepts powerfully transform students in ways that are hard to learn and teach. Moreover, it is important to keep in mind that Meyer and Land were not centrally concerned with teaching about racism. They were looking across academic disciplines in a curricular context, to discover how to teach for deep, enduring conceptual change that would help students 'think like' somebody in that discipline, and ultimately succeed in their degrees. Meyer and Land explored heat transfer in physics, opportunity cost in economics, signification in literary studies, complex numbers in mathematics and presentism in history – concepts students would need to grasp if they were ever to 'think like' a physicist, historian or other expert.

This curricular context offers any teaching initiative continuity, time and sustained contact that enables the development of trust, whereas institutional anti-racist initiatives have tended to be ephemeral and adjunct, using workshops, seminars or self-paced independent online learning. All of these things raise questions about whether threshold concepts theory can be applied to learning about antisemitism. However, educational researchers have applied it to analysing how subjects such as structural racism,[43] anti-racism,[44] otherness[45] and the social model of disability[46] are or could be learned. Students, too, have taken a more capacious view of threshold concepts beyond academic disciplines to include what one has called 'non-academic learning'.[47] These studies indicate that it is not far-fetched to explore what threshold concepts theory can bring to antisemitism education. So, below I will introduce the characteristics of threshold concepts[48] and what they suggest about why contemporary antisemitism is hard to teach and learn about.

Threshold concepts important to understanding antisemitism

Knowledge needs to be active, not inert, so in introducing the concepts below I will aim to take David Perkins' advice to get any tacit presumptions out on the table and examine them 'not just as objects of discursive analysis but as systems of activity to engage'.[49] As you read, you may begin to notice how the concepts I use to illustrate one characteristic are examples of other characteristics too; there are no hard lines to draw here.

Transformative

The transformative characteristic of threshold concepts refers to a striking shift in perception which radically alters a learner's outlook on the subject, or world around them, perhaps even to the extent of changing their identity. As Glynis Cousin puts it:

> Grasping a threshold concept is transformative because it involves an ontological as well as a conceptual shift. We are what we know. New understandings are assimilated into our biography, becoming part of who we are, how we see and how we feel.[50]

Meyer and Land refer to powerful politico-philosophical insights in comprehending, say, aspects of Marxist or feminist analysis, and how emotional the consequent reconstruction of identity can be. Liz Crow[51] gives the example of discovering the existence of a social model of disability:

> Suddenly what I had always known, deep down, was confirmed. It wasn't my body that was responsible for all my difficulties, it was external factors, the barriers constructed by the society in which I live. I was being dis-abled – my capabilities and opportunities were being restricted – by prejudice, discrimination, inaccessible environments and inadequate support. Even more important, if all the problems had been created by society, then surely society could un-create them. Revolutionary!

For Jews, however, becoming conscious of antisemitism in a political form and from the left is likely to bring alienation, self-doubt and a sense of gathering threat. The trope of the hyper-powerful, cunning and parasitic Jew can create distance for Jews in society. Jamie Levine Daniel and colleagues touch on this reserve in their account of redesigning a public affairs curriculum in the light of the Pittsburgh synagogue terror attack, observing that 'a belief in (or inability to recognize) antisemitism undermines the ability of Jewish students to access power without being subject to extra scrutiny'.[52] Even where Jews may seem to have the support of the most powerful figures in a society, the dependence on this support, and its contingent nature, exacerbates the sense of precarity.

How else might learning about antisemitism be transformative? One powerfully transformative way of viewing discrimination is to see it as structural rather than individual. but while this approach is currently adopted widely in the UK, it is rare to see it referenced in relation to antisemitism. In its introduction to structural racism for the sector, for example, Advance HE[53] highlights a gap between, on the one hand, public thinking about racism, which tends to emphasise personal beliefs, and, on the other, campaigners' emphasis on eliminating racism from systemic interactions between institutions, laws, customs and ideas. In a similar vein, Principle 3 of the Race Equality Charter[54] for UK Universities warns against a deficit model focused on perceived shortcomings in individual students rather than the role of structural circumstances outside the student's control in causing the deficit in the first place.

Viewed through this lens, race is taught not as sets of phenotypes or traits in groups of people, but as phenomenon which divides people and enables a hierarchical set of power relations.[55] This prompts a turn away from simple views of racism as a prejudice within individual wrong-headed 'bad apples', and towards a higher-level analysis of power in society. The view that racism has its origins in colonies and the trans-Atlantic slave trade has led to structural racism being referred to as 'whiteness':

> the privileges and opportunities afforded to persons racialized as White are often not recognized as such – they are woven into the basic operating assumptions of society, such that their beneficiaries do not even perceive their existence.[56]

In this description, whiteness as a system facilitates status and power which is also hegemonic, simultaneously unnoticed and ubiquitous. However, this way of thinking about power has dualistic tendencies noted by Cousin and Fine:[57] 'Blackness and Whiteness are primary sources of power and inequality and ... in this dichotomy Jews have generally become advantaged "White ethnics"'. This dualism is the echo of the sharp colour lines of earlier race science which once racialised all Jews as black[58] but which have since transferred Jews into the white category. Consequently, in a climate which seeks to abolish whiteness as an unseen, unspoken, universal authority masquerading as neutral objectivity, Jews are now frequently assumed to be a subspecies of that whiteness. Anyone sensitised to antisemitism can immediately intuit how this viewpoint is likely to compound existing enduring prejudices about Jews as global oppressors. As Moishe Postone observed,[59] in the most fetishised forms of oppositional consciousness, Jews are thought to be conspiring in the oppression of others. For hundreds of years, antisemitic tropes of Jewish hyper-power, world-spanning domination and covert control have been widespread, and can be observed across the political spectrum. Antisemitism has often appeared counter-hegemonic and liberating, and the critical lens of whiteness frequently neglects this.

Unless we are sensitised to antisemitism, adopting whiteness as a tool for understanding the world could compound prejudice against Jews in ways we are unlikely to notice or address. In pursuing the question of 'what Whiteness does to Jewishness', David Schraub[60] finds that 'White power and privilege – valid as far as they go – acted as a sort of accelerant for prejudiced tropes of Jewish power and privilege'. He illustrates this with a dispute that broke out over a Stanford University Student Council motion condemning antisemitism which contained a clause about Jewish control of the media, economy, government and other societal institutions. One student senator reserved the right to bring an analysis of whiteness to bear on 'these potential power dynamics' without being called antisemitic:

> The senator is talking about Jews no differently, he thinks, from how he talks about other members of the White community. How can it be that the argument shifts from valid to illicit simply because the subject is Jews? Meanwhile, the Jewish objectors think that the senator is talking about them in a way no different from any other antisemite. How could the same argument gain legitimacy simply because the senator thought his approach was antiracist in nature?

In attempting to address this 'sense of talking past each other' Schraub exemplifies David Perkins' advice to put any tacit presumptions – 'conceptual submarines' – out on the table for a while, and examine them 'not just as objects of discursive analysis but as systems of activity to engage'.[61]

He does this through a discussion of intersectionality, which I think of as another transformative threshold concept. In the late 1980s, the black feminist lawyer Kimberlé Crenshaw described how legal categories of discrimination based on race and on sex had failed to adequately represent the experiences of black women.[62] Discrimination had been 'defined in terms of the experiences of those who are privileged *but for* their racial or sexual characteristics', meaning that its paradigms tended to be based on the most advantaged members of the class. So black *men* became the normative subjects of the protected category of race, resulting in women's cultural, economic and social characteristics being overlooked in discussions about race. Similarly, *white* women became the normative subjects of the protected category of sex, obscuring the cultural, economic and social characteristics of women of colour. Crenshaw describes how black women can face uniquely compounded discrimination in ways that are 'not the sum of race and sex discrimination, but as Black women'.

I would add here that we can see intersectionality at work in the experience of pale-skinned British Jews who are held under particular suspicion when they get close to power. Moreover, the experiences of British Jews racialised as black bring insights about the nature of antisemitism as it interacts with anti-black racism. Perhaps many Jews in Britain, despite their refugee and migrant background, have become 'functionally white', in the sense that unless they are marked by outward signs such as kippa, tzitzit or magen david, or by an outlandish-sounding name, they can access all systemic benefits accruing to a British ethnic majority with few impediments, and may escape being directly or personally targeted. Yet on Kimberlé Crenshaw's crossroads,[63] this minority of black and dark-skinned British Jews can be hit by racist traffic from both an anti-black direction and an antisemitic one. This is illustrated by the responses to rap artist Wiley's antisemitic tirade, which he underwrote by insisting that 'Black people can't be racist',[64] illuminating differences as well as similarities in how black Jews and white Jews can experience antisemitism and discourse about antisemitism. Racism excludes Jews from whiteness, while anti-racism excludes Jews from the non-white coalition of anti-racists. As the comedian Alex Edelman puts it:[65]

> You might be thinking "Do I think Jews are white?" Here's how you know. If you don't love white people, Jews are white. But if you think being white is awesome – congrats on storming the Capitol! – also you don't think Jews are white.

When these intersections of Jewishness and whiteness, and Jewishness and blackness, conflict with previously held beliefs, they become troublesome knowledge. This can be observed in the support of hundreds of academics for David Miller's work to present the efforts of Jewish organisations[66] as something particularly coordinated, sinister and powerful, decontextualised from other kinds of lobbying. It can be heard in the 'Jewniversity' episode of the JewCL podcast[67] when Jewish students worry about unduly taking up the BAME Officer's time, and hope that somebody in their student union might eventually respond to antisemitism as a structural problem.

Whiteness is one of anti-racism's threshold concepts, and insofar as black and brown people are the normative subjects of anti-racism, the intersection of Jewishness and whiteness has become one of antisemitism's most transformative threshold concepts. This intersection reveals new and troublesome ways of thinking for people with a range of perspectives, for example those already on the side of Jews but maybe less acquainted with the concept of structural racism, people who are habitually sceptical about antisemitism, and those who are agnostic. It also embodies other characteristics of a threshold concept which I have not yet introduced but will turn to now.

Irreversible

A threshold concept is usually irreversible. This does not mean that it is immutable, but rather that it is likely to permanently alter a learner's perspective, and that altered perspective becomes internalised as a new common sense even if a learner eventually refines or rejects it for a rival concept. One example is the widespread, incorrect assumption that Nazi antisemitism characterises antisemitism in general. We are mostly attuned to and unified in our rejection of this kind of biologically essentialist 'Jews as Jews' antisemitism, but it is different from the kinds of political antisemitism addressed in contemporary definitions such as the IHRA. On the other hand, definitions of antisemitism which comprehend left-wing manifestations also recognise forms that, irrespective of intent, lead to indignities, exclusions, harassment and sometimes violence against Jews. Other chapters in this book document how attempts to draw attention to the antisemitism which deforms some pro-Palestine campaigning frequently meet with politicised resistance, discounting even the most egregious examples, defining them out of existence simply by virtue of being in the name of Palestine solidarity. An emphasis on antisemitic effect rather than intent is experienced by such activists as so confronting that some have turned the tables to allege that the accusation of antisemitism itself is actually a disingenuous pro-Israel ploy to obstruct Palestine solidarity. David Hirsh has documented this phenomenon in detail.[68] If the original view of Nazism as the archetypal antisemitism was itself a threshold concept, its irreversibility may to some extent explain this resistance. But in fact, becoming aware of left-wing antisemitism may modify, but will not displace or dilute, a view that antisemitism is a right-wing eugenicist belief that Jews are an alien, socially toxic species that must be exterminated to prevent it polluting the host race. They co-exist, sometimes cross over, and can both be accommodated.

Another important aspect of irreversibility is that often it cannot be pinned to a moment where a threshold is crossed. If you ask left-wing people to remember the moment they first grasped the nature of antisemitism in left-wing movements, they will often struggle. There may have been a striking event but the conceptual change is hard to describe. It is this difficulty in gaining sufficient hindsight[69] to understand afresh what is not simple and obvious about mastering a concept, or what might be in conflict with it, that can make a concept hard to teach, and make it hard for a teacher to become sufficiently aware of the 'conceptual submarines' which stop students from learning.

These qualities of irreversibility suggest that if learners apprehend the threshold concepts of structural racism and whiteness in the absence of any intersectional understandings of contemporary antisemitism, then learning about antisemitism is likely to be experienced as troublesome and disruptive, and it will be much harder to teach in a way that extends people's understanding.

Integrative

A threshold concept often reveals new connections with other concepts which were previously hidden or unknown. These connections allow a learner to start to 'think like' a member of the group they are learning about, whether that be economists, doctors, anthropologists – or indeed like Jews, because a major part of avoiding or contesting antisemitism depends on an understanding of how Jews may experience the world.

Additionally, part of teaching about antisemitism is developing an awareness in the student of how people who are not attuned to antisemitism (or do not comprehend it or suspect it is a ploy) may experience the world. In the following account of an episode of profound misrecognition,[70] Ruth Sheldon describes how one university's Palestine Society had invited a speaker who had repeatedly compared Israelis to Nazis and elided Jews and Zionists. On being accused of contravening the student union's antisemitism policy, he

> railed against this silencing of Palestinian voices, shouting: 'If you criticise Israel, you are antisemite. If you say there's a Zionist lobby in the United States and in Britain, you are an antisemite. If you talk anything about Israeli crimes, you know, you are antisemite.' His rage increased as he went on to claim that Zionism in fact demanded recognition of the nexus of Judaism and Zionism, placing Palestinians like himself in an impossible double bind.

Later a Palestine Society member reminded the university's Israel Society that they were the ones distinguishing between Judaism and Zionism in the first place, by their act of protesting the speaker's conflation of them:

> This is a political and not a religious issue. Zionism is not Judaism, remember? ... Aren't you collating Zionism with Judaism when you claim that there is a need for interfaith dialogue around this issue? ... Please don't refer to the problems of Zionists as being the same as the problems of Jews.

There is no disingenuity here; these protests express incomprehension of antisemitism and suspicion about the claims made around it. At the centre of this double bind is a misunderstanding about Judaism's connection to the *land* of Israel as distinct from, but often overlaying, the connection almost every Jewish student in the IJPR National Survey of Jewish Students summarised above felt with the *state* of Israel, whether religious or not. In the JewCL podcast series, student researchers discuss how interviewees responded to the question of relating to Israel:[71]

> Zionism as it's spoken about, is so intricately linked into the religion of Judaism, and is so deeply in the scriptures and the prayers that we say, there's always a connection to the land of, or idea of, Israel, that any Jew negotiates in some way throughout their life.

A student researcher told a story about interviewing a very orthodox Haredi Jew who said that his specific religious tradition is anti-Zionist for theological reasons, but

> he still felt some sort of kinship ties towards Israel, that there were Jewish people there and therefore he felt a connection even though politically that wasn't quite where he sat. So Israel isn't something that a lot of Jews can talk about in this non-emotional sense.

The connection may be spiritual, familial, existential or antithetical, and is present in many Jewish lives. It resides in what is, even while obscured from view, one of the most troublesome and integrative of antisemitism's threshold concepts, and that is 'Jewishness'. Jewishness is distinct from Judaism, allowing for a more cultural or secular state of being. Historically, Jewishness is not an identity Jews have always adopted voluntarily. Its formative role in Zionism was as an imposed identification – for example the Nazi Party's Nuremberg Laws which targeted secular and religious Jews alike, and Stalin's persecution of the secular Jewish members of the Communist Party. These and other acts taught Jews that they could expect to attract antisemitism whether or not they were religiously observant. A person is targeted by antisemitism if assumed to be Jewish irrespective of how they self-identify. Ultimately, the circumstance which caused Israel to exist was not an intensity of religious worship, but an intensity of antisemitism; a critical mass of Jews had abandoned hope of protection from other states. Since Israel is the world's largest Jewish collectivity, it follows that many Jews, globally, would have connections with Israel. For this reason, Israel was established by its original Zionist Socialist government as a Jewish state even though defining that Jewishness would inevitably be difficult. The sovereign nation state was conceived in Balfour's promise of a 'national home' rather than a religious one.

Given all this, it is unsurprising that Israel should be understood differently by those friendly to it, those hostile to it and those who live in it. An understanding of this threshold concept, that defining who is Jewish and what being Jewish means is complex, contested and contradictory, is integrative because it is required to understand the apparent elisions between Judaism and Zionism made by pro-Israel or anti-antisemitism activists. Palestine activists who do not grasp this threshold concept may well perceive Jewish or Zionist claims about this issue as self-serving sleights of hand, capricious and hypocritical. The realisation that Jewishness exists and is distinct from either Judaism or Zionism is also unforgettable – an example of irreversibility. However, Jewishness is an unstable concept, and difficult to understand, particularly in the context of Israel. Israeli scholar of Jewish sovereignty Yaakov Yadgar has described an Israeli Jewish identity crisis,[72] which is ongoing and shows no sign of resolution. As such, 'Jewishness' may be another of Perkins' 'conceptual submarines'.

Challenges to teaching about antisemitism

I have introduced what I consider to be some key threshold concepts for understanding antisemitism today, including structural racism, whiteness, intersectionality and Jewishness. This chapter aims to provide a basis for further work on the practicality of teaching these concepts. If you were not aware of these ideas before you read this chapter, maybe I have softened up some of your intuitions or disturbed what you take to be common sense. But what I haven't done is taught you about antisemitism. To do that well I would need to be aware of the specific things, in each context, that can interfere with learners crossing such thresholds to a new understanding.

One pitfall to be aware of when preparing to teach is student mimicry: the regurgitation of knowledge without being able to transfer it to new contexts. Consider 'A Lizard's Tale', Marlon Solomon's engaging multimodal talk, which has toured many UK venues.[73] With images, music and emotion, Marlon retells his dawning realisation about the prevalence of antisemitic conspiracy beliefs in society. Yad Vashem's free online course 'Antisemitism: From Its Origins to the Present'[74] is a curriculum that includes presentations and carefully curated talking head interviews with renowned Jewish Studies scholars, activists and public figures. Carefully crafted, well-organised, fluent arguments like these may persuade the learner that because they apprehended it with perfect clarity at the time, they have now learned it.[75] However, the concept is then vulnerable to become stuck – 'inert' knowledge, sequestered in the mind's attic, unable to easily be brought into play in the heat of an antisemitic moment. The magisterial organisation and presentation of a body of knowledge is certainly foundational to teaching about antisemitism, but may not be sufficient for learning to 'think like an anti-antisemite'.

This key difference between lecturing and learning is one of the threshold concepts in the study of education itself. Thinking about how cultural studies students learn about otherness,[76] Glynis Cousin notes the emotional disengagement and 'defendedness' of some students who can 'do sexism' just as they can 'do the Ancient Romans', by correctly and concretely regurgitating what they have been told. Where resigned, performative mimicry is the outcome, Cousin identifies 'domestication wherein the radical, transformative capacity of a concept is tamed'. As Jennifer Booth puts it,[77] 'When information is simply presented to students, they can remain at a distance from it', particularly if the material is 'easily conveyed in an affectively neutral manner'. This can be compounded by the phenomenon Glynis Cousin[78] identifies as voyeurism or spectatorship – an emotional distance and an avoidance of self-examination where a disaffected learner may be 'just trying to work out what boxes you want them to tick'. This may be what Keith Kahn-Harris is referring to in his description of anti-racists who find themselves accused of antisemitism, an example of Perkins' 'alien knowledge'. Kahn-Harris observes that 'it is bewildering and unsettling to be accused of traducing one's deepest beliefs'.[79] In response,

> they will draw on widely available cultural resources in order to deny those claims. We now have decades of experience in developing sophisticated, discursive tools for the denial of racism, and while those on the left may not have been in the avante-garde of the creation of those tools, they are capable of taking advantage of them when needed. Which isn't to say that accusations are always fair, or denials always unreasonable, but that the process of denying antisemitism may be identical regardless of how justified the accusation is.

Another reason that learners may avoid letting go of prior beliefs and crossing the threshold into a more uncertain space is that, as Peter Felten notes,[80] previous educational experiences may have taught them to value being correct and concrete. Felten recommends creating educational settings that, instead of valuing certainty, welcome the ambiguity and confusion intrinsic to learning threshold concepts. This is particularly important, he says, because students' everyday worlds can feel destabilised by encounters with threshold concepts; those who 'often described their own learning process as 'stressful', 'debilitating', 'frustrating' and 'intensely emotional' reported that they were 'shocked', 'upset', 'hopeless' and 'very anxious' in the seminar process he describes. Emotion is frequently overlooked in academic settings, which tend to be predicated on rationalism and restraint, thereby demanding the regulation or avoidance of visceral, intense feelings. As with learning about any form of prejudice, learning about antisemitism can bring self-doubt, mistrust and alienation. It can trouble relationships and make learners feel cut off from each other; in particular it can make Jews feel their Jewishness in new, disturbing ways.

Possibilities for teaching about antisemitism

In the preceding sections, I have introduced some of the concepts important to a contemporary curriculum about antisemitism and some difficulties to overcome. In practice, however, few people will study a curriculum entirely dedicated to this topic, and so alternatives are needed. In common with teaching about other kinds of prejudice and discrimination in universities, teaching about antisemitism is likely to pursue one of two approaches: either adjunct to a curriculum or as specific cases provided within a broader curriculum. I will conclude this chapter by considering the implications for each approach. My evaluation is necessarily tentative and high level, since it would be narrow and technicist to propose strategies decontextualised from teachers' knowledge about their subject and their students.

The first approach is adjunct to the curriculum. One-off events have limited power to change internalised, worked-out anti-antisemitic positions, although if done well they may unsettle them. One powerful example from the Union of Jewish Students' Antisemitism Awareness Training[81] starts with a close-up image of 'Free Palestinie' graffiti on a wall. The facilitator asks the group whether this is antisemitic and only after responding do we discover that the wall is part of a synagogue. This shift in perspective resonates with the threshold concept it presents, is strongly memorable, and is not susceptible to the mimicry described above. These qualities are something to aim for in all such activities, which are particularly susceptible to mimicry where participants feel scrutinised. Where these events are also compulsory or conditional to some other benefit, participants may not arrive in a state of mind to accept the liminality described above. Therefore, teachers need to design opportunities for participants to apply what they learn about antisemitism in ways which anticipate disguised resistance to learning – for example, under cover of playing the game – and design out possibilities for mimicry and regurgitation. Teachers need strategies which bring them opportunities to check for the kinds of conceptual change described above, and adapt the teaching strategies accordingly. As ever, resource is needed to evaluate these events for longer-term outcomes.

Another example of adjunct (or para-curricular) teaching comes from student-organised events about the Israel–Palestine conflict. Ruth Sheldon's ethnography of a student Israel–Palestine Forum meeting is relevant here. Although this event was primarily about history rather than antisemitism, the intensity of energy dedicated to the Israel–Palestine conflict in different student groups (for example, the Federation of Student Islamic Societies considers it central[82]) and the comparatively small numbers of Jews means that, as the IJPR research above noted, these kinds of events affect the atmosphere for Jews at universities. Ruth Sheldon describes a convivial, seminar-like setting of 30 students, open to anyone without prior knowledge or prior registration.[83] Its organisers had decided against the rigid, adversarial structures of meetings elsewhere, and consequently had managed to some extent to sidestep the polarising forces which treat such 'dialogue events' as ideological attempts to undermine pro-Palestine activism by normalising Israeli–Palestinian relations and collaborating with the enemy. At the event, members of the forum showed how it was possible to lay bare their personal connections with Palestine and Israel and respect 'the facts' while at the same time allowing people to 'understand how others learnt about that'. Rather than arguing out the veracity of conflicting historical records, they examined their own experiences of them. Ruth Sheldon notes that one of the forum's initiators 'seemed to have dropped this emphasis on defusing tension, focusing instead on the IPF's educative ambitions'. This seemed to sustain the group through tense conversations which had boiled over into aggression at other meetings she had attended: 'In contrast to the rationalistic containment of the melodramatic frame and the excess of tragic actions turned violent, we stayed in our circle, acknowledging yet not resolving these internal tensions'. This critique of rationalism can be profoundly confronting in academia, particularly in the current anti-intellectual, populist climate. Nevertheless, there is something valuable here about what *to do* when faced with the kinds of emotions I have discussed in this chapter and which, if left unacknowledged, are a threat to the potential of education to sensitise participants about antisemitism, especially within the context of commentary on the Israel–Palestine conflict. The forum is an example of how the formulaic regurgitation and 'defendedness' Glynis Cousin observed in students learning about otherness can be disarmed by adopting pedagogical strategies that ask learners to interrogate their own lives 'without privileging the marginal and marginalising the apparently privileged'.[84]

The second approach is to integrate teaching about antisemitism into existing curricula. In the case of the academics mentioned at the start of this chapter, Jamie Levine Daniel and colleagues[85] designed ways of learning about antisemitism that could advance the existing objectives of their Modern Public Affairs curriculum. This was mainly a matter of bringing antisemitism as examples or case studies to which students would apply core concepts in Modern Public Affairs. Antisemitism could be a lens for examining 'technical rationality' (the excessive emphasis on administrative efficiency which leads to dehumanisation and cruel treatment). An opportunity for students to analyse the influence of stereotypical and prejudiced social constructions on the policy agenda might be found in policymakers' typification of Jewish Americans as 'Contenders' (while casting Black Americans as 'Dependents'). Aspects of critical theory and social construction could be illustrated through analysing national conversations about Jews which are stubbornly impervious to the input of Jews themselves. The aftermath of a terror attack could be a study in different religious community organisations. Knowledge of antisemitism is relevant to learning about culturally responsive evaluation, human resource management and foreign policy critiques related to Israel. These are the opportunities Jamie Levine Daniel and colleagues found. While such approaches may have a valuable role in sensitising students to the presence of antisemitism, the pressure put on most curricula is likely to prevent deep engagement with the threshold concepts of antisemitism unless they already intersect with the learning outcomes and assessment criteria of an existing subject. Modern Public Affairs is a subject which is likely to have threshold concepts of its own, distinct from those of antisemitism and claiming their own priority. So while antisemitism may be present in many curricula in service of their learning outcomes, given the care these concepts require, integrating them would take deft, knowledgeable, confident teaching and a readiness to carry on the discussion beyond timetabled teaching.

Conclusion

Concepts that are necessary for a deep understanding of antisemitism are not islands nor building blocks which can simply be added to a sum of knowledge. Rather, they connect with each other, and if they change, they disturb or distort each other, demanding reconfiguration and a shift in subjectivity which often feels deeply unsettling. I have set out some of what I take to be threshold concepts in anti-racist thinking and how these may disturb or help understanding contemporary antisemitism.

Consequently, when deciding how to go about teaching antisemitism, it may be more straightforward to arrive at what *not* to do than agree on 'what works'. Effective approaches will almost certainly defy very transmissive teaching or rigid technicist approaches which usher students through a series of learning outcomes. Students are likely to respond very differently to learning about these concepts – with insight, resistance, mistrust, shock, recognition or a sense of loss. The most effective strategies, then, will rarely be dislocated techniques; they will be holistic, situated approaches differentiated for a particular context – designs for teaching a particular subject to particular students in a particular environment. Learning about antisemitism depends on staying power, effort, courage and commitment to vitalise the knowledge by applying it to everyday situations, keeping it supple so it can be brought into play in any relevant, often embittered, contexts that arise. Whether adjunct to or integrated into curricula, teaching for conceptual change about antisemitism cannot assume any of these commitments in learners, so needs to encourage them alongside the knowledge, and find ways to check both.

Notes

1 Jamie Levine Daniel, Rachel Fyall, R. and Jodie Benenson, Talking about Antisemitism in MPA Classrooms and Beyond. *Journal of Public Affairs Education,* 26(3), 2020, 313–135. https://doi.org/10.1080/15236803.2019.1646581

2 Higher Education Statistics Agency, *Who's Studying in HE?* (2021). https://www.hesa.ac.uk/data-and-analysis/students/whos-in-he#numbers (accessed 25 February 2023).

3 Higher Education Statistics Agency, *Figure 5: HE Student Enrolments by Personal Characteristics 2015/16 to 2019/20*. https://www.hesa.ac.uk/data-and-analysis/sb258/figure-5 (accessed 25 February 2023).

4 Jonathan Boyd, *Searching for Community: A Portrait of Undergraduate Jewish Students in Five UK Cities*. Institute for Jewish Policy Research (2016). https://archive.jpr.org.uk/object-uk423 (accessed 25 February 2023).

5 David Graham and Jonathan Boyd, *Key Findings from the 2011 National Jewish Student Survey* (2011). https://www.jpr.org.uk/publication?id=34 (accessed 25 February 2023).

6 AdvanceHE, *Equality in Higher Education: Statistical Report 2020*. https://www.advance-he.ac.uk/knowledge-hub/equality-higher-education-statistical-report-2020 (accessed 25 February 2023).

7 Higher Education Statistics Agency, *Table 3: HE Staff by Activity Standard Occupational Classification 2014/15 to 2019/20*. https://www.hesa.ac.uk/data-and-analysis/staff/table-3 (accessed 25 February 2023).

8 Community Security Trust, *Campus Antisemitism in Britain 2018–2020* (2021). https://cst.org.uk/public/data/file/3/6/Antisemitism%20on%20University%20Campuses.pdf (accessed 25 February 2023).

9 All-Party Parliamentary Group against Antisemitism, *Report of the All-party Parliamentary Inquiry into Antisemitism* (2006). https://antisemitism.org.uk/publication/the-all-party-parliamentary-inquiry-into-antisemitism/ (accessed 25 February 2023).

10 David Graham and Jonathan Boyd, *Key Findings from the 2011 National Jewish Student Survey* (2011). https://www.jpr.org.uk/publication?id=34 (accessed 25 February 2023).

11 Paul Weller, Tristram Hooley and Nicki Moore, *Religion and Belief in Higher Education: Researching the Experiences of Staff and Students*, London: Equality Challenge Unit, 2011, pp. 76–80. https://www.advance-he.ac.uk/knowledge-hub/religion-and-belief-he-researching-experiences-staff-and-students (accessed 25 February 2023).

12 National Union of Students, *Hate Crime: Interim Report* (2011). https://www.nusconnect.org.uk/resources/home-office-nus-hate-crime-interim-report (accessed 25 February 2023).

13 Jonathan Boyd, *Searching for Community: A Portrait of Undergraduate Jewish Students in Five UK Cities*. Institute for Jewish Policy Research (2016). https://archive.jpr.org.uk/object-uk423 (accessed 25 February 2023).

14 Stephen Oryszczuk, University to Pay £3,000 for Failure to Tackle Anti-Semitism. *Jewish News*, 3 November 2016. https://www.jewishnews.co.uk/universitys-pay-3000-for-failure-to-tackle-anti-semitism/

15 Cathy Elliott, Manya Eversley, Laura Katan and Sarai Keestra, *JewCL podcast* (2017). https://jewcl.libsyn.com/2017 (accessed 25 February 2023).

16 Josh Salisbury, SOAS 'Ignored Claims of Institutional Antisemitism'. *Jewish News*, 5 August 2021. https://jewishnews.timesofisrael.com/soas-ignored-claims-of-institutional-antisemitism/ (accessed 25 February 2023).

17 Community Security Trust, *Campus Antisemitism in Britain 2018–2020* (2021). https://cst.org.uk/public/data/file/3/6/Antisemitism%20on%20University%20Campuses.pdf (accessed 25 February 2023).

18 Lesley Klaff, Word Crimes: Reclaiming the Language of the Israeli–Palestinian Conflict: Holocaust Inversion. *Israel Studies*, 24(2), 73–90, 2019.

19 Universities UK, *Tackling Antisemitism: Practical Guidance for UK Universities* (2021). https://www.universitiesuk.ac.uk/what-we-do/policy-and-research/publications/tackling-antisemitism-practical-guidance (accessed 25 February 2023).

20 David Miller, The Enemy We Face Here Is Zionism. *YouTube*, 21 February 2021. https://www.youtube.com/watch?v=zrAlJl73NCQ (accessed 25 February 2023).

21 Rachel Hall, Bristol University Sacks Professor Accused of Antisemitic Comments. *The Guardian*, 1 October 2021. https://www.theguardian.com/education/2021/oct/01/bristol-university-sacks-professor-accused-of-antisemitic-comments (accessed 25 February 2023).

22 David Feldman, The David Miller Case: A Textbook Example of Anti Zionism Becoming Vicious Antisemitism. *Ha'aretz*, 4 March 2021. https://www.haaretz.com/israel-news/david-miller-textbook-case-of-anti-zionism-becoming-vicious-antisemitism-1.9585115 (accessed 25 February 2023).

23 Keith Kahn-Harris, *Strange Hate: Antisemitism, Racism and the Limits of Diversity*, Repeater Books, 2019.

24 David Baddiel, *Jews Don't Count*, TLS Books, 2021.

25 Glynis Cousin and Robert Fine, *A Common Cause: Reconnecting the Study of Racism and Antisemitism. European Societies*, 14(2), 166–185, 2012. https://doi.org/10.1080/14616696.2012.676447

26 Smita Jamdar, *Gavin Williamson's Letter to Vice Chancellors on the IHRA Definition of Antisemitism*. Shakespeare Martineau blog, 13 October 2020. https://www.shma.co.uk/our-thoughts/gavin-williamsons-letter-to-vice-chancellors-on-the-ihra-definition-of-antisemitism/ (accessed 25 February 2023).

27 House of Commons Education Committee Oral evidence: Accountability Hearings, HC 262.

28 John Mann, The IHRA Definition Should Not Be Used to Ban Free Speech and that Includes Ken Loach. *Jewish Chronicle*, 10 February 2021. https://www.thejc.com/comment/opinion/the-ihra-definition-should-not-be-used-to-ban-free-speech-and-that-includes-ken-loach-1.511642 (accessed 25 February 2023).

29 Khadija Mohammed, Ibtihal Ramadan and Nighet Riaz, A Brief Introduction to Critical Race Theory. The Anti-racism Curriculum Project Guide (2021). *AdvanceHE*. https://www.advance-he.ac.uk/anti-racist-curriculum-project/project-guide (accessed 25 February 2023).

30 Keith Kahn-Harris, *Strange Hate: Antisemitism, Racism and the Limits of Diversity*, Repeater Books, 2019, p. 122.

31 Community Security Trust, *Antisemitic Incidents*, January–June 2021, p. 3. https://cst.org.uk/research/cst-publications?categories%5BAntisemitic+Incident+Reports%5D= (accessed 25 February 2023).

32 Home Office, United Kingdom Government, Official Statistics, *Hate Crime, England and Wales, 2020–2021*, 12 October 2021, Table 2.2. https://www.gov.uk/government/statistics/hate-crime-england-and-wales-2020-to-2021/hate-crime-england-and-wales-2020-to-2021 (accessed 25 February 2023).

33 David Perkins, Constructivism and Troublesome Knowledge. In: Jan Meyer and Ray Land, eds., Overcoming Barriers to Student Understanding: Threshold Concepts and Troublesome Knowledge, Abingdon: Routledge, 2006.

34 Nadine Batchelor-Hunt, When Wiley Told Me I Wasn't Black. *GQ*, 29 July 2020. https://www.gq-magazine.co.uk/culture/article/wiley-anti-semitism (accessed 25 February 2023).

35 Sander Gilman, Are Jews White? Or, The History of the Nose Job. In: Les Back and John Solomos, eds., *Theories of Race and Racism: A Reader*, Taylor & Francis Group, 2001, pp. 230–231.

36 David Hirsh, How Raising the Issue of Antisemitism Puts You Outside the Community of the Progressive: The Livingstone Formulation. In: Eunice Pollack,

ed., *Anti-Zionism and Antisemitism: Past & Present*, Boston: Academic Studies Press, 2016, ISBN 9781618115652. https://engageonline.wordpress.com/2016/04/29/the-livingstone-formulation-david-hirsh-2/

37 Dermot Shinners-Kennedy, D, How *Not* to Identify Threshold Concepts. In: Ray Land, Jan Meyer and Michael Flanagan, eds., *Threshold Concepts in Practice*, Sense Publishers, 2016. https://doi.org/10.1007/978-94-6300-512-8

38 George Orwell, *Antisemitism in Britain*, The Orwell Foundation, 1945. https://www.orwellfoundation.com/the-orwell-foundation/orwell/essays-and-other-works/antisemitism-in-britain/ (accessed 25 February 2023).

39 Ray Land, Glynis Cousin, Jan Meyer and Peter Davies, Conclusion. In Jan Meyer and Ray Land, eds., *Overcoming Barriers to Student Understanding: Threshold Concepts and Troublesome Knowledge*, Abingdon: Routledge, 2006.

40 David Perkins, Constructivism and Troublesome Knowledge. In Jan Meyer and Ray Land, eds.; *Overcoming Barriers to Student Understanding: Threshold Concepts and Troublesome Knowledge*, Abingdon: Routledge, 2006.

41 Dermot Shinners-Kennedy, D, How *Not* To Identify Threshold Concepts. In: Ray Land, Jan Meyer and Michael Flanagan, eds., *Threshold Concepts in Practice*, Sense Publishers, 2016. https://doi.org/10.1007/978-94-6300-512-8

42 Jan Meyer and Ray Land, Threshold Concepts and Troublesome Knowledge: Linkages to Ways of Thinking and Practising within the Disciplines. *Enhancing Teaching–Learning Environments in Undergraduate Courses Project Occasional Report 4* (2003). http://www.etl.tla.ed.ac.uk//docs/ETLreport4.pdf (accessed 25 February 2023).

43 Erin Winkler, Racism as a Threshold Concept: Examining Learning in a 'Diversity Requirement' Course. *Race Ethnicity and Education*, 21(6), 808–826, 2018. https://doi.org/10.1080/13613324.2017.1294564.

44 William Smith, Ryan M. Crowley, Sara B. Demoiny and Jenna Cushing-Leubner, Threshold Concept Pedagogy for Antiracist Social Studies Teaching. *Multicultural Perspectives*, 23(2), 87–94, 2021. https://doi.org/10.1080/15210960.2021.1914047

45 Glynis Cousin, Threshold Concepts, Troublesome Knowledge and Emotional Capital. In: Jan Meyer and Ray Land, eds., *Overcoming Barriers to Student Understanding: Threshold Concepts and Troublesome Knowledge*, Routledge, 2006.

46 Hannah Morgan, The Social Model of Disability as a Threshold Concept: Troublesome Knowledge and Liminal Spaces in Social Work Education. *Social Work Education*, 31(2), 215–226, 2012. https://doi.org/10.1080/02615479.2012.644964

47 Peter Felten, On the Threshold with Students. In: Ray Land, Jan Meyer and Michael Flanagan, eds., *Threshold Concepts in Practice*, Sense Publishers, 2016. https://doi.org/10.1007/978-94-6300-512-8.

48 Glynis Cousin, An Introduction to Threshold Concepts. *Planet*, 17(1), 4–5, 2006. https://doi.org/10.11120/plan.2006.00170004.

49 David Perkins, Constructivism and Troublesome Knowledge. In: Jan Meyer and Ray Land, eds., *Overcoming Barriers to Student Understanding: Threshold Concepts and Troublesome Knowledge*, Routledge, 2006.

50 Glynis Cousin, An Introduction to Threshold Concepts. *Planet*, 17(1), 4–5, 2006. https://doi.org/10.11120/plan.2006.00170004.

51 Hannah Morgan, The Social Model of Disability as a Threshold Concept: Troublesome Knowledge and Liminal Spaces in Social Work Education. *Social Work Education*, 31(2), 215–226, 2012. https://doi.org/10.1080/02615479.2012.644964

52 Jamie Levine Daniel, Rachel Fyall, R. and Jodie Benenson, Talking about Antisemitism in MPA Classrooms and Beyond. *Journal of Public Affairs*

Education, 21(3), 313–135, 2020. https://doi.org/10.1080/15236803.2019.1646581

53 AdvanceHE, *Understanding Structural Racism in Higher Education: An Introduction* (2021). https://warwick.ac.uk/services/sg/si/diversity/advance_he_-_understanding_racism_report.pdf (accessed 25 February 2023).

54 AdvanceHE. *Race Equality Charter.* https://www.advance-he.ac.uk/equality-charters/race-equality-charter (accessed 25 February 2023).

55 Myriam Francois, *We Need to Talk About Whiteness Podcast, Episode 19, Whiteness and UK BLM with Adam Elliot Cooper* (2021). https://soundcloud.com/myriam-francois-27072150/we-need-to-talk-about-whiteness-with-dr-adam-elliott-cooper (accessed 25 February 2023).

56 David Schraub, White Jews: An Intersectional Approach. *Association for Jewish Studies Review*, 43(2), 379–407, 2019. https://doi.org/10.1017/S0364009419000461

57 Glynis Cousin and Robert Fine, A Common Cause: Reconnecting the Study of Racism and Antisemitism. *European Societies*, 14(2), 166–185, 2012. https://doi.org/10.1080/14616696.2012.676447

58 Sander Gilman, Are Jews White? Or, The History of the Nose Job. In: Les Back and John Solomos, eds., *Theories of Race and Racism: A Reader*, Taylor & Francis Group, 2001, pp. 230–231.

59 Moishe Postone, History and Helplessness: Mass Mobilization and Contemporary Forms of Anticapitalism. *Public Culture*, 18(1), 93–110, 2006. https://doi.org/10.1215/08992363-18-1-93

60 David Schraub, White Jews: An Intersectional Approach. *Association for Jewish Studies Review*, 43(2), 379–407, 2019. https://doi.org/10.1017/S0364009419000461

61 David Perkins, Constructivism and Troublesome Knowledge. In: Jan Meyer and Ray Land, eds., *Overcoming Barriers to Student Understanding: Threshold Concepts and Troublesome Knowledge*, Abingdon: Routledge, 2006.

62 Kimberlé Crenshaw, *Demarginalizing the Intersection of Race and Sex: A Black FeministCritique of Antidiscrimination Doctrine, Feminist Theory and Antiracist Politics*, University of Chicago Legal Forum, 1989. https://chicagounbound.uchicago.edu/cgi/viewcontent.cgi?article=1052&context=uclf (accessed 25 February 2023).

63 Kimberlé Crenshaw, Mapping the Margins: Intersectionality, Identity Politics, and Violence against Women of Color. *Stanford Law Review*, 43(6), 1241–1299, 1999.

64 24th July on a tweet from a suspended account.

65 Alex Edelman, *Dead Jews, Alex Edelman's Peer Group, Series 4, Episode 1* (2021). https://www.bbc.co.uk/programmes/m000vwt4 (accessed 25 February 2023).

66 Marc Goldberg, Why Do So Many Academics Believe in David Miller? *Jewish Chronicle*, 8 October 2021. https://www.thejc.com/comment/opinion/why-do-so-many-academics-believe-in-david-miller-1.521271 (accessed 25 February 2023).
https://www.thejc.com/comment/opinion/why-do-so-many-academics-believe-in-david-miller-1.521271

67 Cathy Elliott, Manya Eversley, Laura Katan and Sarai Keestra, *Jewniversity*, JewCL Podcast (2017). https://jewcl.libsyn.com/2017 (accessed 25 February 2023).

68 David Hirsh, *Contemporary Left Antisemitism*, London, Routledge, 2018.

69 Dermot Shinners-Kennedy, D, How *Not* to Identify Threshold Concepts. In: Ray Land, Jan Meyer and Michael Flanagan, eds., *Threshold Concepts in Practice*, Sense Publishers, 2016. https://doi.org/10.1007/978-94-6300-512-8

70 Ruth Sheldon, *Tragic Encounters and Ordinary Ethics: Palestine–Israel in British Universities*, Manchester: Manchester University Press, 2016, pp. 112–113.

71 Cathy Elliott, Manya Eversley, Laura Katan and Sarai Keestra, *Talking about Israel*, JewCL Podcast (2017). https://jewcl.libsyn.com/2017 (accessed 25 February 2023).

72 Yaacov Yadgar, *What Does It Mean for Israel to Be a Jewish State?* Lecture, Gresham College, 14 October 2021. https://www.gresham.ac.uk/lectures-and -events/jewish-state (accessed 25 February 2023).

73 Marlon Solomon, *Conspiracy Theory: A Lizard's Tale*, https://www.nuscon-nect.org.uk/campaigns/holocaust-memorial-day/a-lizard-s-tale (accessed 25 February 2023).

74 Yossi Kugler, Dafna Dolinko and Dmitry Kolotinenko, *Antisemitism: From Its Origins to the Present*. Online course offered by Yad Vashem on Coursera, November 2021. https://www.coursera.org/learn/antisemitism (accessed 25 February 2023).

75 Shana K. Carpenter, Amber E. Witherby and Sarah K. Tauber, On Students' (Mis)Judgments of Learning and Teaching Effectiveness. *Journal of Applied Research in Memory and Cognition*, 9(2), 137–151, 2020. https://doi.org/10 .1016/j.jarmac.2019.12.009.

76 Glynis Cousin, Threshold Concepts, Troublesome Knowledge and Emotional Capital. In: Jan Meyer and Ray Land, eds., *Overcoming Barriers to Student Understanding: Threshold Concepts and Troublesome Knowledge*, Routledge, 2006.

77 Booth, J., On the Mastery of Philosophical Concepts. In: Jan Meyer and Ray Land, eds., *Overcoming Barriers to Student Understanding: Threshold Concepts and Troublesome Knowledge*, Routledge, 2006.

78 Glynis Cousin, Threshold Concepts, Troublesome Knowledge and Emotional Capital. In: Jan Meyer and Ray Land, eds., *Overcoming Barriers to Student Understanding: Threshold Concepts and Troublesome Knowledge*, Routledge, 2006.

79 Keith Kahn-Harris, *Strange Hate: Antisemitism, Racism and the Limits of Diversity*, Repeater Books, 2019, pp. 66–67.

80 Peter Felten, On the Threshold with Students. In: Ray Land, Jan Meyer and Michael Flanagan, eds., *Threshold Concepts in Practice*, Sense Publishers, 2016. https://doi.org/10.1007/978-94-6300-512-8.

81 Union of Jewish Students, *Antisemitism Awareness Training*, King's College London, 26 November 2021.

82 Federation of Societies of Islamic Students, *Targeting of Muslim Students in the Education Space on the Issue of Palestine*, blog post, 1 June 2021. https://www .fosis.org.uk/news/targeting-of-muslim-students-in-the-education-space-on-the -issue-of-palestine/

83 Ruth Sheldon, *Tragic Encounters and Ordinary Ethics: Palestine–Israel in British Universities*, Manchester: Manchester University Press, 2016, pp. 138–159.

84 Glynis Cousin, Threshold Concepts, Troublesome Knowledge and Emotional Capital. In: Jan Meyer and Ray Land, eds., *Overcoming Barriers to Student Understanding: Threshold Concepts and Troublesome Knowledge*, Routledge, 2006.

85 Jamie Levine Daniel, Rachel Fyall, R. and Jodie Benenson, Talking about Antisemitism in MPA Classrooms and Beyond. *Journal of Public Affairs Education*, 26(3), pp. 313–135. https://doi.org/10.1080/15236803.2019 .1646581.

10

CLIMATE CATASTROPHE, THE 'ZIONIST ENTITY' AND 'THE GERMAN GUY'

An anatomy of the Malm–Jappe dispute

Matthew Bolton

In May 2021, a long-running (and, at the time of writing, still unresolved) legal dispute over the ownership of a number of properties in the Sheikh Jarrah area of East Jerusalem exploded into violence. Clashes between Israeli police and protestors at the Al-Asqa mosque were followed by thousands of rockets being indiscriminately fired at Israeli cities by Hamas militants in Gaza. In response, Israeli forces bombed targets in Gaza, with many civilian casualties. Inter-communal street violence between Jews and Arabs within Israel followed. Large protests were held against Israeli actions in Gaza in numerous cities in Europe and the United States.[1] Multiple violent and verbal attacks on Jewish people, Jewish-owned shops and synagogues were recorded in the wake of the protests.[2] Social media was awash with posts, images and memes, many using antisemitic concepts, signalling opposition to and moral condemnation of Israel.[3] Comparisons between Israel and apartheid South Africa and police violence in the United States were widespread.[4]

In the middle of this febrile period, an online discussion panel was held by the 'Red May' collective in Seattle. The topic of the debate was 'Covid, Climate, Chronic Emergency: Antinomies of the State', and sought to explore different approaches to the state in the midst of the unprecedented interventions of the Covid era.[5] The discussants were the sociologist Alberto Toscano, whose article on the topic was the inspiration for the debate, and the two theorists Toscano's paper had engaged with: Andreas Malm, whose pamphlet 'Corona, Climate, Chronic Emergency' argued that the 'war footing' the state had undertaken to tackle the pandemic should be extended to combat the climate crisis; and Anslem Jappe, whose co-authored book *De Virus Illustribus*, contended that state interventions aimed at 'protecting' a

DOI: 10.4324/9781003222477-11

population – whether from Covid, climate change or economic crisis – are doomed to fail, because the state is an inextricable part of the capitalist social totality which caused the problems in the first place.

The panel opened with Toscano's presentation, before Malm was invited to make his contribution. Flexing a sculpted bicep behind his head, seemingly clad in a Taqqiyah prayer cap, Malm immediately announced that he had just unwillingly "extricated" himself from a Palestine solidarity demonstration in Malmö in order to join the discussion, and "confessed" that he was too choked with "emotion", too "seething" and "boiling", to focus on the topic at hand. The only thing Malm wanted to discuss, he said, the thing he could "not stop himself" from saying, was

> How do we assess the current conjuncture in the Palestinian struggle for liberation? How do we express our admiration for the heroes of the resistance in Gaza, headed by Mohammed Deif? How do we understand the drift of the Zionist entity ever further into the extreme proto-genocidal right?

And neither could he stop himself going on to ask:

> [H]ow does this relate to general trends of fascist-isation in the global north?... How do we learn the lessons from the Palestinian resistance and apply it as a model on other fronts [particularly the ecological crisis]?

At this point Anselm Jappe intervened, declaring that he "was not here to hear hate speeches against the Jewish state", and that if the discussion did not return to the proposed topic – namely Covid, climate and the state – he and his co-authors would leave the Zoom panel. Malm responded with a withering "oh yeah, you're German, right?" before appealing to the moderator, Ajay Singh Chaudhary, to adjudicate on whether anything he had said had been hateful. Referring to his personal heritage as an "Indian Jew", Chaudhary declared he "found nothing hateful" in Malm's comments, and that Malm's focus on the Israel–Palestine conflict was "germane" to the subject of the panel. Malm then continued, gesticulating with a pointed finger, arguing that chants of 'Death to the Arabs' on "the streets of Palestine, 1948 areas" demonstrated that Israel was on the verge of committing genocide, and that "if you Comrade Jappe, as a German, can't take this in, then that's your problem".

Here Jappe again interrupted to declare that, while he acknowledged Israel's actions in Gaza might be criticised as unduly "harsh", he would no longer listen to "somebody making an apology for the antisemitic madmen from Hamas" and left the meeting. Acknowledging that "the German guy" was no longer present, Malm apologised to the rest of the panel for "scaring him off", but that he could not "betray my innermost sentiments" when it came to the question of Palestine. He then began to speak on the issue of the state and the climate, but repeatedly brought the discussion back to Israel, arguing that the "generalised ignorance and indifference to what the science says is necessary" to prevent climate change, and the "affirm[ation]" of the destruction of "the world's tropical forest", is "quite similar" to the world's ignorance and/or affirmation of the "destruction that's going on in Palestine right now".

The reaction to the *contretemps* between Malm and Jappe within the small but by no means insignificant circles of the 'Very Online' radical left leaned heavily in support of Malm, just as it did within the panel itself. Neither Toscano nor the other panellists mentioned the incident, nor sought to defend 'the German guy' from Malm's attack. After the event, moderator Ajay Singh Chaudhary posted a Twitter thread congratulating Malm for showing how the

> Palestinian struggle is part and parcel of the global ecological politics of this moment in the 21st century' [and that] 'there are well and truly only two sides…[and] no way to magic beyond politics which will be violent because conditions are already violent.

Moreover, Chaudhary went on,

> the actual moment of anti-semitism in this panel was when [Jappe] identi-fied Palestine solidarity and critique of "the Jewish state" as anti-semitic. As has long been the case, Zionism itself is actually anti-semitic; it loathes Jews as we really exist in the world as part of becoming an extension of first the European imperial project, as part of the logic of mimicking Christian nation states.
>
> *(@materialist_jew, 16 May 2021)*

For his part, Jappe and his co-authors posted a short response on the Palim Psao website, writing that the event was "another demonstration – to the point of caricature – that the upheavals of the Middle East have a sort of ata-vistic priority for leftism over any other subject". While it would be consoling to "think that the discourse on "left-wing anti-Semitism" was the exaggera-tion of a right that wanted to forget its past", sadly "this is not the case".[6]

Why is this disagreement between Malm and Jappe worth recounting in such detail? Compared with the flood of antisemitism both online and offline that followed the escalation phase, the impact of a minor disagree-ment between two relatively obscure Marxian academics – although Malm has recently won an increasingly broad readership, to the extent that he has been labelled "the first international star of eco-Marxism in the age of climate crisis" – is surely of marginal importance.[7] Quite so; and yet the way the debate unfolded, its conceptual basis, the modes of argumentation, the terminology used and the reaction to the debate, tell us something important about how antisemitism plays out in the intellectual arena, and radical left spaces in particular. The divergence between Malm's and Jappe's positions is by no means arbitrary or contingent: rather it is the result of deep-seated theoretical differences between the distinct traditions of leftist thought both, in an admittedly schematic way, can be said to represent. The theoretical differences that appear at the level of the relation of capitalism and the state – precisely those at stake in the initial debate on the state in the pandemic – play out in their respective analyses of antisemitism, Zionism and the state of Israel.

The debate can thus be recognised as a crystallisation of contemporary forms of antisemitism within the left: indeed, the manner of its unfolding, and the response it generated, will be grimly familiar to many of those who have sought to challenge that antisemitism over the past two or three decades. But it also alerts us to a new front in antisemitic discourse, namely the integration of the image of Israel into the centre of what is rapidly (and rightly) becoming a central focus of leftist activism today, namely climate change and the critique of the 'Capitalocene'. As such the Malm–Jappe debate represents a real-time demonstration of how antisemitic worldviews adapt to new surroundings.

The following section breaks the Malm–Jappe debate down into its component parts, seeking to uncover the conceptual basis of the disagreement. In so doing it will demonstrate how many of the elements of contemporary antisemitism appear throughout this brief interchange. The latter section of the chapter will then interrogate the meaning of Malm's curt dismissal of Jappe's supposedly 'German' response. It traces the historical development of the so-called 'German' stance on antisemitism that Malm takes as given, and shows how Malm's contempt for such a position – one born of intense theoretical reflection and political struggle – unconsciously reproduces the positions of a German right seeking to cast off (Jewish-imposed) guilt for the Holocaust in the name of a revitalised nationalist state. Moreover, the chapter concludes, the summary dismissal facilitated by the ascription of 'German'-ness to Jappe here functions in much the same way as rejections of Jewish (or today, 'Zionist') interlocuters on the grounds of their innate partiality, special pleading or stubborn refusal to conform to new realities. As is often the case, then, such off-hand comments reveal far more than the speaker intends.

Israel: The enemy of 'The State'

The most immediately striking aspect of Malm's intervention is its emotional tenor and frantic urgency. He admits he cannot hold his feelings back; he refuses to allow his "innermost" passion to be restrained by the rigid formalities of 'professional' decorum or the demands of the topic at hand. From the streets of Malmö his love for the Palestinians is such that it overrides any and every other priority, including that of climate change, and negates any attempt at rational debate – indeed the insistence on such abstract rituals is little more than a perpetuation of the oppression under which the Palestinians suffer. Noting, with David Nirenberg, that the opposition Malm sets up between (Christian) inward 'feeling' and 'honesty' and the cold formality and disingenuous politeness of (Jewish) law has been a mainstay of Western 'anti-Judaism' for centuries, it is clear from the outset that Malm's approach to the Israel–Palestine conflict is one driven by inexhaustible moral feeling that can brook no compromise or limitation.[8]

Indeed, it is not a conflict at all, if by 'conflict' is meant what Susie Linfield describes as an "unresolved, frustratingly complex, grievously resilient struggle between two national movements, each with a justified claim to the land".[9] Rather for Malm there is only one legitimate claim to nationhood, to statehood, to the land and to morality itself – and it belongs solely to the Palestinians. Palestinian nationalism is ontological, concrete, eternal and grounded in the soil. Jewish nationalism is transient, abstract, arbitrary, a transparently false concoction. This framing is re-emphasised by Malm's refusal to call Israel by name, instead referring to it as the "Zionist entity". Israel is thus deprived of its statehood: it is not a true nation-state but a usurper, a parody, clownishly aping what Chaudhary later describes as "Christian nation states", the true form of the state. The anti-Arab chants which Malm regards as the precursor to genocidal violence do not take place within Israel, that fictional "entity", but rather on "the streets of Palestine, the 1948 areas". No matter what international law says about the legitimacy of Israel's existence, for Malm the 'Palestine' enduring eternally beneath the ersatz structures of the false Israeli polity represents the 'true state' of the genuine 'people' of the region, one destined in time to be reunited again with its natural land.

No doubt unconsciously, the contrast between the true state and false 'entity' that founds Malm's argument here replicates that made by Nazi ideologue Alfred Rosenberg in his 1922 pamphlet *Der Staatsfeindliche Zionismus*, or 'Zionism, the Enemy of the State'.[10] For Rosenberg, writing long before the State of Israel came into existence, the very idea of a 'Jewish state' undermined the concept of 'the state' of such. The purpose of the state was to unite a national 'people' with the land to which it had an innate, natural – one might say 'indigenous' – connection, and to protect that people from destructive outside forces. A 'Jewish state' was, from this perspective, a contradiction in terms. The Jews could not be considered a 'national people' – they had no connection to any land, but rather existed as a global, cosmopolitan force, an 'anti-nation' whose presence undermined the integral unity of any true nation with the misfortune to host them. Should a 'Jewish state' come into existence, it would necessarily be a despised outlier, a pariah in the community of nations. It would act as the headquarters for the orchestration of the global conspiracy seeking to disintegrate that system of true nation states of which it disingenuously pronounces itself a member. For Rosenberg, such a 'state' cannot be salvaged by political means, by its actions: it is rotten from the inside out, and can only be rejected in its entirety.

The same insistence that Israel is an irredeemable 'historic error', an absolute wrong, reappears in Malm and Chaudhary's contention that the Palestinian struggle against Israel is a microcosm of the fight to save the planet from catastrophic climate change. While in Malm's view 'true' states can and must act as the last line of defence against climate catastrophe by adopting a form of 'war communism', the Israeli state cannot.[11] The 'Zionist entity' is a wholly exploitative and destructive political vehicle, beyond even communist redemption. This is because, as Malm set out in an extensive 2017 article for *Salvage* magazine, the "relation between Palestine and climate change ... is more than one of allegory or analogy. Fossil fuels have been integral to the catastrophe from the very start".[12] The existence of Zionism, and of Israel itself, he suggests, has little to do with theology, antisemitism, the Holocaust or the general rise of nationalism across the 19th century. Rather they are the results of a ploy by the imperialist British to secure access to supplies of fossil fuels in the Middle East, and in particular oil, which was rapidly becoming "the state-of-the-art fossil fuel" in the early decades of the 20th century. The project to establish a 'national home for the Jewish people' is presented here as a necessary precondition for 20th century capitalist development, and the destruction of the natural environment wrought by fossil fuel-based production that followed. The trajectory of the climate crisis is thus set to follow that of Israel itself. Climate change is forcing "millions" of people around the world "along the Palestinian axis", he writes. The entire planet is becoming Palestine.

Malm's main evidence for this claim is the 1932 creation of a pipeline transmitting oil from Iraq to Haifa. Malm extols Arab attacks on the pipeline during the anti-British and anti-Jewish uprising of 1936 as a kind of clairvoyant climate activism *avant la lettre*. Strangely, he fails to mention that Zionist militants also attacked the pipeline a decade later as part of their own anti-colonial struggle, nor that the Haifa pipeline stopped functioning completely after Israeli independence was declared, and has never been reopened. Inconvenient history notwithstanding, the conflation of the existence of Israel and climate catastrophe is further underlined when Malm insists that since its establishment Israel has facilitated "American dominance over the Middle East and untrammelled access to its oil". Again he omits to mention that Israel produces virtually no oil, while the Arab nations responsible for the great bulk of the world's oil production have been, until very recently, as implacably opposed to Israel's existence as Malm is.

If the state of Israel personifies the rapacious destruction of the planet under the 'Capitalocene', then Palestine represents the wounded earth itself, the lost Eden poisoned by Zionist-capitalist development. To "take up [the] Palestinian position", Malm suggests, "is, ultimately, to choose nature as one's last and strongest ally". The *Salvage* essay thus concludes by making a direct parallel between the Palestinian demand for the "right of return" and that of the climate movement for a "C02 concentration" of "350 ppm". The desired result of these conjoined demands, he suggests, is to see "Palestinians living in their own country, much like prior to 1948" – acknowledging that the 'right of return' does indeed necessitate the eradication of Israel – and "the CO2 concentration back below the levels of the late 1980s ... From the river to the sea: CO2 emissions must first be eradicated and then turned negative". For Malm, the destruction of the State of Israel and the salvation of the planet, and thus of humanity itself, are one and the same process.

The romance of reaction

Given the urgency of the situation, it is no surprise that in Malm's view, just as the climate crisis necessitates any and every sort of direct action, so too should any mode of resistance to the 'Zionist entity', from whatever quarter and in whatever form, be unquestionably supported. Thus, in the Red May discussion, Malm does not just express his solidarity with the Palestinians in Gaza facing Israeli attacks, or those in Sheikh Jarrah facing potential eviction, but explicitly extols "the heroes of the resistance in Gaza, headed by Mohammed Deif". Mohammed Deif is the 'Supreme Commander' of the Izz ad-Din al-Qassam Brigades, the military wing of Hamas, the fiercely reactionary and authoritarian Islamist rulers of Gaza. Deif is thought to be the architect of the campaign of suicide bombings targeting Israeli buses and public spaces during the Second Intifada. He was central to the development of Hamas's artillery of Iran-funded Qassam rockets – those being fired indiscriminately at Israeli cities at the time of Malm's speech – as well as the network of tunnels aimed at allowing Hamas militants to enter Israel to perpetrate attacks. Since forcibly taking power in Gaza in 2007, Hamas has ruthlessly suppressed political opposition, public protest and trade union organisation, with arbitrary arrest, abductions, torture and extra-judicial killing of opponents a constant threat.[13] The rights of women have been restricted, while gay people face persecution or even death.[14] The deeply antisemitic content of the organisation's founding charter, which draws heavily on the classic conspiracy theory of the 'Protocols of the Elders of Zion', and of the material pumped out on its propaganda channels on a daily basis, needs little explication here.[15]

Malm's romanticisation of such a reactionary political movement – one which, we can assume, were it of a different 'people' he would not hesitate to assign to the "general trends of fascist-isation" he diagnoses elsewhere – is typical of the Manichean form of 'anti-imperialism' that has dominated the Western left since the 1960s. As is well known, this view of geopolitics begins with the unshakeable premise that anything the United States, the UK, Israel and their allies – the imperialists, a category which for Malm is interchangeable with the more activist-flavoured 'global north' – do is to be *a priori* opposed, and any action by those who purport to oppose them is to be automatically supported, regardless of the political aims or methods of those opponents. Once a state or movement has been admitted to the side of the 'anti-imperialists', everything is permitted. Divisions that elsewhere would be regarded as critical to any social analysis – between left and right, capitalists and workers, secular and theocratic, ecological activist and climate change denier – are here dissolved into the homogenous totality of the 'right side of history'. Once history's backing is secured, there is no longer any moral difference between an autocratic theocracy and a secular democracy – or a non-violent protest, an attack on a tank, the destruction of property or blowing up a bus full of civilians with a suicide bomb.

Malm's support for Hamas and for armed struggle is not mechanical or tinged with regret, but full-throated and celebratory. Indeed, he goes so far as to recommend the methods of Hamas as a model for climate change activists. Recall that these methods of 'resistance' include suicide bombings, indiscriminate rocket fire and, in the words of Hamas official Fathi Hammad, speaking a week before Malm's 'Red May' appearance, "cut[ting] off the heads of the Jews" with "five shekel knives" to "humiliate the Jewish state".[16] Far from distancing himself from such actions, the only time Malm's *Salvage* article voices any criticism of Hamas is for briefly considering *abandoning* violence in favour of a "long-term truce" with Israel in 2015. As with a Jeremy Corbyn or Seumas Milne, expressing public support for (antisemitic) political violence targeted at (Jewish) civilians seems to generate a vicarious thrill for a certain kind of leftist: a frisson of narcissistic wonder at one's own revolutionary toughness, pride at the cultivation of the hardened sensibility and 'higher' morality necessary to accept whatever death and destruction is required in pursuit of the cause. But given Malm's clear authoritarian instincts – his Leninist 'war communist' state would even enforce mandatory veganism – and his explicit commitment to militancy, his bicep-flexing admiration for such 'heroic' resistance, not to mention the satisfaction he takes in 'scaring' Jappe from the panel, takes on a far more threatening hue than the vain and ultimately impotent posing of a Corbyn.

It was, of course, Malm's statement of explicit support for Hamas and Dief – and not, as Chaudhary later claimed, simple "Palestine solidarity" – which prompted Jappe's rejoinder, along with Malm's use of the term "proto-genocidal" to describe Israeli attitudes towards the Palestinians. Despite the 'proto' qualification, the use of the concept of genocide in this context cannot but carry with it the full weight of the Holocaust, implicitly creating an analogy between the actions of the state of Israel (or the hopes of its population) and the Nazi extermination of European Jewry. It opens the pathway to the crude comparisons between Gaza and Auschwitz or the Warsaw Ghetto that are common within certain left spaces, as well as accusations of supposed Zionist collaboration with Hitler, or the graphic conflation of Zionism and Nazism in images that meld the Star of David with the swastika. These modes of Holocaust relativisation, minimisation and victim-blaming combine with older antisemitic notions of Jewish amorality, the idea that, devoid of Christian forgiveness, Jews are incapable of 'learning the correct moral lessons' from past suffering. The distinction between the situation in Gaza, anti-Arab racism within Israel – which certainly exists – and the annihilatory violence of the Holocaust is so great that to brandish the term 'genocide' in the context of an 'emotional' debate about the former amounts to wilful incitement.

The dismissive, even contemptuous, reaction to Jappe's complaint from the rest of the panel, and from Chaudhary as moderator in particular, is also instructive: one wearyingly familiar to anyone who has participated in debates about antisemitism, Israel and Zionism in left spaces over the past three decades. Chaudhary's immediate response to the altercation was to mobilise his Indian-Jewish background in order to give greater moral weight to his rejection of Jappe's concerns. In his later Twitter thread, posted presumably after more considered thought, Chaudhary reiterated that given he was "the only Jewish person (I think) involved in that conversation", he could authoritatively confirm that it was not Hamas, or their advocate Malm, who were antisemitic, but rather Jappe and indeed the entire notion of a 'Jewish state'. Moreover, not only does the antisemitic 'Zionist entity' embody the destruction of the natural world, as Malm asserts, for Chaudhary its "neo-fascist ethnocracy" is "THE model for the global far-right" today. Israel's 'neo-fascism' is not contingently tied, as some apologists might like to pretend, to the particular policies of the Netanyahu government, but rather "dat[es] back to the founding of the country". Zionism *is* fascism for Chaudhary – inherently, in its essence. Nor is it merely one manifestation of fascism today, but rather constitutes the Ur-fascism, the very ground upon which fascism rests.

The logic of this argument is that those who claim to see antisemitism in some form of 'criticism' of Israel – such as, say, the claim that Israel is the only state on earth incapable of fighting climate change and so must be destroyed to save the planet – are defending fascism, colonialism, the destruction of the environment and antisemitism itself. From a leftist perspective, such people cannot be regarded as comrades, and should thus be excluded from the left's 'community of the good'.[17] That the vast majority of the Jewish population around the world fall into this banished category, by virtue of seeing some kind of relation between their Jewish identity and the state of Israel, however despairing they may be of its current political trajectory, is unfortunate. But it is not antisemitic, so this argument goes, because a minority of Jewish people – like Chaudhary himself, or the members of Jewish Voice for Labour in the UK – do pass the left's litmus test on Israel. They are thus free to mobilise their identity to exonerate the left from the false accusations of antisemitism made by those Jews who do not. As David Hirsh puts it, this inverts the standard mantra of identity politics. Instead of claiming that their Jewish identity provides "some special insight, partially hidden from those outside, to the nature of the racism that they suffer", here "membership of the targeted group gives them … special inside knowledge of the self-serving and dishonest claims made by the majority of Jews".[18]

'You're German, Right?'

Of course, as Chaudhary sagely points out, Anselm Jappe is not Jewish. He was born in Germany, moved to Italy as a young man to study philosophy, earned his PhD in France, became a professor and now teaches in France and Italy. But for Andreas Malm, Jappe is simply 'the German guy'. He thrusts the label at Jappe three times throughout their argument: "you're German, right?"; "if you as a German can't take this in, then that's your problem;" "the German guy left". For the uninitiated, Malm's focus on Jappe's Germanness in this context might seem to be merely a distasteful xenophobic insinuation that his place of birth renders him incapable of recognising or standing against genocide. That is indeed part of the work the label is meant to undertake. But for those more *au fait* with the topography of the contemporary Marxian left landscape, it is clear that Malm's 'German' accusation is a reference to the German left's supposed neurotic obsession with antisemitism, and guilt-ridden mechanical defence of Israel. In the second half of this chapter, I want to unpick the concept of 'German-ness' in the accusatory, contemptuous form that it is used by Malm, tracing its political and theoretical genealogy, and the function it fulfils for Malm in this debate.

To do so means acknowledging from the outset that the left in Germany today is indeed a global outlier when it comes to antisemitism, and attitudes to Israel – although the more familiar anti-Zionist positions are by no means absent, and may slowly be becoming dominant.[19] This idiosyncrasy is reinforced by (and to an extent is responsible for) Germany's state-led *Erinnerungskultur*, or 'culture of remembrance', in which the post-reunification state has made Holocaust memorialisation and education a central plank of its existence. The most notorious representation of this tendency is the 'anti-Deutsch' faction, the 'anti-Germans', who rose to brief prominence through the 1990s and 2000s. They became renowned and despised within international leftist circles for waving Israeli flags at demonstrations, disrupting meetings of the anti-Zionist left and confronting pro-Palestine protestors.[20] But a reticence to subscribe to the absolutist anti-Zionism that is the price of entry to the left in the rest of the world is shared by a much wider constituency within the German left than the few activists explicitly affiliated to what remains of the anti-Deutsch.

But far from this being an unthinking 'German reflex', such positions were by no means inevitable, but rather the result of long struggles, at the level of both theory and practice – not only within the left itself, but within Germany more broadly. While aspects of these debates carried specific German resonances, much of what was and is at stake – questions of the meaning and significance of the Holocaust, and how it fits into the broader relationship between antisemitism, genocide, the state, nationalism and capitalist modernity – was and remains of central importance wherever those forms exist. Given this, the contemporary global left's failures on antisemitism – from minor incidents like the Malm–Jappe debate to the major crisis precipitated by Jeremy Corbyn's leadership of the British Labour party – can be, in part, attributed to ignorance of, or failure to understand or engage with, the theoretical and political basis of the German debate, or to take on board the lessons which can be applied in non-German contexts: a failure that Malm's sneering 'German guy' dismissal neatly demonstrates.

Theoretically, the so-called 'German' position on antisemitism can be traced back to the critical theory of antisemitism developed by Theodor W Adorno and Max Horkheimer.[21] In the early years of the Nazi era, Adorno and Horkheimer had subscribed to a version of the orthodox Marxian analysis of antisemitism, whereby antisemitism was explained as a form of ideology consciously and cynically propagated by the ruling class to distract from and thus further their oppression of the working class.[22] Antisemitism here is merely an interchangeable means to a more fundamental end: class domination. But by the early 1940s the centrality, rather than contingency, of exterminatory antisemitism to the Nazi project had begun to become clear, and Horkheimer and Adorno revised their position. Moreover, it was evident that support for antisemitic policies – stretching from economic boycotts to ghettoisations, deportations and eventual annihilation – amongst 'ordinary' Germans, including workers, was not half-hearted or forced, but enthusiastic and authentic. Explaining this embrace of antisemitism across society as a whole meant understanding how antisemitism arose from, or was embedded within, the very foundations of that society – in its concepts, its collective psyche, its mode of existence.

In *Dialectic of Enlightenment*, and throughout the rest of their career, Horkheimer and, in particular, Adorno sought to identify the roots of antisemitism and of Auschwitz in the interplay of universality and particularity, identity and non-identity, rationality and myth across the long development of Western society.[23] While there were historical particularities that meant that Germany was the place where exterminatory antisemitism reached its climax, Adorno argued that the fetishised rationality and identity imposed by the compulsory exchange relations of capitalist modernity, and feelings of powerlessness in the face of the vast state bureaucracies, technological domination and the ceaseless turmoil created by a capitalist world economy, created unprecedented conditions for the exacerbation and political activation of an antisemitism that was never far below the surface. As such, he famously argued in *Negative Dialectics* that "Hitler has imposed a new categorical imperative upon humanity in the state of their unfreedom: to arrange their thinking and conduct, so that Auschwitz never repeats itself, so that nothing similar ever happen again".[24]

In the decades following the end of the war and the construction of the Federal Republic of West Germany, this 'Never Again' imperative entailed constant vigilance against the antisemitism that Adorno suggested remained latent within West German state and society. While the Federal Republic was a democracy, and thus qualitatively distinct from the totalitarian authoritarianism of the Nazi regime, it was fragile and had been imposed from the outside, rather than fought for by the Germans themselves. Adorno argued that in such a context the rise of newly "sanitised" – i.e. no longer explicitly antisemitic – right-wing parties meant that "the survival of National Socialism *within* democracy [was now] potentially more menacing than the survival of fascist tendencies – i.e. explicit neo-Nazi parties – *against* democracy".[25] In particular, Adorno focused on the dangers of what he termed 'secondary antisemitism', whereby attempts are made to minimise the events of the Holocaust, to mitigate the guilt of the perpetrators, to suggest the victims in some instigated or provoked their treatment, or to accuse the victims of seeking to profit, either financially or politically, from the past by continually bringing it up, enforcing a national 'guilt complex' that prevented Germany from moving on.[26]

For all Adorno's influence within German leftist circles until his death in 1969, his critique of the latent fascism within the Federal Republic, and his demand that 'never again' should an Auschwitz be allowed to happen, became subject to interpretations by a new generation of leftists that, in the kind of dialectical twist his own work diagnosed, turned his entreaties on their head – as he privately recognised.[27] In the late 1960s and 1970s, radical left groups within Germany began to regard the Federal Republic as not merely potentially but *actually* fascist – a position Adorno explicitly rejected – while US foreign policy, particularly the brutal war in Vietnam, was routinely characterised as a direct extension of the Nazi regime.[28] This conflation of US 'imperialism' – perhaps better understood as a paranoid, destructive anti-communism – with the Holocaust effectively amounted to a relativisation of the latter, born of a failure to grasp the crucial conceptual distinction between mass murder and extermination, "the administrative murder of millions of innocent people".[29] Conflating the two categories – in much the same way as the German right sought to equate the bombing of Dresden with the gas chambers – implicitly exonerated the older generation of Germans who lived through the Nazi era. If Vietnam was genocide, a new Auschwitz, then neither the Nazis nor the German people need suffer from any exceptional form of guilt.

Moreover, for the German New Left as elsewhere, Israel's surprise victory in the 1967 war against various Arab states seemed to make it clear that Israel too was part of the imperialist project: just one more fascist, Nazi state that had to be defeated, by any means necessary, to 'prevent another Auschwitz'. In fact, as Paul Berman puts it, for much of the German radical left Israel had become "the crypto-Nazi site par excellence, the purest of all examples of how Nazism had never been defeated but had instead lingered into the present in ever more cagey forms. What better disguise could Nazism assume than a Jewish state?"[30] The parallels with Chaudhary's claim that from the moment of its founding Israel has been the model for post-Nazi fascism are clear.

In the wake of 1967, German student movements passed Malm-esque resolutions condemning the 'Zionist entity' as a "bridgehead of imperialism". Guilt over the death of six million Jews, it was argued, should not prevent recognition of the "daily" *Kristallnacht* Israel was imposing on the Palestinians.[31] German revolutionaries travelled to the Middle East to train with Palestinian militants. Direct actions against Jewish and Israeli targets followed. In 1969, the day after the anniversary of *Kristallnacht*, a Jewish community centre in Berlin – built on the site of a synagogue burnt during *Kristallnacht* itself – was bombed by a splinter leftist group, following the desecration of Jewish graves with the words 'Shalom + Napalm'.[32] In 1972, renowned left militant Ulrike Meinhof heralded the murder of 11 Israeli athletes in Munich as an attack on "Israel's Nazi fascism", one brilliantly conducted on the very German soil where the seeds of Israel's criminal existence were first sown.[33] Four years later, German activists helped members of the Popular Front for the Liberation of Palestine (PFLP) – a group whose campaign of plane hijackings, hostage taking and bombings continues to be romanticised by the contemporary left, as Malm does in his *Salvage* article – hijack a plane flying from Tel Aviv to Paris. Landing at Entebbe, Uganda, the hijackers scrupulously separated the Jewish and Israeli passengers from the rest, who were freed, and threatened them with death unless their demands were met. A secret mission by Israeli commando units eventually rescued the abductees.[34]

The grotesque spectacle of German leftists taking part in gunpoint 'selections' of Jews – including at least one survivor of the extermination camps – barely 30 years after the Holocaust was finally too much to take. Discussions within leftist circles, at both intellectual and activist levels, began to reappraise the assumptions underpinning the conflation of US foreign policy, Israeli 'imperialism' and the Nazi extermination of the Jews. The notion that antisemitism was not limited to the far-right or to the ruling class, but was embedded within society as a whole – including, so it seemed, the anti-capitalist left – needed to be taken seriously again.

Marx, Postone and romantic anti-capitalism

For parts of the German left, the tools needed to reappraise the relationship between antisemitism, capitalist society and ostensible opposition to that society were found in a return to Marx. In the midst of the late 1960s activist explosion, a new strand of Marxian theory emerged, heavily indebted to Adorno, and sought to reconstruct Marx's critique of political economy from the original texts, rejecting the distortions imposed by decades of Soviet and official Communist Party filtering. To rather unwisely attempt to summarise an incredibly rich body of literature in a few lines, instead of critiquing capitalism from the perspective of the working class, this 'new reading of Marx' sought to delineate the social forms that structure capitalist society as a whole, including the standpoint of the working class – the commodity, capital, value and money. The movement of these forms, it was argued, creates social conditions, which makes survival dependent on the constant production of ever-increasing value through labour and commodity exchange. These general conditions are out of the control of any particular social actor, no matter how powerful. The capitalist need for more and more profit – a requirement that, as Malm rightly recognises, lies at the heart of today's climate crisis – is not, at root, due to the personal immorality of capitalists, although immoral capitalists no doubt exist. Rather it is the inescapable result of a society in which the reproduction of life itself is inextricably tied up with the reproduction and expansion of value.

Far from the state being the means by which this society can be opposed, as it is for Malm, from this perspective – one shared by Anselm Jappe, whose work draws heavily from the value-critical tradition – the state is "the political form of [capitalist] society" itself, and thus dependent on the continued reproduction of that society.[35] The validity of a particular state in this society does not rest on any ontological connection between a 'people' and a 'land' – the basis of Malm's rejection of the 'Zionist entity' and romanticisation of supposed Palestinian indigeneity – but the extant state's ability to defend its borders, quell internal unrest and integrate its citizens into the capitalist world market. Romantic nationalism does not explain the underlying 'origin' of the state but is rather a consoling fantasy: a secondary response to the division, contradiction and conflict that constitutes a society founded on the movement of capital, an attempt to transcend fragmentation through the imposition of national unity. There are no grounds in such a perspective to reject a Jewish state – aside from the rejection of the state form as such, which thereby precludes support for a state of Palestine.

The most influential attempt to use commodity form theory to comprehend antisemitism and the Holocaust came in the shape of Moishe Postone's seminal 1986 essay 'Anti-Semitism and National Socialism'.[36] Here Postone, who had previously studied in Frankfurt, argued that Nazism should be understood as a romantic form of anti-capitalism, in which the positive, 'concrete' aspects of capitalist society – manual labour, industrial production, the nation-state – were opposed to the intangible yet destructive 'abstract' elements: money, finance, interest, rootless cosmopolitanism. The dramatic, confusing and often traumatic transformations of everyday life wrought by the development of capitalist society were blamed on the contamination of the national community of producers by international finance, interest and money. This 'truncated' critique of capitalism, which does not recognise with Marx that in capitalist society the concrete (use value) and abstract (exchange value) are the necessary preconditions for one other, opens up the pathway to a modern racialised mode of antisemitism, in which the abstract dimension of capitalism is 'biologized' (or concretised) as 'the Jews'. For the Nazis, Postone writes, "The Jews were not seen merely as representatives of capital" – the standard Marxist critique of antisemitism – but "became the personifications of the intangible, destructive, immensely powerful, and international domination of capital as an alienated social form".[37] The attempt to exterminate the Jews was therefore an attempt to salvage the concrete element of capitalism from its abstract deformation in the shape of the Jews.

The connection Postone makes between 'personalised' critiques of capitalism and antisemitism can only ever be one of possibility, not necessity. The association of *Jews* in particular with the secretive yet all-dominating power represented by 'unproductive' finance, interest, usury and so on cannot be explained by the mere existence of a worldview which opposes those phenomena to 'concrete' productive labour. Rather it requires historical analysis of the deep imbrication of anti-Judaism within the conceptual foundations of Western and Christian culture.[38] Moreover, even within the history of antisemitism itself, the exterminatory drive of the Holocaust remains an outlier, demanding explanation at a level of concrete specificity that is beyond the reach of critical theory. Nevertheless, at an abstract level, the basic building blocks of the Nazis' antisemitic worldview – a romantic anti-capitalism, based on the fetishisation of the state as the first line of 'protection' of a national community of producers from destructive global forces, available for political mobilisation within a society shaped at a very deep level by centuries of anti-Jewish thought – are visible in many other cases, including leftist movements.[39] Wherever these elements are present, the possibility of antisemitism is too.

In a later article, Postone built on this analysis to argue that the contemporary 'anti-imperialist' left, still reliant on a Manichean worldview left over from the Cold War, now fetishises the "abstract and dynamic domination of capital … on the global level as that of the United States, or, in some variants, as that of the United States and Israel".[40] The state of Israel here takes on the hated personified form of abstract domination once fulfilled by 'international Jewry'. It is precisely this position which underlies Malm's support for Hamas and abhorrence for the 'Zionist entity'. For both Malm and Chaudhary, Israel is a 'concretisation' of the abstract domination of global capital responsible for climate change. Hamas, on the other hand, represents the rebellion of the concrete against the abstract, the true nation pitted against a legalistic fiction in a last-ditch attempt to salvage nature itself from that "foreign, dangerous, destructive force" which threatens the entire planet.[41]

For Postone, this fetishisation of movements like Hamas or Hezbollah, and the rationalisation of their antisemitism and terroristic forms of 'resistance' as a perhaps regrettable but understandable reaction to Israeli aggression, fatally misunderstands the nature of antisemitism in contemporary Arab societies. The widespread prevalence of classic *Protocols*-style conspiracy theories about Jews here is not due to some supposed backwardness of the 'Muslim world', nor, in the main, to the actual actions of Israel, but rather a consequence of the inability of Arab states to adapt to the demands of neoliberal capitalism. The struggles for democracy that erupted in the Arab Spring was one response to these failures: blaming economic decline on a world conspiracy led by all-powerful 'Zionists' another. The latter constitutes for Postone "a populist antihegemonic movement that is profoundly reactionary and dangerous, not least of all for any hope for progressive politics in the Arab/Muslim world".[42] For the Western left to fail to make any distinction between these two responses, to conflate them both in a single romantic narrative of 'resistance' is, for Postone, a sign of the left's 'helplessness', the total loss of its political and moral bearings.

Postone's initial article on the antisemitic potential of romantic anticapitalism was in part stimulated by what he perceived as the German left's failure to recognise the significance of, or challenge, the 1985 visit of neoconservative US President Ronald Reagan and West German Chancellor Helmut Kohl to the Bitburg cemetery for a memorial ceremony at the graves of Wehrmacht and Waffen SS servicemen. Reagan justified his visit by arguing that German military conscripts, including some in the SS, were as much a victim of Nazism as those who died in the camps, and later suggested that Germany had had for too long "a guilt feeling imposed on them" that was "unnecessary".[43] Polls showed that more than 75%

of the West German population supported the visit. The following year saw the outbreak of the famous *Historikerstreit*, or 'historian's quarrel', in which a succession of right-wing German historians argued that Germany needed to make a 'clean break' with its Nazi past and reject the burden of historic responsibility in order to construct a modern, self-confident national identity. The Nazi era was not the responsibility of the German people as a whole, they suggested, but was the result of a criminal gang taking the nation hostage. Nor were the crimes of the Nazis historically exceptional, but differed only in technicalities from those of the Soviet Union. Indeed, Nazism was in many ways a rational if misguided response to the Bolshevik Revolution. Moreover, the loss of the German Reich and the forced transfer of German populations from Eastern Europe after the war was a 'second *Untergang*' [downfall, ruin] to match that of European Jewry.

For Postone and other Frankfurt School figures such as Jurgen Habermas, this amounted to a concentrated right-wing attempt to 'normalise' and thus sanitise both Nazi antisemitism and the Holocaust itself in name of a new German nationalist project. The urge to exonerate and reconcile Germany to its past, to cast off a guilt which, it was implied, was being forced on it by external forces, was an expression of the kind of 'secondary antisemitism' Adorno had identified 20 years previously. Indeed, for those on the German right less sheepish than the august historians about explicitly identifying who, precisely, was responsible for 'imposing' a guilt complex on the German people, the culprits were, and remain, clear: Israel and its Zionist supporters were exploiting the memory of the Holocaust to extract a moral, political and financial ransom from the German state.[44] This argument was later universalised by Norman Finkelstein in his book *The Holocaust Industry*, published by the leftist Verso Books: for Finkelstein, Israel and its supporters do not merely instrumentalise the Holocaust to seek political and financial reward from Germany but are attempting to blackmail the entire planet.[45]

In Postone's view the failure of the German left to muster any substantive protest against the Bitberg visit or critical intervention in the *Historikerstreit*, while hundreds of thousands of German leftists thronged the streets in protest against US actions in South America, was a manifestation of the same repression and relativisation of the Nazi past expressed by the right. Unless predicated on "an open, ongoing confrontation with and rejection of the Nazi past", he warned, left attempts to force Germany to break with the United States and with NATO, or to seek to recapture the spirit of a pre-Nazi German left radicalism, risked sanctioning a "traditional German rejection of the West, coupled with a return to those Teutonic virtues which have in the past, made Germany the scourge of the earth".[46] There can be no 'new' or radical 'alternative' Germany, unless it is "defined constantly and consciously in opposition to the determinate old of the German past".[47]

It was within this context, then, that the 'anti-German' movement emerged in the wake of the fall of the Berlin Wall and the rising spectre of German reunification. On the one side was a right-wing pushing the idea that the creation of a new German national identity necessitated the downgrading of the Holocaust, the sanitisation of the Nazi era and opposing (implicitly) Israel's supposed hold over German politics. The prospect of a new Germany, casting off the last remnants of historic guilt for the Holocaust in order to take its position on the world stage once more, dominating Europe politically and economically, was, for the anti-Germans, one ripe for a revived far-right. On the other side was a left who sanctioned the right's attempts to sanitise the Nazi past by dissolving it into universal theories of class struggle or imperialism, who denied the legitimacy of Jewish nationalism – and Jewish nationalism alone – and for whom opposition to Israeli 'imperialism' meant – at best – turning a blind eye to antisemitism, or, at worst, the fetishistic romanticisation of reactionary antisemitic political movements. In contrast, the anti-Germans sought to disrupt the ominous "atmosphere of "German informality" and rediscovery", and "insisted on the commemoration of the Holocaust and the confrontation with Germany's National Socialist past as backbones of any left-wing project".[48]

The victory of a left, and a reunified Germany, that took antisemitism seriously in this context was by no means guaranteed. The formation of a new German state with a memorialisation culture at its heart, symbolised by the Memorial to the Murdered Jews of Europe in Berlin – rather than one premised on the reconciliation to the past, the relativisation of the Holocaust and the rejection of historical responsibility – was in great part a triumph for the left, a victory over what might have become a dangerous reprisal of aggressive German nationalism, however pyrrhic for a left opposed to the notion of nation states per se. To naturalise the result of this process – one informed in part by radical critiques of capitalist society, in part by concrete struggles against attempts from both right and left to sanitise German history and the significance of the Holocaust – so as to reduce it to an innate 'German reflex' is to ignore other potential outcomes that were no less, and in many ways more, likely, as well as the continuing – and indeed rising – dangers of antisemitism within Germany today.

It is to also ignore the many divisions within the anti-anti-Zionist left in Germany since the initial emergence of the anti-German current. Ironically, in 2001, Jappe himself wrote a stinging criticism of the anti-Germans' trajectory. He argued that the movement had reverted to a form of inverted German nationalism, moving away from a position which sought to understand the particularities of German history in the light of the general development of capitalist modernity, to one which fetishised the unique evil of German identity at an ontological level, relativised the Holocaust by labelling figures like Saddam Hussein or Yasser Arafat 'new Hitlers', and romanticised Anglo-American capitalism. "Just as the antisemite wants his capitalism without Jews", he suggested, "so the anti-antisemite wants his capitalism without antisemitism and thinks he can find it in the USA" – a mistake that Adorno, for one, never made.[49]

'There Are Only Two Sides'

But for Andreas Malm, none of this complex and contested history matters. Just as the equally complex and contested history of the Middle East is flattened into an eschatological fantasy of a noble 'Palestine' battling a demonic 'Zionist entity', so too does Malm's reified figure of 'the German' erase the ongoing process of theoretical work and political struggle that lies behind Jappe's refusal to leave unchallenged his praise for Hamas. For Malm, Jappe's position is not one borne of considered reflection about the relationship between capitalism, antisemitism and Israel, about the deep imprint of anti-Judaism on the foundations of Western thought, or recognition of the dangers of political movements seeking to blame Jews or Israel for the negative effects of capitalist modernity. Rather it is merely an irrational product of 'the German guy's' roots. From this perspective, awareness of the continued power and pan-political appeal of antisemitism as an explanation and consolation for the turmoil of capitalist society is little more than an inherited pathology, a constitutive weakness, cowardly and laughable, something to be easily 'scared off'. For Malm, this deformed heritage is expressed in an innate character-type – absurdly sensitive, partial, dogmatic and admonitory – which plays out psychologically, theoretically and politically, an identity Jappe cannot escape, however far he physically lives from the German *Gemeinschaft*. It is thus enough for Malm to publicly reveal Jappe's 'German'-ness for everything about the latter's intellectual and political position to be explained, and thereby dismissed without further consideration. That this dismissal functions at a structural level in much the same manner as the antisemite's dismissal of 'the Jew' and 'the Zionist' is perhaps only a coincidence, but it is an unfortunate coincidence nevertheless.

Malm's contempt for the 'German guy' is one shared by that other Germany, the Germany that drops entirely out of sight in his analysis: a Germany that has long sought to reconcile to rather than reject its past, and to overcome guilt and historical responsibility in the name of a reinvigorated nationalism. For this Germany, the continued failure to recreate the 'true state' demanded by the romantic imaginary can be blamed on those outsiders seeking political and financial gain through the imposition of a guilt complex – and the cowardice of those Germans who submit to such demands, those, like Jappe, without the pride and fortitude needed to finally 'close the books on the past' and move on. For Malm, of course, it is not the restoration of an old Germany that is supposedly blocked by the cynical leveraging of historical suffering for present political and financial gain, accompanied by endless, groundless, manipulative cries of antisemitism, but the creation of a new Palestine. And as his impassioned writings and intervention makes clear, for Malm this Palestine-to-come, premised on the destruction of the 'Zionist entity', will not be merely one more state among many but rather the symbol of an emancipated world, the harbinger of a reconciled nature and a redeemed humanity. As so many times in the past, here a stubborn, recalcitrant Jewish particularity is presented as the obstacle to the restoration of natural harmony. 'There are well and truly only two sides' in this struggle for salvation, and the fact that all but a slither of the world's Jewish population find themselves, once again, cast as the misfortune of the world is something that cannot be helped.

Notes

1 The London protest featured a speech from former British Labour Party leader Jeremy Corbyn, delivered next to a huge 'jewified' inflatable caricature of Sheikh Mohamed bin Zayed bin Sultan Al Nahyan of the United Arab Emirates, complete with exaggerated nose, horns and red claws. Bin Zayad had been pivotal to the normalisation of UAE's relations with Israel as part of the 2020 'Abraham Accords'. Cf. Georgia Gilholy, The chilling scenes outside the Israeli embassy show the urgency of tackling anti-Semitism. *CapX*, 18 May 2021. https://capx .co/the-chilling-scenes-outside-the-israeli-embassy-show-the-urgency-of-tackling-anti-semitism (accessed 25 February 2023).

2 Community Security Trust, *The Month of Hate: Antisemitism & extremism during the Israel–Gaza conflict*, Research Briefing, July 2021. https://cst.org.uk /news/blog/2021/07/15/the-month-of-hate (accessed 25 February 2023).

3 ADL, Antisemitism on Facebook, Instagram and TikTok in Response to Middle East Violence, 19 May 2021. https://www.adl.org/blog/antisemitism-on-facebook-instagram-and-tiktok-in-response-to-middle-east-violence (accessed 25 February 2023).

4 Cf. Susie Linfield, Palestine Isn't Ferguson. *The Atlantic*, 24 October 2021. https://www.theatlantic.com/ideas/archive/2021/10/israeli-palestinian-conflict -ferguson/620471 (accessed 25 February 2023).

5 Red May TV, Covid, Climate, Chronic Emergency: Antinomies of the State. *YouTube*, 14 May 2021. https://www.youtube.com/watch?v=p_pamp3oi78 (accessed 25 February 2023). Malm's contribution begins at 21 minutes.

6 Anselm Jappe, Sandrine Aumercier and Gabriel Zacarias, Israel, Still the Number One Obsession. *Palim Psao*, 17 May 2021. http://www.palim-psao.fr/2021/05/ israel-still-the-number-one-obsession-by-anselm-jappe-sandrine-aumercier-and -gabriel-zacarias.html (accessed 25 February 2023).

7 Bue Rübner Hansen, 'The Kaleidoscope of Catastrophe: On the Clarities and Blind Spots of Andreas Malm. *Viewpoint Magazine*, 14 April 2021. https:// viewpointmag.com/2021/04/14/the-kaleidoscope-of-catastrophe-on-the-clari-ties-and-blind-spots-of-andreas-malm (accessed 25 February 2023).

8 My thanks to Marcel Stoetzler for this point. Cf. David Nirenberg, *Anti-Judaism*, London: Head of Zeus, 2013, *passim*.

9 Linfield, Palestine Isn't Ferguson.

10 This discussion of Rosenberg and the state draws on Marcel Stoetzler, Capitalism, the Nation and Societal Corrosion: Notes on 'Left-Wing Antisemitism'. *Journal of Social Justice*, 9, 1–45, (2019)

11 Andreas Malm, *Corona, Climate, Chronic Emergency: War Communism in the Twenty-First Century*, London, New York: Verso, 2020.

12 Andreas Malm, The Walls of the Tank: On Palestinian Resistance. *Salvage*, 1 May 2017. https://salvage.zone/in-print/the-walls-of-the-tank-on-palestinian-resistance (accessed 25 February 2023).

13 Jakob Erikkson, Why Hamas Still Relies on Violent Repression to Control Gaza. *The Conversation*, 8 June 2015. https://theconversation.com/why-hamas-still-relies-on-violent-repression-to-control-gaza-42461 (accessed 25 February 2023). Imogen Lambert, Facing Years of Repression, Palestinians Continue to Flee Gaza. *The New Arab*, 3 December 2019. https://english.alaraby.co.uk/analysis/facing-years-repression-palestinians-continue-flee-gaza (accessed 25 February 2023).

14 AP News Wire, Hamas 'Guardian' Law Keeps Gaza Woman from Studying Abroad. *The Independent*, 5 November 2021. https://www.independent.co.uk/news/world/americas/hamas-gaza-gaza-city-human-rights-watch-islamic-b1952015.html (accessed 25 February 2023). Diaa Hadid and Majd Al Waheidi, Hamas Commander, Accused of Theft and Gay Sex, Is Killed by His Own. *New York Times*, 1 March 2016. https://www.nytimes.com/2016/03/02/world/middleeast/hamas-commander-mahmoud-ishtiwi-killed-palestine.html (accessed 25 February 2023).

15 Meir Litvak, The Anti-Semitism of Hamas. *Palestine–Israel Journal of Politics, Economics, and Culture* 12(2–3), 41–46, 2005. Bassam Tibi, From Sayyid Qutb to Hamas: The Middle East Conflict and the Islamization of Antisemitism. In: Charles A. Small, ed., *The Yale Papers: Antisemitism in Comparative Perspective*, Createspace Independent Pub, pp. 457–483, 2015.

16 Memri TV, Senior Hamas Offical Fathi Hammad to Palestinians in Jerusalem: Buy 5-Shekel Knives and Cut Off the Heads of the Jews. *Memri.org*, 7 May 2021. https://www.memri.org/tv/snr-hamas-official-fathi-hammad-urges-people-jerusalem-cut-off-heads-jews-knives-day-reckoning-moment-destruction (accessed 25 February 2023).

17 Cf. David Hirsh, *Contemporary Left Antisemitism*, London: Routledge, 2017, 52 ff and *passim*.

18 David Hirsh, It Was the New Phenomenon of Israel-focused Antisemitism that Required the New Definition. *Fathom*, January 2021. https://fathomjournal.org/it-was-the-new-phenomenon-of-israel-focused-antisemitism-that-required-the-new-definition-of-antisemitism-david-hirsh-responds-to-a-recent-call-to-reject-the-ihra (accessed 25 February 2023).

19 See Sebastian Voigt, Antisemitic Anti-Zionism within the German Left: *Die Linke*. In: Charles A. Small, ed., *Global Antisemitism: A Crisis of Modernity*, Leiden: Brill, 2013, pp. 335–343.

20 The most comprehensive (albeit for the most part unsympathetic) historical analysis of the anti-German movement in English is Raphael Schlembach, Towards a Critique of Anti-German 'Communism'. *Interface: A Journal for and about Social Movements*, 2(2), 199–219, 2010.

21 See Lars Fischer, Antisemitism and the Critique of Capitalism. In: Beverley Best, Werner Bonefeld, and Chris O'Kane, eds., *The SAGE Handbook of Frankfurt School Critical Theory*, Los Angeles, London: Sage, 2018, pp. 916–931.

22 For a critique of this 'class instrumentalist' theory of antisemitism in relation to the Corbyn crisis, see my 'Conceptual Vandalism, Historical Distortion: The Labour Antisemitism Crisis and the Limits of Class Instrumentalism'. *Journal of Contemporary Antisemitism*, 3(2), 11–30, 2020.

23 Theodor W. Adorno and Max Horkheimer, *Dialectic of Enlightenment*, Stanford: Stanford University Press, 2002 (1944).

24 Theodor W. Adorno, *Negative Dialectics*, London: Routledge, 1990 (1966), 365.
25 Theodor W. Adorno, The Meaning of Working through the Past. In: Rolf Tiedemann, ed., *Can One Live after Auschwitz?*, Stanford: Stanford University Press, 2003, pp. 3–18.
26 Cf. Lars Rensmann, *The Politics of Unreason*, New York: SUNY Press, 2017, Chapter 8.
27 See Hans Kundnani, *Utopia or Auschwitz*, London: Hurst & Co, 2009, p. 79.
28 Cf. Stefan Muller-Doohm, *Adorno: An Intellectual Biography*, Polity Press, p. 456.
29 Adorno, 'Meaning', p. 5.
30 Paul Berman, *Power and the Idealists*, New York: Norton & Co, 2007, p. 54.
31 Kundnani, p. 90.
32 Kundnani, pp. 88–91.
33 Ibid., pp. 112–113.
34 Ibid., p. 134
35 Anslem Jappe, *The Writing on the Wall*, Alresford: Zero Books, 2017. Werner Bonefeld, *The Strong State and the Free Economy*, Maryland: Rowman and Littlefield, 2017, *passim.*
36 Moishe Postone, Anti-Semitism and National Socialism. In: Anson Rabinbach and Jack Zipes, eds., *Germans and Jews since the Holocaust*, New York: Holmes and Meier, 1986, 302ff.
37 Ibid., p. 311.
38 Cf. Nirenberg, *Anti-Judaism.*
39 The antisemitism within leftist movements should not, then, be equated with that of the Nazis, for this too amounts to a form of Holocaust relativisation and minimisation. The same is true for Islamist antisemitism – it is a striking irony that recent portrayals of Islamist movements, or Muslims more generally, as direct successors to Hitler by anti-Deutsch splinter groups mirrors the anti-imperialist left's Holocaust-relativising attribution of Nazism to the United States and Israel.
40 Moishe Postone, History and Helplessness: Mass Mobilization and Contemporary Forms of Anticapitalism. *Public Culture*, 18(1), 93–110, (2006).
41 Postone, Anti-Semitism and National Socialism, p. 305.
42 Postone, History and Helplessness, p. 102.
43 Gerald M. Boyd, Reagan Weighs Visit to Concentration Camp. New York Times, 16-April 1985. https://www.nytimes.com/1985/04/16/world/reagan-weighs-visit-to-concentration-camp.html (accessed 18 August 2023).
44 For many contemporary examples of such arguments from ordinary members of the German public, see Monika Schwarz-Friesel and Jehuda Reinharz, *Inside the Antisemitic Mind*, Massachusetts: Brandeis University Press, 2017, pp. 309–316.
45 Norman Finkelstein, *The Holocaust Industry*, London: Verso, 2000.
46 Moishe Postone, Bitburg: May 5, 1985 and after – A Letter to the German Left. *Radical America*, 19(5), 10–17 (1985).
47 Ibid., p. 15.
48 Schlembach, Towards a Critique of Anti-German 'Communism', p. 205.
49 Anselm Jappe, Es gibt sie noch, die guten Deutschen. *Exit*, March 2001. https://www.exit-online.org/link.php?tabelle=autoren&posnr=330 (accessed 25 February 2023). My translation; Theodor W. Adorno et al., *The Authoritarian Personality*, London: Verso, 2019 (1950).

11

WHITHER LIBERAL ZIONISM?

Anthony Julius

I contribute my chapter in comradeship with, and esteem for, Dr. David Hirsh, the editor of this volume. No greater single contribution than David's has been made to arguing the anti-academic boycott case. In the clarity of his analysis, with no sacrifice of complexity, and in his patient combativeness, with no resort to nastiness of tone or false charge, he is the model of an engaged intellectual.

The question I pose in this chapter is a simple one. What is the character of my Zionism? It's a personal question and the answer to it has all the limitations of a personal response. (Though it is among my fields of study, I am not a *scholar* of Zionism.) And yet, because I regard myself as typical of the anti-academic boycott crowd, and think it likely that my Zionism may be a lot like my fellow activists', the chapter may serve as a contribution to a group portrait.

I

I pose the question with a certain sense of belatedness; I should have asked it of myself earlier on in the fight. Why didn't I? I was not alone in my delay. It is, I think, interesting to ponder why, when contesting the academic boycott, we anti-boycotters typically did *not* trouble to clarify the nature of our attachment to the Zionist project – other than by reference, in a general sort of way, to 'the two-state solution'.

In summary terms, I answer as follows. The imperative to resist the academic boycott was so strong, and the justifications of an anti-academic boycott stance so plain, the prompt to self-interrogation was just not felt.

I will unpack this answer, just a little.

DOI: 10.4324/9781003222477-12

First, the academic boycott case collapsed in the face of objections variously empirical and principled. Nothing was left of it after consideration of the principle of the universality of science; the independence of Israel's universities from the state; their historical alignment with irenic stances (*Brit Shalom*, *Ihud* etc.); the integration of Israeli science in the world economy. The collapsed state of the case was never conceded by the boycotters – on the contrary, they made no concessions at all. In their blinkeredness, they shared the characteristics of Bernard Williams's imaginary hyper-traditional society – maximally homogeneous and minimally given to general reflection.[1] They spoke as one; they allowed no challenge to violate their certainty.

Second, the analysis supporting the boycott call was weak and compromised. It was pseudo-theological (Israel was conceived in sin, the Israel–Palestine conflict is Manichean etc.); it was derived from unthought-through ideological legacies of pre-1989 Leftism (a derivative of anti-Americanism, a residue of anticolonialism, a Soviet provenance);[2] it could not be universalised (the pursuit of national goals was held a vice for Jews, but a virtue for Palestinians).[3] Boycotters comprised of a division of the larger BDS movement, with its thought-terminating clichés and slogans – 'Apartheid state,' 'settler colonialists' (surely, 'resettler nationalists'?), 'From the river to the sea, Palestine will be free' and so on. Theirs was not a vocabulary of elucidation but of indictment, and supported a preoccupation without knowledge.[4]

Third, their objective, when acknowledged, was the overrunning of the Jewish state – that is, a rematch of 1947–1948, but with a different outcome, and even greater death and destruction. Of course, a state could not be built out of such wreckage; but even if the Palestinians were to succeed, the Jews would not be safe in that state;[5] and even if they *were* safe, the state would no longer be a guarantor of last resort for Jews elsewhere. The distant prospect was terrifying, even if dim. But the immediate consequences were bad enough – demoralised Jewish students; Jewish academics driven out of the UCU; high levels of anxiety in the wider Jewish community.

Fourth, their advocates were deaf to our remonstrances and to our arguments anyway. These deafnesses were disincentives to engagement. I experienced them myself across the weeks of the Ronnie Fraser case and then in the tribunal's self-admiring, feckless judgement; Anglo-Jewry experienced them across the years of the Corbyn ascendancy. Whatever we said was taken to be a cover for uglier purposes. It was assumed we were lying when we complained about antisemitism, intending a smear, not reporting any genuine fears. We were twisty, not to be trusted. This disparaging, dismissive posture was a balancing excess to the servility shown by boycotters towards what they took to be the demands of Palestinian civil society.

Fifth, the disincentive to engagement was strengthened by the boycotters' indignantly denied antisemitism, which admitted no self-interrogation on their part. At the very least they had a case to answer, given: what they shared with antisemitism; what was antisemitic about the academic boycott; the substitution of 'Zionist' for 'Jew' as a common device in current antisemitic discourse ('the Zionists have always been a plague etc.').[6] Indeed, so dominant was this indignation in the presentation of the pathology that it merits its own term – 'indignation antisemitism'. In consequence, we experienced a certain disgust when contemplating contact with the boycotters – David Hirsh was always admirable in his ability to swallow that disgust.

Last, because it would have brought us into public conflict with fellow Jews, offering an unwelcome, even slightly ignominious spectacle – with the unhappiest associations. I have in mind not just those spectacles of hostile witnessing against communities of the faithful by converts, but the more common demonstrations of competitive piety within Jewish communities. We recoiled when Jews, typically self-identifying for the occasion, (a) endorsed boycott calls, and (b) denied even the possibility that these calls were contaminated by antisemitism. We recoiled further at their manner of expression, placatory and condescending towards our adversaries, and dismissive of our own worries for the safety and peace of mind of the Jews in our own community. It was precisely this recoil, made even more extreme whenever their endorsements and denials took on an ingratiating, self-promoting quality (admire our superior fidelity to Jewish values), that deflected us from any open intra-communal contestation.

What is problematic then, what could give pause for thought, about rallying to the defence of academic freedom and to the defence of Jews? That a boycott of universities is a bad thing, and a boycott of *Israeli* universities is an aggravated version of that bad thing; that the BDS movement, both in the opacity of its objectives and in its unreflective embrace of all the clichés of what today passes for 'antizionism,' is a threat to Jewish morale; that this threat could escalate into threats of a more immediately destructive character (abuse, intimidation, violence) – what is difficult about any of this? Indeed, it is precisely the obviousness of these considerations that allows us to identify in BDS positions so many vices – malice, ignorance, self-admiration, conformism. This has been noticed many times.[7]

II

There were, however, more questionable motives for the absence of self-examination, which we may gather under the general observation that in a hostile environment people tend to recoil from explaining themselves, especially when they find themselves under direct attack.

But again, to unpack.

First, I identify a certain aversion to offering explanations. We knew who we were; we knew to what collectivities we belonged. What more was there to say? We were Jews, we were academics. To defend Israeli universities against boycott calls – what could be more natural? We looked at things from the Jewish point of view and from the academic point of view. We were dismissive of equivocators. Attachment to the Zionist project and attachment to free intellectual inquiry were basic to our identity. Attacks on them demanded not self-interrogation but courage, resoluteness, resourcefulness and an unflinching loyalty, both to persons (fellow Jewish academics) and entities (Israel's universities). As Ahad Ha'am wrote: '[I am ready to] proclaim from the rooftops that my kith and kin are dear to me wherever they are, without feeling constrained to find forced and unsatisfactory excuses'. He went on: 'I at least know why I remain a Jew – or rather, I can find no meaning in such a question, any more than if I were asked why I remain my father's son'.[8]

Second, I identify a certain complacency, a sense that inquiry is *redundant* – that everything that matters is already well-known, established beyond doubt, obvious. We knew that a boycott of Israel's universities would constitute, in Baruch Kimmerling's formulation, 'a mortal blow to the concepts of academia and academic freedom'.[9] We knew that the Zionist project was and remains a just one.

Third, there was perhaps also a hesitation before the risks posed by elaboration of an affirmative position, both in respect of concessions that might have to be made (reluctance in times of contention to make concessions aiding the enemy is natural enough) and in respect of the fear that elaboration might require us to choose at some point between liberal and Zionist loyalties.

Last, there was a sense that anything other than entirely defensive labour, anything that asserted a positive case about Zionism, Israel etc., would be subject to the gravitational pull of partisanship (that it could never be, so to speak, our best work). This partisanship standardly works in a dual motion of (a) moralism (our side justly prosecutes a just cause; supporting the cause is a moral duty) and (b) realism (in the competition for scarce resources, each group strives to secure the resources for itself – some will win, others will fail).[10] Double standards are everywhere present: our crimes are excusable and contingent to our undertaking; *their* crimes are inexcusable and constitutive of their undertaking; our most deplorable utterances are atypical of us, when not mere polemical excesses; *theirs* are constitutive of their political philosophy. And throughout there is an opportunism that will always privilege one's own side, even at the price of a sacrifice of intellectual standards. This is more than a matter of 'disregarding the difficult details'.[11]

III

Notwithstanding all the good reasons, and precisely because of the other, somewhat uncompelling reasons, I think we *should* clarify the character of our attachment to the Zionist project.

First, and if only, as a break from the negativity of opposing BDS. And in particular, from the tiresomeness of opposing indignation antisemitism. (Of course, we don't think that 'criticism of Israel' is antisemitic; the IHRA definition expressly allows for criticism of Israel; etc. etc.) I keep returning to the inadequacy of Saul Lieberman's 'While rubbish is rubbish, the study of rubbish can be scholarship'. This witticism, too often cited (including by me), does not take account of the dispiriting effect on scholars thus engaged. It can generate a certain obsessiveness, an immoderate magnification of the importance of the adversarial undertaking. At the very least, it can lead to a certain hypertrophying of the defiance aspect of one's Jewish identity. One can become, indeed, a 'defiance Jew' – Jewish because of antisemitism.[12] It also conditions one's prose – the risk reminds me of F.R. Leavis's remark about Matthew Arnold. He said that Arnold always endeavoured in his prose writings to make 'his argument carefully fool-proof, *insultingly* fool-proof'.[13] Armour-plated, offensive – it's not a good style.

Second, because the relentlessness of the fight, if not relieved by self-criticism, will for sure generate a certain vulgarity. I mean, the vulgarity of unreflective disparagement, in which one attributes low intelligence and unworthy motives to everyone on 'the other side'. (A negative exemplarity of this vulgarity? Hannah Arendt's remark, arriving in Jerusalem: 'Everyone, with very few exceptions, is idiotic, often to an outlandish degree'.)[14] When we are not in the fight, the vulgarity of this 'superiority' is immediately obvious. In the generalised contempt for stupid positions taken by our adversaries, we risk stupidity ourselves. We stupidly mistake as stupidity their good arguments, we stupidly disparage their worthy motives. Moreover, we lose the right to be indignant about what is truly stupid in their positions if we are stupid about our own.

Third, to meet the demand, made precisely by virtue of our group membership, that we honour independence of mind. History is full of justifications of party before principle (or rather, party *as* principle). They all overlook the elementary moral truth that our special regard for family, friends and other groups is built upon our foundational regard for humanity. Humanity is the first 'group' to which we belong, in virtue of our own species identity. To affirm a special regard for our family while denying a foundational regard for humanity is to conjure sky-castles.[15]

Fourth, history matters. While it is true that even if:

> Jewish settlement harmed Arab interests, and the Arab fears on this score were warranted, it does *not* follow that that harm, and those fears, placed

a moral obligation on the Jewish people not to return to their homeland; and/or

there was no justification for the creation of a Jewish state in 1948, it does *not* follow that the preservation of Israel as a Jewish state is unjustified today,[16]

it is *also* true that a proper understanding of the past (that is, both in its factuality and in terms of the rights, interests and liberties of the various parties) must condition the understanding of present possibilities – including what should be conceded. So while I don't dismiss Emma Lazarus's profession of faith (the 'study of Jewish history is all that is necessary to make a patriot of an intelligent Jew'),[17] because that would merely substitute cynicism for credulity, I would move the adjective: the study of Jewish history makes an intelligent patriot of a Jew – where 'intelligent' here stands for the critical, the unillusioned, the liberal.

Fifth, self-examination is the Zionist way. At least, it is in the nature of the best version of Zionism. In his essay 'Truth from Palestine', Ahad Ha'am was unconcerned about any jubilation his report might cause in non-Zionist circles. Anita Shapira adds: There was an aspect to Zionist thinking of a certain 'merciless self-exposure'.[18] Ahad Ha'am's essay, writes Baruch Kimmerling, himself committed to 'the continued legitimate existence and prosperity of Israel', initiated 'Hebrew critical writing'.[19] *Self*-critical, I emphasise – as for that other kind of criticism, criticism of others, with which the history of Zionism is heavy, this has only rarely reflected its 'best version'.[20] Zionism is not an inheritance. Each one of us has to become a Zionist in our own way, on our own terms, by our own route.

Sixth, because otherwise we risk being confused with a type of Zionist that we are not. I have in mind both the illiberal Zionists and the religious redemptionist Zionists. My Zionism is not tied to advocacy of American interests, nor does it have any Messianic aspect. The illiberal Zionists, like members of the Comintern (who followed every snaking turn of the Soviet Union), tend to defend without reservation or exception. They muddle government and state; they treat every criticism as an existential threat; for them, antisemitism is an explanation of first resort; their 'Israel' is somewhat reified, while their 'Left' is entirely reified. To the religious redemptionist Zionists, settlement in the Occupied Territories distils the meaning of Judaism and Zionism in our time; the redemption of the land is the holy path, and takes precedence over the value of individual life; if the state turns against redemption, one must turn against the state; these Zionists regard themselves as 'commanded by the Torah, not the government'.[21]

Seventh, because the more of us there are who make clear the grounds of our Zionism, the less compelling that hostile caricature of 'Zionism' becomes in the public square. If it is indeed the case that 'Zionism is one of the most controversial ideologies in the world',[22] then it is so only because the caricature is mistakenly taken for a proper account. (There is no reason why Zionism, correctly understood, in all its density and diversity, should be any more 'controversial', notwithstanding its density etc. than the national sentiments that bind, say, the citizens of the United States or of Australia.)

Last, in contribution to the further realisation of the Zionist project, which is *not* over. Zionism has never been less than a Jewish phenomenon; it was born of the active creative forces of Jewish life;[23] it is now central to contemporary Jewish identity, and shares in the creativity of that identity. It drives decisions in Israel. It has a future; it is still fertile.

IV

I consider myself a liberal Diaspora Zionist Jew. It is a constitutive part of my identity. It has an elective quality, even though it is grounded in childhood and adolescent experiences. It derives from many sentiments and solidarities, and is expressed in admiration and dismay, esteem and hope. It is a politics of loyalty, not enmity. I have other loyalties, other commitments, which I endeavour to integrate with my Zionist identity (recognising that a full integration is not possible).

The essential ground of my liberal Diaspora Zionism is my identity as a Jew. This identity is marked on my body, and it structures my life. I feel an intense solidarity with Jewish people. The will to be a Jew is strong in me, one that I experience as a natural force, a source of life.[24]

I have an inwardness with Judaism, Jewish culture, Jewish jokes – the intimacies of expression, the shared references, the participation in ceremonies. The Jewish tradition provides me with materials, resources. It stimulates me to thought. Jewish questions are *my* questions. They are the questions that have been set for me, the ones that I feel impelled to answer. I have a Jewish sensibility. I consider myself bound to the Jewish people; they comprise a source of obligation for me. I have duties to Jews. I have never been alienated from them, and so I cannot say, like the Moses Hess of *Rome and Jerusalem*: 'After twenty years of estrangement I have returned to my people'.[25] There has been no period of estrangement. I am now as I was as a child.

This identity is an aspect of my fidelity to my parents' memory – their way of life, their traditions, their own sense of a Jewish past. It finds expression in study, in the weekly marking of Shabbat, in the celebration of holidays and anniversaries, in communal rituals and gatherings, in the High Holy Days (the blowing of the shofar; the Yom Kippur fast). My people have done these things for centuries and centuries.[26] I do not agree with A.B. Yehoshua's remark that we Jews express our identity with consciousness alone;[27] though he made it as a concession (in a polemic against Diaspora existence), by omitting this collective aspect, he conceded too much.

Where does Zionism come in? My Jewish identity is responsive to an understanding of Jews as a people, and Zionism is in turn the ideology that gives best recognition to this understanding. This was clear to Jews from the very inception of the movement. It did not make the performance of ritual practices, the holding of theological positions, the preconditions of membership. As Ahad Ha'am explained: it is possible to be a Jew in the national sense without accepting many things in which religion requires belief.[28] (I note in passing that the secular antizionist effects a reversal – not, 'I am a Zionist because I am a Jew', but rather, 'I am a Jew because I am an antizionist'. The antizionism typically comes from no greater solidarity with Jews, no greater engagement with Jewish life.)

I am a Zionist *in part* because I regard the Jews as a nationality, and hold that, all things being equal, each nationality should have its own state; and *in part* because I recognise that Jews are vulnerable to abuse and worse, that *when* abused or worse, they cannot rely on others to defend them, and that a Jewish state is the most effective vehicle for their self-reliance; but *principally* because I am a Jew. And this in turn means that to be a Zionist one does not need to be an Israeli Jew.

My Zionism is a Zionism of the Diaspora. Israel is a state of the Jewish people and not only of the Jews living in Israel. (Denying to Diaspora Jews the right to comment on Israel's affairs has never made sense to me – and it is always politically motivated.)[29] The focus of Diaspora Zionism has to be on antisemitism, of course. But it is also Diaspora-positive – that is, in several of the Diaspora's iterations. It rejects that tendency in certain versions of Zionism to disparage Diaspora existence; it does not regard Diaspora life as conditioned by 'political servitude', still less, 'enslavement'; it does not welcome the prospect of abolition.[30] It celebrates Diaspora creativity – a 'national art' (an art coloured by Jewish concerns) does *not* need 'a unified community from which it arises and which it represents'.[31] It rejoices in the relative absence of rabbinic oppression in Diaspora communities – what a violation of Herzl's ambition in this regard is Netanyahu's December 2022 cabinet! ('Our clergy, on whom I most especially call … must, however, clearly understand from the outset, that we do not found a theocracy, but a tolerant modern civil state',[32] Herzl declared.) It takes a conservative, limited view of the *benefits* of Jewish self-government – there are pleasures to be taken in social marginality. And it is responsive to what I will call the exogamous imagination. Being amongst one's 'own' has its gratifications and benefits, of course; being among others, in cooperative harmony, offers gratifications and benefits of another kind.

To be even more specific: I am an *English* Diaspora Zionist. I am not taken with that current project, a neo-Babylonian bipolarity, which designates the United States and Israel as the two centres of contemporary Jewish existence.[33] Let me substitute 'English' for 'German' in this passage by the German-Jewish philosopher and literary critic Gustav Landauer (1870–1919):

I feel my Judaism in the expressions of my face, in my gait, in my facial features. Judaism is alive in everything that I am and do. Being a Jew and an Englishman at the same time does me no harm, but actually a lot of good. I experience this strange and yet intimate unity in duality within myself as something precious. I do not distinguish one element of the relationship within myself as primary, and the other, secondary. I have never felt the need to simplify myself or to create an artificial unity by way of denial; I accept my complexity and hope to be an even more multifarious unity than I am now aware of.[34]

I am English. Englishness is also an essential aspect of my identity, a fundamental fact of my consciousness.[35] The language,[36] its literature, the life of a Londoner, all are fundamental. I cannot quite imagine leaving England for Israel for good. England gives to me what Israel cannot – or can only inadequately replicate. But of course – England's appeal is also something *internal* to Zionism. Let's not forget Ahad Ha'am's letter to his friend Simon Dubnov, written from Tel Aviv in 1923: 'In these ideal conditions, I sit and long for London!'[37] For me it is more than a longing – it is a *belonging*. But I have *also* never doubted that I 'belong' to the Jewish people.

Finally, it is a *liberal* Zionism. I am a liberal because of what I value in liberalism.

First, liberalism recognises the complexities of a person's identity, which comprises many elements, commanding distinct loyalties, making their own demands, requiring distinct defences against external challenge, demanding to be reconciled with each other and which at best can only deliver a provisional, fragile and incomplete sense of autonomy – better, self-mastery.[38] 'Israel is a country where I feel I have a natural affinity with the inhabitants', declared Isaiah Berlin. 'I remain totally loyal to Britain, to Oxford, to Liberalism, to Israel, to a number of other institutions with which I feel identified'.[39] My own list is different – though there is some overlap. I 'remain totally loyal', for example, to Mishcon de Reya, the law firm where I have worked for over 40 years.

Second, I want to live in a liberal state because I have a liberal soul. That is, I want to live in a state that respects the need to promote the coexistence of conflicting powers and interests, because I respect that need in my own self. The illiberal Plato shows the way in the *Republic*.[40]

Wouldn't we say that morality can be a property of whole communities as well as all the individuals? Yes. And a community is larger than a single person? Yes. It's not impossible, then, that morality might exist on a larger scale in the larger entity and be easier to discern. So if you have no objection, why don't we start by trying to see what morality is like in communities? And then we can examine individuals too, to see if the larger entity is reflected in the features of the smaller entity.

But for me, the larger entity is not so much *reflected* in the features of the smaller entity as the *solution* to an aspect of those features – namely, their commonly conflicting character.

Third, a liberal utilitarianism (each to count for one, and none more than one) means that I am alive to the *costs* of Zionism. Palestinian nationalism might not have emerged in the absence of Zionism, but it has been frustrated by Zionism. My liberalism encourages me to support a Palestinian state-hood compatible with, and thriving alongside, a vigorous, free Jewish state-hood. (Liberal Zionists will differ among themselves on the detail here.)

Fourth, liberalism is critical. In a certain sense, indeed, liberalism *is* criticism. It can only ever be imperfectly realised; this further realisation requires a relentless self-interrogation.

Last, because Judaism itself is best lived under liberal conditions – not least, because life itself is best lived under liberal conditions.

V

I feel driven especially at this time to affirm the strongly, stalwartly liberal quality of my Zionism. While liberal Zionism has always been both foundational and marginal, only now is it embattled.

What are the moods of my liberal Zionism?

It is first, and still, celebratory. I am with Michael Walzer: Zionism is one of the success stories of 20th century national liberation. In the first decades, notwithstanding the military rule over the western Galilee and its mostly Arab inhabitants, it was a liberal regime, with opposition parties, a highly critical press and free universities.[41] And I am with Emil Fackenheim:

> June 7, 1967, the third day of the Six-Day War. On that day, Israeli troops returned to the Western Wall in Jerusalem, after having been forced out of the ancient part of the city by the Jordanian army in 1948. For Jews worldwide it was an event of destiny and arguably the most profound Jewish religious experience since the beginning of the second exile.[42]

It is vigilant. I experience the threats to Israel as threats to me and to my family. But one needs to moderate one's sense of threat: 'If American Jews were denied opportunities to act out vigilance for Israel, what would be left of their Judaism?'[43] The intensity of attention means affront not just at unwarranted attacks on Israel, but at Israel's failure to meet its own best standards.

It is also, of course, combative. Simon Goldhill, a Classics professor at Cambridge, writes in lament: To be Jewish is now inevitably not just to be associated with Israel and the violent disagreements about its policies, but also to be held publicly responsible. It is not an area where nuanced positions about affiliation, belonging and political justice are rhetorically easy to maintain. He concludes his observation: 'For any minority, there is always a cost in asserting a politicized identity'.[44] I understand his point, but for myself, I do not mind this. The price for me has not so far been a high one.

And it is utopian. Here I can leave my Diaspora deference behind. No one is a citizen of utopia – so speculation is freely available to us all. Utopianism historically ran in a quasi-religious direction. See Syrkin, for example – his talk of merging the vision of a better world with the renascence of the Jewish people.[45] (Call it 'light unto the nations' utopianism.) My utopianism is secular, and more moderate. It simply dreams of a more liberal democratic Israel. We liberal Zionists are once again elaborating utopian programmes.[46] In his 26 October 2004 Knesset speech, advocating his Gaza disengagement plan, Ariel Sharon said: 'We have no desire to permanently rule over millions of Palestinians, who double their numbers every generation. Israel, which wishes to be an exemplary democracy, will not be able to bear such a reality over time'.[47] I understand why Sharon said this, but it was an overstatement. Israel does not have to be an *exemplary* democracy. It would be enough were Israel a *full*, rather than a *hybrid*, democracy (see the Democracy Index 2022).[48] The Jewish State does not have a duty to be a light unto the nations – still less, a Kookian redemption of humanity in statehood. At present, we might settle for its government behaving with decency, consistently. For any government to behave decently – now *that's* a challenge.

VI

There are many liberal Zionisms; and all comprise just one version among many versions of Zionism itself. (There has always been a quantum of 'theoretical chaos'[49] in Zionist thinking.) Common in all versions, however, are two imperatives, which address questions of survival and revival, respectively, and which I term 'safe-haven' and 'self-government'.

'Safe-haven'

It has been well observed: The disastrous consequences for Jews of the conjunction of relative economic advantage, cultural identifiability and political and military weakness are too well-known to require repetition. These consequences range from expulsion to genocide.[50] To put the point simply: Jews could not survive, or if survived, could not flourish, or if flourished, only for now, and not reliably for the future too, without a state of their own as a refuge. Jews in Europe had been 'lambs among wolves' (Ahad Ha'am) – they may become so again.[51] They need a safe-haven, and while that could mean several possible things, it will always comprise a measure of independence.

What would a secure haven look like? It would accept Jews immediately and unconditionally; it would consider its own interests served when receiving them; it would be ready to issue passports to them. 'What gives Zionists the courage to begin this labour of Hercules?' asked Nordau in 1897. 'They wish to save eight to ten million of their kin from intolerable suffering'.[52] And in August 1900:

> Why have we become Zionists? Because of a mystic desire for Zion? We have become Zionists because the distress of the Jewish race has appealed to our hearts, because we see with sorrow a steadily-increasing misery which will lead to sudden and calamitous catastrophes, because our earnest and painful investigations show us but one way out of the labyrinth of affliction, and that is the acquisition of a legally assured and guaranteed home for the persecuted Jewish millions. [53]

The imperative is responsive to four moments:

> *Pre-Shoah* From the 1881 pogroms to the 1918–1921 pogroms, and in between, the 1894–1900 Dreyfus trials, the 1903 Kishinev massacre, the 1905 Aliens Act (Britain, 'the last place of refuge completely available to us', declared Herzl).[54] These horrors provided the impetus for political Zionism, though Zionism did not originate in this moment – it was not brought into existence by the wish to escape torments.[55] It is, however, the moment of the Uganda scheme, of Max Nordau's 'temporary refuge', his *Nachtasyl*.
> *Shoah* The year 1933 to the aftermath of World War II made the case unchallengeable.[56] The perpetrator Nazis were killing the Jews; the bystander Allies were denying the Jews a safe-haven (including in Palestine).[57] In consequence, there was an utter collapse of trust in the non-Jewish world among Jews.[58]
> *Foundation* In the years 1947–1978, the safe-haven imperative stood as a defence of necessity – the Jews were like a 'man jumping out of a building' (Deutscher), or a 'man drowning' (Oz). They were entitled to 'the survival right of the endangered' (Yehoshua). The safe-haven itself had to be kept safe, otherwise it would become a death trap.[59]
> *Post-Foundation* Here, the struggle is to keep the safe-haven case compelling for the non-Jewish world and operative for Jews themselves. That is, to demonstrate both that Israel can perform a function for Jews that would not otherwise be performed (say, Operations Moses, Joshua and Solomon – the airlifts of Ethiopia's Jews), and that Jews continue to be a people at risk.

In 1936, Jabotinsky addressed the Peel Commission, and the world beyond it: Zionism may include all kinds of dreams – a model community, Hebrew culture – but all this is nothing in comparison with that tangible momentum of distress and need by which we are propelled. We are facing an elemental calamity, a kind of social earthquake. It is actually impossible to bring to the Commission a picture of what this Jewish hell looks like. What are you going to advise us? Where is the way out? Our demand is that we should be saved.[60] It is to Israel's glory that such an address no longer needs to be made.

'Self-government'

Throughout Zionist writing, one finds strong language evoking a collective purpose: 'The Jewish people is still alive and full of the will to live' (Ahad Ha'am); 'we shall refresh ourselves, renew our blood and be heartened' (Epstein); 'authentic Jewish energy' (Jabotinsky); 'ancient Judaism's commanding will to create the true community', 'the Jewish will to realisation' (Buber);[61] 'the Jewish spirit' (Weizmann);[62] 'the natural right of the Jewish people to be masters of their own fate' (Declaration of Independence). The language is echoed in those provisions of the Mandate that obliged Britain to facilitate 'the development of [Jewish] self-governing institutions'.[63]

The fullest realisation of national life is a self-governing one, even if not always a state. This does not rule out coexistence with minority groups, of course. In one formulation, the path we choose will not be dictated, as has been the case for virtually all of Jewish history, by our external enemies. It will be determined by us.[64] Yeshayahu Leibowitz made all the essential points: Zionism is best defined as the program for the attainment of political and national independence. The object is to live a life free of domination by non-Jews. The State of Israel in its ideal version completely satisfies the demand for freedom from domination by others.[65]

(There are two risks internal to the self-government imperative: (a) the withering of the exogamous imagination, which of course Zionism itself wishes to guard against; (b) the instrumentalising of relations with the Diaspora. But consideration of these risks would take me beyond the limits of this chapter.)

$SH + SG \approx Z$

There is a patent tension here. How could Jews persecuted into seeking a safe-haven have the wherewithal to be self-governing? How could fearful Jews also be confident Jews? In safe-haven Zionism, there is an acknowledged failure of will, a certain defencelessness, a collapse of morale, leading to the retreat to a redoubt. In self-governing Zionism, we find a superb assertion of will – post-Shoah, one of exceptional, perhaps even unique, strength and intensity of force, a taking of what is theirs, a surmounting of every challenge and obstacle.

Yet now, at least, the need for safe-haven supports, even when it does not drive, the will to collective self-government. To the extent that anti-semitism is intensified by the very existence of the Jewish State, the Jews are in a better position by virtue of that state to respond to threats and acts of violence. (Antisemitism may go up from 3 to 5; but the Jews' ability to deal with it will go up from 2 to 8.) Gideon Levy misses just this point: 'Israel is less secure than anywhere else, but Jews are being called upon to come and save themselves here of all places, in this crowded and troubled land'.[66] It is by the adoption of the state form that Jews may secure a safe-haven *and* manage their own affairs.

On this point, at least, I am in agreement with Yoram Hazony: 'If Israel could do no more than offer diplomatic and military assistance to Jews in need, this would be sufficient reason to maintain it as a Jewish state'. He argues for a safe-haven *version* of the self-government principle, relying on this passage of Rousseau's:

> [The unfortunate Jews] feel themselves to be at our mercy. The tyranny practised against them makes them fearful [...] I shall never believe that I have seriously heard the arguments of the Jews until they have a free state, schools, and universities, where they can speak and dispute without risk. Only then will we be able to know what they have to say.[67]

Further, there is an undeniable spiritual affirmation that lives in the con-ception of Israel as a place of safety. Medieval in its first, developed form alludes to a unity of Torah, land and people, which echoes in even the most secular of Zionisms (if only as cultural memory).[68]

VII

What is the liberal Zionist version of these imperatives? It accents safe-haven over self-government, in part because it regards it as the more fundamental of the two, and in part because it finds in self-government the danger that the Jewish part of one's life might become too insistent in its demands and overwhelm all other parts.

I find in the work of Judith Shklar the best way of thinking through this liberal version. Shklar was born in Riga in 1928, but left at the age of 11; she was educated in Canada, and then at Harvard, where she then taught; she died of a heart attack in 1992. She took up political theory as a way of making sense of the experiences of the 20th century. Though Shklar was a Jewish liberal thinker, however, she did not write very much about Zionism, nor has she been much written about in a Zionist context.

However, in a short, private note that Shklar prepared after her return from a visit to Israel, she discussed the political situation in Israel and Palestine, and how it impacted on the positioning of liberal American Jews *vis-à-vis* Israel and the United States. This note, entitled 'delusion and sanity in Israel', was written in 1987 and intended for friends and selected colleagues. It focused on states of mind rather than traditional left-right distinctions. She separated out positions on a political-psychological continuum, ranging from the 'deluded' to the 'sane'. The 'deluded' positions were those oblivious to the fact that Israel finds itself in an Arab and Palestinian environment, which will not simply disappear from the map. Not to relate to this environment is therefore 'irrational' and not a viable political option. On the 'sane' side, however, there are many opinions and options, from military intervention to negotiation. What distinguishes the 'sane' from the 'deluded' is that only 'sane' positions contend against fatalism, the conviction that there is basically nothing that can be done. Against such illusions, Shklar rallied for liberal support, not of parties and partisan politics, but of individuals and individual positions that would have enough courage to reject the status quo. Liberal Jews should support those Israelis who have not given up on the idea that things can still be influenced and changed.

The Zionist project sought to get rid of fatalism and permanent victimhood. 'The Jews of Israel have achieved one of the aims of Zionism: They are [now] no different, neither worse not better, than the rest of mankind', Shklar wrote. In consequence,

> liberal American Jews may have to learn to lower their expectations. It is not because Israel is a moral beacon, but because we have an historical title as citizens, Jews all, that we ought to do our best to support those who share our political values.

She went on:

> The sane certainly know a lot of Jewish history. One cannot suffer from historical amnesia in Israel. [The sane Israelis] have not forgotten the past and all its burdens, but they know that democratic government depends upon a degree of present mindedness and that one cannot allow memory to obliterate all one's other mental faculties.[69]

In her general orientation, however, Shklar was taken to be contemptuous of any and all nationalisms. Sanford Levinson recalls her responding 'with almost palpable outrage' to a conference paper arguing for liberal nationalism. She seemed to view nationalism, Levinson relates, 'as being essentially irrational and almost inevitably dangerous, characterized first by excessive attention to blood ties and then, all too often, by bloodshed of those not within the requisite tribal connection'.[70]

And yet, her principal idea, the 'liberalism of fear', fortifies the Zionist safe-haven imperative. She asks: What would a carefully thought-through political theory that puts cruelty first look like? Liberalism's deepest grounding, in place from the outset, is that cruelty is an absolute evil. For the liberalism of fear, the basic units of political life are the 'weak' and the 'powerful'. The freedom this liberalism wishes to secure is freedom from the abuse of power and intimidation of the defenceless that this difference invites. This includes, but is not limited to, the extremity of institutional violence. The liberalism of fear takes the condition of life without terror as its first requirement.[71]

Now, Jews for centuries have been among the class of the weak, and in consequence at the mercy of the class of the powerful. They have not been free, because they have been in others' power. The 'institutions of primary freedom' that Shklar makes the precondition for everything else that liberalism seeks (say, 'more communal or more expansively individual personalities') were not reliably protective of Jews. In consequence, Jews needed to establish their own institutions of primary freedom, in their own state.

Bernard Williams drew out a somewhat counter-intuitive implication of Shklar's theory. The politics of fear can, 'in good times', he wrote, be the 'politics of hope too'.[72] I would add, if only as an implication of that implication, the 'politics of courage too'. What then does a Zionism of courage look like? It has a certain quality of creative audacity, one equal to the task of making a break in history, of remoulding Jews as citizens of a new polity, and warriors vigilant in its defence.[73] Of course, it's the precondition of the self-government aspect of Zionism. But safe-haven Zionism *also* requires courage. We fear the hostile attention of other nations, an attention we must address in a way that ensures our survival. There is a logic of courage, then, inside safe-haven Zionism too.

As well as demanding that we rise to the challenge of external threats, a Zionism of courage makes three further demands on us.

First, that we acknowledge the Jewish State's strength. This means settling accounts with the Shoah, and reaching a proper understanding of contemporary antisemitism, in every distinguishable local context. It means resisting the temptation to pick quarrels, the temptation to take the lowest view of political adversaries, and the temptation to treat the charge of antisemitism as anything other than one of last resort.

Second, that we endeavour to grasp Israel's history, in all its complexity and influence, and confront its current government, in all its deplorableness.[74] The estimable Chaim Gans writes:

> The fact that Israel has not stopped its policies of territorial expansion and discriminatory practices undermines its capacity to now invoke the necessity defence in good faith. This defence is crucial for the justification of Zionism. The State of Israel's current actions and policies not only undermine its moral standing in the present and in the future, they also affect the legitimacy of relying on the justice of the Zionist past.[75] Though I disagree with his analysis of the necessity defence,[76] I fully share his liberal recoil.

Third, that we go up against the rabbinic-coercive and secular-illiberal elements in Israel – and indeed, wherever it is found in Jewish communities worldwide. We want a Jewish state, but we do *not* want it to be a clerical state (see the new Netanyahu cabinet).[77] We want Jewish self-government, but not of a type contemptuous of the Rule of Law (again, see the new Netanyahu cabinet).[78] Specifically, the State has an obligation to protect the rights of all its citizens, to treat them fairly and with respect, and to provide equally for the security and welfare of its majority Jewish population and non-Jewish minorities. Jewish hegemony does not entail Jewish exclusivity; it does not justify budgetary or political discrimination. Denying Arabs any representation in state symbols is as alienating as denying them autonomy in determining how their children should be educated.[79]

A Zionism of courage – that is, a liberal Zionism – strives to act justly. For sure, some injustices cannot be fully remedied – neither by the perpetrator nor his descendants nor by third parties. But all can be *tackled*. In *The Faces of Injustice* (1990), Shklar wrote against what she termed 'passive injustice'. Passive citizens who turn away from actual and potential victims contribute their share to the sum of iniquity. Who does not prevent or oppose wrong when he can is just as guilty of wrong as if he deserted his country. Passive injustice is more than failing to be just, it is to fall below personal standards of citizenship. It ignores the ills that we cause by letting matters not our immediate concern take their course. As a failing, this is typical of people who enjoy the benefits of constitutional democracy but do nothing to maintain it. Citizens who say nothing about laws and ordinances they regard as unjust and oppressive are passively unjust. They ignore the claims of victims of injustice; they prefer to see only bad luck where victims perceive injustice.[80]

An example of citizens who refuse this passivity? The 130,000 citizens who protested on 21 January across Israel. David Grossman told them, in a language that echoed Shklar's: 'Our house is burning, no less. We understand the rule of law is being critically wounded, and if you didn't feel the same way, you wouldn't be here. You are refusing to be cynical, to be passive'.[81]

VIII

Given present circumstances, and Israel's political trajectory, it is possible that the Jewish State will lose its centrality in the Jewish imagination – that it will so diminish itself, it will merely have the status of one Jewish community among others. This will mark the moment of separation of 'Zionism' as an ambition from 'Israel' as an actually existing state. We are not there; we are not nearly there; but the destination is now *imaginable*.

Notes

1 *Ethics and the Limit of Philosophy*, Harvard, MA, 1985, p. 142.

2 Baruch Kimmerling, *Marginal at the Center*, New York, 2012, p. 192.

3 One can imagine either as a general position, but not *both* held at the same time, at the level of principle. See Alasdair MacIntyre, *Is Patriotism a Virtue?* Kansas, 1984, p. 3.

4 See Arthur Hertzberg, ed., *The Zionist Idea*, Philadelphia, PA, 1997, p. 491.

5 [Ari Shavit:] 'Knowing the region and the history of the conflict, do you think … a Jewish minority would be treated fairly? [Edward Said:] I worry about that. The history of minorities in the Middle East has not been as bad as in Europe, but I wonder what would happen. It worries me a great deal. The question of what is going to be the fate of the Jews is very difficult for me. I really don't know. It worries me'. The Palestinian Right of Return: An Interview with Ari Shavit. *Raritan*, Winter, 20(3), 46, 2001. I do not admire this – not least, because it invites admiration.

6 Say, the tweets of Ayatollah Ali Khamenei, Iran's Supreme Leader: '"Zionism is an obvious plague for the world of Islam. The Zionists have always been a plague, even before establishing the fraudulent Zionist regime. Even then, Zionist capitalists were a plague for the whole world. Now they're especially a plague for the world of Islam'." And a Trump-rally attendee: '"We need to end Zionism, which is huge, and it's probably the biggest problem that we have in this country today and around the globe, which is a few people controlling pretty much everything— – all the money, all the business, brainwashing all the people from the education systems'. …" See Yair Rosenberg, "Why Twitter Won't Ban Its Most Powerful Anti-Semite.," *Atlantic*, 9 June 2022.

7 Susie Linfield, *The Lions' Den*, New Haven, Ct., 2019, p. 7 ('[the] idealisation, misrepresentation and distortion of the Palestinian national movement and the evasion, if not defence, of its most inhuman acts'; 'today's debate is a remarkably ignorant one'; 'the glib pseudo-history endlessly regurgitated'; etc.) and p. 13 ('the impossibility of analysing the Arab-Israeli conflict when a major aspect of it is swathed in idealisation or ignorance'; 'glib, often uncritical "solidarity" offered [to Palestinians]'; etc.).

8 Slavery in Freedom (1891). In: Leon Simon, ed., *Selected Essays of Ahad Ha'am*, New York, 1962, pp. 193–194.

9 *Marginal at the Center*, New York, 2012, p. 204.

10 Ernest Gellner's point: Not only is the number of nations greater than the number of independent or autonomous political units, the number of nations is greater than the combined number of *potential* and *actual* political units. See *Nations and Nationalism*, Oxford, 1983, p. 2. If this is so, then why *not* prefer one's own nation-claimant over other nation-claimants to 'independent etc. unit' status? Ruth Wisse takes just this position: 'Every country, emphatically including every one of the many Arab countries, can be said to exist at the expense of another. Arabs, having conquered more civilisations than any other people in history, are in the weakest position of all to deny the rights of conquest to a single, tiny Jewish state'. *If I Am Not For Myself* …, New York, 1992, p. 119.

11 Hillel Cohen, *Year Zero of the Arab–Israeli Conflict 1929*, Lebanon: New Hampshire, 2015, p. 133.

12 'The stance the Jew, suffering and reacting, assumes towards the non-Jewish world … does not constitute a basic element of his inner Judaism. Otherwise he would be a Jew merely by defiance, a Jew not by his very essence but by proclamation of the nations'. Martin Buber, *On Judaism*, New York, 1972, p. 13.

13 Leavis's Downing Seminars. In: Ian MacKillop and Richard Storer, eds., *F.R. Leavis: Essays and Documents*, Sheffield, 1995, p. 83.

14 Lotte Kohler, ed., *Within Four Walls*, (New York, 2000), p. 282.

15 See Christine Korsgaard, *The Sources of Normativity*, Cambridge, 1996, *passim*. I prefer this to Michael Walzer's formulation: Precisely *because* I have a special concern for my own children, my friends, my comrades, my co-religionists and my fellow citizens, I recognise the legitimacy of these repeated acts of moral specialisation in others too. I make some people special; I ought to acknowledge that other people are special for you. See: Nation and Universe. *Thinking Politically*, New Haven, CT, 2007, pp. 198–199.

16 See Ruth Gavison, The Jewish State: A Justification. In: David Hazony, Yoram Hazony and Michael B. Oren, eds., *New Essays on Zionism*, Jerusalem, 2006, pp. 10–12 and 32 (fn. 11).

17 *An Epistle to the Hebrews*, New York, 2022, p. 38.

18 Anita Shapira, *Land and Power*, Stanford, CA, 1992, pp. 27, 42. 'The Zionist movement undoubtedly fits within [the national liberation] tradition of self-critique, which it sometimes raised to an extreme pitch. There are several reasons for this, including the Jews' culture of analytic thought and sceptical argument; in addition, many Zionists were strongly influenced by Bolshevik vanguardism. Zionism aimed not only for political independence but for a profound psychic and cultural transformation'. Susie Linfield, *The Lions' Den*, New Haven, CT, 2019, p. 87.

19 *Marginal at the Center*, New York, 2012, pp. 25, 69. 'This is how I want to write too', Kimmerling remembers thinking, when he first read the essay at high school.

20 Very little of the criticism that was once turned outwards, against the Diaspora (mostly, an ideologically conditioned distortion of reality), or inwards, against political rivals, and now concerns itself with polemicising against Jews taken to be inadequately pro-Israel, brings credit to the critics. It is important for us not leave the ground of affirmation to these crass types. On criticism of the Diaspora, see Yehezkel Kaufman, Anti-Semitic Stereotypes in Zionism: The Nationalist Rejection of Diaspora Jewry. *Commentary*, March 1949, and Susie Linfield: 'During several periods in his exceedingly turbulent life, Arthur Koestler was a fiercely committed Zionist. But he was a peculiar sort of Zionist, for he viewed Israel not as the site for the Jewish people's regeneration but, rather, as a means to that people's disappearance. ... As he aged, Koestler's views on the Jewish Question became increasingly extreme and peculiar. Yet those views ... raise important issues about the role of Jewish self-criticism within the Zionist movement. And outside it, too, for many of Koestler's views endure within the Diaspora today, especially among Jews on the left who are most critical of Zionism'. *The Lion's Den*, New Haven, CT, 2019, p. 81 (also see pp. 88–89).

21 Gadi Taub, *The Settlers*, New Haven, CT, 2010, pp. 1, 3, 43, 47 ('commanded': R' Zvi Yehuda Kook), 67, 70–71. Taub argues that the Jewish Underground, a terrorist group, 'was not born outside the logic of the settlers' worldview', but 'came from its very heart' (pp. 72–73).

22 Michael Stanislawski, *Zionism*, Oxford, 2017, p. 1.

23 Marie Syrkin, *Nachman Syrkin, Socialist Zionist*, New York, 1961, p. 279.

24 See Gideon Shimoni, *The Zionist Ideology*, Hanover, New England, pp. 272, 439 and fn. 6.

25 Compare Moses Hess, in *Rome and Jerusalem* (1862): 'Here I am again, after twenty years of estrangement, in the midst of my people. I take part in its days of joy and sorrow, in its memories and hopes, its spiritual struggles within its own house, and among the civilised peoples in whose midst it lives'. Quoted, Isaiah Berlin, The Life and Opinions of Moses Hess. *Against the Current*, Princeton, 2013, p. 292.

26 'National holidays are a good indicator as to whether continuity in national identity actually exists'. Eyal Chowers, *The Political Philosophy of Zionism*, Cambridge, 2012, p. 87, fn. 27.

27 'The meaning of homeland' (2006). In: Paul Mendes-Flohr and Jehuda Reinharz, eds., *The Jew in the Modern World*, 3rd ed., Oxford, 2011, p. 867.

28 Gideon Shimoni, *The Zionist Ideology*, Hanover, New England, pp. 26, 273. 'Zionist ideology ... redefined the nature of Jewish identity in nationalist terms. It was the legacy of emancipation and enlightenment ... that made this nationalist redefinition possible' (p. 269).

29 Nathan Rotenstreich, *Zionism*, New York, 2007, p. 126.

30 Compare: 'The *Galut* has returned to its starting point. It remains what it always was: political servitude, which must be abolished completely. The attempt which has been considered from time to time, to return to an idea of the *Galut* as it existed in the days of the Second Temple – the grouping of the Diaspora around a strong centre in Palestine – is today out of the question'. Y. Baer, *Galut*, New York, 1947, p. 118 (also see p. 9).

31 Martin Buber, Zionism and Jewish Art (1903). In: Paul Mendes-Flohr and Jehuda Reinharz, eds., *The Jew in the Modern World*, 3rd ed., Oxford, 2011, p. 615.

32 A solution of the Jewish Question. *Jewish Chronicle*, 17 January 1896. In: Paul Mendes-Flohr and Jehuda Reinharz, eds., *The Jew in the Modern World*, 3rd ed., Oxford, 2011, p. 600.

33 E.g., 'it is America where emancipation has, arguably, been most successful, and only in Israel is there a full engagement with political sovereignty'. Michael Walzer, Preface. In: Walzer, ed., *Law, Politics and Morality in Judaism*, Princeton, NJ, 2006, p. x.

34 A 1913 text, in Paul Mendes-Flohr and Jehuda Reinharz, eds., *The Jew in the Modern World*, 3rd ed., Oxford, 2011, p. 827 (I have edited the passage for clarity).

35 'The country, as an inescapable group into which we are born ... seems to be a fundamental fact of our consciousness, an irreducible minimum of social feeling'. Randolph Bourne 'The State', *The Radical Will*, Los Angeles, CA, 1992, p. 357.

36 For sure – we understate at our peril the centrality of language in identity-formation. But it cannot constitute an *exclusive* identity. In the case of English, this incapacity is deepened by the language's quasi-global character. Fichte was wrong, then, when making the *general* case that 'the first, original, and truly natural frontiers of states are undoubtedly their inner frontiers. Those who speak the same language ... are joined together ... with a multitude of invisible ties ...; they understand one other and are able to communicate ever more clearly; they belong together and are naturally one, an indivisible whole'. See Gregory Moore, ed., *Addresses to the German Nation*, Cambridge, 2008, p. 166. To speak English as one's mother tongue is to be given the privilege, among other gifts, of being able to accommodate multiple national loyalties.

37 Leon Simon, *Ahad Ha'am*, New York, 1960, pp. 263, 301.

38 This is very far from the account of liberalism as derived from the fantasy of being an entirely sovereign individual. See Raymond Geuss, *Not Thinking Like a Liberal*, Cambridge, MA, 2022, pp. 8, 24, 157–158.

39 Ramin Jahanbegloo *Conversations with Isaiah Berlin*, London, 1992, p. 87.

40 *Republic*, Oxford, 1993, trans. Robin Waterfield, p. 58 (369d).

41 *The Paradox of National Liberation*, New Haven, CT, 2015, pp. 34, 69.

42 The Zionist Imperative. www.firstthings.com, February 1995.

43 Bernard Avishai, *The Tragedy of Zionism*, New York, 1985, p. 353.

44 Simon Goldhill, *What Is a Jewish Classicist?* London, 2022, pp. 60, 61.

45 Marie Syrkin, *Nachman Syrkin, Socialist Zionist*, New York, 1961, p. 238.

46 Liberal Zionists, the liberal Zionist Omri Boehm argues, are committed to the Two-State Solution, which is untenable, while the One-State Solution is perceived as antizionist. He proposes, against both these 'solutions', 'an alternative to two-state politics from within a liberal Zionist perspective', that is, 'Jewish self-determination in a binational republic'. This is in the line of Zionist thinking (and follows the 1977 Begin Plan), which accepted 'the distinction between national self-determination and national sovereignty'. His proposal 'recognises the right of both Jews and Palestinians to national self-determination, even sovereignty, in their own states, separated along the '67 border, and yet regulating their separate sovereignty by a joint constitution ensuring basic human rights, freedom of movement, and economic liberties throughout the territory. Such a plan could allow many settlers to remain in their homes. And it would enable Palestinians to exercise rights commonly associated with the right of return'. See *Haifa Republic*, New York, 2021. pp. 9, 11, 14, 15, 19.

47 https://www.jewishvirtuallibrary.org/prime-minister-sharon-address-to-the-knesset-on-the-disengagement-plan-october-2004

48 Frontline democracy and the battle for Ukraine. Democracy Index 2022, *EIU*.

49 See Marie Syrkin, *Nachman Syrkin, Socialist Zionist*, New York, 1961, p. 243.

50 Ernest Gellner, *Nations and Nationalism*, Oxford, 1983, pp. 105, 107.

51 The Negation of the Diaspora (1907). In: Arthur Hertzberg, ed., *The Zionist Idea*, Philadelphia, PA, 1997, p. 270.

52 Speech to the First Zionist Congress (1897). In: Arthur Hertzberg, ed., *The Zionist Idea*, Philadelphia, PA, 1997, p. 244.

53 *Max Nordau to His People*, New York, 1941, p. 117.

54 Theodor Herzl, The Uganda Plan. In: Paul Mendes-Flohr and Jehuda Reinharz, eds., *The Jew in the Modern World*, 3rd ed., Oxford, 2011, p. 619.

55 Michael Stanislawski, *Zionism*, Oxford, 2017, p. 9.

56 In May 1939, the German liner St. Louis sailed from Hamburg, Germany, to Havana, Cuba. The ship's 937 passengers were almost all Jewish refugees. Cuba's government refused to allow the ship to land. The United States and Canada were unwilling to admit the passengers. They were finally permitted to land in western European countries rather than return to Nazi Germany. Two hundred fifty-four St. Louis passengers were killed in the Holocaust. Emil Fackenheim writes: 'Suppose that the captain of the St. Louis has turned away from America and is heading back to Europe, as slowly as the engines permit. He hears a news item on the radio: a Jewish state has been proclaimed in Palestine. He shouts to the engine room, 'Change course, and full steam ahead!' The news spreads to the hapless refugees and, hapless no more, they sing and dance without let-up until the blessed coast comes into sight, and with it, thousands of people waiting on the beach to welcome and celebrate them-those nine hundred whom the world has despised and rejected'. The Zionist Imperative. www.firstthings.com, February 1995.

57 'Rescue had become for the Jews a matter of life and death. If the Nazi ring could not be sprung open and the Jews brought to a safe destination, they would die in mounting numbers as the catastrophe quickened. The British government and its helpers were not moved to drastic action by this situation'. In a 1939 speech, Hitler made these mocking remarks: 'It is a shameful example to observe today how the entire democratic world dissolves in tears of pity but then, in spite of its obvious duty to help, closes its heart to the poor, tortured Jewish people'. See Raul Hilberg, *The Destruction of the European Jews*, New York, 1985, pp. 39, 1113–1114.

58 See Raul Hilberg, *The Destruction of the European Jews*, New York, 1985, pp. 1049, 1057. The condemnations of persecution, the freedom propaganda and the expressions of sympathy for the oppressed were hedged in by reservations that preserved more basic Allied interests. These reservations were responsible for the functional blindness that afflicted the Allies during decisive moments of the Jewish catastrophe. The repressive pattern manifested itself primarily in the refusal to recognise either the special character of German action or the special identity of the Jewish victims.

59 And not just in 1947–1948. Arthur Koestler, reporting from Palestine in 1937, in the midst of the so-called Arab Revolt ('only a few among the terrorists are real fanatics, most of them were paid gunmen with a salary of from £4 to £6 a month, £5 reward for killing a casual Jew, and £200 reward for killing a British official or an Arab belonging to a clan hostile to those of the instigators'), told his readers that Palestine would become a 'death trap' for Jews who 'had gone to Palestine on the basis of [the Balfour Declaration', if Britain did not 'act, and act quickly'. See: A Sentimental Journey through Palestine. In: Wilfred Hyde, ed., *Foreign Correspondent*, London, 1939, pp. 69–70, 79.

60 Shlomo Avineri, *The Making of Modern Zionism*, New York, 2017, p. 193. Arthur Hertzberg, ed., *The Zionist Idea*, Philadelphia, PA, 1997, pp. 559–570.

61 *On Judaism*, New York, 1972, pp. 115, 140.

62 See Paul Mendes-Flohr and Jehuda Reinharz, eds., *The Jew in the Modern World*, 3rd ed., Oxford, 2011, pp. 607, 633, 673, 677.

63 Mandate for Palestine (24 July 1922). In: Paul Mendes-Flohr and Jehuda Reinharz, eds., *The Jew in the Modern World*, 3rd ed., Oxford, 2011, p. 671.

64 See Nathan Rotenstreich, *Zionism*, New York, 2007, p. 99, fn. 8.

65 *Judaism, Human Values, and the Jewish State*, Cambridge, MA, 1992, pp. xxxiv, 77, 116, 211, 214.

66 Gideon Levy, Hey Israel, Let's Become a Normal Country. *Ha'aretz*, 24 July 2022.

67 *Emile, or On Education*, New York, 1979, p. 304. Rousseau continues, 'At Constantinople, the Turks state their arguments, but we do not dare to state our own. There it is our turn to crawl'.

68 See Y. Baer, *Galut*, New York, 1947, pp. 34, 51.

69 Andreas Hess, *The Political Theory of Judith N. Shklar*, New York, 2014, pp. 192–193.

70 Is Liberal Nationalism an Oxymoron? An Essay for Judith Shklar. *Ethics*, 105(3), 626, 627, 1995.

71 The Liberalism of Fear. *Political Thought and Political Thinkers*, Chicago, 1998, pp. 3–20.

72 The Liberalism of Fear. *In the Beginning Was the Deed*, Princeton, New Jersey, 2005, p. 61.

73 See Eyal Chowers, *The Political Philosophy of Zionism*, Cambridge, 2012, p. 101.

74 'A number of racists, misogynists, homophobes and theocrats have taken powerful ministerial posts in [Netanyahu's] government, and the whole spirit of their enterprise is visibly hostile toward the culture of democratic tolerance and rationality'. Paul Berman, Martin Peretz, Michael Walzer and Leon Wieseltier, We Are Liberal American Zionists. We Stand with Israel's Protesters. *Washington Post*, 2 February 2023. The cabinet recalls to mind David Hume's 'society of ruffians' – 'such a disregard for equity, such contempt of order, such stupid blindness to future consequences'. See *An Enquiry Concerning the Principles of Morals*, Oxford, 1998, p. 15.

75 *A Just Zionism*, Oxford, 2008, pp. 147–148 (I have slightly edited the sentences).

76 First, because for the defence of necessity to be made good, it need only be good for the moment at which it is relied upon; it cannot be undone by subsequent actions ('policies of territorial expansion and discriminatory practices'), which instead fall to be dealt with in their own terms. Secondly, because in any event, the defence of necessity in respect of a Jewish state (questions of constitution and boundaries aside) continues to be a good one.

77 (1) Mordy Miller, Jewish Law Above All: Recordings Reveal Far-Right Knesset Member's Plan to Turn Israel into a Theocracy. *Ha'aretz*, 20 January 2023. Avigdor Maoz, deputy minister in the Prime Minister's Office, responsible for establishing 'identity security': 'We must protect our people and our state from the infiltration of the alien bodies that arrive from foreign countries, foreign bodies, foreign foundations ... I would be very happy to have sufficient power to be appointed minister of education, to cleanse the entire education system of all foreign influences and to add Judaism, tradition, heritage and Zionism to the education system'. (2) Yael Darel, 'They Want to Set Women Back 500 Years': Israel's Rabbinical Courts Now Set to Enjoy 'Horrifying' Power'. *Ha'aretz*, 6 February 2023.

78 'Prime Minister Benjamin Netanyahu fired his ally Aryeh Dery "with a heavy heart" from his roles as health and interior minister at a cabinet meeting on Sunday, following a High Court ruling barring the ultra-Orthodox leader from holding these posts. The High Court's decision on Wednesday barred the Shas party chair from serving in the cabinet following his criminal conviction on tax evasion charges last year and subsequent suspended sentence. In a letter read by Netanyahu at the cabinet meeting, he expressed regret over the decision and described Dery as an 'anchor of experience, intelligence and responsibility'. 'The High Court decision ignores the will of the nation, and I am intending to find every possible legal means to allow you to contribute to the country', the prime minister continued. Michael Hauser Tov, Netanyahu Fires Loyalist Dery. *Ha'aretz*, 22 January 2023. Netanyahu's gesture towards legality must be understood in the context of his government's plans for a 'hostile takeover of the judiciary'. See Alon Pinkas, Israel's Chief Justice Is Left in Charge of 'Fortress Democracy (quoting Chief Justice Esther Hayut), and Michael Hauser Tov, The Netanyahu-led Gov't's Four-step Plan to Trample Israel's Judiciary, both in *Ha'aretz*, 22 January 2023.

79 *A Just Zionism*, Oxford, 2008, pp. 138–139, 141 and fn. 33.

80 *The Faces of Injustice*, Yale, NJ, 1988, pp. 40–49.

81 Josh Breiner et al., 'Dictatorship of Criminals': Over 130,000 Israelis Protest Netanyahu Government's Anti-democratic Reforms, *Haaretz*, 21 January 2023. 'Where the law is subject to some other authority, and has none of its own', wrote Plato, 'the collapse of the state is not far off' (*Laws*, 715d-e). See John M. Cooper, ed., *Plato: Complete Works*, Indianapolis, IN, 1997, p. 1402.

INDEX

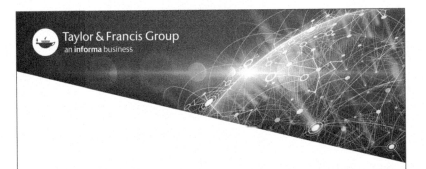